Building Classroom Discipline

Seventh Edition

C. M. Charles
San Diego State University, Emeritus

Allyn and Bacon
Boston   London   Toronto   Sydney   Tokyo   Singapore

Series Editor: Arnis E. Burvikovs
Editorial Assistant: Matthew Forster
Marketing Manager: Kathleen Morgan
Editorial-Production Administrator: Michael Granger
Composition Buyer: Linda Cox
Manufacturing Buyer: Julie McNeill
Cover Administrator: Linda Knowles
Editorial-Production Service: Chestnut Hill Enterprises
Electronic Composition: Omegatype Typography, Inc.

Copyright © 2002 by Allyn and Bacon
Earlier edition copyright © 1999 by Addison Wesley Longman, Inc.
A Pearson Education Company
75 Arlington Street
Boston, Massachusetts 02116

Internet: www.ablongman.com

Library of Congress Cataloging-in-Publication Data

Charles, C. M.
   Building classroom discipline / C. M. Charles. — 7th ed.
      p. cm.
Includes bibliographical references and index.
   ISBN 0-321-07691-5
   1. School discipline.   2. Classroom management.   I. Title.
   LB3012 .C46 2002
   371.5—dc21

                                                    2001022426

Printed in the United States of America
10 9 8 7 6 5 4 3 2 1   05 04 03 02 01

Contents

Preface   *xiii*

CHAPTER 1   **Classroom Discipline: The Problem and the Struggle**   *1*

Behavior and Misbehavior   *2*
Five Types of Misbehavior   *3*
Discipline and Misbehavior   *3*
Is Discipline Really Such a Serious Matter?   *4*
Why Is Misbehavior Becoming Worse?   *4*
Schools' Efforts to Make Adjustments   *6*
Improving Discipline in the Classroom   *7*
Formal Systems of Classroom Discipline   *10*
Building Your Own System of Discipline   *11*
References and Recommended Readings   *11*

CHAPTER 2   **Great Pioneers in Modern Discipline**   *17*

Fritz Redl and William Wattenberg: Discipline through Influencing
Group Behavior   *18*
    Redl and Wattenberg's Principal Teachings   *18*
    Analysis of Redl and Wattenberg's Contributions   *19*
B. F. Skinner: Discipline through Shaping Desired Behavior   *20*
    Skinner's Principal Teachings   *20*
    Analysis of Skinner's Contributions   *21*
William Glasser: Misbehavior as Student Choice   *22*
    Glasser's Principal Teachings   *22*
    Analysis of Glasser's Contributions   *23*
Jacob Kounin: Improving Discipline through Lesson Management   *23*
    Kounin's Principal Teachings   *24*
    Analysis of Kounin's Contributions   *24*
Haim Ginott: Discipline through Congruent Communication   *25*
    Ginott's Principal Teachings   *26*
    Analysis of Ginott's Contributions   *27*

Rudolf Dreikers: Discipline through Democratic Teaching   *28*
Dreikurs's Principal Teachings   *29*
Analysis of Dreikurs's Contributions   *30*
Key Terms Used by the Pioneers in Modern Discipline   *31*
Questions and Activities   *31*
References   *32*

CHAPTER 3   **Lee and Marlene Canter's *Assertive Discipline***   **33**
Preview of Lee and Marlene Canter's Work   *33*
About Lee and Marlene Canter   *34*
The Canters' Contributions to Discipline   *34*
The Canters' Central Focus   *34*
The Canters' Principal Teachings   *35*
Analysis of the Canters' *Assertive Discipline*   *35*
    Needs and Rights in the Classroom   *36*
    Types of Teachers and Their Effects on Students   *36*
    Moving toward Good Discipline   *37*
    Developing a Solid Basis of Trust and Respect   *37*
    Teaching Students How They Are Expected to Behave in the Classroom   *37*
    Establishing a Discipline Plan That Provides Structure
    and Identifies Behavior Limits   *38*
    The Discipline Hierarchy   *39*
    Teaching the Plan   *40*
    Providing Positive Recognition   *40*
    Redirecting Nondisruptive Off-Task Behavior   *41*
    Invoking Consequences   *41*
    Working with Difficult Students   *42*
    Reaching Out to Difficult Students   *42*
    Building Trust with Difficult Students   *43*
    Meeting Difficult Students' Needs   *43*
    Providing Positive Support   *44*
    Redirecting Nondisruptive Misbehavior   *45*
    Interacting with Difficult Students   *45*
Strengths of the Canters' *Assertive Discipline*   *46*
Initiating the Canters' *Assertive Discipline*   *47*
Review of Selected Terminology   *47*
Application Exercises   *48*
    Concept Cases   *48*
Questions and Activities   *48*
Primary References   *49*
Recommended Viewing and Reading   *49*

CHAPTER 4   Fredric Jones's *Positive Classroom Discipline*   51

Preview of Jones's Work   51
About Fredric Jones   51
Jones's Contributions to Discipline   52
Jones's Central Focus   52
Jones's Principal Teachings   52
Analysis of Jones's Positive Classroom Discipline   53
    Misbehavior and Loss of Teaching-Learning Time   53
    Skill Clusters in Jones's Model   54
    Skill Cluster 1: Classroom Structure to Discourage Misbehavior   55
    Skill Cluster 2. Limit-Setting through Body Language   56
    Skill Cluster 3: Using Say, See, Do Teaching   57
    Skill Cluster 4: Responsibility Training through Incentive Systems   57
    Skill Cluster 5: Providing Efficient Help to Individual Students   62
Strengths of Jones's *Positive Classroom Discipline*   63
Initiating Jones's *Positive Classroom Discipline*   64
Review of Selected Terminology   64
Application Exercises   65
    Concept Cases   65
Questions and Activities   65
Primary References   66
Recommended Viewing and Guides   66

CHAPTER 5   Linda Albert's *Cooperative Discipline*   67

Preview of Albert's Work   67
About Linda Albert   67
Albert's Contributions to Discipline   68
Albert's Central Focus   68
Albert's Principal Teachings   69
Analysis of Albert's *Cooperative Discipline*   69
    The Goal of Classroom Discipline   70
    Why Students Misbehave   70
    Albert's Plethora of Strategies   72
    The Three C's of *Cooperative Discipline*   72
    The First C—Capability   72
    The Second C—Helping Students Connect   74
    The Third C—Helping Students Contribute   75
    The Classroom Code of Conduct   76
    Teaching the Code of Conduct   76
    Enforcing the Code of Conduct   77
    Reinforcing the Code of Conduct   78

Involving Students and Parents as Partners   78
Avoiding and Defusing Confrontations   79
Dealing with More Severe Confrontations   80
Implementing Consequences   81
Strengths of Albert's *Cooperative Discipline*   82
Initiating Albert's *Cooperative Discipline*   82
Review of Selected Terminology   82
Application Exercises   83
Concept Cases   83
Questions and Activities   83
Primary References   83
Recommended Readings and Viewing   84

CHAPTER 6   **Thomas Gordon's *Discipline as Self-Control*   85**

Preview of Gordon's Work   85
About Thomas Gordon   85
Gordon's Contributions to Discipline   86
Gordon's Central Focus   86
Gordon's Principal Teachings   87
Analysis of Gordon's *Discipline as Self-Control*   89
Authority   89
Rewards and Punishment   89
What Is Misbehavior, and Who Owns the Problem?   90
The Behavior Window   90
Strengths of Gordon's *Discipline as Self-Control*   98
Initiating Gordon's *Discipline as Self-Control*   99
Review of Selected Terminology   100
Application Exercises   100
Concept Cases   100
Questions and Activities   101
Primary References   101
Recommended Reading   101

CHAPTER 7   **Jane Nelsen, Lynn Lott, and H. Stephen Glenn's *Positive Discipline in the Classroom*   103**

Preview of Nelsen, Lott, and Glenn's Work   103
About Jane Nelsen, Lynn Lott, and H. Stephen Glenn   104
Nelsen, Lott, and Glenn's Contributions to Discipline   104
Nelsen, Lott, and Glenn's Central Focus   104
Nelsen, Lott, and Glenn's Principal Teachings   105
Analysis of Nelsen, Lott, and Glenn's *Positive Discipline in the Classroom*   105
The Significant Seven   106

The Three Empowering Perceptions   *106*
Four Essential Skills   *106*
Developing the Significant Seven   *106*
The Importance of Caring   *108*
Barriers to Relationships   *108*
Eight Building Blocks to Effective Class Meetings   *109*
Beyond Consequences   *112*
Standard Format for Class Meetings   *114*
Remember That the Process Takes Time   *114*
Respectful Classroom Management   *114*
Putting It All Together   *116*
Strengths of *Positive Discipline in the Classroom*   *116*
Initiating *Positive Discipline in the Classroom*   *116*
Review of Selected Terminology   *117*
Application Exercises   *117*
Concept Cases   *117*
Questions and Activities   *118*
Primary References   *118*
Recommended Reading and Viewing   *119*

CHAPTER 8   **William Glasser's *Noncoercive Discipline*   121**

Preview of Glasser's Work   *121*
About William Glasser   *121*
Glasser's Contributions to Discipline   *122*
Glasser's Central Focus   *123*
Glasser's Principal Teachings   *123*
Prior to 1985   *123*
Since 1985   *124*
Analysis of Glasser's *Noncoercive Discipline*   *125*
What School Offers   *125*
Students' Needs   *126*
Curriculum and Quality Work   *127*
Quality Teaching   *127*
Boss Teachers and Lead Teachers   *128*
The Relation of Quality Teaching to Discipline   *130*
When Rules Are Broken   *131*
Strengths of Glasser's *Noncoercive Discipline*   *132*
Initiating Glasser's *Noncoercive Discipline*   *133*
Review of Selected Terminology   *133*
Application Exercises   *134*
Concept Cases   *134*
Questions and Activities   *134*
Primary References   *135*
Recommended Readings   *135*

CHAPTER 9   Richard Curwin and Allen Mendler's *Discipline with Dignity*   137

Preview of Curwin and Mendler's *Discipline with Dignity*   137
About Richard Curwin and Allen Mendler   138
Curwin and Mendler's Contributions to Discipline   138
Curwin and Mendler's Central Focus   138
Curwin and Mendler's Principal Teachings   139
Analysis of Curwin and Mendler's *Discipline with Dignity*   139
   Why Students Misbehave   139
   Dignity   140
   Students Who Are Behaviorally At-Risk   140
   Why Behaviorally At-Risk Students Are Difficult to Control   141
   Helping Students Regain Hope   142
   Disciplining Difficult-to-Control Students   142
   Consequences   143
   Preventing Escalation   144
   Motivating Difficult-to-Manage Students   145
   Dealing with Aggression, Hostility, and Violence   146
   A Four-Phase Plan for Schools and Educators   146
   Techniques for Dealing with Violence in the Classroom   148
   Suggestions to Help Teachers Retrain Themselves   149
   Specific Suggestions for Dealing with Conflict   149
Strengths of Curwin and Mendler's *Discipline with Dignity*   149
Initiating Curwin and Mendler's *Discipline with Dignity*   150
   Principles You Must Accept   150
   Establishing the Social Contract   150
   Providing Motivation and Helpfulness   151
Review of Selected Terminology   151
Application Exercises   151
   Concept Cases   151
Questions and Activities   152
Primary References   152
Recommended Readings   153

CHAPTER 10   Barbara Coloroso's *Inner Discipline*   155

Preview of Coloroso's *Inner Discipline*   155
About Barbara Coloroso   155
Coloroso's Contributions to Discipline   156
Coloroso's Central Focus   156
Coloroso's Principal Teachings   156
Analysis of Coloroso's *Inner Discipline*   158
   Three Types of Schools and Teachers   158

Tenets of Inner Discipline   *159*
Discipline, Not Punishment   *159*
Three Types of Misbehavior   *159*
Effective Classroom Discipline Leads to Inner Discipline   *162*
Teaching Decision Making   *162*
The Three Cons   *163*
Problem Solving   *164*
Natural Consequences   *165*
Reasonable Consequences and RSVP   *166*
Strengths of Coloroso's *Inner Discipline*   *166*
Initiating Coloroso's *Inner Discipline*   *166*
Review of Selected Terminology   *168*
Application Exercises   *168*
Concept Cases   *168*
Questions and Activities   *169*
Primary References   *170*

CHAPTER 11   **Patricia Kyle, Spencer Kagan, and Sally Scott's**
Win-Win Discipline   *171*

Preview of Kyle, Kagan, and Scott's *Win-Win Discipline*   *171*
About Patricia Kyle, Spencer Kagan, and Sally Scott   *172*
Kyle, Kagan, and Scott's Contributions to Discipline   *172*
Kyle, Kagan, and Scott's Central Focus   *173*
Kyle, Kagan, and Scott's Principal Teachings   *173*
Analysis of Kyle, Kagan, and Scott's *Win-Win Discipline*   *174*
Applying the *Win-Win Discipline* Process   *175*
Identifying the Type of Disruptive Behavior—ABCD   *176*
Identifying the Student's Position   *177*
Discipline Structures for the Moment, Follow-Up,
and Long-Term   *178*
Matching Discipline Structures to Student Positions   *180*
The Role of Logical Consequences   *182*
Identifying and Dealing with Whole Class Patterns   *182*
The Big Three   *183*
Parent and Community Alliances and Schoolwide Programs   *183*
Strengths of Kyle, Kagan, and Scott's *Win-Win Discipline*   *184*
Initiating Kyle, Kagan, and Scott's *Win-Win Discipline*   *184*
Review of Selected Terminology   *185*
Application Exercises   *186*
Concept Cases   *186*
Questions and Activities   *187*
Primary Reference   *187*
Suggested Readings   *187*

CHAPTER 12   **Alfie Kohn's** *Beyond Discipline*   189

Preview of Kohn's Work   *189*
About Alfie Kohn   *190*
Kohn's Central Focus   *190*
Kohn's Contributions to Discipline   *190*
Kohn's Principal Teachings   *191*
Analysis of Kohn's *Beyond Discipline*   *192*
     The Trouble with Today's Teaching   *192*
     How Instruction Should Be Done   *193*
     Where Discipline Fits in Kohn's Views on Teaching   *194*
     The Trouble with Compliance   *195*
     The Changes That Are Needed   *196*
     The Value of Conflict   *197*
     Regarding Structure and Limits   *198*
     Class Meetings   *198*
     Making Decisions   *199*
     School as a Community   *200*
Strengths of Kohn's Views   *201*
Implementing Kohn's *Beyond Discipline*   *201*
Review of Selected Terminology   *203*
Application Exercises   *203*
     Concept Cases   *203*
Questions and Activities   *204*
Primary References   *204*
Recommended Reading   *204*

CHAPTER 13   **C. M. Charles's** *Synergetic Discipline*   205

Preview of Charles's *Synergetic Discipline*   *205*
About C. M. Charles   *206*
Charles's Contributions to Discipline   *206*
Charles's Central Focus   *206*
Charles's Principal Teachings   *207*
Analysis of Charles's *Synergetic Discipline*   *208*
     Elements of the Synergetic Approach   *208*
     Discipline in the Synergetic Classroom   *212*
Strengths of Charles's *Synergetic Discipline*   *214*
Initiating Charles's *Synergetic Discipline*   *215*
Review of Selected Terminology   *217*
Application Exercises   *218*
     Concept Cases   *218*
Questions and Activities   *219*
Primary Reference   *219*
Recommended Readings   *219*

CHAPTER 14   Clarifying Your Philosophy and Theory of Discipline   *221*

Philosophy of Discipline   *222*
Theory of Discipline   *224*
The Practice of Discipline   *228*
Review of Selected Terminology   *234*

CHAPTER 15   Finalizing a Personal System of Discipline   *235*

What You and Other Teachers Want   *235*
Your Plan of Action   *236*
    Preventive Discipline   *236*
    Supportive Discipline   *236*
    Corrective Discipline   *237*
Sample Discipline Plans   *237*
    Approach 1. A Plan That Emphasizes Rules and Consequences   *238*
    Deborah Sund's Third-Grade Discipline Program   *238*
    Approach 2. A Plan That Emphasizes Prevention and Human Relationships   *241*
    Gail Charles's Discipline Plan—Eighth Grade English   *242*
Schoolwide Discipline Plans   *244*
    Recommended Components of a Schoolwide System   *244*
    Two Examples of Schoolwide Systems of Discipline   *245*
Implementing Your Personal System   *250*
    The First Days   *250*
    Keeping Your System Flexible   *251*

APPENDIX A   Classroom Scenarios for Analysis and Practice   *253*

Scenario 1: Fifth Grade   *253*
Scenario 2: High School Biology   *254*
Scenario 3: Middle School Library   *255*
Scenario 4: Second Grade   *256*
Scenario 5: High School Special Education   *257*
Scenario 6: Continuation High School Photography Lab   *258*
Scenario 7: Sheltered English Kindergarten   *259*
Scenario 8: Junior High World History   *260*
Scenario 9. High School American Literature   *261*
Scenario 10. Sixth Grade, Student Teacher   *262*

APPENDIX B   Synopses of Models of Discipline Analyzed in This Book   *265*

Assertive Discipline (The Canters)   *265*
Behavior as Student Choice (William Glasser)   *265*

Beyond Discipline to Community (Alfie Kohn)   *265*
Congruent Communication (Haim Ginott)   *266*
Cooperative Discipline (Linda Albert)   *266*
Dealing with the Group (Fritz Redl and William Wattenberg)   *266*
Democratic Discipline (Rudolf Dreikurs)   *267*
Discipline as Self-Control (Thomas Gordon)   *267*
Discipline with Dignity (Richard Curwin and Allen Mendler)   *267*
Inner Discipline (Barbara Coloroso)   *267*
Managing Lessons and the Class (Jacob Kounin)   *268*
Noncoercive Discipline (William Glasser)   *268*
Positive Classroom Discipline (Fredric Jones)   *268*
Positive Discipline in the Classroom (Jane Nelsen, Lynn Lott,
and H. Stephen Glenn)   *269*
Shaping Desired Behavior (B. F. Skinner and his followers)   *269*
Synergetic Discipline (C. M. Charles)   *269*
Win-Win Discipline (Patricia Kyle, Spencer Kagan, and Sally Scott)   *270*

APPENDIX C   **Authorities in Discipline Included in This Book**   *271*
Albert, Linda   *271*
Canter, Lee, and Marlene Canter   *271*
Charles, C. M.   *271*
Coloroso, Barbara   *272*
Curwin, Richard, and Allen Mendler   *272*
Dreikurs, Rudolf (1897–1972)   *272*
Ginott, Haim (1922–1973)   *272*
Glasser, William   *272*
Gordon, Thomas   *273*
Jones, Fredric   *273*
Kohn, Alfie   *273*
Kounin, Jacob   *273*
Kyle, Patricia, Spencer Kagan, and Sally Scott   *273*
Nelsen, Jane, Lynn Lott, and H. Stephen Glenn   *274*
Neo-Skinnerians   *274*
Redl, Fritz, and William Wattenberg   *274*

APPENDIX D   **Major Themes in Discipline, Arranged Alphabetically**   *275*

APPENDIX E   **Glossary of Terms Related to Discipline**   *279*

Bibliography   *289*

Index   *297*

Preface

Most teachers believe that a pleasant classroom environment where students are well-behaved is essential for high-quality teaching and learning. In order to support such an environment, teachers at times exert influence on students to help them behave responsibly and interact positively with others. This type of influence is commonly called *discipline*. In the past, discipline techniques were often demanding and occasionally harsh; they helped keep students in line but produced undesirable side effects such as fearfulness, loss of motivation, and dislike for school. That kind of discipline is no longer required and can now be replaced with discipline techniques that promote student self-direction and positive attitudes toward school and teachers. The techniques for doing so are presented in this book.

Regarding This Book

Beginning with the first edition of *Building Classroom Discipline*, the overriding purpose of this book has been to help teachers develop personal systems of discipline tailored to their individual philosophies and personalities as well as to the needs, traits, and social realities of their schools and communities. None of the commercial models of discipline described in this book is likely to provide a perfect match for all teachers' needs. However, teachers can make excellent use of all the models by selecting judiciously from the information presented and then organizing the strategies and techniques in ways that suit them best.

Over the past 20 years, many advances have been made in discipline. Whereas earlier discipline hinged on reward and punishment, newer techniques encourage students to behave acceptably because they see that doing so is advantageous to themselves and their classmates. *Building Classroom Discipline,* seventh edition, describes a variety of such approaches set forth by leading authorities. These approaches show teachers how to work with students helpfully and respectfully, ensuring learning while preserving student dignity and good teacher–student relationships.

Building Classroom Discipline, seventh edition, is designed for use in pre-service courses in discipline and classroom management, learning and instruction, methods of teaching, and educational psychology. It is equally appropriate for teachers already in service who are seeking more effective and enjoyable ways of working with students. Instructors in school district training programs and teacher institutes will also find the book useful. The book is comprehensive enough to serve as a single or primary text, yet compact enough for use with other texts. It describes for analysis 17 models of discipline developed by some of the most astute educational thinkers of the past half century. Six of these models, all influential predecessors of today's approaches, are summarized and reviewed in historical perspective, which enables readers to follow the developmental trends that have led to today's approaches. An additional 11 models, some widely in use and others just coming onto the scene, are presented in greater detail. These 11, called *application models,* reflect the spectrum of current thought on how discipline is most effectively organized and used. Information presented in the models is further clarified through exercises involving application to realistic problems and situations.

How Application Models Are Presented

Application models are presented in individual chapters organized for maximum clarity, understanding, and applicability. The chapters review the work of individual authorities or teams of authorities and consist of the following:

1. A preview of the authority's discipline scheme, including focus, logic, contributions, and principal suggestions
2. A brief biographical sketch of the authority
3. The authority's contributions to discipline
4. The authority's central focus
5. The authority's principal teachings
6. Analysis of the authority's discipline model
7. Strengths of the model
8. Initiating the model in the classroom
9. Review of terminology particular to the model
10. Application exercises
11. Primary references
12. Recommended reading and viewing (when appropriate)

Review and Feedback from Authorities

Authorities whose discipline approaches are presented as application models have, prior to publication herein, had the opportunity to review the chapter that presents their work and approve the descriptions of concepts, approaches, and terminology central to their models. These authorities and others are continually developing new approaches, updating techniques, and adding new terminology. The ongoing cooperative liaison between discipline authorities and the author of this book ensures that authorities' views are presented accurately.

Material Related to the Models of Discipline

Chapters on important discipline matters not addressed in the application models are provided for the following purposes: (1) to establish the general context of concerns about discipline; (2) to identify trends in discipline techniques and establish relationships between historical models and application models; (3) to make the suggestions given in the application models more understandable and effective; and (4) to make important names, terms, and trends easily identifiable and accessible. These ends are accomplished in the following sections.

Chapter 1 reviews types of behavior that disrupt teaching and prevent learning. The nature of "misbehavior" is discussed and its effects on students and teacher is described. Schools' attempts to deal with behavioral problems are reviewed.

Chapter 2 presents condensed analyses of historical models of discipline, allowing readers to comprehend earlier attempts at dealing with inappropriate classroom behavior, recognize the origins of important concepts and approaches, and identify the trends that have led to today's application models.

Chapter 14, following the presentation of historical and application models, provides assistance in helping readers clarify their own personal philosophy and theory of discipline, an essential phase in developing a personal system of discipline.

Chapter 15 provides guidance to help teachers develop personal systems of discipline that are consistent with their individual philosophy and theory of discipline, as well as with the realities of the students and community with whom they work.

Appendix A presents a group of classroom scenarios involving misbehavior at different grade levels and subject areas. These scenarios provide practice in determining how suggested discipline techniques can be used to resolve problems.

Appendixes B through E present highly summarized information related to discipline. Appendix B gives brief summaries of each of the discipline models presented in the book. Appendix C provides brief professional and contact information about each of the authorities whose work is reviewed in the book. Appendix D reviews the predominant themes evident in modern discipline. And Appendix E presents a comprehensive glossary of terms used in discipline. These appendixes are organized for easy reference.

New to This Edition

Since publication of the previous edition of *Building Classroom Discipline,* new and promising approaches to discipline have appeared that enable educators to work with students in ways that are ever more humane and productive. At the same time, certain older models of discipline have ceased to be used in their entirety, although portions of them can be seen in the newer approaches. *Building Classroom Discipline,* seventh edition, has been reorganized to present newer application models while minimizing, though still identifying, their historical antecedents. The following are new to this edition.

1. Models that are no longer used in their entirety have been summarized and presented in Chapter 2, "Great Pioneers in Modern Discipline." This chapter now provides brief descriptions of six models that in former editions were presented and analyzed in chapters of their own.

2. In the previous edition, the discipline models developed by Barbara Coloroso (*Inner Discipline*) and Alfie Kohn (*Beyond Discipline*) were presented together and were called "emerging models of discipline." The works of those two authorities have attracted wider audiences and are now analyzed in chapters of their own.

3. Two new application models have been added in this edition. They are Patricia Kyle, Spencer Kagan, and Sally Scott's *Win-Win Discipline,* which puts teachers and students on the same side in finding nondisruptive ways for students to meet legitimate needs, and C. M. Charles's *Synergetic Discipline,* which emphasizes disciplinary techniques based on ethics and trust within the context of energized classrooms.

4. Chapter 14, which deals with helping readers clarify their own philosophy and theory of discipline, as well as understand how application is derived accordingly, has been added to serve as a preliminary step in formulating personal systems that are consonant with teacher needs and beliefs as well as with the realities of students being served.

5. Chapter 15, "Building a Personal System of Discipline," has been revised so it now follows naturally from Chapter 14.

6. The reference value of the book has been enhanced with the additions of Appendix B (brief summaries of historical and application models), Appendix C (biographical and contact information for authorities whose work is reviewed in the book), Appendix D (gives predominant themes in today's discipline that cross over from model to model), and Appendix E (an updated glossary of special terms used in discipline). In addition, the comprehensive bibliography of works important in discipline has been updated.

Acknowledgments

The author gratefully acknowledges the valuable contributions made to this and the previous edition by the following people:

Teachers and Administrators

Roy Allen
Constance Bauer
Linda Blacklock
Tom Bolz
Michael Brus
Gail Charles
Ruth Charles
Diana Cordero

Keith Correll
Barbara Gallegos
Nancy Girvin
Kris Halverson
Leslie Hays
Elaine Maltz
Colleen Meagher
Nancy Natale

Linda Pohlenz
David Sisk
Deborah Sund

Mike Straus
Virginia Villalpando

Critical Reviewers

Linda Albert, Cooperative Discipline Institute
Dale Allee, Southwest Missouri State University
Lee and Marlene Cantor, Canter and Associates, Inc.
Barbara Coloroso, *Kids Are Worth It!*
Richard Curwin, Discipline Associates
Philip DiMattia, Boston College
Karen M. Dutt, Indiana State University
Carolyn Eichenberger, St. Louis University
Janne D. Ellsworth, Northern Arizona University
Sara S. Garcia, Santa Clara University
William Glasser, William Glasser Institute
Thomas Gordon, Effectiveness Training International
Marci Green, University of South Florida at Ft. Myers
C. Bobbi Hansen, University of San Diego
Fredric Jones and JoLynne Jones, Fredric H. Jones and Associates, Inc.
David I. Joyner, Old Dominion University
Deborah Keasler, Southwestern Oklahoma State University
Alfie Kohn, Author and Critic
Patricia Kyle, Spencer Kagan, and Sally Scott, *Win-Win Discipline*
Thomas J. Lasley, The University of Dayton
Lawrence Lyman, Emporia State University
Bernice Magnus-Brown, University of Maine
Vick McGinley, West Chester University
Janey L. Montgomery, University of Northern Iowa
Janice L. Nath, University of Houston
Jane Nelsen, Lynn Lott, and H. Stephen Glenn, Empowering People
Merrill M. Oaks, Washington State University
Jack Vaughan Powell, University of Georgia
Elizabeth Primer, Cleveland State University
Mary C. Shake, University of Kentucky
Alma A. Shearin, University of Central Arkansas
Terry R. Shepherd, Southern Illinois University at Carbondale
JoAnne Smatlan, Seattle Pacific University
Bruce Smith, Henderson State University
Kay Stickle, Ball State University
Sylvia Tinling, University of California, Riverside
Gwen Webb-Johnson, University of Texas at Austin
Bill Weldon, Arizona State University
Kathleen Whittier, State University of New York at Plattsburgh

CHAPTER 1

Classroom Discipline
The Problem and the Struggle

The scene is an inner-city school. Classroom 314 is quiet as students listen attentively to the teacher's questions about a recent lesson. Suddenly, eager hands begin to wave and bodies twist out of their seats amidst shouts of "ooh me," "I know," "ooh-oh." Quiet returns when one student is chosen to answer. As soon as she has responded, others begin to yell out refutations or additions and compete again for teacher recognition. As they participate wholeheartedly in class, several students are simultaneously but secretly passing notes and candy and signalling to each other in sign and face language. When the questions end and seat work begins, some students offer to help others who are unsure of how to proceed.

But across the hall in room 315, chaos reigns. The room is noisy with the shouting, laughter, and movement of many children. Though most students are seated, many are walking or running aimlessly around the classroom. Some stop at others' desks, provoke them briefly, and move on. Several students who are lining up textbooks as "race courses" for toy cars laugh when the teacher demands their attention. As the teacher struggles to ask a question over the noise, few if any students volunteer to answer. When one student does respond correctly, others yell out, "You think you're so smart." (Schwartz 1981, p. 99)

By most teachers' standards, the discipline in Room 314 is acceptable, while that in Room 315 is not. But what is the difference? In both rooms, students are making noise and behaving in ways not usually condoned. Yet the teacher in Room 314 is probably satisfied with the lesson, while the teacher in Room 315 is not. Why? The answer lies in the teacher's sense that the classroom situation is productive. The students in 314 are showing initiative, but are still responsive to the teacher. Their personal interactions are positive and reasonably respectful. The teacher feels progress is being made and is happy to see students displaying reasonable manners while actively involved in the lesson.

In contrast, the students in 315 are barely in touch with the lesson. They are accomplishing little that is worthwhile. They are doing more or less what they want, disregarding what the teacher says. Their behavior is haphazard and their interactions frequently disrespectful of teacher and each other. The teacher is rightfully concerned about the behavior in this class, for it is keeping students from learning and is encouraging habits that are self-defeating for students. An impartial judge would consider the lesson a failure.

If you were the teacher in Room 315, what would you hope to see? Think about this a moment. How would you want students to respond to your lessons? To you? How would you want them to relate to each other? What would, or could, you do to make things as you'd like them to be? Could you work out a detailed plan concerning how you'd work with the class so it would be productive and rewarding? Suppose you did make such a plan and found that students disregarded what you asked them to do. Then what? Questions such as these are difficult to answer, and in truth are more difficult to answer in a real classroom than when discussing imaginary situations. If the answers were easy, we'd have no teachers feeling unfulfilled or ready to leave teaching because they could no longer tolerate dealing with disrespectful, unmotivated students.

By the time we complete this chapter's review of the nature and frequency of classroom misbehavior, you may find the overall picture dismal and be asking yourself how teaching could possibly be worth it. Be assured that there is another side to the picture. We have great numbers of very successful teachers, working in all types of schools with all types of students, who find teaching joyful and rewarding. They are proud to see their students interacting positively and behaving considerately. They feel a closeness to many of them and enjoy trusting relationships. To be sure, they experience some stress. That will always be the case when one works with energetic students. But stress does not damage us if its overall negativity remains within limits.

In short, if you are like most teachers, your greatest continuing problem will involve dealing with misbehavior—with maintaining control in the class. You are not going to fail because you have an insufficient knowledge of composition or algebra or world history, nor will you leave teaching because you can't recite the cardinal principles of education or make a lesson plan. If you fail in teaching it will almost certainly be because you cannot keep students engaged in class lessons. We are going to make sure this doesn't happen to you. In this chapter and those that follow, you will find information and suggestions that will enable you to get the most from teaching, including the greatest prize of all, esteem from your students. You will begin by becoming aware of the good, the bad, and the ugly in discipline. As you learn more about discipline, you will find misbehavior less daunting than it first appears and certainly far from unmanageable.

Behavior and Misbehavior

Behavior refers to everything people do, good or bad, right or wrong, helpful or useless, productive or wasteful. **Misbehavior** is the same as behavior except that, first, it is *inappropriate* for the setting or situation in which it occurs, and second, it is done *willfully,* that is, on purpose, or else out of ignorance of what is expected. An accidental hiccup during quiet work time is not misbehavior, even if the class breaks up laughing. But when feigned in order to gain attention or disrupt a lesson, the same hiccup is justifiably considered misbehavior. If you look back to what students were doing in Room 315, you will see that some of their actions seem to suggest a careless disregard for expectations while others seem to be intentional transgressions.

Five Types of Misbehavior

Teachers contend with five broad **types of misbehavior.** In descending order of seriousness, as judged by social scientists, they are as follows:

1. Aggression: physical and verbal attacks on teachers, students, or property
2. Immorality: acts contrary to accepted morality, such as cheating, lying, and stealing
3. Defiance of authority: refusal to do as the teacher requests
4. Class disruptions: talking loudly, calling out, walking about the room, clowning, tossing things
5. Goofing off: fooling around, out of seat, not doing assigned tasks, dawdling, daydreaming

Teachers generally agree with social scientists' judgments about the relative seriousness of the five categories of misbehavior, and indeed they dread having to deal with aggression, immorality, and defiance. But in practice the misbehavior that predominates in their classrooms is usually much less serious. Mostly it consists of goofing off, talking, and inattention. These are relatively innocuous behaviors that nevertheless waste much instructional time and interfere with learning.

Discipline and Misbehavior

The word **discipline** has several different definitions, but two predominate in education. The first refers to school misbehavior; for example, "The discipline in that room is pretty bad." The second refers to what teachers do to help students behave acceptably—"Mr. Smythe's discipline system is one of the best I've seen." Both meanings are used in these discussions; the context will indicate which is which. You can see that discipline is interconnected with misbehavior. Where there is no misbehavior, discipline is not a consideration.

Discipline (what teachers do) is intended to prevent, suppress, and redirect misbehavior. All teachers know that students sometimes behave with sweetness, kindness, gentility, consideration, helpfulness, and honesty. Their doing so makes teaching one of the most satisfying of all professions. But students also behave at times with hostility, abusiveness, disrespect, disinterest, and cruelty, all of which can devastate personal feelings and severely damage the learning climate of the classroom. Ideally, the goal of discipline is to reduce the need for teacher intervention over time by helping students become self-disciplined, that is, able to control their own behavior appropriately. When teachers apply various discipline techniques, they hope not only that misbehavior will cease but that students will further internalize self-discipline and display it in the classroom and elsewhere.

Is Discipline Really Such a Serious Matter?

Phi Delta Kappa, a professional organization for educators, annually sponsors a Gallup Poll of the public's attitudes toward education. One question on the survey asks: "What do you think are the biggest problems with which the public schools of this community must contend?" In the overwhelming majority of the polls conducted so far, discipline has been listed as the top problem. For example, the 29th annual poll (Rose, Gallup, and Elam 1997) revealed that the public believes lack of discipline and uncooperative students are two of the most troublesome problems in public education. This continues a trend that began many years ago showing the public is very concerned about discipline, drugs, and violence in the schools.

Of course, public opinion can be suspect because it is influenced by sensational occurrences, such as physical attacks on teachers and wanton vandalism of schools. In the case of discipline, however, little disagreement exists between educators and the public. Administrators report a widespread increase in school violence, and for years, teachers have maintained that misbehavior interferes significantly with their teaching (Elam 1989). The frustration that comes from continually dealing with misbehavior produces stress that affects some teachers as severely as battle fatigue does combat soldiers, producing symptoms such as lethargy, exhaustion, tension, depression, and high blood pressure.

The concern about discipline is not declining, but continues to increase. Numerous studies list discipline among the most serious problems with which teachers must contend and a significant factor in their leaving the profession. It is largely responsible for the teacher dropout rate of between 30 and 40 percent within the first three years on the job ("Study backs" 1987; Curwin 1992; Brownell, Smith, and McNellis 1997; Halford 1998). Adding to the problem is the fact that experienced teachers tend to transfer away from schools that have high levels of misbehavior, leaving those schools staffed by teachers not yet skilled in discipline.

Why Is Misbehavior Becoming Worse?

Given that misbehavior seems to be growing steadily worse, one feels compelled to ask why. After all, schools everywhere are using powerful new programs of discipline designed to foster genteel behavior and reduce violence. Are these programs having no effect? Could it possibly be that, contrary to common sense, they are actually making the situation worse? That was the conclusion reached for earlier authoritarian systems that were judged to be in direct conflict with the democratic goals of education (Peterson 1996; Schimmel 1997), and the same complaint is being heard today about the newer systems (Kohn 1996, Peterson 1996).

Most authorities place blame at the feet of society. Schools reflect, more than reform, the nature of the society they serve. Where society is humane, gentle, and caring, so are students in the schools. Where society is hostile and uncaring, students behave in the same manner. At present, societies around the world are experiencing a progressive decline in humane behavior—that is, in individuals' willingness to help and show consideration for each other. That same change is evident among students. The fundamental proposition of mass education is that schooling improves society, and no one would suggest that democratic societies would be better off if left uneducated. But society is more powerful than school when it comes to establishing norms of behavior. Many people have argued that the media must assume much of the blame for misbehavior, particularly violence. In 1998, President Clinton scolded the motion picture industry for their unending emphasis on violence, maiming, and killing which, he said, leaves teenage children numbed to violence (Broder 1998). It is not likely schools can correct all that society has done wrong.

Thirty years ago, the vast majority of schools were barely touched by serious student misbehavior. Occasionally one would hear of students being expelled for violations of dress code, but rarely for violent behavior. Today, it is a rare school, even in the best neighborhoods, that remains free from aggressive, sometimes criminal behavior by its students. A study on victimization in grades 6 through 12 reported that unsafe conditions at school are a reality for most U.S. students (Nolin 1996). A few years ago it was unthinkable to bring a weapon into school. Suddenly students began bringing weapons in such numbers that schools had to implement stringent measures of weapons detection and confiscation. This phenomenon is not limited to secondary schools; guns have appeared in many elementary schools as well (Collins 1995). In 1996, it was reported that over 100,000 teachers and 200,000 students are physically assaulted at school each year in the United States (Mazin and Hestand 1996). In 1996–1997, more than one-half of all U.S. public schools reported at least one crime and one in ten reported a violent crime. In that same year, more than 6,000 students were expelled for bringing guns to school, and in 1998, 42 students were killed in school violence (Egan 1999). Where once student violence was seen only in inner city schools, it has now spread into the suburbs, even into posh schools (see Zeitlin and Parrilla 1999). For the most part, students responsible for this violence come from homes where parents use violence in handling stress and resolving conflict (Massey 1998). There was a time when teacher stress occurred mainly in secondary schools. Now, elementary teachers report even greater stress than do secondary teachers (McCormick 1997). By 1993, stress was being reported as a major concern of prekindergarten teachers (Micklo 1993) and now we are beginning to hear university faculty complaining about unacceptable and disruptive student behavior, so serious in some cases that assistance is required to help professors cope (Schneider 1998).

One must take care not to tar all students and school with this brush. The truth is, the majority of students remain well-intentioned, willing to learn, and inclined to cooperate. But that does not negate the fact that misbehavior, even if it does come from a minority of students, presents an increasingly serious problem for teachers and students (Shen 1995).

How are teachers contending with the increasing pressures of misbehavior? As noted, a surprising number of teachers suffer stress and leave the profession because of it. Many of those who remain are asking for help. Greenlee and Ogletree (1993) surveyed 50 elementary and secondary teachers. Of the respondents, 41 said they needed more training in handling disruptive behavior, and 39 said they were suffering undue stress because of the difficulties in dealing with misbehavior. It is important to note that in this survey the teachers were not referring to criminal or violent behavior. They identified the behaviors that most seriously interfered with their work as student disrespect for others, disinterest in school, lack of attention, and excessive talking.

Misbehavior, as we have seen, produces harmful physical and psychological effects on teachers. It also affects their job performance. Rancifer (1993) reported that teachers who are poor in controlling misbehavior experience little job satisfaction and become increasingly ineffective in their work. Shreeve (1993) surveyed 91 school districts in Washington State and found that between 1984 and 1987, 153 teachers were placed on probation. Sixty-nine percent of that group were then dismissed or else retired or were reassigned to other duties, most of them because of inability to control their classes. Ehrgott and associates (1992) explored "marginal teachers" in 518 elementary and secondary schools in California. They concluded that somewhere between 5 and 20 percent of all teachers in those schools were considered marginal, being especially poor at maintaining discipline, establishing adequate relations with students, and conveying subject matter. Generally speaking, novice teachers seem not to anticipate the difficulties they will encounter. At first, they are preoccupied with how to present the content of lessons. But later, misbehavior and discipline become overriding concerns (Richardson 1993; Gibbons and Jones 1994; Byrne 1998).

Related to teacher dropout is the perplexing matter of teacher burnout. Terry (1997) points out that approximately 40 percent of U.S. teachers leave teaching before they reach retirement age, most because of burnout. Byrne (1998) studied burnout and found that it tended to hit teachers hardest in years 7 and 10. Its presence was devastating to teachers and their relationships with others. The main causes of burnout were feckless or uncaring administrators and uncaring students. On the positive side, there is evidence that special programs provided in the schools for new teachers—programs that emphasize discipline expectations, classroom management, and peer support—can improve new teachers' chances of success and longevity in the profession (Loucks 1993; Rancifer 1995).

Schools' Efforts to Make Adjustments

Schools and community agencies have begun taking action to curb violently disruptive behavior. Some urban schools are merging the school police force with that of the city, for increased training and authority (Dowdy 1995). To help allay teacher fear of violence, some schools are implementing "zero-tolerance" policies against weapons and violence, that bring immediate suspension for violators ("Teachers fear...1995). In 1995, New York State enacted automatic one-year suspensions for bringing weapons to school (Dao 1995).

Schools' efforts are not limited to sanctions against students. Most are implementing special programs and designating special schools for students with serious misbehavior ("A place for.. 1994). In 1995, New York City Schools took over direct control of 16 city schools especially troubled with misbehavior and chronic low achievement (Newman 1995) and, in 1999, began operating certain "charter schools" formerly plagued with poor discipline and low achievement. In many schools where misbehavior has not reached serious levels, school boards are reimplementing programs that teach values and ethics, including self-discipline, respect, honesty, responsibility, and integrity ("Classroom discipline...1990; "Fighting violence...1993; Weirs 1995; Woo 1995; Harrow 1995; Shen 1995; Schmidt 1996). But it is still behavior in the classroom that troubles teachers most. For years teachers have felt they were fighting a lonely and losing battle, but now parents and even students are raising voices against classroom behavior that damages learning (Nealon 1995). It remains to be seen whether these schoolwide measures will have a positive effect on disruptive (or more frequently, noncooperative) classroom behavior that interferes strongly with teaching and learning.

Improving Discipline in the Classroom

Teachers want to teach well and help students learn. Since misbehavior often prevents their doing so, the fundamental question for teachers is· "What can I do to promote attention, cooperation, and civil behavior among the students under my direction?" Happy to say, new suggestions are appearing regularly for helping teachers, novice and experienced, understand misbehavior and deal with it more effectively.

In recent years, we have seen a number of well-organized easily-applied discipline programs made available to educators. They began most notably with Lee and Marlene Canter's *Assertive Discipline* (1976) and have continued to appear regularly. The most widely-recognized of those programs are analyzed in this book in Chapters 3 through 13. Those mainstream programs are highly touted, but even so some of them have begun drawing criticism. Some have been labelled "overly authoritarian," what most of them were trying *not* to be in the first place. In response to that criticism some are being progressively modified. Most now make evident a new thrust in discipline—one that emphasizes bringing in students as partners in deciding on matters of class behavior and instruction. This emphasis urges teachers to treat students with respect and dignity while encouraging personal development and self-discipline (Charles 1996). Burton (1998) describes the movement as rejecting the "psychological theory" of discipline while espousing a more "critical theory" of discipline. In the former, emphasis is placed on student behavior and what the teacher can do to improve it, with the teacher clearly directing the process. In the latter, students' feelings and emotions are brought to the fore as teachers implement a cooperative democratic climate in the classroom, where students are allowed responsible input into decisions about their behavior and learning.

Teachers are beginning to take this newer approach to heart. Lumsden (1996), in an article entitled "Motivating Today's Students: The Same Old Stuff Just Doesn't Work," reported interviews with two teachers and a principal recognized for their in motivation and instructional effectiveness. Those educators believe that acceptable classroom behavior occurs naturally when students are kept highly interested and engaged in activities. They say teachers will have little discipline trouble if they provide enthusiasm, excitement, student choice, responsibility, cooperative learning, activity-based instruction, authentic learning tasks, real-life applications, caring relationships, individual goals, and student-led conferences. Gootman (1997) has written a book for teachers that focuses on student self-control as opposed to control imposed by the teacher. She stresses such topics as caring teachers making a difference by creating a community of caring listeners and talkers and problem-solving as a tool for students.

Others have added to the newer approach to discipline by attending to certain facets of the broader picture. For example, Phillips-Hershey and Kanagy (1996) provide suggestions concerning nonviolent options that students can use in dealing with anger. They remind us that student inability to control and channel anger appropriately usually underlies violence. Lickona (1996) and Curwin and Mendler (1997) address school violence per se, arguing that if we are to counter the surge of youth violence we must begin instilling ethical values in students and call on families, churches, and communities to work with us as partners.

Character development seems to be part and parcel of suggestions about newer approaches to discipline. Crossner (1997) says that students have had too much authoritarian and permissive control and now require a democratic approach in which they must exercise both choice and responsibility. She urges teachers to be better listeners to what students say and take time to offer much student choice, explain why certain decisions are made, negotiate reasonable solutions to problems, and value the contributions of students. Schneider (1996) describes the Educational Responsibility program used in many New York State schools. In that program, teachers strive to organize their programs to meet student needs, offer choices, focus on improvement, and provide value for effort. Peterson (1996) says that because most of the well-known discipline systems are not working as we had hoped, teachers should emphasize "discipleship," encouraging their students to become "teachers of others," which brings increased decision making, attention to the well-being of others, and responsibility. Kohn (1998) urges teachers to give up "doing to" students in favor of "working with" them, emphasizing among other things good listening, responsiveness, and a collaborative effort to build a sense of community in the classroom. Miller (1997) urges teachers to make regular use of class meetings, provides directions for incorporating class meetings into the ongoing curriculum, and shows teachers how to overcome concerns about not having sufficient time for meetings. Wade (1997) tells about a school in Connecticut that became dissatisfied with its discipline program and discarded it in favor of giving students a sense of ownership in the educational process. When students misbehave teachers help them reflect on their behavior, consider its effects, and decide how to proceed from that point. The program includes a spirit committee, classroom buddies, school-community breakfasts, and school assemblies to build community.

The changes advocated in such approaches to discipline move students from what Freiberg (1996) calls "tourists" in the classroom to "citizens" of the classroom. Freiberg characterizes effective discipline as that which combines instructional effectiveness with student self-discipline, developed cooperatively with the teacher (see also Sudzina 1997). But in order to be effective, such programs often require support from the community. A 1997 column entitled "Parents as Partners" in the journal

Our Children, urges schools to bring parents into the ongoing programs as long-term partners. Ideally, parents would not only support the program but would agree to model appropriate behaviors and attitudes, provide guidance, communicate love, teach responsibility, and demonstrate a balanced approach to discipline.

Experience has taught that if teachers are to replace their older ideas about discipline with new ones that are more effective, they must hear convincing evidence and receive clear instructions on how to do so. It is a waste of time for critics to cajole and philosophize if they provide no guidance for change. Teachers remain greatly concerned about what to do when students misbehave—in other words, what they do or say, specifically, to correct the problem. This concern is particularly obvious among new teachers. In the absence of clear, effective, easily-applied methods of countering misbehavior, beginning teachers usually fall back on what they themselves experienced as students. Weinstein, Woolfolk, and Dittmeier (1994) found that while student teachers seemed eager to view discipline as preventive and nonpunitive, they were more comfortable when assuming an authoritarian role in the classroom. Johnson (1994) discovered that when student teachers were asked to judge the comparative merits of dominance, rule-based, and nurturing styles of discipline, they indicated a clear preference for a rule-based approach, but readily admitted they didn't really understand how to implement that approach. One means of attending to this problem is reported by Teasley (1996) who describes how to help pre-service teachers determine, first, how they want to "be" in the classroom (their self-image as teacher in all its aspects) and, second, how they can, from that self-image, strategically deal with classroom misbehavior.

The authoritarian approach to discipline dies hard. Beginning teachers usually revert back to it quickly. It is interesting to note that teachers designated as outstanding may be more nurturing than other teachers in dealing with students. Agne, Greenwood, and Miller (1994) compared "teachers of the year" against matched in-service teachers and explored the effects of gender, years of service, grade levels taught, and highest degrees earned. They found teachers of the year to be significantly more humanistic than others in their dealings with students.

What does it mean to be "humanistic?" Curwin (1995) describes it as schools reducing cynicism, making all students feel welcome, replacing reward and punishment with strong values, and asking students to contribute ideas for resolving problems. These suggestions are carried forward by Kohn (1996) who advises moving beyond the usual conception of discipline in favor of developing a sense of community in the classroom, and by Charles (2000) who believes that in order to be effective in today's classroom, discipline must involve shared responsibility based on teacher ethics and the development of trust.

Being humanistic does not imply that schools should abandon standards of order. To the contrary, Blendinger (1996) maintains that an orderly classroom is a primary determinant of teaching success. He advocates an approach to discipline that includes the following: (1) develop a discipline plan, (2) establish classroom rules, (3) determine consequences for violating rules, (4) recognize and celebrate good behavior, and (5) involve parents in helping children behave well. While the outline of such an approach may smack of the old-fashioned, the difference lies in its emphasizing good instruction and positive human relations. Kounin, back in 1971, urged teachers to use certain teaching and management techniques to keep misbehavior under control. That line of thought continues. Martens and Kelly (1993) advocate instructional practices that reduce misbehavior by emphasizing engaged learning. Castle and Rogers (1993) say that student participation in rule-making encourages active involvement, respect for rules, cooperation, and sense of ownership in the classroom, the same as was found when eight middle schools implemented a program to improve adolescent conduct through clarity of rules, school-home communication, and reinforcement of positive behavior (Gottfredson, Gottfredson, and Hybl 1993).

Conflict resolution has been emphasized in recent years as an important component of classroom discipline. When students learn and practice skills of conflict resolution, they become more inclined to work out problems among themselves before the problems escalate (Castle and Rogers 1993; Bozzone 1994; Johnson, Acikogz, and Johnson 1994). Johnson and Johnson (1996) point out that there are positive aspects to conflict and that most conflict, rather than being allowed to deteriorate into serious misbehavior, can be resolved amicably with mutual satisfaction. They present directions for helping students resolve disputes and show how to use conflict as an opportunity for learning.

Also characterizing the newer discipline is the teaching of values, ethical behavior, and decision making. Fuhr (1993) stresses the importance of helping students distinguish between right and wrong. Stone (1993) recommends patiently teaching social and moral understanding. Black (1994) surveyed 40 classroom management studies and found that in most of them teachers were being asked to design lessons that helped students make ethical judgments and decisions. Charles (2000) maintains that ethics and trust are essential in discipline. Teachers have also learned the value of procedures that promote students' sense of self-worth ("La Disciplina Positiva" 1994) and that focus on personal growth and academic progress (Hindle 1994; Powell and Taylor 1994). This requires that teachers give up some of their traditional control and allow more student decision making, an option that is gaining favor everywhere (Blank and Kershaw 1993; Kohn 1996).

Formal Systems of Classroom Discipline

It has been only a few decades since educators began looking seriously for ways to promote good student behavior by means other than intimidation and punishment. Educators began to recognize the limitations of the traditional approach to discipline and together with occasional scholars began identifying and clarifying nonpunitive approaches to behavior management. Several important discipline schemes appeared between 1951 and 1972, as we will note in Chapter 2. Those views opened educators' minds to new possibilities and contributed significant elements that have become components of today's powerful systems of discipline. As concern about discipline continued to grow, other educators, psychologists, and psychiatrists developed still more effective and workable approaches. The best known and most widely used of these programs are presented in Chapters 3 through 13 of this book.

Building Your Own System of Discipline

The purpose of this book has remained constant since its inception—to assist readers in organizing and implementing their own personal systems of discipline. The conviction underlying this purpose is that the best system of discipline for meeting individual teachers' needs is not any of the models described herein, but rather ones that teachers compose for themselves, ones they tailor to fit their particular personality, their philosophy of teaching, and the realities of the students, school, and community where they teach. The information needed for accomplishing that end is provided in the chapters, appendixes, and glossary that follow. There you will find workable concepts and tactics you can assemble to make your own effective discipline system. Chapters 14 and 15 are designed to help you put your discipline system together.

References and Recommended Readings

A *handbook of alternatives to corporal punishment*. 4th ed. 1994. Oklahoma City: Oklahoma State Department of Education.

A place for problem students: Separate school proposed for disruptive teenagers. 1994. *Washington Post.* January 13.

Agne, J., G. Greenwood, and L. Miller. 1994. Relationships between teacher belief systems and teacher effectiveness. *Journal of Research and Development in Education*, 27(3), 141–152.

Black, S. 1994. Throw away the hickory stick. *Executive Educator,* 16(4), 44–47.

Blank, M., and C. Kershaw. 1993. Perceptions of educators about classroom management demands when using interactive strategies. Paper presented at the annual meeting of the American Educational Research Association (Atlanta, April 12–16).

Blendinger, J. 1996. *QLM: Quality leading & managing. A practical guide for improving schools.* Dubuque, Iowa: Kendall Hunt.

Blumenfeld-Jones, D. 1996. Conventional systems of classroom discipline (the patriarchy speaks). *Journal of Educational Thought/Revue de la Pensee Educative*, 30(1), 5–21.

Boothe, J., L. Bradley, and T. Flick. 1993. The violence at your door. *Executive Educator,* 15(1), 16–22.

Bozzone, M. 1994. Spend less time refereeing and more time teaching. *Instructor,* 104(1), 88–93.

Broder, J. 1998. Clinton blames Hollywood, access to firearms, and lax supervision for school violence. *The New York Times.* June 14.

Brownell, M., S. Smith, and J. McNellis. 1997. Reflections on "Attrition in Special Education: Why Teachers Leave the Classroom and Where They Go." *Exceptionality,* 7(3), 87–91.

Burton, M. 1998. Teachers action—students lives: The silent voice of discipline. Position Paper available from ERIC. ERIC Identifier: ED423215.

Byrne, J. 1998. Teacher as hunger artist: Burnout: Its causes, effects, and remedies. *Contemporary Education,* 69(2), 86–91.

Canter, L. 1996. Discipline alternatives. First, the rapport—then, the rules. *Learning,* 24(5), 12, 14.

Canter, L., and M. Canter. 1992. *Assertive discipline: Positive behavior management for today's classroom.* 2nd ed. Santa Monica, CA: Lee Canter & Associates.

Castle, K., and K. Rogers. 1993. Rule-creating in a constructivist classroom community. *Childhood Education*, 70(2), 77–80.

Charles, C. 2000. *The synergetic classroom: Joyful teaching and gentle discipline.* New York: Longman.

Charles, M. 1996. A note on school reform. *Canadian Social Studies*, 30(3), 19–20.

Classroom discipline and lessons in social values. 1990. *The New York Times*, B, 7.3, January 31.

Clawson, P. 1995. Hispanic parents demonstrate to protest students' expulsions. *Chicago Tribune*. October 24.

Collins, R. 1995. Dover takes action. *Boston Globe*. November 12.

Coloroso, B. 1994. *Kids are worth it! Giving your child the gift of inner discipline*. New York: William Morrow.

Crossner, S. 1997. Helping young children to develop character. *Early Childhood News, 9(2)*, 20–24.

Curwin, R. 1992. *Rediscovering hope…Our greatest teaching strategy*. Bloomington, IN: National Educational Service.

———. 1995. A humane approach to reducing violence in schools. *Educational Leadership, 52(5)*, 72–75.

Curwin, R., and A. Mendler. 1997. *As tough as necessary. Countering violence, aggression, and hostility in our schools*. Alexandria, VA: Association for Supervision and Curriculum Development.

Dao, J. 1995. Suspension now required for taking gun to school. *New York Times*. August 1.

Dowd, J. 1997. Refusing to play the blame game. *Educational Leadership, 54(8)*, 67–69.

Dowdy, Z. 1995. School officers to merge with Boston police force. *Boston Globe*. March 16.

Downing, J. 1996. Establishing a discipline plan in elementary physical education. *Journal of Physical Education, Recreation, and Dance, 67(6)*, 25–30.

Egan, T. 1999. Violence by youths: Looking for answers. *The New York Times*. April 22.

Ehrgott, et al. 1992. A study of the marginal teacher in California. Paper presented at the annual meeting of the California Educational Research Association (San Francisco, November).

Elam, S. 1989. The second Gallup/Phi Delta Kappa Poll of teachers' attitudes toward the public schools. *Phi Delta Kappan 70(10)*, 785–798.

Elam, S., L. Rose, and A. Gallup. 1995. The 27th annual Phi Delta Kappa/Gallup Poll of the public's attitudes toward the public schools. *Phi Delta Kappan, 76(1)*, 41–56.

Ellis, D., and P. Karr-Kidwell. 1995. A study of assertive discipline and recommendations for effective classroom management methods. Paper. Washington, DC: U.S. Department of Education. ERIC Clearinghouse #35596.

Farner, C. 1996. Discipline alternatives. Mending the broken circle. *Learning, 25(1)*, 27–29.

Feldman, D. 1994. The effect of assertive discipline procedures on preschool children in segregated and integrated settings: A longitudinal study. *Education and Training in Mental Retardation and Developmental Disabilities, 29(4)*, 291–306.

Fighting violence with values. 1993. *Atlanta Journal*. December 23.

Foltz-Gray, D. 1996. The bully trap: Young tormentors and their victims find ways out of anger and isolation. *Teaching Tolerance, 5(2)*, 18–23.

Freiberg, H. 1996. From tourists to citizens in the classroom. *Educational Leadership 54(1)*, 32–36.

Fuhr, D. 1993. Effective classroom discipline: Advice for educators. *NASSP Bulletin, 76(549)*, 82–86.

Gardner, P. 1996. The giant at the front: Young teachers and corporal punishment in inter-war elementary schools. *History of Education 25(2)*, 141–163.

Gibbons, L., and L. Jones. 1994. Novice teachers' reflectivity upon their classroom management. Paper. Washington, DC: U.S. Department of Education. ERIC Clearinghouse #SP036198.

Glasser, W. 1969. *Schools Without Failure*. New York: Harper and Row.

———. 1993. *The Quality School Teacher*. New York: Harper Perennial.

———. 1996. Then and now. The theory of choice. *Learning, 25(3)*, 20–22.

Good, P. 1996. Discipline alternatives: It's not your job. *Learning, 25(3)*, 36–37.

Gootman, M. 1997. *The caring teacher's guide to discipline: Helping young students learn self-control, responsibility, and respect*. Thousand Oaks, CA: Corwin Press, Inc.

Gottfredson, D., G. Gottfredson, and L. Hybl. 1993. Managing adolescent behavior: A multi-year, multischool study. *American Educational Research Journal, 30(1)*, 179–215.

Gratch, A. 1998. Growing teaching professionals: Lessons taught by first-year teachers. Paper presented at the Annual Conference on Qualitative Research in Education (Athens, GA, January 8–10).

Greenlee, A., and E. Ogletree. 1993. Teachers' attitudes toward student discipline problems and classroom management strategies. Washington, DC: U.S. Department of Education. ERIC Clearinghouse #PS02185 1.

Halford, J. 1998. Easing the Way for Teachers. *Educational Leadership: 55(5)*, 33–36.

Heaviside, S., C. Rowand, C. Williams, and E. Farris. 1998. *Violence and discipline problems in the U.S. public schools: 1996–97.* Evaluative Report. Washington, DC: U.S. Government Printing Office.

Henley, M. 1997. Six surefire strategies to improve classroom discipline. *Learning, 26(1)*, 43–45.

Hindle, D. 1994. Coping proactively with middle years students. *Middle School Journal, 25(3)*, 31–34.

Horne, A. 1994. Teaching children with behavior problems takes understanding, tools, and courage. *Contemporary Education, 65(3)*, 122–127.

Hughes, H. 1994. From fistfights to gunfights: Preparing teachers and administrators to cope with violence in school. Paper presented at the annual meeting of the American Association of Colleges for Teacher Education (Chicago, February).

Johnson, D., K. Acikogz, and R. Johnson. 1994. Effects of conflict resolution training on elementary school students. *Journal of Social Psychology, 134(6)*, 803–817.

Johnson, D., and R. Johnson. 1996. Peacemakers: Teaching students to resolve their own and schoolmates' conflicts. *Focus on Exceptional Children, 28(6)*, 1–11.

Johnson, V. 1994. Student teachers' conceptions of classroom control. *Journal of Educational Research, 88(2)*, 109–117.

Jones, F. 1996. Discipline alternatives. Did not did, too. *Learning, 24(6)*, 24, 26.

Kohn, A. 1996. *Beyond discipline: From compliance to community.* Alexandria, VA: Association for Supervision and Curriculum Development.

———. 1998. Beyond bribes and threats: How not to get control of the classroom. *NAMTA Journal, 23(1)*, 6–61

La discipline positiva. 1994. ERIC Digest. Urbana, IL: ERIC Clearinghouse on Elementary and Early Childhood Education.

Landen, W. 1992. Violence and our schools: What can we do? *Updating School Board Policies, 23*, 1–5.

Lickona, T. 1996. Teaching respect and responsibility. *Reclaiming Children and Youth: Journal of Emotional and Behavioral Problems, 5(3)*, 143–151.

Loucks, H. 1993. Teacher education: A success story. *Principal, 73(1)*, 27–29.

Lumsden, L. 1996. Motivating today's students: The same old stuff doesn't work. *Portraits of Success, 1(n2)*, November 1996.

Mackenzie, R. 1997. Setting limits in the classroom. *American Educator, 21(3)*, 32–43

Martens, B., and S. Kelly. 1993. A behavioral analysis of effective teaching. *School Psychology Quarterly, 8(1)*, 10–26.

Massey, M. 1998. Early childhood violence prevention. *ERIC digest.* ERIC Identifier: ED424032.

Mazin, L., and J. Hestand. 1996. This gun is loaded. *Learning, 25(2)*, 44, 46.

McCormick, J. 1997. Occupational stress of teachers: Biographical differences in a large school system. *Journal of Educational Administration, 35(1)*, 18–38.

Micklo, S. 1993. Perceived problems of public school prekindergarten teachers. *Journal of Research in Childhood Education, 8(1)*, 57–68.

Miller, F. 1997. A class meetings approach to classroom cohesiveness. Perspectives. *Social Studies and the Younger Learner, 9(3)*, 18–20.

Morris, R. 1996. Contrasting disciplinary models in education. *Thresholds in Education, 22(4)*, 7–13.

Nealon, P. 1995. *Boston Globe.* March 14, 17:2.

Nelsen, J., L. Lott, and H. Glenn. 1993. *Positive discipline in the classroom.* Rocklin, CA: Prima Publishing.

New Hampshire schools begin program to teach ethics, values. 1989. *Boston Globe.* August 31.

Newman, M. 1995. Sixteen city schools are taken over by chancellor. *The New York Times.* October 20.

Newman, W., and Newman, J. 1996. Teacher education and classroom discipline: A candid conversation between a teacher and a professor. *Thresholds in Education, 22(4),* 2–6.

Nolin, M. 1996. Student victimization at school. *Journal of School Health, 66(6),* 216–221.

O'Harrow, R. 1995. Reading, writing, right and wrong. *Washington Post.* September 8.

Ozvold, L. 1996. Does teacher demeanor affect the behavior of students? *Teaching and Change, 3(2),* 159–172.

Paradise, R. 1994. Spontaneous cultural compatibility: Mazahua students and their teachers constructing trusting relationships. *Peabody Journal of Education, 69(2),* 60–70.

Parents as partners. 1997. *Our Children, 22(3),* 36–37.

Peng, S. 1993. Fostering student discipline and effort: Approaches used in Chinese schools. Paper presented at the annual meeting of the American Educational Research Association (Atlanta, April 12–16).

Peterson, T. 1996. Discipline for discipleship. *Thresholds in Education, 22(4),* 28–32.

Petrie, G., P. Lindauer, B. Bennett, and S. Gibson. 1998. Nonverbal cues: The key to classroom management. *Principal, 77(3),* 34–36.

Phillips-Hershey, E., and B. Kanagy. 1996. Teaching students to manage personal anger constructively. *Elementary School Guidance & Counseling, 30(3),* 229–234.

Powell, T., and S. Taylor. 1994. Taking care of risky business. *South Carolina Middle School Journal,* (Spring), 5–6.

Rancifer, J. 1993. Effective classroom management: A teaching strategy for a maturing profession. Paper presented at the annual conference of the Southeastern Regional Association of Teacher Educators (Nashville, October 27–30).

———. 1995. Revolving classroom door: Management strategies to eliminate the quick spin. Paper presented at the annual meeting of the Southern Regional Association of Teacher Educators (Lake Charles, LA, November 2–4).

Rich, J. 1992. Predicting and controlling school violence. *Contemporary Education, 64(1)* 35–39.

Richardson, G. 1993. Student teacher journals: Reflective and nonreflective. Paper presented at the annual Mid-South Educational Research Association (New Orleans, November 10–12).

Richardson, R., D. Wilcox, and J. Dunne. 1994. Corporal punishment in schools: Initial progress in the bible belt. *Journal of Humanistic Education and Development, 32(4),* 173–182.

Rose, L., A. Gallup, and S. Elam. 1997. The 29th Annual Phi Delta Kappa/Gallup Poll of the Public's Attitudes toward the Public Schools. *Phi Delta Kappan, 79:* 41–56.

Ryan, E. 1994. From rod to reason: Historical perspectives on corporal punishment in the public schools. *Educational Horizons, 72(2),* 70–77.

Schimmel, D. 1997. Traditional rule-making and the subversion of citizenship education. *Social Education, 61(2),* 70–74.

Schmidt, S. 1996. Character in the classroom. *The San Diego Union.* May 19.

Schneider, A. 1998. Insubordination and intimidation signal the end of decorum in many classrooms. *Chronicle of Higher Education, 44(29),* A12–A14.

Schneider, E. 1996. Giving students a voice in the classroom. *Educational Leadership, 54(1),* 22–26.

Schwartz, F. 1981. Supporting or subverting learning: Peer group patterns in four tracked schools. *Anthropology and Education Quarterly, 12(2),* 99–120.

Sesno, A. 1998. *97 savvy secrets for protecting self and school: A practical guide for today's teachers and administrators.* Thousand Oaks, CA: Corwin Press, Inc.

Shen, E. 1995. Educators get tough on violence. *Washington Post.* August 24.

Shreeve, W. 1993. Evaluating teacher evaluation: Who is responsible for teacher probation? *NAASP Bulletin, 77(551),* 8–19.

Stein, N. 1996. From the margins to the mainstream: Sexual harassment in K-12 schools. *Initiatives, 57(3),* 19–26.

Stone, S. 1993. Issues in education: Taking time to teach social skills. *Childhood Education, 69(4),* 194–195.

Study backs induction schools to help new teachers stay teachers. 1987. *ASCD Update, 29(4),* 1.

Sudzina, M. 1997. From tourists to citizens in the classroom: An interview with H. Jerome Freiberg. *Mid-Western Educational Researcher, 10(2),* 35–38.

Susi, F. 1996. Becoming a behavior-minded art teacher. *Art Education, 49(5),* 62–68.

Taking action against violence. *Instructor, 103(6),* 41–43.

Teachers fear violence in schools. 1994. *Atlanta Journal Constitution.* March 20.

Teaching children with attention deficit/ hyperactivity disorder: Update 1998. *ERIC Digest* E569. ERIC Identifier: ED423633.

Teasley, A. 1996. Dealing effectively with student behavior (new teachers). *English Journal, 85(4),* 80–81.

Terry, Paul M. (1997). Teacher burnout: Is it real? Can we prevent it? Paper presented at the Annual Meeting of the North Central Association of Colleges and Schools (Chicago, IL, April 8, 1997).

Wade, R. 1997. Lifting a school's spirit. *Educational Leadership, 54(8),* 34–36.

Weinstein, C., A. Woolfolk, and L. Dittmeier. 1994. Protector or prison guard? Using metaphors and media to explore student teachers' thinking about classroom management. *Action in Teacher Education, 16(1),* 41–54.

Weirs, M. 1995. Clayton County adds boot camp to school program. *Atlanta Constitution.* October 19.

Wesley, D., and D. Vocke. 1992. Classroom discipline and teacher education. Paper presented at the Annual Meeting of the Association of Teacher Educators (Orlando, FL, February 15–19).

Winik, L. 1996. Students want more discipline, disruptive classmates out. *American Educator, 20(3)* 12–14.

Woo, E. 1995. New math: Dividing school day differently. *Los Angeles Times.* September 29.

Zeiger, A. 1996. 10 steps to a happier classroom. General music. *Teaching Music 4(1),* 38–39.

Zeitlin, E., and L. Parrilla. 1999. Malibu High has "a coming of age." *Los Angeles Times.* October 10.

Zeller, N., and M. Gutierrez. 1995. Speaking of discipline...: An international perspective. *Thresholds in Education, 21(2),* 60–66.

Great Pioneers in Modern Discipline

Prior to the middle of the Twentieth Century, teachers for the most part used a single method of discipline, one that was forceful and demanding, often harsh and punitive. Those teachers were not evil. They were people of good intent doing the best they could to help students learn. Their control tactics were reflective of the times. Everyone expected teachers to make their requirements clear, perhaps reward students who complied, and scold or punish those who didn't. Teachers possessed authoritative power and thought they should use it. But in doing so, they caused students to be fearful, to dislike school, and often to subvert teachers' efforts.

Why did teachers use methods that caused student resentment rather than encouraging cooperation? The answer lies in tradition, ignorance, and desire for success. Although they tried not to show it, teachers were also afraid of losing control, of being terrorized by their students, of being failures as teachers. They didn't yet know that humane procedures, properly used, could deflect student resistance and replace it with cooperation.

But the years following World War II brought many societal changes toward equality and democracy. Correspondingly society's view of teaching and classroom discipline changed. That change became evident in the early 1950s though it took a while to catch on, slowed by an absence of formalized discipline procedures that were gentle, yet effective.

What we now call modern discipline consists of techniques that entice, persuade, and assist students, rather than relying on intimidation and punishment to force student compliance. It received a major push in 1951 when Fritz Redl and William Wattenberg set forth the first organized, systematic set of humane discipline techniques that could be used reliably in place of the old-fashioned approaches. Their work opened educators' minds to new possibilities and set a pattern for changes to come.

In this chapter we examine the contributions of Redl and Wattenberg and other great pioneers in modern discipline. We begin with Redl and Wattenberg's conclusions concerning group behavior and proceed to the pivotal discoveries by B. F. Skinner on behavior shaping, William Glasser on behavior as student choice, Jacob Kounin on lesson management, Haim Ginott on communication in discipline, and Rudolf Dreikurs on discipline through democratic teaching.

<table>
<tr><td>

**FRITZ REDL
AND
WILLIAM
WATTEN-
BERG:
DISCIPLINE
THROUGH
INFLUENC-
ING GROUP
BEHAVIOR**

</td><td>

Fritz Redl and William Wattenberg (1951) presented the first set of theory-based suggestions designed specifically to help teachers understand and deal considerately with classroom misbehavior. Their work inaugurated the modern era in classroom discipline. Both Redl and Wattenberg were specialists in human behavior. Redl, born in Austria, emigrated to the United States in 1936 and devoted his career to research, therapy, and teaching, principally as professor of behavioral science at Wayne State University. Wattenberg, born in 1911, received his doctorate from Columbia University in 1936. He specialized in educational psychology and held professorships at Northwestern University, Chicago Teacher's College, and Wayne State University.

</td></tr>
</table>

Fritz Redl

Redl and Wattenberg's Principal Teachings

William Wattenberg

- *People in groups behave differently than they do individually.* Students in classrooms do things they would not do if by themselves, and will not do certain things they would do if by themselves. When teachers understand individual behavior in the context of the group, they can become more effective in providing guidance.
- *Group dynamics, defined as the generation of forces by and within groups, produce the group currents that strongly affect behavior.* Redl and Wattenberg claimed that if teachers are to deal effectively with group behavior, they must understand group dynamics, how they develop, and how they affect students in the classroom. Group dynamics, which are influenced by teacher behavior and attitude, produce such effects as group spirit, imitative behavior, desire to excel, scapegoating of certain students, hiding places for nonachievers, group norms and expectations, and the adoption of certain roles by members of the group.
- *Students adopt identifiable roles in the classroom.* Within any group, students take on roles such as leaders, followers, clowns (the show-offs), instigators (those who provoke misbehavior), and scapegoats (those on whom blame is placed even when not deserved). Individuals may play different roles in different groups. Teachers should be watchful for the emergence of these roles, bring them to the class's attention, be prepared to encourage or discourage them as appropriate, and know how to limit their detrimental effects.
- *Teachers are also cast into many different roles that affect student behavior.* Students see teachers as role models, sources of knowledge, referees, judges, and surrogate parents. Teachers must be aware that students hold these expectations of them. They can discuss these matters with students for clarification.
- *Teachers should give students a clear say in helping set class standards and deciding how transgressions should be handled.* They should do the following: Keep student attitude in mind at all times; show a desire to be helpful, never hurtful;

be as objective as possible; maintain a sense of humor; and remember that all of us are human.

- *Diagnostic thinking is teachers' best tool for resolving behavior problems.* Diagnostic thinking involves (a) forming a first hunch about the cause of the misbehavior, (b) quickly gathering facts about it, (c) exploring hidden factors, such as background information about students, (d) taking action, (e) evaluating the results, and (f) remaining flexible and open to other possibilities.

- *When teachers identify problems in class behavior, they should make use of positive influence techniques, leaving punishment as a last resort.* Positive techniques include *(a) supporting student self-control,* such as helping them stay on-task, pay attention, and complete their work, *(b) offering situational assistance,* such as providing immediate help when students are stuck on work assignments or providing a break when students become overly tired, *(c) appraising reality,* where teachers point out the underlying causes of students' behavior and in a friendly way remind them of their obligations and request continued cooperation.

- *Punishment is a last resort in dealing with class misbehavior.* Punishment is a last-resort tactic. If used, it should never be physically hurtful, but should consist of pre-planned consequences that are unpleasant to the student, such as sitting by themselves, making up work that has not been done, or not being allowed to participate in certain class activities. Never should it involve angry outbursts from the teacher or attempts to teach the student a lesson. Teachers should maintain their composure and show students they are sincerely trying to help. Redl and Wattenberg emphasize that punishment has a detrimental effect on student self-concept and relations with the teacher and is, in addition, a poor model for teaching students how to resolve personal problems.

Analysis of Redl and Wattenberg's Contributions

Redl and Wattenberg made five notable contributions that have helped teachers work more effectively with students. First, they described how groups behave differently from individuals, thus helping teachers understand classroom behaviors that are otherwise perplexing. Second, they provided the first well-organized, systematic approach to improving student behavior in the classroom, replacing aversive techniques with humane approaches that promoted long-term working relationships. Third, they showed how to diagnose the causes of student misbehavior, believing that by attending to causes teachers could eliminate most misbehavior. Fourth, they established the value of involving students in making decisions about discipline, now advocated by all authorities. And fifth, they pointed out the detrimental effects of punishment and showed why it should not be used in class discipline. These five contributions established a pattern that newer, more humane discipline would emulate.

But despite its remarkable advances and contributions to later developments in classroom discipline, Redl and Wattenberg's approach was never put widely into practice. Teachers couldn't seem to get a handle on the concept and implications of group dynamics, nor did they understand how to deal with roles they and students assumed in the group. They found they could not put the diagnostic thinking procedure into effect quickly enough, given the harried context of the classroom, and that they had insufficient expertise to carry it out properly. Thus, while Redl and Wattenberg's work broke new ground in discipline and while teachers found it interesting, persuasive, and in many ways helpful, the approach was all in all too cumbersome to implement efficiently. It remained for later innovators to build its valuable components into discipline systems that teachers could use.

B. F. SKINNER: DISCIPLINE THROUGH SHAPING DESIRED BEHAVIOR	Even before Redl and Wattenberg published their suggestions for working with the group, a Harvard psychologist named Burrhus Frederic Skinner was making interesting findings about how our voluntary actions are affected by what happens to us immediately after we perform a given act. Skinner is respected as perhaps the greatest behavioral psychologist of all time. He earned his doctorate in psychology at Harvard in 1931 and from that time almost until his death in 1990 published articles and books based on his findings and beliefs about human behavior. During all those years, Skinner never concerned himself with classroom discipline.

B. F. Skinner

However, his followers saw the applicability of his findings, especially in regard to encouraging students to behave acceptably in the classroom. Those followers, sometimes referred to as "Neo-Skinnerians," devised and popularized the procedure of behavior modification which is used extensively in different realms of human learning. Behavior modification came strongly into vogue in the early 1960s and, though no longer the force it once was, it still figures prominently in teaching and learning.

Skinner's Principal Teachings

- *Much if not most of our voluntary behavior is shaped as we receive reinforcement immediately after we perform an act.* (For our purposes here, reinforcement can be thought of as reward, though "reward" is a term Skinner avoided.) We do something, and if rewarded for it, become more likely to repeat the act.
- *Most reinforcing stimuli, if they are to have an effect on behavior, must be received soon after the behavior occurs.* Reinforcing stimuli common in behavior modification as used in the classroom include knowledge of results, peer approval, awards and free time, and smiles, nods, and praise from the teacher.
- *Behavior modification (not a term Skinner used) refers to the overall procedure of **shaping** student **behavior** intentionally through reinforcement.* This procedure still comprises a major part of many teachers' discipline systems, particularly at the primary grade level.
- *Constant reinforcement, provided every time a student performs a desired act, helps new learnings become established.* The teacher might praise Jonathan

every time he raises his hand, or privately compliment Mary every time she turns in required homework.

- *Intermittent reinforcement, in which rewards are supplied only occasionally, is sufficient to maintain desired behavior once it has become established.* After students have learned to come into the room and get immediately to work, the teacher will only occasionally need to express appreciation.
- *Behaviors that are not reinforced soon disappear or, as Skinner said, become* **extinguished.** If Roberto raises his hand in class but is never called on, he will sooner or later stop raising his hand.
- **Successive approximation** *refers to a behavior-shaping progression in which behavior comes closer and closer to a preset goal.* This process is evident when skills are being built. Here students are rewarded regularly for improvement.
- **Punishment** *often has negative effects in behavior modification and hence is not used in the classroom.* Skinner believed punishment could not extinguish inappropriate behavior.

Analysis of Skinner's Contributions

Although Skinner did not concern himself with classroom discipline per se, his discoveries concerning the shaping of desired behavior through reinforcement led directly to behavior modification, still used to speed and shape academic and social learning. Years ago many primary grade teachers used behavior modification as their entire discipline system, rewarding students who behaved properly and ignoring those who misbehaved. Very few teachers now use behavior modification as their discipline system, yet Skinner's principles of reinforcement are applied in classrooms everywhere.

In the 1960s, teachers very much liked behavior modification. They found it unusually effective in promoting desirable behavior, especially at the primary grade level, and many built it into every aspect of their daily teaching. After a few years, however, behavior modification was being used not so much for discipline as for encouraging and reinforcing learning. Even teachers who enjoyed its effectiveness began to worry that they might be simply bribing students to behave properly. Beyond primary grades, teachers had found behavior modification unsuitable as a total discipline package for several reasons. A major concern was that while it was effective in teaching students desirable behavior, it was inefficient in teaching them what *not* to do. Unlike laboratory pigeons, school students comprehend the meaning of "don't do that." Teachers grew tired of hoping that by ignoring misbehaving students they could get them to behave properly; they saw that misbehavior often brought enough rewards from peers to keep it in full bloom. Also, students can be taught or shown almost instantly how to behave desirably. They don't have to learn it through lengthy nonverbal and nonimitative processes as do pigeons and rats. And while behavior modification works well with young children, older ones are embarrassed by being singled out for praise in front of their classmates. For those reasons, plus the burden of continually having to dispense reinforcers, few teachers now use behavior modification as their complete system of discipline.

A few years after behavior modification burst onto the scene, a new approach to discipline appeared. It came from psychiatrist William Glasser, whose contributions came at an appropriate time. In the 1960s, advocates of behavior modification implied that teachers really worth their salt could use reinforcement to control their classes, and if they couldn't, they were to blame for classroom misbehavior, not the students. Thus almost overnight, teachers became the focus of blame when students failed to learn or behave properly.

William Glasser

This was tremendously disconcerting to teachers, who felt they had no politically correct tools other than behavior modification to use in discipline. When students misbehaved, behavior modification didn't tell teachers what to do. It is no wonder that so many furtively resorted to old-style intimidation. Then William Glasser's monumental book *Schools Without Failure* (1969) appeared. Glasser contended that students chose to behave as they did—that nothing "made" then do so. That being the case, teachers could improve students' behavior simply by helping them make better choices. Glasser showed teachers how to do that. After 1984, Glasser turned his emphasis from discipline to effective teaching. His post-1984 views are analyzed in Chapter 8.

Glasser's Principal Teachings

- *Students are rational beings who choose to behave as they do.* While many come from poor backgrounds and dysfunctional homes, those conditions do not force them to behave unacceptably. Students always choose to act as they do.
- *Educators can think of behavior choices as good or bad, depending on their outcomes.* Good choices equal approved behavior. Bad choices equal disapproved behavior. Teachers must help students understand that their well-being depends on making good choices.
- *The teacher's role in discipline is to help students make good choices, continually, throughout the day.* They do this by helping students see the effects of poor choices, helping them identify better choices for themselves, showing they must live with the choices they make, whether good or bad, and insisting they assume personal responsibility for making proper choices.
- *Every class should have an agreed-upon, printed set of **class rules**.* Students are allowed much input into establishing the rules that govern class behavior, as well as how the rules are enforced.
- *Teachers should accept no excuses for student misbehavior.* When students break class rules, they almost always make excuses. Teachers who truly care about their students must never accept those excuses, must never intimate that it is all right to make bad choices. Instead, they should see that students live with the consequences of their misbehavior, but at the same time do all they can to help students make better choices in the future.

- *Teachers must see to it that **reasonable consequences** follow student behavior, good or bad.* Consequences should be discussed and agreed to by the class. Reasonable consequences for good choices can include such things as the pleasure of learning something well, positive attention from teacher or peers, and being allowed to engage in a favorite activity. Reasonable consequences for bad choices can include such things as making up for what was done wrong, working out a plan to ensure better behavior in the future, and not being allowed to participate in favorite group activities.

Analysis of Glasser's Contributions

Glasser made several significant contributions to discipline. He contended that students choose to behave as they do; nothing forces them. He described misbehavior as a bad choice and appropriate behavior as a good choice. He urged teachers to formulate class rules and consequences and involve students in the process. He insisted that teachers never accept excuses for misbehavior and always see that students experience the reasonable consequences, pleasant or unpleasant, of the choices they make. He maintained that the teacher's role in discipline consists of continually helping students to make better behavior choices. He also popularized **class meetings**, now incorporated in almost all systems of discipline and advocated that those meetings be conducted with students and teacher seated in a close circle.

Teachers were at first enthralled with Glasser's views of discipline. They appreciated the concept of misbehavior as poor choice and the teacher's role as helping students make better choices. In fact, they wholeheartedly agreed with virtually everything Glasser said. Yet Glasser's scheme of discipline, as a total system, never became widely used. Practically all teachers wove bits and pieces of it into their classroom practice, especially the written rules, reasonable consequences for breaking rules, and class discussions about proper behavior. But most teachers felt they did not have sufficient time to follow through properly with every student who misbehaved, counseling them over and over on making productive choices, as Glasser suggested. Moreover, teachers found that students paid little attention to benign consequences and so continued to misbehave when they felt like it. The major limitation of Glasser's system of discipline was its unwieldiness. Busy teachers just couldn't get a handle on it well enough to work all of it into their daily teaching.

| JACOB KOUNIN: IMPROVING DISCIPLINE THROUGH LESSON MANAGEMENT | Shortly after Glasser introduced the concept of behavior as choice, a new work appeared that opened a new window on classroom discipline. Previously, teaching and discipline had been seen as separate aspects of education. Although everyone knew they affected each other, teaching was thought of as helping students acquire information and skills, while discipline was what the teacher did to keep students working, paying attention, and behaving themselves. This changed somewhat following the 1971 publication of Jacob Kounin's book entitled *Discipline and Group Management in Classrooms*. |  *Jacob Kounin* |

Kounin was an educational psychologist who earned his doctorate at Iowa State University in 1939. In 1946, he was appointed professor of educational psychology at Wayne State University, where he spent most of his academic career. Kounin became best known for his detailed investigations into the effects of classroom management and lesson management on student behavior.

Kounin's Principal Teachings

- *Teachers need to know what is going on in all parts of the classroom at all times.* Kounin verified that teachers good in discipline displayed this trait, which he called **withitness.**
- *Good lesson momentum helps keep students on track.* Kounin used the term **momentum** to refer to teachers' starting lessons with dispatch, keeping lessons moving ahead, making transitions among activities efficiently, and bringing lessons to a satisfactory close.
- *Smoothness in lesson presentation helps keep students involved.* The term **smoothness** refers to steady progression of lessons, without abrupt changes or disturbing incidents.
- *Effective teachers have systems for gaining student attention and clarifying expectations.* Kounin called this tactic **group alerting.**
- *Effective teachers keep students attentive and actively involved.* Such **student accountability** is maintained by regularly calling on students to respond, demonstrate, or explain.
- *Teachers good in behavior management are able to attend to two or more events simultaneously.* This skill, which Kounin called **overlapping,** is shown when teachers answer questions for students doing independent work while at the same time instructing a small group of students.
- *Effective teachers see to it that students are not given overexposure to a particular topic.* Overexposure produces **satiation,** meaning students have had their fill of the topic as shown through boredom, resistance, and misbehavior.
- *Effective teachers make instructional activities enjoyable and challenging.* Kounin described how fun and challenge delay satiation.

Analysis of Kounin's Contributions

Kounin was able to identify a number of teacher strategies that engaged students in lessons and thus reduced misbehavior. His work placed emphasis on how teachers could manage students, lessons, and classrooms so as to reduce the incidence of misbehavior. The interconnection he identified between ways of teaching and control of behavior led to a new line of thought—that teaching influences discipline to a much greater degree than previously believed and that the best way to maintain good discipline is to keep students actively engaged in class activities, while showing them individual attention.

Kounin's commentary on his research is interesting and illuminating. He concluded that teacher personality has little to do with classroom control. Referring to teacher traits such as friendliness, helpfulness, rapport, warmth, patience, and the like, he declared that contrary to popular opinion such traits are of little value in managing a classroom.

He also explained that in his research he had hoped and expected to find a relationship between what teachers did when students misbehaved and the subsequent misbehavior of those same students. But no such findings emerged. Kounin wrote:

> That unexpected fact required unlearning on my part, in the sense of having to replace the original question by other questions. Questions about disciplinary techniques were eliminated and replaced by questions about classroom management in general, [and] *preventing* misbehavior was given higher investigative priority than *handling* misbehavior. (p. 143, italics added)

He went on to describe what his research suggested must be considered by teachers in operating their classrooms:

> ...the business of running a classroom is a complicated technology having to do with developing a nonsatiating learning program; programming for progress, challenge, and variety in learning activities; initiating and maintaining movement in classroom tasks with smoothness and momentum; coping with more than one event simultaneously; observing and emitting feedback for many different events; directing actions at appropriate targets; maintaining a focus upon a group; and doubtless other techniques not measured in these researches. (pp. 144–145)

Kounin made outstanding contributions concerning how lesson management can forestall misbehavior, and he provided a valuable service in drawing attention to the close connection between teaching and discipline. However, teachers never found his approach satisfactory as a total system of discipline. They agree that what he suggests can cut down markedly on the incidence of class misbehavior. But misbehavior does occur even in the best of circumstances, and Kounin provides no help in what teachers should do when a lesson is being spoiled. Kounin stated that he couldn't identify teacher tactics that, when used in response to misbehavior, did anything to improve the behavior. Improve it or not, teachers feel they must be able to put a stop to disruptive or defiant behavior simply in order to continue with their lessons. Unfortunately they found little in Kounin's work that helped in that regard.

HAIM GINOTT: DISCIPLINE THROUGH CONGRUENT COMMUNICATION

In the same year that Kounin published his work on lesson management, there appeared another small book that had even greater influence. That was Haim Ginott's *Teacher and Child* (1971) in which Ginott illuminated the critical role of communication in discipline, especially concerning how teachers talk to and with their students. Just as Kounin's influence is evident in subsequent models of classroom discipline, so is Ginott's. In many ways, Ginott did more than anyone else to set the tone for today's systems of classroom discipline.

Ginott (1922–1973) was born in Tel Aviv, Israel. A classroom teacher early in his career, he later earned his doctorate

Haim Ginott

at Columbia University and went on to hold professorships in psychology at Adelphi University and at New York University Graduate School. He also served as a UNESCO consultant in Israel, was resident psychologist on the "Today" show, and wrote a weekly syndicated column entitled *Between Us* that dealt with interpersonal communication.

Ginott's Principal Teachings

- *Learning always takes place in the present tense,* meaning teachers must not prejudge students or hold grudges.
- *Learning is always a personal matter to the student.* Large classes often make teachers forget that each student–learner is an individual who must be treated as such.
- *Teachers should always endeavor to use congruent communication,* which is communication that is harmonious with students' feelings about situations and themselves.
- *The cardinal principle of congruent communication is that it addresses situations.* It never addresses students' character or personality.
- **Teachers at their best,** *using congruent communication, do not preach or moralize, nor impose guilt or demand promises.* Instead, they **confer dignity** on their students by treating them as social equals capable of making good decisions.
- **Teachers at their worst** *label students, belittle them, and denigrate their character:* They usually do these things inadvertently.
- *Effective teachers* **invite cooperation** *from their students by describing the situation and indicating what needs to be done.* They do not dictate to students or boss them around, which provokes resistance.
- *Teachers have a* **hidden asset** *upon which they should always call, namely, "How can I be most helpful to my students right now?"* Most classroom difficulties are avoided when teachers remember to call upon that asset.
- *Teachers should feel free to express their anger, but in doing so should use* **I-messages** *rather than* **you-messages.** Using an I-message, the teacher might say "I am very upset." Using a you-message, the teacher might say "You are being very rude."
- *It is wise to use* **laconic language** *when responding to or redirecting student misbehavior.* Laconic means short, concise, and brief, which describes the sort of responses Ginott advocates.
- **Evaluative praise** *is worse than none at all and should never be used.* An example of evaluative praise is "Good boy for raising your hand."
- *Teachers should use* **appreciative praise** *when responding to effort or improvement.* This is praise in which the teacher shows appreciation for what the student has done, without evaluating the student's character (e.g., "I can almost smell those pine trees in your drawing").
- *Always respect students' privacy.* Teachers should never pry when students do not wish to discuss personal matters, but should show they are available should students need to talk.

- *When correcting students, teachers should provide directions concerning the behavior desired.* Instead of reprimanding students, teachers should help them behave properly.
- *Teachers should not use **why questions** when discussing behavior.* Why questions only make students feel guilty. An example of a "why question" is, "Why did you speak to Susan that way?"
- *Sarcasm is almost always dangerous and should not be used when discussing situations with students.*
- *Punishment should not be used in the classroom.* Punishment only produces hostility, rancor, and vengefulness, while never making students really desire to improve.
- *Teachers should strive continually for **self-discipline** in their work with students.* They must be careful not to display the very behaviors they are trying to eradicate in their students, such as raising their voice to end noise, using force to break up fighting, showing rudeness to students who are impolite, and berating students who have used bad language.
- *Classroom discipline is attained gradually, as a series of little victories* in which the teacher, through self-discipline and helpfulness, promotes humaneness and self-control within students.

Analysis of Ginott's Contributions

Ginott insisted that the only true discipline is self-discipline, which all teachers should try to promote in their students. He made a number of especially helpful contributions concerning how teachers can communicate with students to foster positive relations while reducing and correcting misbehavior. He showed the importance of the teacher always being self-controlled and, beyond that, the value of congruent communication, which is teacher communication that is harmonious with student feelings and self-perception. Ginott urged teachers to use sane messages when addressing misbehavior, messages that focus calmly on what needs to be corrected without attacking the student's character or personality. He helped clarify his contentions by describing teachers at their best and teachers at their worst, pointing out the positive effects that accrue from treating students considerately and helpfully as well as the negative effects that result when teachers lose self-control, berate students, or speak to them sarcastically. He cautioned educators that his suggestions would not produce instantaneous results, that guidance through communication had to be used repeatedly over time for its power to take effect. Although misbehavior can be squelched, **genuine discipline** (by which Ginott meant self-discipline) never occurs instantaneously, but rather over time, in a series of small steps that result in genuine changes in student attitude.

Ginott's overall view on teaching and working with students is summarized in the following excerpt from *Teacher and Child:*

> As a teacher I have come to the frightening conclusion that I am the decisive
> element in the classroom. It is my personal approach that creates the climate. It is

my daily mood that makes the weather. As a teacher I possess tremendous power to make a child's life miserable or joyous. I can be a tool of torture or an instrument of inspiration. I can humiliate or humor, hurt or heal. In all situations it is my response that decides whether a crisis will be escalated or de-escalated, and a child humanized or dehumanized. (p. 13)

It would be difficult to find a teacher who does not agree with Ginott's views on the value of communication and his suggestions concerning how it should be done. Indeed, his ideas are evident in classrooms everywhere and can be found in virtually all of today's popular systems of discipline. Yet, teachers who have tried to use Ginott's suggestions as their total system of discipline have found something lacking. Teachers would like to have a solid discipline system on which to rely. They want it to be humane, but they also want it to be effective. They want it to make absolutely clear what sort of behavior is appropriate for the classroom. They want that behavior to be discussed and formulated into class agreements or rules. They want everyone to know, up front, what will happen when students transgress the rules. And above all, they want to be sure they have the power to put an immediate stop to behavior that is offensive or disruptive. They can find some, but not all, of those qualities in Ginott's proposals. Ginott doesn't provide adequate suggestions for rules and consequences, nor does he indicate how teachers can put an immediate stop to atrocious behavior. While teachers find much of value in Ginott's proposals, especially if their students are well-mannered, they find the suggestions more helpful in maintaining good relationships with students than in dealing with students who are disruptive in the classroom.

RUDOLF DREIKERS: DISCIPLINE THROUGH DEMOCRATIC TEACHING	On the heels of the influential books by Jacob Kounin and Haim Ginott there appeared yet another approach to discipline, one which emphasized seeking out and dealing with underlying causes of misbehavior. That was the highly influential contribution from yet another psychiatrist, Rudolf Dreikurs, who also provided strategies for helping students acquire self-discipline based on understanding of its social value. Dreikurs taught that these outcomes could best be achieved within the context of a democratic classroom.

Rudolf Dreikers

Dreikurs (1897–1972) was born in Vienna, Austria. After receiving his medical degree from the University of Austria, he entered into a long association with the renowned Austrian psychiatrist Alfred Adler, with whom he worked in family and child counseling. Dreikurs immigrated to the United States in 1937 and eventually became director of the Alfred Adler Institute in Chicago. He also served as professor of psychiatry at the Chicago Medical School. In keeping with his interest in child and family counseling, he turned his attention to misbehavior and discipline in school classrooms.

Dreikurs's Principal Teachings

- *Discipline at its best is defined as self-control, based on **social interest**.* Self-controlled students are able to show initiative, make reasonable decisions, and assume responsibility in ways that benefit both themselves and others. Social interest refers to students' efforts to make the classroom comfortable and productive, based on understanding that such classrooms better meet their personal needs.

- *Good discipline occurs best in a **democratic** classroom.* A democratic classroom is one in which teacher and students work together to make decisions about how the class will function.

- *Good discipline cannot occur in autocratic or permissive classrooms.* In **autocratic** classrooms, the teacher makes all decisions and imposes them on students, leaving no opportunity for student initiative and responsibility. In **permissive** classrooms, the teacher fails to require that students comply with rules, conduct themselves humanely, or endure consequences for their misbehavior.

- *Almost all students have a compelling desire to feel they are a valued member of the class, that they belong.* Students sense **belonging** when the teacher and others give them attention and respect, involve them in activities, and do not mistreat them.

- *When students are unable to gain a sense of belonging in the class, they often turn to the **mistaken goals** of attention, power, revenge, and inadequacy.* When seeking attention, students talk out, show off, interrupt others, and demand teacher attention. When seeking power, they drag their heels, make comments under their breath, and sometimes try to show that the teacher can't make them do anything. When seeking revenge, they try to get back at the teacher and other students, by lying, subverting class activities, and maliciously disrupting the class. When seeking to display inadequacy, they withdraw from class activities and make no effort to learn.

- *Teachers should learn how to identify mistaken goals and deal with them.* When teachers see evidence that students are pursuing mistaken goals, they should point out the fact by identifying the mistaken goal and discussing the faulty logic involved. They should do this in a friendly, nonthreatening manner. Dreikurs suggests calmly asking "Do you need me to pay more attention to you?" or "Could it be that you want to show that I can't make you do the assignment?"

- *Rules for governing class behavior should be formulated jointly by teacher and students. Tied to those rules should be the **logical consequences** of compliance or violation.* It is the teacher's responsibility to see that stipulated consequences are invoked. Good behavior (following the rules) brings pleasant consequences such as enjoyment of learning and associating positively with others. Misbehavior brings unpleasant consequences such as having to complete work at home or being excluded from normal class activities.

- *Punishment* *should never be used in the classroom.* Punishment is just a way for teachers to get back at students and show them who's boss, and is usually humiliating to the student. Punishment has many bad side effects and therefore should be supplanted with logical consequences agreed to by the class.

Analysis of Dreikurs's Contributions

Dreikurs contributed several valuable concepts and strategies, many of which are important components of today's most popular systems of discipline. He identified **true discipline** as synonymous with self-discipline and was the first to base his discipline scheme on the premise of social interest, that is, of concern for the well-being of the group as well as the individual. He was among the first to clarify how democratic teachers and democratic classrooms promote sound discipline. He was the first to pinpoint a prime goal (that of belonging) as an underlying motivator of student behavior, and to identify the mistaken goals of attention, power, revenge, and inadequacy that students turn to when unable to achieve the primary goal of belonging. He urged that teachers and students jointly should formulate rules of class behavior and link those rules with logical consequences that occur as students comply with, or break, the class rules.

Dreikurs also provided a number of more specific suggestions concerning how teachers should interact with students. He said teachers should never use punishment and should avoid using praise, which he felt made students dependent on teacher reactions. Instead of praise, Dreikurs would have teachers use **encouragement**. Praise, by its nature, is directed at the character of the student. Encouragement, by its nature, is directed at what the student does or can do. Instead of saying "You can certainly play the piano well," an enlightened teacher would say, "I notice a great deal of improvement," or "I can see you enjoy playing very much." Dreikurs gave encouragement a very strong role in how teachers should speak with students. He made the following suggestions (Dreikurs and Cassel, 1972):

- Always speak in positive terms; never be negative.
- Encourage students to strive for improvement, not perfection.
- Emphasize a student's strengths while minimizing weaknesses.
- Help students with how to learn from mistakes. Show that mistakes are valuable in learning.
- Encourage independence and the assumption of responsibility.
- Let students know you have faith in them; offer help in overcoming obstacles.
- Encourage students to help each other.
- Show pride in students' work; display it and share it with others.
- Be optimistic and enthusiastic—a positive outlook is contagious.
- Use encouraging remarks such as "You have improved." "Can I help you?" "What did you learn from that mistake?" (pp. 51–54)

Dreikurs contributed so much valuable information for discipline, it seems at first glance strange to think that teachers did not adopt his approach wholeheartedly. Yet they did not, though almost all teachers use many of Dreikurs's ideas every day. For teachers, the most appealing aspects of Dreikurs's contributions are his suggestions on how to treat students. But all in all, they found his system a bit daunting. It seemed too grand, somehow, to implement easily. It focused on approaches that didn't seem, on the surface, related to each other, such as democracy, prime motive, mistaken goals, social interest, and logical consequences. But most of all, teachers found it lacking in the ingredient they most wanted; namely, what do you do to put an immediate stop to student disruptions, aggression, and defiance? They felt Dreikurs offered good advice on working with students positively, but little to help with major behavior problems.

Key Terms Used by the Pioneers in Modern Discipline

The following terms and concepts are essential to understanding the contentions of the pioneers in modern discipline. The majority of these terms and concepts are incorporated into systems of discipline now in use.

From Redl & Wattenberg's Group Dynamics: appraising reality, diagnostic thinking, group behavior, group dynamics, influence techniques, situational assistance, student roles, supporting self-control, teacher roles.

From Skinner's Behavior Shaping: behavior modification, constant reinforcement, extinction, intermittent reinforcement, positive reinforcement, punishment, reinforce, reinforcement, reinforcer, shaping behavior, successive approximations.

From Glasser's Behavior as Choice: behavior as choice, class rules, class meetings, reasonable consequences, good choices, no excuses, poor choices, teacher role.

From Kounin's Lesson and Group Management: accountability, group alerting, momentum, overlapping, satiation, smoothness, withitness.

From Ginott's Discipline through Communication: appreciative praise, conferring dignity, congruent communication, evaluative praise, genuine discipline, I-messages, invite cooperation, laconic language, sane messages, teacher self-discipline, teachers at their worst, teachers at their best, teachers' hidden asset, why questions, you-messages.

From Dreikurs's Discipline through Democratic Teaching: attention, autocratic teacher, belonging, democratic classroom, democratic teacher, encouragement, inadequacy, logical consequences, mistaken goals, permissive teacher, power, revenge, self-control, social interest, true discipline.

Questions and Activities

1. Review the lists of terms and concepts presented in the previous paragraphs. See how many of them you can explain. Look up the meanings of those you can't remember.

2. It was noted that none of the discipline systems described in this chapter found widespread use *as a total system*. What do you understand to be the reason for this, given the number of excellent suggestions they contain?

3. Of the approaches reviewed in the chapter, which seemed most useful to you? Which seemed least useful? Why?

4. Despite the presence today of many effective systems of discipline, one can still see teachers who try to maintain discipline by outshouting their students, speaking sarcastically, and treating students disrespectfully. Why do you believe they persist with these tactics? How effective do you think those tactics are with today's students?

Primary References

Dreikurs, R., and P. Cassel. 1995. *Discipline without tears.* New York: Penguin-NAL. Originally published in 1972, this is a book for teachers that presents Dreikurs's ideas for maintaining democratic discipline in the classroom.

Ginott, H. 1971. *Teacher and child.* New York: Macmillan.

———. 1972. I am angry! I am appalled! I am furious! *Today's Education, 61,* 23–24. A short article in which Ginott explains how teachers should express their emotions in a way that doesn't attack students' sense of self.

———. 1973. Driving children sane. *Today's Education, 62,* 20–25. An article in which Ginott explains the use of sane messages and the positive effects they have on students.

Glasser, W. 1969. *Schools without failure.* New York: Harper and Row. Glasser's first great book in education, in which he explains the detrimental effects of failure on student self-concept and motivation and sets forth the concepts of class meetings and behavior as student choice.

Kounin, J. 1977. *Discipline and group management in classrooms.* Rev. ed. New York: Holt, Rinehart & Winston. Originally published in 1971, this small book reports Kounin's research from which he concluded that lesson management was more important than any other factor in maintaining good classroom behavior.

Redl, F., and W. Wattenberg. 1959. *Mental hygiene in teaching.* Rev. ed. New York: Harcourt, Brace & World. Originally published in 1951, this book presents Redl and Wattenberg's views on group dynamics and how they can be used as the basis for a more effective system of discipline.

Skinner, B. 1953. *Science and human behavior.* New York: Macmillan. A book in which Skinner reports the major findings he had made up to that time in reinforcement theory and how that principle could be applied to human learning.

———. 1954. The science of learning and the art of teaching. *Harvard Educational Review, 24,* 86–97. A classic article in which Skinner describes why knowledge about learning can be considered a science and how teachers can use the science of learning in teaching the young.

———. 1971. *Beyond freedom and dignity.* New York: Knopf. Skinner's widely read book in which he presents his contentions that freedom and dignity are illusory concepts that no longer deserve credibility—he maintains that people are never really free to choose but instead make choices based on what has happened to them in the past and further that they should not take credit for their accomplishments because they really could not have acted differently.

Lee and Marlene Canter's
Assertive Discipline

Focus

- Maintaining a calm, productive classroom environment.
- Meeting students' needs for learning and ensuring that their rights are attended to.
- Helping the teacher remain calmly, nonstressfully in charge in the classroom.

Lee Canter

Logic

- Teachers have a right to teach as they see best, without disruption.
- Students have a right to learn in a safe, calm environment, with full teacher support.
- These ends are best met by in-charge teachers who do not violate students' best interests.
- Trust, respect, and perseverance enable teachers to earn student cooperation.

Contributions

- A classroom control strategy that places teachers humanely in charge in the classroom.
- A system that allows teachers to invoke positive and negative consequences calmly and fairly.
- Techniques for teaching students how to behave and for dealing with difficult students.

Marlene Canter

Canters' Suggestions

- Remain always in charge in the classroom, but not in a hostile or authoritarian manner.
- Take specific steps to teach students how to behave acceptably in the classroom.
- Identify students' personal needs and show your understanding and willingness to help.
- Continually strive to build trust between yourself and your students.

About Lee and Marlene Canter

Lee Canter is founder of Canter & Associates, an organization that provides training in classroom discipline and publishes related materials for educators and parents. Marlene Canter collaborates in the work. For many years the Canters have been refining their system of discipline, which they call *Assertive Discipline*, to help teachers interact with students in a calm, helpful, and consistent manner. The goal of their program is to help teachers establish classrooms where students may learn and teachers may teach effectively. Through workshops and graduate courses, the Canters have brought *Assertive Discipline* to well over a million teachers and administrators. In addition to offering books, tapes, and training programs in discipline, the Canters produce materials and offer graduate-level courses on topics such as motivation, instructional strategies, homework, dealing with severe behavior problems, and activities for positive reinforcement. For more information on *Assertive Discipline*, contact Canter & Associates, P.O. Box 2113, Santa Monica, CA 90406; telephone 310-395-3221; e-mail canter.net; website: www.canter.net

The Canters' Contributions to Discipline

The Canters have made several major contributions to classroom discipline. They popularized the concept of rights in the classroom—the rights of students to have teachers who help them learn in a calm, safe environment and the rights of teachers to teach without disruption. They explained that students need and want limits that assist their proper conduct and that it is the teacher's responsibility to set and enforce those limits. The Canters were the first to insist that teachers have a right to backing from administrators and cooperation from parents in helping students behave acceptably, and also the first to provide teachers with a workable procedure for correcting misbehavior efficiently through a system of easily administered consequences, positive and negative. The Canters continually modify their approach to ensure that it remains effective as social realities change. Earlier they focused on teachers being strong leaders in the classroom, while now they emphasize the building of trusting, helpful relationships between teachers and students.

The Canters' Central Focus

The Canters' model focuses on establishing a classroom climate in which needs are met, behavior is managed humanely, and learning occurs as intended. This climate is accomplished by attending closely to student needs, formalizing good class rules of behavior, teaching students how to behave properly, regularly giving students positive attention, talking helpfully with students who misbehave, and establishing a sense of mutual trust and respect.

The Canters' Principal Teachings

- *Today's students have clear rights and needs that must be met if they are to be taught effectively.* These **students' rights** and needs include a caring teacher who persistently works to foster the best interests of students.
- *Teachers have rights and needs in the classroom as well.* **Teachers' rights** include teaching in a classroom that is free from disruption, with support from parents and administrators as they work to help students.
- *The most effective teachers are those who remain in control of the class while always remembering that their main duty is to help students learn and behave responsibly.*
- *Teachers must continually model through their own behavior the kind of trust and respect for students that they want students to show toward others.*
- *A good discipline plan, built upon trust and respect, is necessary for helping students limit their own counterproductive behavior.* Such a discipline plan contains rules and consequences, and it must be fully understood and supported by students and their parents.
- *Teachers should practice* **positive repetitions.** Positive repetitions involve repeating directions as positive statements to students who are complying with class rules, for example, "Fred remembered to raise his hand. Good job."
- **Negative consequences** *are penalties teachers invoke when students violate class expectations.* They are brought to bear only when all else fails. They must be something students dislike (staying in after class, being isolated from the group) but must never be physically or psychologically harmful.
- **Positive consequences** *are rewards, usually words or facial expressions, that teachers offer when students comply with class expectations.* The Canters consider positive consequences to be very powerful.
- *Today's teachers must both model and directly teach proper behavior.* It is not enough for teachers simply to set limits and apply consequences. They must go well beyond that to actually teaching students how to behave responsibly in the classroom.
- *Teachers can have success with a majority of students deemed difficult-to-manage.* They can accomplish this by reaching out to those students, learning about their needs, interacting with them personally, and showing a constant willingness to help.

Analysis of the Canters' *Assertive Discipline*

In 1976, the Canters first set forth the basic premises and practices of *Assertive Discipline,* designed to bring relief to teachers beleaguered by classroom misbehavior. They have progressively modified their approach over the years by developing several new concepts and techniques, described in the following paragraphs.

Needs and Rights in the Classroom

Canter and Canter (1996) explain that students have a need for and the right to a warm, supportive classroom environment in which to learn, where teachers do all in their power to help students be successful. Teachers have needs and rights in the classroom as well, which include the need and right to teach as they believe correct without interruption, with support from their administrators.

Types of Teachers and Their Effects on Students

The Canters describe three types of teachers, differentiated on the basis of how they relate, proactively and reactively, to students. They call the three types hostile teachers, nonassertive teachers, and assertive teachers.

Hostile teachers view students as adversaries. They feel if they are to maintain order and teach properly, they must keep the upper hand, which they attempt to do by laying down the law, accepting no nonsense, and using loud commands and stern facial expressions. They make needlessly strong statements such as: "Sit down, shut up, and listen!" Such messages suggest a dislike for students and cause students to feel they are being unjustly controlled.

Nonassertive teachers take a passive approach to students. They seem unable to state their expectations clearly and are inconsistent in their dealings with students, allowing certain behaviors one day while forbidding them the next. They come across as wishy-washy, making statements such as "For heaven's sake, please try to behave like ladies and gentlemen" or "How many times do I have to tell you no talking?" After a time students learn not to take these teachers seriously. Yet, the same teachers, once they finally get fed up, come down hard on students. This inconsistency leaves students confused about expectations and enforcement.

Assertive teachers clearly, confidently, and consistently express class expectations to students. They attempt to build trust, they teach students how to behave so learning can progress, and they implement a discipline plan that encourages student cooperation. Such teachers help students understand exactly what is acceptable and unacceptable, and they make plain the consequences that follow student behavior. Assertive teachers are not harsh taskmasters. They recognize students' needs for consistent limits on behavior, but at the same time are ever mindful of students' needs for warmth and encouragement. They also know that students may require direct instruction in how to behave acceptably in the classroom. An assertive teacher might be heard to say "Our rule is no talking without raising your hand. Please raise your hand and wait for me to call on you."

Each of the response styles produces certain effects on teachers and students. The **hostile response style** takes away most of the pleasure teachers and students might otherwise enjoy. Its harshness curtails the possibility of developing trusting relationships with students and can produce negative student attitudes toward teachers and school. The **nonassertive response style** leads to feelings of frustration and inadequacy. Nonassertive teachers cannot get their needs met in the classroom, which produces high levels of stress. These teachers frequently develop hostility toward chronically misbehaving students, a hostility they ordinarily keep suppressed but occasionally release explosively. Students of nonassertive teachers often come to feel frustrated, manipulated, and angry, and they develop little respect for their teachers. The **assertive response style** provides several benefits that are absent in the other styles. Assertive teachers create a classroom atmosphere that helps both teacher and students meet their needs. They invite student collaboration and help students practice acceptable behavior. This produces a climate which meets the teacher's needs and gives them a feeling of pleasure and accomplishment. Students learn to trust assertive teachers because they provide clear expectations, consistency, and an atmosphere of warmth and support.

Moving toward Good Discipline

The Canters (Canter 1996) stress that good discipline does not depend on ever more rules and harsher consequences, which have no effect on students who see rules as meaningless and have no fear of the consequences. Instead, good discipline must grow out of mutual trust and respect. The Canters provide abundant advice to help teachers develop good discipline in their classrooms, summarized in the paragraphs that follow.

Developing a Solid Basis of Trust and Respect

In order to develop trust and respect in the classroom, teachers must always model the trust and respect they wish to see in their students. The Canters specifically suggest that teachers listen carefully to students, speak respectfully to them, and treat everyone fairly. Further, teachers should get to know their students as individuals and acknowledge them as such. Toward this end the Canters suggest that teachers greet students by name with a smile, acknowledge birthdays and other important events in students' lives, learn about students' interests and what motivates them, and chat with students individually in and out of the classroom. They also suggest establishing strong ties by communicating purposefully with parents or guardians. This can be done by sending positive notes home with students and making occasional phone calls to parents with positive comments about the student.

Teaching Students How They Are Expected to Behave in the Classroom

Students do not automatically know how to behave in all settings and situations. Therefore, teachers must make sure to teach acceptable behavior to students through modeling, explanation, and practice. The Canters say that the most important classroom rule is "Follow directions," but students can't be expected to know automatically how to do so in all the many classroom activities. Recognizing that different teachers have their own ways of doing things, the Canters (1992, p. 122) say "Your students need to follow your expectations, not another teacher's expectations." The Canters advise teachers to identify the academic activities, routine procedures, and special procedures for which directions are needed and then determine the specific directions that students need. The following are two examples, one for an academic activity and one for a routine procedure: (Canter and Canter 1992)

Teacher conducting a directed lesson, teaches students how to follow these directions:

1. Please clear your desks of everything but paper and pencil.
2. Eyes on me. No talking while I'm talking.
3. Raise hand and wait to be called on before speaking.

For routine procedure for entering the room, the teacher teaches students how to:

1. Walk into the room.
2. Go directly to their seat and sit down.
3. Cease talking when the bell rings. (pp. 126–127)

The best time for teaching directions is immediately prior to the first (or next) time the activity is to take place. For young children, give demonstrations and have children act them out. Frequent reteaching and reinforcement are necessary.

For older students, explain the reasons behind the directions and the benefits they provide. The Canters (1992) suggest the following procedure:

1. Explain the rationale for the direction.
2. Involve the students by asking questions.
3. Explain the specific directions.
4. Check for student understanding (by asking questions or having students role play). (pp. 131–138)

Once taught, the specific directions should be reinforced regularly through **positive repetition.** This means that rather than identify and correct a student who is not following directions, the teacher repeats the desired behavior. For example, a primary grade teacher notes one or more who are following directions and says, "Joshua has remembered to raise his hand. So has Elsa." A secondary teacher addresses the class rather than individuals: "Practically everyone began work quickly. I appreciate that very much." Directions should be reviewed each time the activity is repeated during the first two weeks. For the next month the directions should be reviewed each Monday as a refresher, and for the remainder of the year they should be reviewed after vacations and before special events such as holidays and field trips.

Establishing a Discipline Plan That Provides Structure and Identifies Behavior Limits

The Canters advocate a formalized, written discipline plan that includes rules, positive recognition, and consequences. **Rules** state exactly how students are to behave. They should indicate observable behaviors such as "Keep your hands to yourself" rather than vague ideas such as "Show respect to other students." Rules remain always in effect, in contrast to **directions** which only last for a given activity. Rules should be limited in number (three to five) and refer only to behavior, not to academic issues. **Positive recognition** refers to giving sincere personal attention to students who behave in keeping with class expectations. Recognition should be used frequently, as it can increase self-esteem, encourage good behavior, and build a positive classroom climate. Common ways of providing recognition include praise, expressing appreciation, and positive notes and positive phone calls to parents. **Consequences** are results teachers apply following student behavior. **Positive consequences** are given when students behave appropriately. **Negative consequences** are applied when students interfere with others' right to learn. While unpleasant to students, negative consequences are never harmful physically or psychologically. The Canters stress that it is not severity that makes consequences effective, but rather the teacher's consistency in applying consequences. Students have full knowledge of probable consequences in advance. When consequences must be invoked, students are reminded that, by their behavior, they have chosen the consequence. Teachers usually don't like to invoke consequences, but the Canters (1992) say:

> There is perhaps nothing more harmful we can do to children than allow them to disrupt or misbehave without showing them we care enough to let them know their behavior is not acceptable. (p. 79)

The Discipline Hierarchy

With advance preparation, misbehavior can be dealt with calmly and quickly. The Canters advise making what they call a **discipline hierarchy** that lists consequences and the order in which they will be imposed within the day. (Each day or secondary class period begins afresh.) Each consequence in the hierarchy is a bit more unpleasant than its predecessor. The Canters (1992) illustrate the discipline hierarchy with the following examples:

First time a student disrupts. Consequence: "Bobby, our rule is no shouting out. That's a warning."

Second or third time the same student disrupts. Consequence: "Bobby, our rule is no shouting out. You have chosen 5 minutes time out at the back table."

Fourth time the same student disrupts. Consequence: "Bobby, you know our rules about shouting out. You have chosen to have your parents called." The teacher informs Bobby's parents. This is done by phone and is especially effective if Bobby is required to place the call and explain what has happened.

Fifth time the same student disrupts. Consequence: "Bobby, our rule is no shouting out. You have chosen to go to the office to talk with the principal about your behavior."

Severe clause. Sometimes behavior is so severe that it is best to invoke the *severe clause*—being sent to the principal—on the first offense. Consequence: "Bobby, fighting is not allowed in this class. You have chosen to go to the principal immediately. We will talk about this later." (p. 85)

To employ the discipline hierarchy effectively, teachers must keep track of offenses that students commit. This is done by recording on a clipboard students' names and the number of violations. Other options include recording this information in the plan book or, in primary grades, using a system of colored cards that students "turn" or change after each violation. The Canters advise that names of offending students *not* be written on the board.

Teaching the Plan

The Canters stress this point: In order to make a discipline plan work effectively, teachers must actually teach the discipline plan to their students. It is not enough just to read it aloud or display it on a poster. The Canters provide a number of sample lessons showing how the plan can be taught at different grade levels (Canter and Canter 1992). All the plans they suggest follow this sequence:

1. Explain why rules are needed.
2. Teach the specific rules.
3. Check for understanding.
4. Explain how you will reward students who follow rules.
5. Explain why you have consequences.
6. Teach the consequences.
7. Check again for understanding. (pp. 98–115)

Providing Positive Recognition

The Canters (1992, p. 146) say that the best way to build responsible behavior is to "continually provide frequent positive recognition to those students who are on task." By positive recognition, they mean praise and support, both of which should be integrated naturally into lessons being taught. They go on to say (1992) that **praise** is the most effective technique teachers have for encouraging responsible behavior, and they provide guidelines for its use:

- Effective praise is personal. The student's name is mentioned along with the desired behavior: "Jack, thank you for working quietly back there."
- Effective praise is genuine. It must be related to the situation and behavior, and the teacher's demeanor should show that it is sincere.
- Effective praise is descriptive and specific. It lets students know when and why they are behaving appropriately: "Good, Susan. You went right to work on your essay."
- Effective praise is age appropriate. Young children like to be praised publicly. Older students like praise but usually prefer to receive it privately.The Canters make several recommendations concerning how to go about providing positive praise and support, such as scanning the room to note students who are working appropriately, circulating around the classroom to give one-on-one attention, and writing names on the board of students who are behaving responsibly. They suggest setting a goal with the class for getting at least 20 names on the board each day. (pp. 148–150)

Redirecting Nondisruptive Off-Task Behavior

Often students fail to behave responsibly, but not in a way that disrupts the class. They may look out the window instead of working, read a book instead of doing their assignment, doodle instead of completing their work, do work for another class, or daydream or sleep. Instead of applying consequences for these benign misbehaviors, teachers should redirect students back to the assigned task. The Canters (1992) describe four techniques teachers can use in these circumstances:

1. Use "the look": Make eye contact and use an expression that shows awareness and disapproval.
2. Use **physical proximity:** Move beside the student. Usually there is no need to do more.
3. Mention the offending student's name. The teacher says, "I want all of you, including Tanya and Michael, to come up with the answer to this problem."
4. Use **proximity praise:** Jason is not working, but Alicia and Maria, seated nearby, are. The teacher says, "Alicia and Maria are doing a good job of completing their work." (pp. 164–166)

Normally, these redirecting techniques are quite effective. If they do not produce the needed results, the teacher should assume that the offending student needs more help for self-control and should turn to the discipline hierarchy and issue a warning.

Invoking Consequences

Students will have been clearly informed of both positive recognition and negative consequences associated with class rules, and they may have role-played situations involving both. They realize that consequences naturally follow misbehavior. The Canters (1992) make these suggestions for invoking negative consequences:

1. Provide consequences calmly in a matter-of-fact manner: "Nathan, speaking like that to others is against our rules. You have chosen to stay after class."
2. Be consistent: Provide a consequence every time students choose to disrupt.
3. After a student receives a consequence, find the first opportunity to recognize that student's positive behavior: "Nathan, I appreciate how you are working. You are making a good choice."
4. Provide an escape mechanism for students who are upset and want to talk about what happened: Allow the student to describe feelings or the situation in a journal or log.
5. When a younger student continues to disrupt—move in: Nathan again speaks hurtfully to another student. The teacher moves close to Nathan and quietly and firmly tells him his behavior is inappropriate. She reminds him of the consequences he has already received and of the next consequence in the hierarchy.
6. When an older student continues to disrupt—move out: Marta once again talks during work time. The teacher asks Marta to step outside the classroom, where she reminds Marta of the inappropriate behavior and its consequences. All the while, the teacher stays calm, shows respect for Marta's feelings, and refrains from arguing. (pp. 170–186)

Working with Difficult Students

The Canters have found that the techniques described to this point help almost all students behave in a responsible manner, but they recognize that a few students require additional consideration. Those are the difficult-to-handle students the Canters (1993) describe as:

> ...students who are continually disruptive, persistently defiant, demanding of attention or unmotivated. They are the students who defy your authority and cause you stress, frustration and anger. Many of these students have severe emotional or behavioral problems. They may have been physically or psychologically abused, or born substance-addicted to alcohol, crack or other drugs. Many of them come from home environments where parents have minimal, if any, influence or control over their behavior.
>
> Difficult students are *not* the students in your class who act up occasionally. They're not the ones who once in a while may cause you to lose your temper. Difficult students are those who engage in disruptive, off-task behavior with great intensity and frequency. (p. 6)

Teachers do not like having to contend with these students, but they are the students most in need of attention and adult guidance. The Canters acknowledge that "You can't 'cure' or change these students, but you can create an environment that will help (them) achieve" (1993, p. 11). This is accomplished in three phases, which the Canters call (1) reaching out to difficult students, (2) meeting the special needs of difficult students, and (3) communicating with difficult students.

Reaching Out to Difficult Students

Teachers must take the initiative. Instead of continually reacting to the misbehavior of difficult students, teachers will have to reach out to them and try to gain their trust. The Canters (1993, p. 13) remind us that most students arrive in the classroom feeling they can trust the teacher, and they therefore accept teacher guidance. But difficult students are different. For a number of reasons, they do not see teachers as positive, caring role models. They do not trust teachers, do not like school, and do not see any point in behaving nicely in school. They find satisfaction in ignoring teacher requests and behaving impudently. A teacher's first priority in working with such students is, therefore, to build a sense of trust.

The process is not an easy one. Teachers can begin by trying to put themselves in the student's place, trying to see teachers and schools from the student's point of view. Then they can change the ways they *respond* to the difficult student. They need to know beforehand what they will do when the student behaves defiantly or confrontationally. The Canters contrast **reactive teacher behavior** with **proactive teacher behavior.** When responding reactively to a difficult student, teachers usually lose their tempers, fail to impose their will on the student, and end up sending the student to the principal's office. This accomplishes nothing positive. The teacher feels bad, stress is increased, and a sense of frustration and failure remain. The student does not become more willing to comply with teacher requests, but rather more resistant and untrusting, and the class is left feeling uneasy.

By preparing proactive responses, teachers can avoid much of the uneasiness and begin building a sense of trust. The Canters (1993) advise teachers as follows:

1. Anticipate what the difficult student will do and say. Think through how you will respond.
2. Remember that you have a choice in your responses. You can choose *not* to respond angrily or defensively. You can choose *not* to let your feelings get hurt.
3. Do not give up on difficult students. They need to see that you care about them. (pp. 32–34)

Building Trust with Difficult Students

Teachers can show that they care about students as individuals by treating every student as they would want their own child to be treated. Further, they can reach out to students in ways such as the following:

1. Take a student interest inventory. Find out about brothers and sisters, friends, preferred activities, hobbies, favorite books and TV shows, future hopes, and what students like their teachers to do.
2. Greet students individually at the door. Say something special to each, personally.
3. Spend some individual time with students. Give one-on-one attention when possible.
4. Make a phone call to the student after school and express appreciation, empathy, or regret, as appropriate.
5. When a student is ill, send a get-well card or use the phone to convey best wishes.

Meeting Difficult Students' Needs

Although all students have similar needs, certain strongly felt needs of difficult students are not being adequately met at school. In order to be successful with these students, teachers need to help them meet those needs. The Canters explain that three kinds of special needs underlie the behavior of difficult students: (1) a need for extra attention, (2) a need for firmer limits, and (3) a need for motivation. When a difficult student is disruptive or noncompliant, he or she is attempting to fulfill a need for either extra attention, firmer limits, or extra motivation.

How does a teacher identify the particular need that a student seems to be striving to satisfy? By doing three things, the Canters say: (1) Look at the student's behavior, (2) look at your own response to the student's behavior, and (3) look at the student's reaction to your response. Suppose fourth-grader Jonathan continually makes silly noises, gets out of his seat, makes irrelevant comments, shouts out, and grins at others. His behavior annoys you greatly, and after days of it you feel he is driving you crazy. Every time you reprimand Jonathan, he gets quiet for a little while, then begins disrupting again. Jonathan is annoying you (a sign of persistent attention-seeking behavior) and is satisfied temporarily when you give him attention. It is clear that Jonathan has a **need for extra attention.**

Suppose ninth-grader Alicia talks back to you, argues with others, and refuses to do what you ask of her. She doesn't want you or anyone else telling her what to do. Alicia's behavior makes you angry, and after a time you feel threatened. You want to put her in her place. When you reprimand and redirect her, she refuses to comply with your reasonable requests. Alicia shows a **need for firmer limits.**

Suppose eleventh-grader Arthur is always reluctant to begin an assignment, never completes one, continually makes excuses, and has an "I-can't" attitude. Arthur's behavior over time frustrates you; you try everything you know to get him going. He doesn't fight back, but nothing you do seems to work. Arthur, the Canters would say, has a **need for extra motivation.**

Fulfilling the Student's Primary Need

Once a difficult student's predominant need is identified, the teacher can address it in a beneficial manner (Canter and Canter 1993, pp. 68–73).

If the student needs *attention,* provide the maximum amount of attention in the shortest amount of time. Plan some proactive steps, such as greeting the student at the door, taking him or her aside for occasional brief chats, giving personal attention during directions and work time, and providing positive recognition for effort and attentiveness. Through the process, help the student see how to obtain recognition through appropriate, rather than inappropriate, behavior.

If the student needs *firmer limits,* enforce class rules in a nonconfrontational way. Do not give these students occasion to show how tough and defiant they can be. Quietly and privately remind them of rules and show appreciation when they comply.

If the student needs *greater motivation,* let him or her know you have faith in their ability. Make sure the assignment is within the student's capability. Break the task down into small parts if possible. Compliment the student on any effort or progress he or she makes.

Providing Positive Support

Positive interactions with difficult students are one of the keys to success, but most teachers find this an especially difficult task, since they are so often provoked by the students' misbehavior. The Canters (1993, pp. 100–116) provide a number of suggestions, including:

1. In the plan book, enter reminders of whom you wish to praise, what for, and when.
2. Post reminders at strategic points in the classroom, such as beside the clock.
3. Put a sticker on your watch face, so that every time you look at your watch you will be reminded to provide positive recognition to someone in need of it.
4. Walk around the room and look for positive behavior, then supply recognition.

The Canters believe positive support is best provided in the form of *praise*. It can also be given effectively in notes and phone calls home, special privileges, behavior awards, and tangible rewards.

Redirecting Nondisruptive Misbehavior

Difficult students often misbehave in ways that do not disrupt the class, such as day-dreaming, doodling, looking out the window, and withdrawing. Teachers usually react to this kind of misbehavior by either ignoring it or giving an immediate consequence. The Canters suggest, however, that nondisruptive misbehavior offers a good opportunity to build positive relationships with the student. The strategy proceeds this way (Canter and Canter 1993, pp. 120–124): The teacher says quietly to the student, "Your behavior is inappropriate, but I care about you and I'm going to give you the chance to choose more appropriate behavior." This gives the student an opportunity to meet the teacher's expectations. Probably further help will be needed, which the teacher provides by establishing eye contact, moving into physical proximity, or softly calling the student's name. If this is not sufficient, the student can be reminded of the rules and seated near the teacher. Teachers must remember to give plenty of encouragement as the student shows signs of complying with the rules.

Interacting with Difficult Students

The Canters make a number of suggestions about how to interact with difficult-to-manage students, including how to handle oneself, how to defuse confrontations, and how to use one-to-one problem solving. They begin by cautioning against "reactive responses" which usually make relationships worse, not better. They remind us that when a student becomes increasingly upset or defiant, we can stay calm and deescalate the situation. When meeting in a problem-solving conference with a student, we can communicate both firmness and caring. And by using effective communication skills we can build trust with a student even in difficult circumstances. (1993, p. 190)

Defusing Confrontations

The Canters point out that when you set limits and hold difficult students accountable, there will be confrontations. Teachers intensely dislike confrontations with students, which put teachers on the defensive and stir up heated emotions. How do you deal with them? The Canters (1993, pp. 162–175) make suggestions that include the following:

1. Tell yourself to stay calm. Do not speak for a moment or two. Take a slow deep breath and count to three, four, or five. This will help you relax.
2. Depersonalize the situation. Realize that the student is not attacking you personally, but rather the situation. Think of it as a scene in a movie. The calmer you remain, the harder it is for the student to remain upset.

3. Differentiate between covert and overt confrontations. In covert confrontations, the student mumbles or sneers but does not attack you verbally. In this case, step away from the student, but later speak to him or her privately. Overt confrontations are treated differently. Here, the student reacts defiantly to the teacher's requests, drawing other students' attention. In this case, remain calm and refuse to engage the student hostilely. Instead, acknowledge the student's emotion and restate what the student needs to do. If the student remains hostile, take him or her apart from the class, acknowledge the student's feelings, and again request cooperation.

4. If the student is especially hostile, you should back off. Drop the matter temporarily so the class may continue. Later, talk with the student privately.

Difficult though it may be, teachers should not view confrontations as setbacks, but rather as new opportunities to show commitment to the student. A calm, caring attitude will do much toward building trust between teacher and student.

One-to-One Problem Solving

Students who continue to misbehave seriously require more in-depth, personal guidance from the teacher. This can be provided in what the Canters call one-to-one problem-solving conferences, useful when the student's misbehavior is chronic, or when there is a sudden change in behavior, or when there is a serious problem (such as fighting) that cannot be overlooked. The Canters (1993, pp. 180–189) provide these guidelines for personal conferences:

1. Meet privately with the student and keep the meeting brief.
2. Show empathy and concern. The meeting is about the student's behavior, not your classroom and not about you.
3. Focus on helping the student gain insight into the misbehavior and into more appropriate behavior that will meet the student's needs. Try to find out why the problem behavior persists—is there a problem at home, with other students, with the difficulty of assignments? Listen and show respect for the student.
4. Help the student determine how his or her behavior can be improved.
5. Disarm the student's criticism of you. Ask for specific examples of what you are doing that bothers the student. Show empathy. Focus on the student's needs.
6. State your expectations about how the student is to behave. Make it clear (in a calm, friendly manner) that you will not allow the student to continue disruptive behavior.

Strengths of the Canters' *Assertive Discipline*

The Canters have developed and refined a system of discipline for helping promote a pleasant, supportive classroom environment that frees teachers to teach and students to learn. Their approach has broken new ground in several ways—ease of implementation, meeting teachers' and students' needs, teaching students how to behave responsibly, and insistence on support from administrators and parents. A great many teachers are very enthusiastic about *Assertive Discipline* because it helps them deal with students positively and teach with little interruption. It also helps relieve the annoyance of verbal confrontations and preserves instructional time. In the past, *Assertive Discipline* was criticized for being unnecessarily harsh and too focused on suppressing unwanted behavior rather than on helping students learn to control their own behavior. The Canters have been sensitive to those concerns and have taken pains to make sure that teachers understand this central point: Students must be taught, in an atmosphere of respect, trust, and support, how to behave responsibly. Perhaps the most telling evidence of the strength of *Assertive Discipline* is its continued widespread popularity, which suggests that it provides educators skills that work well for their students and themselves.

Initiating the Canters' *Assertive Discipline*

Assertive Discipline can be introduced in the class at any time, although the first few days of a new school year or semester are especially appropriate. Decide on behaviors you want from students, what you will do to build trust, and what positive recognitions you will provide and consequences you will invoke. Meet with your class and discuss the kinds of behavior that will make the classroom pleasant, safe, and productive. Solicit student ideas. Using their input, jointly formulate three to five rules to govern behavior. Sincerely ask all students if they can agree to abide by the rules. Discuss with students the positive recognitions you will provide and the hierarchy of consequences that you will invoke. Make sure students realize that the rules apply to every member of the class all the time. Take your plan to the principal for approval and administrative support. Send a copy of the discipline plan home for parents to read. Ask parents to sign and return a slip indicating their approval and support. With students, role-play rules, recognitions, and consequences, and emphasize repeatedly that the plan helps everyone enjoy a safe, positive environment.

Review of Selected Terminology

The following terms are emphasized in the Canters' *Assertive Discipline:*

Rights: of students, of teachers

Types of teachers, their response styles, and their behavior: assertive, hostile, nonassertive; reactive, proactive

Student needs: for extra attention, for firmer limits, for extra motivation

Discipline components: setting limits, directions, rules, consequences, praise, severe clause

Useful tactics: teaching the discipline plan, teaching proper behavior, behavior journal, physical proximity, positive recognition, positive repetitions, proximity praise

Application Exercises

Concept Cases

Case 1: Kristina Will Not Work ■ Kristina, a student in Mr. Jake's class, is quite docile. She socializes little with other students and never disrupts lessons. However, despite Mr. Jake's best efforts, Kristina will not do her work. She rarely completes an assignment. She is simply there, putting forth no effort at all. ***How would the Canters deal with Kristina?***

They would advise Mr. Jake to do the following: Quietly and clearly communicate class expectations to Kristina. Redirect her to on-task behavior. Have private talks with her to determine why she is not doing her work and what Mr. Jake might do to help. Provide personal recognition regularly and try to build a bond of care and trust with Kristina. Contact Kristina's parents about her behavior. See if they can provide insights that will help Mr. Jake work with Kristina. If necessary, make an individualized behavior plan for helping Kristina do her work.

Case 2: Sara Cannot Stop Talking ■ Sara is a pleasant girl who participates in class activities and does most, though not all, of her assigned work. She cannot seem to refrain from talking to classmates, however. Her teacher, Mr. Gonzales, has to speak to her repeatedly during lessons,

to the point that he often becomes exasperated and loses his temper. ***What suggestions would the Canters give Mr. Gonzales for dealing with Sara?***

Case 3: Joshua Clowns and Intimidates ■ Joshua, larger and louder than his classmates, always wants to be the center of attention, which he accomplishes through a combination of clowning and intimidation. He makes wise remarks, talks back (smilingly) to the teacher, utters a variety of sound-effect noises such as automobile crashes and gunshots, and makes limitless sarcastic comments and put-downs of his classmates. Other students will not stand up to him, apparently fearing his size and verbal aggression. His teacher, Miss Pearl, has come to her wit's end. ***Would Joshua's behavior be likely to improve if the Canters' techniques were used in Miss Pearl's classroom? Explain.***

Case 4: Tom Is Hostile and Defiant ■ Tom has appeared to be in his usual foul mood ever since arriving in class. On his way to sharpen his pencil, he bumps into Frank, who complains. Tom tells him loudly to shut up. Miss Baines, the teacher, says, "Tom, go back to your seat." Tom wheels around, swears loudly, and says heatedly, "I'll go when I'm damned good and ready!" ***How would the Canters have Miss Baines deal with Tom?***

Questions and Activities

1. Each of the following exemplifies an important point in the Canter model of discipline. Identify the point illustrated by each.

   a. Miss Hatcher, on seeing her class list for the coming year, exclaims, "Oh no! Billy Smythe in my class! Nobody can do a thing with him! There goes my sanity!"

   b. "If I catch you talking again during the class, you will have to stay an extra five minutes."

   c. "I wish you would try your best not to curse in this room."

   d. Students who receive a fourth check mark must go to the office and call their parents to explain what has happened.

   e. If the class is especially attentive and hard-working, students earn five minutes they can use for talking quietly at the end of the period.

2. For a grade level and/or subject you select, outline an *Assertive Discipline* plan that includes the following:

   • Four rules

- Positive recognition and consequences associated with the rules
- The people you will inform about your system, and how you will inform them

3. Examine Scenario 3 or 4 in Appendix A. How could *Assertive Discipline* be used to improve behavior in Mrs. Daniels's library or Mrs. Desmond's second grade?

Primary References

Canter, L. 1976. *Assertive Discipline: A take-charge approach for today's educator.* Seal Beach, CA: Lee Canter & Associates. The first edition, which describes assertive discipline, and which took the discipline world by storm.

———. 1978. Be an assertive teacher. *Instructor, 88(1),* 60. Canter instructing teachers on what it means to be an assertive teacher and how you become one.

———. 1988. Let the educator beware: A response to Curwin and Mendler. *Educational Leadership, 46(2),* 71–73. Canter's response to criticisms leveled at Assertive Discipline by Curwin and Mendler.

———. 1996. First, the rapport—then, the rules. *Learning, 24(5),* 12, 14. Canter's short article showing his movement toward building trusting relationships with students.

Canter, L. & M. Canter. 1992. *Assertive Discipline: Positive behavior management for today's classroom.* Santa Monica, CA: Lee Canter & Associates. Third edition, 1996. The third edition of the basic text on Assertive Discipline, containing many modifications from the original version, especially concerning relationships between teacher and students.

———. 1993. *Succeeding with difficult students: New strategies for reaching your most challenging students.* Santa Monica, CA: Lee Canter & Associates. A small book that outlines how to work more effectively with students who are difficult to manage.

Recommended Viewing and Reading

Canter, L., and M. Canter. 1986. *Assertive Discipline Phase 2: In-service media package* [videotapes and manuals]. Santa Monica, CA: Lee Canter & Associates.

———. 1989. *Assertive Discipline for secondary school educators: In-service video package and leader's manual.* Santa Monica, CA: Lee Canter & Associates.

Hill, D. 1990. Order in the classroom. *Teacher Magazine, 1(7),* 70–77.

Fredric Jones's *Positive Classroom Discipline*

Focus

- Using effective body language to help students pay attention and remain on task.
- Using incentive systems to motivate responsibility, good behavior, and productive work.
- Teaching in a manner that reduces the likelihood of misbehavior.
- Providing help efficiently to students needing teacher guidance during independent work.

Logic

- The easiest and best way to deal with behavior problems is to prevent their occurrence.
- Teachers are most effective in managing behavior when they remain calm and poised.
- Good body language is the single most effective control strategy available to teachers.
- Interactive teaching (Say, See, Do) has the potential to reduce misbehavior significantly.

Contributions

- Clarified the value and techniques of effective body language.
- Explained how to use Say, See, Do Teaching as a means of limiting misbehavior.
- Showed how to use incentive systems and PAT to motivate responsible behavior.
- Explained how to provide help efficiently to students during independent work.

Jones's Suggestions

- Use Say, See, Do teaching which calls for frequent student response.
- Make it a priority to eliminate the vast time wasting that is evident in most classrooms.
- Use good classroom organization and efficient help to forestall most behavior problems.
- Use effective body language and incentive systems to deal with incipient misbehavior.
- Teach responsibility; don't do for students what they are capable of doing for themselves.

Fredric Jones

About Fredric Jones

Fredric H. Jones is the developer and disseminator of Positive Classroom Management. He is based in Santa Cruz, California. A clinical psychologist, Jones has worked for many years to develop training procedures for improving teacher effectiveness in motivating, managing, and instructing school students. His procedures have grown from extensive field observations of effective teachers he conducted while on the faculties of the UCLA Medical Center and the University of Rochester School of Medicine and Dentistry. An independent consultant since 1978, Jones now devotes full efforts to his training programs.

Jones's management system is described in his books, *Positive Classroom Discipline* (1987), *Positive Classroom Instruction* (1987), and *Fredric Jones's Tools for Teaching* (2001). Jones also makes available two video courses of study called *Positive Classroom Discipline* (2001) and *Positive Classroom Instruction* (2001). The manuals for the videos are authored by JoLynne Talbott Jones. These materials and others for Jones's programs are available from Fredric H. Jones & Associates, Inc., 103 Quarry Lane, Santa Cruz, CA 95060; telephone 408-425-8222; fax 408-426-8222; e-mail FHJ123@aol.com, website: www.fredjones.com

Jones's Contributions to Discipline

While other authorities have devoted much attention to the role of verbal communication in promoting classroom discipline, Jones was the first to place major emphasis on the importance of *nonverbal communication* such as teachers' body language, facial expressions, gestures, eye contact, and physical proximity. He was also the first to note how teachers reinforce students he calls "helpless handraisers," and the first to prescribe the cure. He has reemphasized the value of good classroom organization and management, and is now stressing the importance of teaching students to behave responsibly. More recently, Jones has proposed what he calls *Say, See, Do Teaching*, an instructional approach that calls for frequent student response during lessons.

Jones's Central Focus

The main focus of Jones's efforts is on helping students support their own self-control so that they behave properly and maintain a positive attitude. Toward that end he emphasizes good classroom management, teaching in a way that calls for much student interaction, the effective use of body language, providing incentives that motivate desired behavior, helping students assume personal responsibility, and providing efficient help to students during independent work time.

Jones's Principal Teachings

- *Approximately 95 percent of all student misbehavior consists of talking to neighbors and being out of one's seat, as well as generally goofing off, such as daydreaming and making noise.* But it is this behavior that most often disrupts teaching and learning.

- *On the average, teachers in typical classrooms lose approximately 50 percent of their teaching time because students are off-task or otherwise disrupting learning.* This amounts to massive time wasting.
- *Most teaching time that is otherwise lost can be recouped when teachers use Say, See, Do Teaching, provide efficient help to students, use effective body language, and use incentive systems.* These are the hallmarks of good behavior management.
- *Say, See, Do Teaching is an instructional method that calls for frequent student response to teacher input.* It keeps students actively alert and involved in the lesson.
- *Efficient arrangement of the classroom improves the likelihood of successful teaching and learning.* This includes seating arrangements that permit the teacher to "work the crowd" as they supervise student work and provide help.
- *Proper use of body language is one of the most effective discipline skills available to teachers.* Body language includes eye contact, physical proximity, body carriage, facial expressions, and gestures.
- *Teachers set limits on student behavior not so much through rules as through subtle interpersonal skills.* These are the skills that convey that teachers mean business.
- *Students will work hard and behave well when given incentives to do so.* These incentives are teachers' promises that students will receive, in return for proper behavior, rewards in the form of favorite activities that can be earned by all members of the group for the enjoyment of all members of the group.
- *To be effective, an incentive must be attractive to the entire group and be available equally to all.* Incentives that are available only to certain members of the class will affect only the behavior of those few individuals and leave the class as a whole little changed.
- *Students must learn to do their work without the teacher hovering over them.* Jones calls students' reliance on teacher presence "helpless handraising." He devised a method of providing help very efficiently to students who call for teacher assistance during independent work. Jones says to "be positive, be brief, and be gone."
- *The goal of discipline is for students to assume responsibility for their actions.* All aspects of learning are improved when students do so.

Analysis of Jones's *Positive Classroom Discipline*

Misbehavior and Loss of Teaching-Learning Time

Since the early 1970s, Jones and his associates have spent thousands of hours observing and recording in hundreds of elementary and secondary classrooms. Jones's main interest has been in identifying the methods of classroom management used by highly successful teachers, especially the methods for keeping students working on-task, providing individual help when needed, and dealing with misbehavior.

Jones's observations led him to several important conclusions. Principal among them was that discipline problems are usually quite different from the way they are depicted in the media and perceived by the public. Even though many of the classrooms studied were located in inner-city schools and alternative schools for students with behavior problems, Jones found very little hostile student defiance—the behavior that teachers fear and that many people believe predominates in schools. Instead, he found what he called massive time wasting, in which students talked when they shouldn't, goofed off, daydreamed, and moved about the room without permission. Jones found that in well-managed classrooms, one of those disruptions occurred about every two minutes. In loud, unruly classes the disruptions averaged dozens every minute. In attempting to deal with those misbehaviors, teachers lost an average of almost 50 percent of the time available for teaching and learning (Jones 1987a).

Jones also discovered a critical time during lessons in which misbehavior was most likely to occur. He found that most lessons go along fairly well until students are asked to work on their own. That is when, Jones (1987b) says, "the chickens come home to roost." Until that point, students seem to pay attention and give the impression they are learning perfectly. But when directed to continue work on their own, hands go up, talking begins, students rummage around or stare out the window, and some get out of their seats. The teacher often doesn't know what to do except nag and admonish. This, Jones says, is "another day in the life of a typical classroom" (1987b, p. 14) where the teacher ends up reteaching the lesson to **helpless handraisers** during time that should be devoted to supervising independent work.

Teachers everywhere relate to that scenario as one that leaves them feeling frustrated and defeated. When discussing the phenomenon, many express bitterness over never having received training in how to deal effectively with such misbehavior. New teachers say they expected that they would quickly learn to maintain order in their classrooms but were only partially successful and found themselves resorting to punitive measures.

Jones concluded that teachers were correct about not receiving training in behavior management and, further, that many, if not most, were unable to develop needed skills while working on the job. Jones decided to observe and document the methods used by teachers who were notably successful with discipline. Those observations provided the basis of Jones's system of discipline.

Skill Clusters in Jones's Model

Jones says that the purpose of discipline is to help students engage in learning, and it should be as positive and unobtrusive as possible. His analysis of the numerous classroom observations uncovered five clusters of teacher skills that keep students productively at work, thus preventing misbehavior or allowing teachers to deal with it efficiently. Those skill clusters have to do with (1) classroom structure to discourage misbehavior, (2) limit-setting through body language, (3) using Say, See, Do Teaching to maximize student attention and involvement, (4) responsibility training through incentive systems, and (5) providing efficient help to individual students. Let us explore these skill clusters further.

Skill Cluster 1: Classroom Structure to Discourage Misbehavior

Jones emphasizes that the best way to manage behavior problems is to prevent their occurrence. In turn, the best way to prevent their occurrence is by providing a **classroom structure** that gives specific attention to room arrangement, class rules, classroom chores, and routines to begin class.

Room Arrangement

An effective way to prevent students' goofing off is to minimize the physical distance between teacher and students. This allows teachers to "work the crowd." Through movement and proximity with an occasional pause, look, or slow turn, teachers cause most students most of the time simply to rule out inattention or misbehavior.

Teachers with minimum discipline problems constantly move among students during seat work, group discussions, and cooperative learning. This calls for room arrangements with generous walkways that allow teachers to move easily among the students. Jones suggests the "interior loop" as ideal: There, desks or tables are set with two wide aisles from front to back and enough distance between side-to-side rows for teachers to walk comfortably among the students.

Classroom Rules

Classroom rules should be both general and specific. **General rules,** fairly few in number, define the teacher's broad guidelines, standards, and expectations for work and behavior. They can be reviewed and posted. **Specific rules** describe procedures and routines, detailing specifically what students are to do and how they are to do it. These rules must be taught and rehearsed until they are learned like any academic skill. Jones advocates spending the first two weeks making sure students understand the specific rules.

Classroom Chores

Jones believes in assigning as many classroom chores to students as possible. This gives them a sense of buy-in to the class program and helps develop a sense of responsibility.

Opening Routines

Typically, class sessions begin in a fragmented way, with announcements, taking attendance, handling tardies, and the like. This produces delays during which students waste time and misbehave. Jones says that, on average, about five to eight minutes are wasted in most classrooms immediately after the bell rings. It is much preferable that teachers begin lessons promptly. Jones suggests beginning the class with **bell work,** which does not require active instruction from the teacher. Bell work engages and focuses students on the day's lesson. Students can begin on their own upon entering the room. Examples of bell work are review questions, warm-up problems, brain teasers, silent reading, and journal writing.

Skill Cluster 2: Limit-Setting through Body Language

Jones maintains that good discipline depends in large measure on teachers using **body language** effectively. Therefore, his approach concentrates on helping teachers learn to use physical mannerisms in setting and enforcing behavior limits. Jones says teachers are most effective in **setting limits** when they use their bodies correctly but say nothing and take no other action. He reminds teachers that they cannot discipline with their mouths. He says if that were possible nagging would have fixed every kid a million years ago. When you open your mouth, he says, you run the risk of slitting your own throat. The specific body language that Jones emphasizes is discussed in the following paragraphs.

Proper Breathing

Teachers do well to remain calm in all situations, as calm conveys strength. Calm is attained in part through proper breathing. The way teachers breathe when under pressure signals how they feel and what they are likely to do next. Skilled teachers breathe slowly and deliberately before responding to situations. Jones noted that some teachers take two deep breaths before turning to a misbehaving student, enabling them to maintain self-control.

Eye Contact

Miss Remy is demonstrating and explaining the process of multiplying fractions. She sees that Jacob has stopped paying attention. She pauses in her explanation. The sudden quiet causes Jacob to look at Miss Remy and find that she is looking directly at his eyes. He straightens up and waits attentively. Few physical acts are more effective than **eye contact** for conveying the impression of being in control. Jones says that turning and pointing both the eyes and the feet toward talking students shows teacher commitment to discipline.

Physical Proximity

Miss Remy has completed her demonstration of the multiplication of fractions. She has directed students to complete some exercises on their own. After a time she sees from the back of the room that Jacob has stopped working and has begun talking to Jerry. She moves toward him. Jacob unexpectedly finds Miss Remy's shadow at his side. He immediately gets back to work, without Miss Remy having to say anything. Jones observed that teachers who use **physical proximity** rarely need to say anything to the offending students to get them to behave.

Body Carriage

Jones also found that posture and **body carriage** are quite effective in communicating authority. Students read body language and are able to tell whether the teacher is feeling in charge, tired, disinterested, or intimidated. Good posture and confident carriage suggest strong leadership; a drooping posture and lethargic movements suggest resignation or fearfulness. Effective teachers, even when tired or troubled, tend to hold themselves erect and move assertively.

Facial Expressions

Like body carriage, teachers' **facial expressions** communicate much to students. Facial expressions can show enthusiasm, seriousness, enjoyment, and appreciation, all of which tend to encourage good behavior; or they can reveal boredom, annoyance, and resignation, which may encourage misbehavior. Perhaps more than anything else, facial expressions such as winks and smiles demonstrate a sense of humor, the trait that students most enjoy in teachers.

Skill Cluster 3: Using Say, See, Do Teaching

Jones says that many teachers beyond primary grades spend major portions of their class periods presenting information to students while the students remain relatively passive. Finally, toward the end of the lesson, students are asked to do something with the information they have received. Jones (2001) graphically depicts this approach as follows:

(Teacher) input, input, input, input, input → (Student) output

This instructional approach contains some built-in factors that contribute to student misbehavior, including:

1. The large amount of teacher input produces cognitive overload in students, which makes them disengage from the lesson.
2. The students sit passively for too long. The urge to do something builds up.
3. The teacher does not adequately "work the crowd," that is, interact with individual students, particularly in the back of the classroom.

Teachers who are more effective, Jones contends, put students to work from the beginning. They present information and then quickly have students do something with it. This approach is "doing" oriented, with activities occurring often at short intervals, and is depicted as follows:

Teacher input → student output → teacher input → student output → teacher input → student output

Jones explains that he calls the approach **Say, See, Do Teaching.** The teacher says (or does), the students see, and the students do something with the input. This approach greatly reduces the amount of student fooling around because the students are kept busy while the teacher circulates and interacts with students at work.

Skill Cluster 4: Responsibility Training through Incentive Systems

Jones observed that teachers have three different management styles: Some teach well and reward well; some nag, threaten, and punish; and some lower their standards and accept whatever they can get from students. These management styles are closely related to success in the classroom. Mr. Sharpe tells his class that if all of them complete their work in 45 minutes or less, they can work on an enrichment activity or play a learning game. Mr. Naeve tells his class he will allow them to begin the period by discussing their work with a friend, provided they promise to work very hard afterward. Which teacher is likely to get the best work from his students? This question has to do with incentives and how they affect responsibility.

An **incentive** is something outside of the individual that prompts the individual to act. It is something that is promised as a consequence for desired behavior but is held in abeyance to occur or be provided later. It might be a preferred activity in the form of a learning game or an enrichment activity. A PAT is never a free time. It is structured and the teacher is a participant. It is an effective incentive if students behave as desired in order to obtain it later. Jones gives a prominent place in his classroom management program to incentives as a means of motivating students. He found that some of the most effective teachers use incentives systematically but that most teachers use them ineffectively or not at all.

What, then, are characteristics of effective incentives, and how should they be used? Responsibility training gains most of its strength, Jones says, from the "bonus" portion of the incentive. Bonuses encourage students to save time they would normally waste in order to get it back in the form of preferred activity time. It gives members of the class a shared vested interest in cooperating to save time rather than wasting it in small snippets throughout the period or day. Jones suggests that in order to make best use of incentives, teachers should carefully consider (1) Grandma's rule, (2) student responsibility, (3) genuine incentives, (4) preferred activity time, (5) educational value, (6) group concern, (7) ease of implementation, (8) omission training, and (9) backup systems. Let us see what is involved in each.

Grandma's Rule

Grandma's rule states: "You have to finish your dinner before you can have your dessert." Applied to the classroom, this rule requires that students first do what they are supposed to do, and then for a while after that they can do what they want to do. Just as children (and most adults) want their dessert first, promising to eat their vegetables afterward, students ask to have their incentive first, pledging on their honor to work feverishly afterward. As we all know, even the best intentions are hard to remember once the reason for doing so is gone. Thus, teachers who wish to use effective incentive systems must, despite student urging, delay the rewards until last and make the reward contingent on the students' doing required work acceptably. In other words, if they don't eat their broccoli, they don't get their ice cream.

Student Responsibility

Jones believes that incentives, used correctly, can help everyone take responsibility for their actions. For example, one way students can show responsibility is through cooperating with others. However, cooperation is voluntary; it is difficult to force anyone to cooperate. Students who enjoy goofing off and daydreaming, when asked to cooperate, can ask themselves, "Why should I? What's in it for me?" Jones suggests that when students show responsibility by doing what teachers ask them to do, it is because teachers have used encouragement and incentives, rather than trying to force responsibility through nagging, threatening, or punishing.

Genuine Incentives

There is a wide difference between what many teachers hope will be incentives (e.g., "Let's all work in such a way that we will later be proud of what we do") and what students consider **genuine incentives** (e.g., "If you complete your work on time, you can have five minutes of preferred activity time"). Jones cautions against allowing students to earn "free time" to do whatever they wish: He says students won't work for long to earn free time, but they will for *activity* time they enjoy. This shows that what teachers believe to be an incentive may, in actuality, not work for most students in the class. Further examples: A teacher may say, "The first person to complete a perfect paper will receive two bonus points." This may motivate a few of the most able students, but all the others know they have little chance to win so there is no reason to try. Or the teacher may say, "If you really work hard, you can be the best class I have ever had." This sounds good to the teacher but means little to the students and is not sufficient to keep them diligently at work.

Jones believes that activities students enjoy are the best overall incentives. Students respond well to the anticipation of activities such as art, viewing a film, or having time to pursue personal interests or play a learning game. Such group activities are genuine incentives in that, first, almost all students desire them sufficiently to make extra effort to obtain them and, second, they are available to all students, not just a few. Tangible objects, awards, and certificates should not be used as incentives. They tend to be costly or difficult to dispense or, worse, have little educational value.

Preferred Activity Time

Preferred activity time is time allotted for any activity that can serve as an incentive. "Preferred activity" means that the activity is one students enjoy, such as learning games, activities, and projects—activities they prefer to most others. Jones uses the abbreviation **PAT** (preferred activity time) and advises that when selecting and introducing PAT, teachers must make sure that students want the activity, that they earn the activity by showing responsibility, and that the teacher can live with the PAT.

PAT may be earned in a number of different ways. Mr. Jorgensen gives his fourth graders three minutes to put away their language arts materials and prepare for math: Any time left over from the three minutes goes to later PAT. In Mrs. Nguyen's room, if everyone is seated and ready when the bell rings, the class earns two additional minutes of PAT. Some PAT may be used the day it is earned, while other PAT may be accumulated for a future activity, such as a field trip. In some instances, PAT may be earned as individual bonuses. When Mickey continues to be unprepared and consequently loses PAT for the class, Mr. Duncan decides to work with him individually. Mickey's irresponsibility no longer penalizes the entire class, but as he improves, he might earn PAT for the entire class which improves his status with peers.

Educational Value

To the extent feasible, every class period should be devoted to activities that have **educational value.** Work that keeps students occupied but teaches them nothing can seldom be justified. This principle applies equally to incentive systems. While few educators would be loath never to allow a moment of innocent frivolity, the opposite extreme of daily or weekly parties as incentives is difficult to condone. What then should one use as PAT?

There are many activities with educational value that students enjoy greatly (see PAT section at www.fredjones.com). Students are not left to do just anything, nor do they proceed without guidance. The freedom lies in being able to choose from a variety of approved activities. Activities can be chosen by vote, and all students engage in the same activity during the time allotted. Elementary school students often select physical education, art, music, drama, construction activities, or being read to by the teacher. Secondary students often choose team games such as Jeopardy, College Bowl, or Academic Baseball, hold class discussions on special topics, or watch performances by class members. JoLynne Talbott Jones (1993) gives suggestions for a large number of educationally sound activities that students of various grade levels enjoy greatly and that therefore serve as good preferred activities.

Group Concern

Jones emphasizes the importance of making sure every student has a stake in earning the incentive for the entire class. This **group concern** motivates all students to keep on task, behave well, and complete assigned work. Here is how it is done.

The teacher agrees to set aside a period of time in which students might be allowed to engage in a preferred activity. In keeping with Grandma's rule, this PAT period must come after a significant amount of work time has been devoted to the standard curriculum. The PAT can be at the end of the school day for self-contained classes—perhaps 15 to 20 minutes. For departmentalized classes, the time can be set aside at the end of the week—perhaps 30 minutes on Friday. The students can decide on the activity for their dessert time, and to earn it they have only to work and behave as expected.

The teacher manages the system by keeping track of the time that students earn. Of course, it is possible that a single student, by misbehaving, can prevent the class from earning full PAT. Teachers often think it unfair to penalize the entire class for the sins of a few. In practice, this is rarely a problem, because the class quickly understands that this is a group, not an individual, effort. The group is rewarded together and punished together regardless of who might transgress. A strength of this approach is that it brings peer pressure to bear against misbehavior. Ordinarily a misbehaving student obtains reinforcement from the group in the form of attention, laughter, or admiration. With proper PAT, the opposite is true. The class is likely to discourage individual misbehavior, because it takes away something the class members want. Nevertheless, some students do occasionally misbehave to the detriment of other responsible students. When this occurs, the teacher may decide to work with the offending student individually.

Ease of Implementation

Incentive systems will not work unless they are easy to implement. Jones (2001) suggests:

1. Establish and explain the system.
2. Allow the class to vote from time to time on the approved activities they wish to enjoy during incentive time.
3. Keep track of the bonus time students have earned for PAT.
4. Be prepared when necessary to conduct the class in low preference activities for the amount of time that students might have lost from the time allotted to their preferred activity.

Omission Training

Generally speaking, incentives and PAT bonuses are earned by the entire class. Teachers cannot possibly monitor incentives for all students individually. The exception lies in the occasional student whose misbehavior repeatedly ruins PAT for the rest of the class. For those few students Jones describes **omission training,** a plan that allows a student to earn PAT for the entire class by omitting a certain misbehavior.

Kevin is one such student. In Ms. VanEtten's class he simply does not seem to care about PAT, and consequently is late, loud, and unprepared, thus ruining PAT for the others. Ms. VanEtten privately explains to Kevin that he doesn't have to participate in PAT, particularly since he doesn't care about it, but she does want him to be successful with his own work and behavior. She explains that she will use a timer, and when Kevin behaves in accordance with class rules, he will earn time for himself, and also PAT for the class. When he misbehaves, he loses time for himself but not for the class.

Backup Systems

As a last option for students like Kevin, Jones suggests **backup systems,** which are hierarchical arrangements of sanctions intended to put a stop to unacceptable student behavior. Jones identifies three levels of backup.

1. As teachers work the crowd they are able to camouflage their small backup responses by speaking privately or semiprivately to the student: "I expect you to stop talking so we can get on with our work." With such low-keyed messages the student knows the teacher means business. Whispering privately is a constructive way of protecting students' dignity.
2. Medium backup systems are those sanctions that we all grew up with and that any student in the classroom can see: loss of privilege, staying after school, and parent conferences.
3. Large backup responses require at least two professionals, usually the teacher and an administrator, and deal with chronically repeated disruptions or other intolerable behavior. Large backup responses include trips to the office, in- or out-of-school suspension, special class, and special school.

Skill Cluster 5: Providing Efficient Help to Individual Students

One of the most interesting, important, and useful findings in Jones's research has to do with the way teachers help students who are stuck during seatwork. Suppose a grammar lesson is in progress. The teacher introduces the topic, explains the concept on the board, asks a couple of questions to determine whether the students are understanding, and then assigns exercises for students to complete at their desks. Very soon Arnell raises his hand signaling that he needs help. If only three or four students raise hands during work time, the teacher has no problem. But if 20 students fill the air with waving arms, most sit for several minutes doing nothing while waiting for the teacher. This waiting time is pure waste and an invitation to misbehave.

Jones asked teachers how much time they thought they spent on the average when providing help to individuals who signaled. The teachers felt that they spent from one to two minutes with each student, but when Jones's researchers timed the episodes, they found that teachers actually spent around four minutes with each student. This consumed much time and made it impossible for the teacher to attend to more than a few students during the work period. Even if the amount of time were only one minute per contact, several minutes would pass while some students sat and did nothing.

Jones noted an additional phenomenon that compounded the problem. He called it **helpless handraising** wherein some students routinely raised their hands for teacher help even when they did not need it. To have the teacher unfailingly come to their side and give personal attention proved rewarding for those students, and the constant reinforcement furthered their dependency.

Jones therefore concluded that independent seatwork is typically beset with four problems: (1) insufficient time for teachers to answer all requests for help; (2) wasted student time; (3) high potential for misbehavior; and (4) perpetuation of dependency. Consequently, he gives this matter high priority in *Positive Classroom Discipline*.

Jones determined that all four problems can be solved through teaching teachers how to give **efficient help,** which is accomplished as follows:

First. Organize the classroom seating so that students are within easy reach of the teacher. The interior loop seating arrangement previously described is suggested because it gives the teacher free, easy movement in the room. Unless able to get quickly from one student to another, the teacher uses too much time and energy.

Second. Use graphic reminders, such as models or charts, that provide clear examples and instructions. These reminders might show steps in algorithms, proper form for business letters, or written directions for the lesson. The reminders are posted and can be consulted by students before they call for teacher help.

Third. Reduce to a minimum the time used for giving students individual help. To see how this can be accomplished, consider that teachers normally give help very inefficiently through a questioning tutorial that proceeds something like this:

"What's the problem?"

"All right, what did we say was the first thing to do?" *[Waits; repeats question.]*

"No, that was the second. You are forgetting the first step. What was it? Think again." *[Waits until student finally makes a guess.]*

"No, let me help you with another example. Suppose…"

In this manner, the teacher often reteaches the concept or process to each student who requests help. Four minutes can be unexpectedly spent in each interaction. If help is to be provided more quickly, this questioning method must be replaced. Jones trains teachers to give help in a very different way, and he insists that it be done in 20 seconds or less for each student, with an optimal goal of about 10 seconds. To reach this level of efficiency, the teacher should do the following when arriving beside the student:

1. (Optional). Quickly find anything that the student has done correctly and mention it favorably: "Your work is very neat" or "Good job up to here."
2. Give a straightforward prompt that will get the student going: "Follow step two on the chart" or "Regroup here." Jones says teachers are to help students continue working instead of tutoring them through the whole task. They can do this by using a visual instruction plan or simply telling students what they are to do next.
3. Leave immediately. As Jones says, "Be positive, be brief, and be gone."

Help provided in this way solves the time and attention problems that teachers face during instructional work time. Every student who needs help can receive proper attention. Students waste little time waiting for the teacher. Misbehavior is much less likely. Helpless handraising is diminished, especially if the teacher gives attention to students who work without calling for assistance. Rapid circulation by the teacher also permits better monitoring of work being done by students who do not raise their hands. When errors are noted in those students' work, the teacher should provide help just as for students who have raised their hands.

Strengths of Jones's *Positive Classroom Discipline*

The Jones model provides effective tactics for preventing misbehavior and supporting proper behavior, and does so in a balanced way. Jones has been successful in identifying and compiling discipline techniques used by teachers who are so effective they are often called "naturals." That is why teachers' heads nod in agreement with his suggestions. Jones has found that the strategies he advocates are all teachable, though many teachers do not learn them well within the pressures of day-to-day teaching. Through specific training episodes, most teachers can acquire the techniques that are normally used only by their most effective colleagues.

The tactics Jones describes must be understood and then practiced repeatedly. Fortunately, teachers can assess their classroom behavior in light of Jones's suggestions and isolate certain control tactics they would like to incorporate into their teaching. They can practice what Jones suggests and apply their new skills in the classroom. That is one of the most appealing qualities of Jones's suggestions: The entire *Positive Classroom Discipline* program does not have to be put into place as a full-blown system but can instead be practiced, perfected, and added incrementally.

Initiating Jones's *Positive Classroom Discipline*

Jones (1987a, p. 321) suggests that his model of discipline be initiated as a five-tiered system of closely related management methodologies: (1) classroom structure, (2) limit setting, (3) Say, See, Do teaching, (4) incentives, and (5) backup systems. All five tiers are carefully planned out in advance and introduced simultaneously. It is important to understand that *Positive Classroom Discipline* is a system in which the parts interrelate. For example, if classroom structure is inadequate, some of the unmanaged behavior is likely to surface as misbehavior, and to deal with it the teacher must stop teaching. If this happens often, the cost in time and effort skyrockets. Say, See, Do teaching keeps students attentive and actively involved with smaller bits of input, thus preventing problems that occur when input becomes more than students can handle. If potential discipline problems are not circumvented at this point, they end up requiring responsibility training, which again consumes much instructional time.

To introduce *Positive Classroom Discipline* to students, you can begin with a discussion of limit setting, which leads to the formulation of agreements (rules) about what students may and may not do in the classroom. Explain to the students that when they violate rules, their behavior will be corrected with body language that does nothing more than make the misbehaving student feel uncomfortable. Examples such as eye contact, stares, and physical proximity are given and demonstrated.

To make limit setting work effectively, mild discomfort is counterbalanced with incentives and social rewards, such as acknowledgment and approval, in return for students' observing rules and agreements. Desirable incentives are discussed, and procedures for managing incentives are described. Students are reminded that the incentives they select are to have instructional value.

You will also need to discuss with students the **backup systems** you will use when students misbehave seriously and refuse to comply with your requests. Such sanctions receive relatively little attention in Jones's system, which attempts to move teachers away from reliance on admonition and threat, yet Jones acknowledges that at times the teacher may be unable to get misbehaving students to comply with the rules. At those times, teachers may tell the student, "If you are not going to do your work, sit there quietly and don't bother others." And for yet more serious situations of defiance or aggression, teachers must have a plan by which they isolate the student or call for help as needed.

Review of Selected Terminology

The following terms are central to Jones's *Positive Classroom Discipline*. Check yourself to make sure you can explain their meanings:

Major discipline problem: massive time wasting

Preferred instructional style: Say, See, Do Teaching

Limit-setting: the body language of meaning business, in particular relaxing, slowing down, committing to dealing with a problem and following through by using body carriage, facial expressions, gestures, eye contact, breathing.

Classroom structure: room arrangement, working the crowd, general rules, specific procedures and structures.

Providing help efficiently: steps in, interior loop, avoiding helpless handraising

Individual and group tactics: genuine incentives, preferred activity time (PAT), group concern, Grandma's rule, omission training, physical proximity, bell work, nonverbal communication, backup systems

Application Exercises

Concept Cases

Case 1: Kristina Will Not Work ■ Kristina, a student in Mr. Jake's class, is quite docile. She socializes little with other students and never disrupts the class. However, Mr. Jake cannot get Kristina to do any work. She rarely completes an assignment. She is simply there, putting forth almost no effort at all. *How would Jones deal with Kristina?*

Jones would probably suggest that Mr. Jake take the following steps to improve Kristina's behavior:

1. Make frequent eye contact with her. Even when she looks down, Mr. Jake should make sure to look directly at her. She will be aware of it, and it may make her uncomfortable enough that she will begin work.
2. Move close to Kristina. Stand beside her while presenting the lesson.
3. Give Kristina frequent help during seatwork. Check on her progress several times during the lesson. Give specific suggestions and then move quickly on.
4. Increase the amount of Say, See, Do teaching with Kristina so she has less information to deal with and is called on to respond frequently.
5. Set up a personal incentive system with Kristina; for example, a certain amount of work earns an activity she especially enjoys.
6. Set up a system in which Kristina can earn rewards for the entire class. This brings her peer attention and support.

Case 2: Sara Cannot Stop Talking ■ Sara is a pleasant girl who participates in class activities and does most, though not all, of her assigned work. She cannot seem to refrain from talking to classmates, however. Her teacher, Mr. Gonzales, has to speak to her repeatedly during lessons, to the point that he often becomes exasperated and loses his temper. *What suggestions would Jones give Mr. Gonzales for dealing with Sara?*

Case 3: Joshua Clowns and Intimidates ■ Joshua, larger and louder than his classmates, always wants to be the center of attention, which he accomplishes through a combination of clowning and intimidation. He makes wise remarks, talks back (smilingly) to the teacher, utters a variety of sound-effect noises such as automobile crashes and gunshots, and makes limitless sarcastic comments and put-downs of his classmates. Other students will not stand up to him, apparently fearing his size and verbal aggression. His teacher, Miss Pearl, has come to her wit's end. *What specifically do you find in Jones's suggestions that would help Miss Pearl with Joshua?*

Case 4: Tom Is Hostile and Defiant ■ Tom has appeared to be in his usual foul mood ever since arriving in class. On his way to sharpen his pencil, he bumps into Frank, who complains. Tom tells him loudly to shut up. Miss Baines, the teacher, says, "Tom, go back to your seat." Tom wheels around, swears loudly, and says heatedly, "I'll go when I'm damned good and ready!" *How effective do you believe Jones's suggestions would be in dealing with Tom?*

Questions and Activities

1. For each of the following scenarios, first identify the problem that underlies the undesired behavior, then describe how Jones would have the teacher deal with it.

   a. Mr. Anton tries to help all of his students during independent work time but finds himself unable to get around to all who have their hands raised.

   b. Ms. Sevier wants to show trust for her class. She accepts their promise to work hard if she will allow them first to listen to a few favorite recordings. After listening, the students talk so much that they fail to get their work done.

   c. Mr. Gregory wears himself out every day dealing ceaselessly with three class clowns who disrupt his lessons. The other students always laugh at the clowns' antics.

   d. Mrs. Swanson, who takes pride in her lectures, is becoming frustrated because students begin to gaze out the window and whisper before she has completed what she wants to tell them.

2. Examine Scenario 2 or 10 in Appendix A. What changes would Jones suggest that Mr. Platt or Miss Thorpe make in order to provide a more efficient and satisfactory learning environment?

Primary References

Jones, F. 1979. The gentle art of classroom discipline. *National Elementary Principal, 58,* 26–32. An early article by Jones that describes his views on discipline and how discipline should be implemented.

———. 1987a. *Positive classroom discipline.* New York: McGraw-Hill. Jones's detailed description of discipline problems and his scheme for helping teachers deal with them effectively.

———. 1987b. *Positive classroom instruction.* New York: McGraw-Hill. A companion volume to *Positive classroom discipline* that explores how instruction can be made most effective and how that effectiveness, in turn, reduces misbehavior.

———. 1996. Did not! Did, too! *Learning, 24*(6), 24–26. A short article in which Jones explains how to deal effectively with class squabbles.

———. 2001. *Fredric Jones's Tools for Teaching.* Santa Cruz, CA: Fredric H. Jones & Associates. Jones's revised edition that combines earlier editions of *Positive Classroom Discipline* and *Positive Classroom Instruction.* It interrelates discipline and instruction more closely and describes in detail Say, See, Do Teaching.

Recommended Viewing and Guides

Jones, F. 1996. *Positive Classroom Discipline— a video course of study.* Santa Cruz, CA: Fredric H. Jones & Associates.

Jones, J. 1993. *Instructor's guide: Positive classroom discipline—a video course of study.* Santa Cruz, CA: Fredric H. Jones & Associates.

———. 1996. *Instructor's guide: Positive classroom discipline—a video course of study.* Santa Cruz, CA: Fredric H. Jones & Associates.

Jones, F. (2001). *Tools for Teaching: A Video Toolbox.* Santa Cruz, CA: Fredric H. Jones and Associates.

Linda Albert's
Cooperative Discipline

Focus

■ A cooperative approach to help students connect with others, contribute, and feel capable.
■ A class code of conduct that fosters an optimal climate for learning and teaching.
■ Student-parent partnership in sustaining a quality learning environment.

Linda Albert

Logic

■ Behavior is based on choice: Students choose to behave the way they do.
■ Teachers are in a powerful position to influence the choices students make.
■ Teachers best influence students through encouragement, intervention, and collaboration.
■ Students behave better when they and their parents help establish the behavior code.

Contributions

■ Established teacher–student–parent cooperation as a key to positive classroom behavior.
■ Extended Rudolf Dreikurs's discipline concepts to the classroom in a more useful form.
■ Devised the Three C's—capable, connect, contribute—to help students feel they belong.
■ Clarified dozens of teacher interventions for application at the moment of misbehavior.

Albert's Suggestions

■ Help every student feel they belong in the class, that they have a place and are valued.
■ Help every student connect with others, contribute to the class, and feel capable.
■ Involve students and parents in planning class code of conduct and the consequences for misbehavior.
■ Turn every misbehavior into an opportunity to help students learn to behave better.

About Linda Albert

Linda Albert, author and disseminator of *Cooperative Discipline,* is an educator, counselor, syndicated columnist, and former classroom teacher who works nationally and internationally with educators and parents. She has authored regular columns in *Working Mother* and *Family* magazines and has made featured appearances on NBC's "Today Show," CBS's "This Morning," and CNN's "Cable News."

Albert has produced a quantity of materials and programs for educators and parents, including *An Administrator's Guide to Cooperative Discipline* (1992), *Coping with Kids* (1993), *Cooperative Discipline* (1996), *A Teacher's Guide to Cooperative Discipline* (1996), and *Cooperative Discipline Implementation Guide: Resources for Staff Development* (1996). She has also produced two video series, *Responsible Kids in School and at Home: The Cooperative Discipline Way* (1994), and *Cooperative Discipline Staff Development Videos* (1996), with separate materials for elementary and secondary teachers. Albert lives in Tampa, Florida, and can be contacted via fax 813-265-3399 or website: www.cooperativediscipline.com

Albert's Contributions to Discipline

Influenced by Adlerian psychology and the work of Rudolf Dreikurs, Albert became convinced that students' behavior—and misbehavior—is a consequence of students' attempts to meet certain needs. By attending to those needs and providing much encouragement, teachers can reduce misbehavior greatly and establish classrooms where students participate cooperatively with the teacher and each other. Albert shows how this is accomplished and provides clear techniques and strategies for classroom use. She has contributed the concepts of the Three C's (capable, connected, contributing), the classroom code of conduct, the Six-D conflict resolution plan, and the Five A's of helping students connect with teachers and peers. She has also contributed a vast number of specific suggestions on what to do and say in order to prevent and redirect misbehavior.

Albert's Central Focus

Albert's main focus is on helping teachers meet student needs so that students will choose to cooperate with the teacher and each other. This obviates the adversarial roles so often evident between teacher and student. Albert believes cooperation is made likely when students truly feel they belong to and in the class. To ensure that students acquire that feeling, she gives heavy attention to what she calls the Three C's—helping all students feel capable, helping them connect with others, and helping them make contributions to the class and elsewhere. Albert also shows how parental support can be obtained and used to advantage. Although Albert places major emphasis on developing a classroom climate that significantly diminishes misbehavior, she acknowledges that some misbehavior will occur even in the best-managed classrooms. Therefore, she explains carefully how to intervene effectively when misbehavior occurs. Beyond that, she provides strategies that minimize classroom conflict and permit teachers to deal with it in a positive manner.

Albert's Principal Teachings

- *Students choose their behavior.* How they behave is not outside their control. Virtually all can behave properly when they see the need to do so.
- *Students need to feel that they belong in the classroom.* This means they must perceive themselves to be important, worthwhile, and valued.
- *When students misbehave, their goal is usually either to gain attention, gain power, exact revenge, or avoid failure.* At times, misbehavior can also occur because of exuberance or simply not knowing the proper way to behave.
- *Teachers can only influence student behavior; they cannot directly control it.* By knowing which goal students are seeking teachers can exert positive influence on behavior choices that students make.
- *Teachers in general reflect three styles of classroom management: permissive, autocratic, and democratic.* Of the three, the democratic style best promotes good discipline. Albert refers to these three styles as the *hands-off, hands-on,* and *hands-joined* styles.
- *The Three C's—capable, connect, and contribute—are essential in helping students feel a sense of belonging.* When students feel capable, they are able to connect personally with peers and teachers and able to make contributions to the class and elsewhere. With the three C's in place, the incidence of misbehavior drops dramatically.
- *Teachers should work cooperatively with students to develop a classroom code of conduct.* The code of conduct stipulates the kind of behavior expected of everyone in the class.
- *Teachers should also work cooperatively with students to develop a set of consequences to be invoked when the classroom code of conduct is transgressed.* When students participate in developing consequences, they are more likely to accept them as fair and reasonable.
- *When conflicts occur between teacher and students, the teacher should remain cool and relaxed.* Teachers should adopt a businesslike attitude and use a calm yet firm tone of voice.
- *Encouragement is the most powerful teaching tool available to teachers.* Few things motivate good behavior as much as does teacher encouragement.
- *Teachers should remember that in order to develop a good system of discipline, they require the cooperation of students and parents.* Both should be valued as partners and their contributions brought meaningfully into cooperative discipline.

Analysis of Albert's *Cooperative Discipline*

Albert has found teachers everywhere are overwhelmed by student misbehavior. They feel incapable of dealing effectively with special-needs students, are dismayed by the number of severe classroom disruptions, and are increasingly frightened by violence against teachers. These conditions are ruining the quality of teaching for many teachers and are wiping away job satisfaction.

Albert says that in order to reverse this picture, teachers require a discipline approach that permits them to work cooperatively with students and parents. She believes a true cooperative understanding brings two prized results: The classroom can be transformed into a safe, orderly, inviting place for teaching and learning, and students have a good chance of learning to behave responsibly while achieving more academically.

The Goal of Classroom Discipline

Albert says the goal of classroom discipline is the same everywhere—helping students learn to choose responsible behavior. Developing a positive relationship between teachers and students that extends to include parents, other teachers, and administrators helps that goal become a reality. It is the combination of intervention strategies to deal with the moment of misbehavior, encouragement strategies to build self-esteem, and collaboration strategies that involve students as partners that enables teachers to reach the goal of helping students choose positive behavior.

Why Students Misbehave

Albert contends that most misbehavior occurs as students attempt unsuccessfully to meet a universal psychological need—the *need to belong*. Students want to feel secure, welcome, and valued, and to a large extent their behavior influences how well those needs are met in the classroom. While most students behave acceptably and thus get their needs met, some seem unable to do so. When that happens, many direct their behavior toward **mistaken goals,** so-called because students have the mistaken idea that through misbehavior they can somehow fulfill the need to belong. Albert believes students pursue four mistaken goals—attention, power, revenge, and assumed disability. Albert calls behavior that students direct at those mistaken goals **attention-seeking, power-seeking, revenge-seeking,** and **avoidance-of-failure.**

Attention-Seeking Behavior

As noted, most students receive all the attention they need in the classroom. Some do not, however, and so seek it, actively and passively. Active attention seeking involves what Albert calls *AGMs*, attention-getting mechanisms. The variety of AGMs is enormous—pencil tapping, showing off, calling out, asking irrelevant questions. Passive attention-seeking is evident in students who dawdle, lag behind, and are slow to comply. They behave in these ways to get attention from the teacher.

Albert says there is a silver lining to attention-seeking: It shows that the offending student desires a positive relationship with the teacher, but does not know how to connect appropriately. For such students, Albert suggests providing abundant recognition when they behave properly. For misbehavior that becomes excessive, she provides 31 intervention techniques for dealing with attention-seeking. Two examples are standing beside the offending student, and using I-messages such as "I find it difficult to keep my train of thought when talking is occurring."

Power-Seeking Behavior

When they do not receive enough attention to feel they belong in the classroom, some students resort to power-seeking behavior. Through words and actions they try to show that they cannot be controlled by the teacher, that they will do as they please. They may mutter replies, disregard instructions, comply insolently, or directly challenge the teacher. Active power-seeking may take the form of temper tantrums, back-talk, disrespect, and defiance. Passive power-seeking may take the form of quiet noncompliance with directions, with the student willing to hide behind labels such as lazy, forgetful, and inattentive.

Power-seeking behavior makes teachers angry and frustrated. They worry they will lose face or even lose control of the class. Albert says that power-seeking has its silver lining, too, in that many students who display this behavior show good verbal skills and leadership ability, as well as assertiveness and independent thinking. Keeping the silver lining in mind, teachers can prevent much power-seeking behavior by giving students options from which to choose (you may do this or do that), delegating responsibilities to them, and granting them legitimate power when appropriate. For dealing with power struggles that have begun, Albert advises teachers to use graceful-exit, time-out, and consequence strategies, techniques described later in the chapter.

Revenge-Seeking Behavior

When students suffer real or imagined hurts in the class, a few may set out to retaliate against teachers and classmates. This is likely when teachers have dealt forcefully with students. It sometimes happens when students are angry at parents or others, people too risky to rebel against. The teacher is a convenient, relatively nonthreatening target. Revenge-seeking usually takes the form of verbal attacks on the teacher, for example, "You really stink as a teacher!" or in destruction of materials or room environment or, most frightening of all, in direct physical attacks on teachers or other students.

All of the strategies that were previously mentioned for dealing with power-seeking behavior are effective when students misbehave for revenge. Two additional tactics are helpful for decreasing revenge-seeking behavior. The first is to work at building caring relationships with all students. This includes students whose behavior is often unacceptable. The second is to teach students to express hostility in acceptable ways, such as through talking about their problems or developing a personal anger management plan.

Avoidance-of-Failure Behavior

Many students have an intense dread of failure. A few, especially when assignments are difficult, withdraw and quit trying, preferring to appear lazy rather than stupid. Albert advises teachers not to allow students to withdraw. She says instead to alter assignments and provide plentiful encouragement. Specific suggestions include: (1) using concrete learning materials that students can see, feel, and manipulate; (2) using computer-based instruction, taking advantages of the latest technology and many students' natural in computers; (3) teaching students to accomplish one step at a time so they enjoy small successes; and (4) teaching to the various intelligences described by Howard Gardner (1983). This last strategy encourages students to use particular talents they might have—linguistic, mathematical, visual, kinesthetic, rhythmic, intrapersonal, and interpersonal. In addition, special help can be provided by the teacher or by remedial programs, adult volunteers, peer tutoring, or commercial learning centers. It is important that withdrawn students be constantly encouraged to try. The teacher must show belief in them and help remove their negative thoughts about such students' ability to succeed.

Albert's Plethora of Strategies

Albert puts great stock in strategies that serve to prevent misbehavior, but she puts equal emphasis on strategies teachers can employ at what she calls "the moment of misbehavior." She states that her intention is to give teachers so many specific strategies that they are never at a loss for what to do next when a student misbehaves. Space within this chapter does not permit presentation of the numerous strategies she describes. Readers are directed to the Appendixes of *Cooperative Discipline* (1996b), especially Appendix C which provides a summary chart of the numerous effective interventions she advocates.

The Three C's of *Cooperative Discipline*

The fundamental approach to *Cooperative Discipline* is embodied in what Albert calls the *Three C's*—helping students see themselves as capable, connected with others, and contributing members of the class.

The First C—Capability

Albert contends that one of the most important factors in school success is what she calls students' **I-can level.** The I-can level refers to the degree to which students believe they are capable of accomplishing work given them in school. Albert suggests teachers consider the following approaches to increase students' sense of capability.

1. *Make mistakes okay.* The fear of making mistakes undermines students' sense of capability, and, when fearful, many stop trying. To minimize this fear, Albert would have teachers talk with students about what mistakes are, help them understand that everyone makes mistakes, and show students that mistakes are a natural part of learning. Teachers can point out that the more an individual undertakes, the more mistakes he or she will make. Albert urges teachers to be careful how they correct students' mistakes. Too many corrections are overwhelming, especially so when papers come back covered with red ink. Teachers should correct mistakes in small steps, focusing only on one or two mistakes at a time.

2. *Build confidence.* In order to feel capable, students must have confidence that success is possible. To raise student confidence, teachers should think of learning as a process of improvement, not as an end product, and when improvement occurs it should be acknowledged. The student's work is compared only to his or her own past efforts, not against other students or grade-level expectations. It should be remembered that people can be successful in a number of ways that do not involve written work. Students may show neatness, good handwriting, persistence, and any number of other talents. Teachers can capitalize on these qualities and provide activities that bring them into play.

   New tasks seem difficult to practically everyone, so there is little point in calling a task "easy" or saying "Oh, anybody can do this." It is better to tell students, "I know this may seem difficult at first, but keep at it. Let's see how you do." When students succeed in tasks they consider difficult, their sense of capability rises.

3. *Focus on past successes.* Very few people are motivated by having their mistakes pointed out. When they know they are being successful, however, they like to proceed. Success grows from a combination of two factors—belief in one's ability and effort expended. Albert says teachers should ask students why they think they were successful in assigned tasks. If they say it was because the task was easy, teachers can say "It seemed easy because you had developed the skills to do it." If they say it was because they tried hard, teachers can say "You surely did. That is one of the main reasons you were successful."

4. *Make learning tangible.* Teachers should provide tangible evidence of student progress. Grades such as "B" and "satisfactory" are ineffective because they tell little about specific accomplishments. Albert suggests more effective devices such as I-can cans, accomplishment albums and portfolios, and talks about yesterday, today, and tomorrow. She describes these devices as follows:

   I-can cans are empty coffee cans, decorated and used by primary-grade students, in which students place strips of paper indicating skills they have mastered, books they have read, and so forth. As the cans fill, they show how knowledge and skills are accumulating. These cans are useful for sharing in parent–teacher conferences.

   Accomplishment albums and portfolios are better for older students. Students can place in them evidence of accomplishments, such as papers written, books read, projects completed, and special skills attained. Students should not be allowed to compare their accomplishment albums against each other. The emphasis is solely on personal growth, drawing attention to what individuals can do now that they couldn't do before.

   Talks about yesterday, today, and tomorrow help students visualize improvements they have made. "Remember when you couldn't spell these words? Look how easy they are now. You are learning fast. By the end of the year you will be able to...." Or, "Remember three weeks ago when you couldn't even read these Spanish verbs? Now you can use all of them in present tense. By next month, you'll be able to use them in past tense as well."

5. *Recognize achievement.* Albert believes that a sense of capability increases when students receive attention from others for what they've accomplished. She suggests having the class acknowledge each other's accomplishments, recognize students at awards assemblies, set up exhibits, and make presentations for parents and other classes. Other suggestions include positive time out in which students are sent to administrators, counselors, or librarians for a few minutes of personal attention, and giving self-approval for achievements.

The Second C—Helping Students Connect

Albert feels it is essential that all students **connect,** meaning that they initiate and maintain positive relationships with peers and teachers. As students make these connections, they become more cooperative and helpful with each other and more receptive to teachers. In discussing making connections, Albert uses the term the **Five A's,** which are acceptance, attention, appreciation, affirmation, and affection.

Acceptance means communicating that it is all right for each student to be as he or she is, regarding culture, abilities, disabilities, and personal style. Teachers need not pretend that whatever students do is all right, but should always indicate that the student is a person of potential, worthy of care.

Attention means making oneself available to students, by sharing time and energy with them. Albert suggests greeting students by name, listening to what they say, chatting with them individually, eating in the cafeteria with them occasionally, scheduling personal conferences, recognizing birthdays, making bulletin boards with students' baby pictures on them, sending cards and messages to absent students, and showing real interest in students' work and hobbies.

Appreciation involves showing students that we are proud of their accomplishments or pleased by their behavior. It is made evident when we give compliments, express gratitude, and describe how students have helped the class. Appreciation can be expressed orally, in writing, or behaviorally in how we treat others. In showing appreciation, it is important to focus on the deed, not the doer. Albert suggests making statements of appreciation that include three parts: (1) the action, (2) how we feel about it, and (3) the action's positive effect. For example, a teacher might say "Carlos, when you complete your assignment as you did today, it makes me very pleased because we can get all our work done on time."

Affirmation refers to making positive statements about students that recognize desirable traits, such as courage, cheerfulness, dedication, enthusiasm, friendliness, helpfulness, kindness, loyalty, originality, persistence, sensitivity, and thoughtfulness. By consciously looking for such traits, teachers can find something positive to say about every student, even those with difficult behavior problems. Albert suggests phrasing affirmations as follows: "I have noticed your thoughtfulness" and "Your kindness is always evident."

Affection refers to displays of kindness and caring that people show each other. Albert points out that affection differs from reward, where kindness is shown only when the student behaves as desired. Affection is freely given, with nothing required in return. As Albert (1996b, p. 117) puts it: "[affection] is a gift with no strings attached. It is not 'I like you when' or 'I'd like you if.' Instead, it is simply 'I like you.' " Unlike appreciation, which is directed at what the student has done, affection is always addressed to the student personally, regardless of the deed. It helps students believe that their teacher likes them even when they make mistakes.

The Third C—Helping Students Contribute

People who do not feel they are needed often see school as purposeless, with no need to try or progress. Albert suggests that one of the best ways to help students feel they are needed is to help them to contribute to the class. Some of the ways she suggests to do this are:

1. *Encourage students' contributions in the class.* Ask students to state their opinions and preferences about class requirements, routines, and other matters. Students can also furnish ideas about improving the classroom environment. Sincerely indicate you need their help and appreciate it.
2. *Encourage students' contributions to the school.* Albert suggests creating **three C committees** whose purpose is to think of ways to help all students feel more capable, connecting, and contributing. Teachers and administrators can assign school service time, in which students perform such tasks as dusting shelves, beautifying classrooms, and cleaning the grounds, all of which help build a sense of pride in the school.
3. *Encourage students' contributions to the community.* Albert makes a number of suggestions in this regard, including the following:
   - Adopting a health care center and providing services such as reading, singing, and running errands for residents of the center
   - Contributing to community drives such Meals on Wheels, Toys for Tots, and disaster relief funds
   - Promoting volunteerism in which students volunteer their services to local institutions
   - Encouraging random acts of kindness, such as opening doors for people and providing help with their packages.
4. *Encourage students to work to protect the environment.* One of Albert's suggestions is for the class to adopt a street or area of the community and keep it litter free.
5. *Encourage students to help other students.* Albert's suggestions include:
   - Establishing a **circle of friends** who make sure that everyone has a partner to talk with, to sit with during lunch, and to walk with between classes
   - Doing peer tutoring, in which adept students help students who are having difficulty
   - Doing peer counseling, in which students talk with other students who are experiencing certain difficulties in their lives
   - Providing peer mediation where students mediate disputes between other students
   - Giving peer recognition, in which students recognize efforts and contributions made by fellow students.

The Classroom Code of Conduct

Albert strongly advises teachers to work together with their classes to establish a classroom **code of conduct** which specifies how everyone is supposed to behave and interact, including the teacher. In accordance with the code of conduct, every person is held accountable for his or her behavior all the time. Albert would have this code of conduct replace the sets of rules that teachers normally use. Rules, she says, cause difficulty because students interpret the word *rule* as meaning what teachers do to control students. Moreover, rules are limited in scope, while classroom code of conduct covers a wider variety of behavior. The code of conduct is developed as follows:

1. *Envision the ideal.* Spend time thinking about how you would like your classroom to be, if everything were as you wanted. What would it look and sound like? How would the students behave toward each other?
2. *Ask students for their vision of how they would like the room to be.* Usually, students want the same conditions that teachers want. It will be easy to merge the two visions.
3. *Ask for parents' input.* Albert suggests involving parents by sending them a letter summarizing the ideas students have expressed and asking for comments and suggestions. This increases parental support for the code of conduct.

Albert presents several examples of codes of conduct developed in elementary, middle, and secondary schools. They are quite similar at the various grade levels. This is one such example for the secondary level: (Albert 1996b, p. 131)

I am respectful.

I am responsible.

I am safe.

I am prepared.

Because "Excellence in Education" is our motto, I will:

- Do nothing to prevent the teacher from teaching and anyone, myself included, from participating in educational endeavors
- Cooperate with all members of the school community
- Respect myself, others, and the environment.

Teaching the Code of Conduct

The code of conduct can be taught in three steps:

1. *Identify appropriate and inappropriate behaviors.* Begin by asking students to identify specific behaviors that are appropriate for each operating principle. For example, in discussing what one does when "treating everyone with courtesy and respect," students might suggest:

   - Use a pleasant tone of voice.
   - Listen when others are speaking.

- Use proper language.
- Respond politely to requests from teachers and classmates.

Behaviors that these same students might list as inappropriate might include making obscene gestures, putting others down, pushing and shoving, ridiculing others, and making ethnic jokes.

Albert says it doesn't matter if these lists become long. They are not for memorizing. Their purpose is to help students develop the judgment and understanding needed for evaluating their own behavior choices and for accepting responsibility for all their behavior all the time.

2. *Clarify appropriate and inappropriate behaviors.* It is not enough simply to list student suggestions. They must be clarified so that every student knows exactly what each suggestion means. This is accomplished through explanation, modeling, and role-playing.

3. *Involve parents.* Students can write a letter to parents explaining the code of conduct and listing the appropriate and inappropriate behaviors they have identified. The teacher can add a postscript to the letter asking parents to save the letter for discussions with their children.

Enforcing the Code of Conduct

Albert advises teachers to do the following when misbehavior occurs:

1. *Check for understanding.* Ask questions to make sure students grasp that their behavior is inappropriate as relates to the code. Examples of questions are:

- What behavior are you choosing at the moment?
- Is the behavior you are choosing right now appropriate to our code of conduct?
- Is this behavior on our *appropriate list* or *inappropriate list* of behaviors?
- Can you help me understand why you are violating our code of conduct at this moment?
- Given our code of conduct, what should I say to you right now?

These questions are asked in a businesslike manner, without implying accusation.

2. *Problem-solve when disagreements occur.* Students may at times disagree with the teacher about whether a behavior is appropriate or inappropriate. These disagreements should be resolved in one of three ways:

- With a student–teacher conference;
- In a class meeting dealing with the behavior; or
- By any other mediation or conflict resolution process.

3. *Post the code of conduct.* It is a good idea to keep the code of conduct displayed in the classroom. When prominently displayed, the teacher can:

- Walk to the display, point to the operating principle being violated, and make eye contact with the offending student.

- Write the number of the principle being violated on an adhesive note and put it on the student's desk.
- Point to the operating principle and say, "Class, notice principle number three, please."
- Point to the operating principle being violated and say, "Tell me in your own words, Clarissa, what this principle means."

Reinforcing the Code of Conduct

Regular repetition and review are needed in helping students become proficient in monitoring and judging their behavior. Albert makes these suggestions:

- Review the code of conduct daily or weekly.
- Model self-correction. When the teacher makes a mistake, such as yelling at the students, the violation should be admitted, with a description of how it will be done correctly the next time.
- Encourage student self-evaluation. Ask students to make lists of their own behaviors that show how they are complying with or violating the code of behavior.

Involving Students and Parents as Partners

The effectiveness of *Cooperative Discipline* is increased when supported by students and parents. Albert makes many suggestions for obtaining their invaluable support.

For enlisting students as partners—

1. *Teach students about the fundamental concepts in cooperative discipline, which are:*

   - Behavior is based on choice. Students choose to behave as they do.
   - Everyone needs to feel they belong in the class, and will be helped to do so.
   - The four goals of misbehavior are attention, power, revenge, and avoidance of failure.
   - The three C's help everyone feel capable, connected, and contributing.

2. *Involve students in formulating the classroom code of conduct.*
3. *Involve students in establishing consequences for misbehavior.*
4. *Involve students in decision-making about classroom and curriculum.*

For enlisting parents as partners—

1. *Inform parents about cooperative discipline and the class code of conduct that teacher and students have been discussing. Ask for parents' comments.* This is best done through newsletters sent home to parents and may be reinforced through parent group presentations.
2. *Establish guidelines for the style of communicating with parents.* Teachers should use objective terms when referring to students and their behavior, limit

the number of complaints made to parents, and anticipate student success because every parent needs to have hope for their child's improvement.

3. *Notify parents when behavior problems occur.* Begin with a positive statement about the student, then identify the problem, and end with another positive statement about the student.

4. *Structure parent–teacher conferences for success.* When it is necessary to conference with a parent, use the **Five A's** strategy, which is:

   - Accept the parent without prejudice.
   - Attend carefully to what the parent says.
   - Appreciate the parent's efforts and support.
   - Affirm the child's strengths and qualities.
   - Affection for the child is made evident to the parent.

Avoiding and Defusing Confrontations

Teachers greatly dislike having to deal with situations in which students defy their authority. It is important to think through and practice how you want to conduct yourself when students exhibit power or revenge behaviors and defiantly challenge you. The situation can either be calmed or made worse by how you react. Albert suggests practicing how to:

1. *Focus on the behavior, not the student.* To do this, a teacher can

   - Describe the behavior that is occurring, but without evaluating it. Use objective terms to tell the student exactly what he or she is doing. Do not use subjective words such as bad, wrong, or stupid.
   - Deal with the moment. This means talking only about what is happening now, not what happened yesterday or last week.
   - Be firm, but friendly. Being firm means indicating that the misbehavior must stop, but at the same time, show the student that you have continuing care and interest.

2. *Take charge of negative emotions.* This refers to teachers' negative emotions. In confrontations, teachers feel angry, frustrated, or hurt, but acting in accord with those emotions is counterproductive. One should therefore:

   - Control negative emotions. Teachers should practice responding in a calm, objective, noncombative manner. This blocks the student's intent to instigate conflict and helps everyone calm down so the problem can be resolved.
   - Release negative emotions. Emotions, though controlled, will remain after the confrontation. Albert suggests that teachers release those emotions as soon as possible by physical activity such as walking, playing tennis, or doing house or yard work.

3. *Avoid escalating the situation.* This recommendation dovetails with controlling negative emotions. Certain reactions make the situation worse, not better. Albert provides an extensive list of behaviors teachers should avoid, such as

raising the voice, insisting on the last word, using tense body language, using sarcasm or put-downs, backing the student into a corner, holding a grudge, mimicking the student, making comparisons with siblings or other students, and commanding or demanding.

4. *Discuss the misbehavior later.* At the time of the confrontation, make a brief, direct, friendly intervention that will defuse tensions. When feelings are strong, the matter cannot be resolved instantly. Wait an hour or until the next day when both parties have cooled down.

5. *Allow students to save face.* Students know teachers have the ultimate power in confrontations, so eventually they comply with teacher expectations. However, to save face with their peers and make it seem they are not backing down completely, they often mutter, take their time complying, or repeat the misbehavior one more time before stopping. Albert advises teachers to overlook these behaviors rather than confront the student anew. When allowed to save face students are more willing to settle down and behave appropriately.

Dealing with More Severe Confrontations

Suppose that a very upset student is having a real tantrum, yelling and throwing things. What does the teacher do then? Albert offers a number of suggestions which she calls **graceful exits,** which allow teachers to distance themselves from the situation. These exits are made calmly, with poise, and without sarcasm.

- *Acknowledge the student's power.* Recognize that you can't make the offending student do anything and be willing to admit it to the student. But also state your expectation: "I can't make you write this essay, but it does need to be turned in by Friday. Let me know your plan for completing the assignment."

- *Move away from the student, putting distance between the two of you.* Try stating both viewpoints, such as: "To *you* it seems I'm being unfair when I lower your grade for turning in an assignment after the due date. To *me* it's a logical consequence for not meeting an important deadline."

- *Remove the audience.* By this, Albert means removing the onlookers' attention when a confrontation arises. This can be done by making an announcement or raising an interesting topic for discussion.

- *Table the matter.* When emotions are running high or when the entire class is likely to become embroiled in a confrontation, say "You may be right. Let's talk about it later." Or "I am not willing to talk with you about this right now."

- *Call the student's bluff and deliver a closing statement.* "Let me get this straight. I asked you to _____ and you are refusing. Is this correct?" The teacher stands with pencil and clipboard, to write down what the student says. Albert also suggests using a closing statement, which she calls a one-liner to communicate that the confrontation has ended, for example, "You've mistaken me for someone who wants to fight. I don't."

- *If you feel yourself losing control, take a teacher time-out.* Say something like "What's happening right now is not okay with me. I need some teacher time-out to think about it. We'll talk later."

- *If you see that the student will not calm down, have the student take time out in the classroom, principal's office, or designated room.*

Implementing Consequences

When a student seriously or repeatedly violates the classroom code of conduct, particularly with power or revenge behavior, consequences are invoked in keeping with previous agreement. Consequences are a teaching tool, designed to help students learn to make better behavior choices in the future. They are usually unpleasant to the student but not harmful physically or psychologically. Albert refers to the **four R's of consequences**—related, reasonable, respectful, and reliably enforced. By *related*, she means that the consequence should involve an act that has something to do with the misbehavior. Betsy continues to talk disruptively; her consequence is isolation in the back of the room where she cannot talk to others. She should not be kept after class for talking, as the penalty has no logical connection with the offense. By *reasonable*, Albert means that the consequence is proportional to the misbehavior. She reminds us that consequences are used to teach students to behave properly, not to punish them. If Jonathan fails to turn in an assignment, the consequence should be to redo the assignment. By *respectful*, Albert means that the consequence is invoked in a friendly but firm manner, with no blaming, shaming, or preaching. By *reliably enforced*, Albert means that teachers consistently follow through and invoke consequences.

Albert describes four categories of consequences for teachers to discuss with their class:

- Loss or delay of privileges, such as loss or delay of a favorite activity
- Loss of freedom of interaction, such as talking with other students
- Restitution, such as return, repair, or replacement of objects, doing school service, or helping other students that one has offended
- Reteaching appropriate behavior, such as practicing correct behavior and writing about how one should behave in a given situation

Resolution of more serious misbehaviors or repeated violations of the class code of conduct should be done in a conference with the student. The purpose of the conference is never to cast blame, but rather to work out ways for helping the student behave responsibly. Albert presents a **Six-D conflict resolution plan** to help resolve matters under dispute, for use in conferences or between students in the classroom. The plan is as follows:

1. *Define* the problem objectively, without blaming or using emotional words.
2. *Declare* the need, that is, tell what makes the situation a problem.
3. *Describe* the feelings experienced by both sides.
4. *Discuss* possible solutions. Consider pros and cons of each.
5. *Decide* on a plan. Choose the solution with the most support from both sides. Be specific about when it will begin.
6. *Determine* the plan's effectiveness. A follow-up meeting is arranged after the plan has been in use for a time in order to evaluate its effectiveness.

Strengths of Albert's *Cooperative Discipline*

Cooperative Discipline is a powerful way of helping students achieve their ultimate goal of belonging in the class, which in turn reduces their amount of misbehavior. For times when students do misbehave, Albert has developed approximately 70 proven procedures for dealing with misbehavior, procedures that stress teaching proper behavior rather than punishing transgressions. She has provided a clear rationale for cooperative discipline and a detailed guide for implementing and maintaining the program. She recognizes the importance of strong support from administrators and parents and provides many suggestions for ensuring that support.

Initiating Albert's *Cooperative Discipline*

Cooperative Discipline can be put into effect at any time. Teacher and class, working together, envision the sort of environment that would best meet their needs. They identify specific behaviors that would contribute to such an environment as well as behaviors that would work against it. They clarify these behaviors through discussion, demonstration, and role-playing. Teachers and students jointly decide on the consequences to be invoked for violations of the standards they have agreed to, remembering that consequences should be related to specific misbehaviors. They write out the agreement, which becomes known as the code of classroom conduct, and before it is finalized, the teacher sends copies to parents and asks for input and support. In final form, the code of conduct is posted in the room. The behaviors it calls for must be taught, not taken for granted, and the code should be discussed regularly. This keeps it in the foreground where it is useful in reminding students and in correcting misbehavior. When serious violations of the code occur, procedures of conflict resolution are applied. All the while, teachers make ongoing efforts to help students feel capable, connected with others, and contributors to the class and elsewhere.

Review of Selected Terminology

The following terms and concepts are important in Albert's *Cooperative Discipline*. Check yourself to make sure you understand their meanings.

Cooperative Discipline: nature of

Goals of student behavior and misbehavior: genuine, mistaken, belonging, attention-seeking, power-seeking, revenge-seeking, avoidance-of-failure

The Three C's of Cooperative Discipline: capable, connected, contributing, accomplishment albums and portfolios, I-can cans, circle of friends, the three C committee, the Five A's of connecting

Teacher behavior to deal with misbehavior and confrontations: classroom code of conduct, self-control, graceful exits, Four R's of consequences, Six-D conflict resolution plan

Application Exercises

Concept Cases

Case 1: Kristina Will Not Work ■ Kristina, a student in Mr. Jake's class, is quite docile. She socializes little with other students and never disrupts lessons. However, despite Mr. Jake's best efforts, Kristina will not do her work. She rarely completes an assignment. She is simply there, putting forth no effort at all. *How would Albert deal with Kristina?*

Albert would advise Mr. Jake to do the following: Work hard at the Three C's with Kristina. Give her work she can do easily so she begins to feel more capable, then gradually increase the difficulty, teaching one new step at a time. Help her connect through a buddy system with another student and through participation in small group work. Give her opportunities to contribute by sharing information with the class about hobbies, siblings, and the like. Perhaps she has a skill she could teach to another student. Encourage her at every opportunity. Talk with her; ask her if there is something that is preventing her from completing her work. Show that you will help her however you can.

Case 2: Sara Cannot Stop Talking ■ Sara is a pleasant girl who participates in class activities and does most, though not all, of her assigned work. She cannot seem to refrain from talking to classmates, however. Her teacher, Mr. Gonzales, has to speak to her repeatedly during lessons, to the point that he often becomes exasperated and loses his temper. *What suggestions would Albert give Mr. Gonzales for dealing with Sara?*

Case 3: Joshua Clowns and Intimidates ■ Joshua, larger and louder than his classmates, always wants to be the center of attention, which he accomplishes through a combination of clowning and intimidation. He makes wise remarks, talks back (smilingly) to the teacher, utters a variety of sound-effect noises such as automobile crashes and gunshots, and makes limitless sarcastic comments and put-downs of his classmates. Other students will not stand up to him, apparently fearing his size and verbal aggression. His teacher, Miss Pearl, has come to her wit's end. *Would Joshua's behavior be likely to improve if Albert's techniques were used in Miss Pearl's classroom? Explain.*

Case 4: Tom Is Hostile and Defiant ■ Tom has appeared to be in his usual foul mood ever since arriving in class. On his way to sharpen his pencil, he bumps into Frank, who complains. Tom tells him loudly to shut up. Miss Baines, the teacher, says, "Tom, go back to your seat." Tom wheels around, swears loudly, and says heatedly, "I'll go when I'm damned good and ready!" *How would Albert have Miss Baines deal with Tom?*

Questions and Activities

1. For a grade level and/or subject you select, outline your vision of how you would prefer that teacher and students behave and interact.

2. Indicate and describe the student and parent support structures you would implement to make *Cooperative Discipline* maximally effective.

3. Examine your choice of Scenario 4 or 8 in Appendix A. How could *Cooperative Discipline* be used to improve behavior in Mrs. Desmond's second grade or Mr. Jaramillo's world history class?

Primary References

Albert, L. 1996a. *A teacher's guide to cooperative discipline.* Circle Pines, MN: American Guidance Service. A guidebook for teachers that accompanies the basic book entitled *Cooperative Discipline.*

———. 1996b. *Cooperative discipline*. Circle Pines, MN: American Guidance Service. Albert's basic text that describes Cooperative Discipline, its rationale, its advantages, and how it is applied in the classroom and school.

Recommended Readings and Viewing

Albert, L. 1992. *An administrator's guide to cooperative discipline*. Circle Pines, MN: American Guidance Service.

———. 1993. *Coping with kids*. Tampa, FL: Alkorn House.

———. 1994. *Bringing home cooperative discipline*. Circle Pines, MN: American Guidance Service.

———. 1994. *Responsible kids in school and at home: The cooperative discipline way* (Videotape series). Circle Pines, MN: American Guidance Service.

———. 1996. *Cooperative discipline implementation guide: Resources for staff development*. Circle Pines, MN: American Guidance Service.

———. 1996. *Cooperative discipline staff development* (Videotape series). Circle Pines, MN: American Guidance Service.

Thomas Gordon's *Discipline as Self-Control*

**PREVIEW OF
GORDON'S
WORK**

Focus

- Participative management in the classroom and its positive effect on student self-control.
- Identification and clarification of interpersonal problems and problem ownership.
- Helping teachers acquire positive influence with students and make the best use of it.

Logic

- The best classroom discipline occurs when students' have an inner sense of self-control.
- Authority can be used to control others, but teachers should only influence, not control.
- Neither punishment nor reward is effective in promoting lasting change in behavior.

Contributions

- Championed participative management, where teachers and students share decision making.
- Popularized the no-lose method of conflict resolution, which preserves self-esteem.
- Identified roadblocks, which suppress students' willingness to discuss problems.
- Demonstrated how to clarify problems, determine ownership, and deal with the problems.

Gordon's Suggestions

- Involve students in problem solving and decision making about class rules and procedures.
- Use the behavior window to identify interpersonal problems and determine ownership.
- Use helping skills when students own problem, confrontive skills when teachers own it.
- Learn to see misbehavior simply as student actions the teacher considers undesirable.

Thomas Gordon

About Thomas Gordon

Thomas Gordon, a clinical psychologist, is founder of Gordon Training International, one of the largest human relations training organizations in the world. He is known for pioneering the teaching of communication skills and conflict resolution to parents, teachers, youth, and managers of organizations. More than 1.5 million

persons have taken his training programs worldwide. His organization has representatives in 27 countries, and his books have sold nearly 6 million copies in 30 languages. Gordon is the author of eight books, including *Parent Effectiveness Training:
A Tested New Way to Raise Responsible Children* (1970), *P.E.T. in Action* (1976),
T.E.T.: Teacher Effectiveness Training (1987), and *Discipline That Works: Promoting Self-Discipline in Children* (1989). In his books and training programs, Gordon
offers parents and teachers strategies for helping children become more self-reliant,
self-controlled, responsible, and cooperative. Gordon, a fellow of the American Psychological Association, has received numerous honors including the 1999 American
Psychological Foundation's Gold Medal Award for Enduring Contributions to Psychology in the Public Interest. He has been a guest on the "Today Show," the "To-
night Show," "Donahue," and many other TV and radio programs. Catalogs and
information about his programs are available from Gordon Training International,
531 Stevens Avenue West, Solana Beach, CA 92075; telephone 800-359-5915; e-mail
info@gordontraining.com; website: www.gordontraining.com

Gordon's Contributions to Discipline

Gordon has made several important contributions to discipline. His work as a clinical
psychologist and his analyses of research have convinced him that power-based methods of discipline are ineffective in the long run. He concluded that such methods more
often than not create new problems that range from rebellion to withdrawal, and that
praise and reward do little to change student behavior for the better. He therefore
urges teachers to strive for cooperation with students, while avoiding power, punishment, praise, and reward.

As a way of helping teachers with their management efforts, Gordon created a
graphic device he called the **behavior window.** This device helps teachers visualize
situations and student behavior so that they may determine whether a problem exists,
who owns it, and which skills should be applied to handle the situation. Related to the
behavior window, Gordon devised a series of skills for teachers to implement as appropriate. **Confrontive skills** are used when teachers own the problem. **Helping skills**
are used when students own the problem, and **preventive skills** are used to prevent
the occurrence of possible problems. Gordon also pushed for **participative classroom
management** where teachers and students share in planning and decision making.

Gordon's Central Focus

Gordon has taken a leadership role in the recent trend in school discipline that places
primary emphasis on development of student responsibility and self-control. His con-
victions grew from his work in Parent Effectiveness Training and led to his conclusion
that effective discipline cannot be achieved through either coercion or reward and
punishment but rather must be developed within the character of each individual.

Gordon's 1989 book, *Discipline That Works,* presents his views on discipline, emphasizing that the punitive actions prevalent in traditional discipline harmed children by leading to self-destructive and antisocial behavior. But he was quick to state that permissiveness in dealing with children is just as misguided as authoritarianism. In place of power or permissiveness, Gordon offers middle-ground strategies designed to help children make positive decisions, become more self-reliant, and control their own behavior. Gordon (1989) summed up his concerns about current discipline practices and their results as follows:

> As a society we must urgently adopt the goal of finding and teaching effective alter–
> natives to authority and power in dealing with other persons—children or adults—
> alternatives that will produce human beings with sufficient courage, autonomy, and
> self-discipline to resist being controlled by authority when obedience to that authority
> would contradict their own sense of what is right and what is wrong. (p. 98)

Gordon has maintained that the only truly effective discipline is self-control that occurs internally in each child. The development of such self-control, he says, can be strongly assisted by teachers. To help children control their own behavior and become self-reliant in making positive decisions, teachers must first give up their "controlling" power over students. As Gordon (1989) says,

> You acquire more influence with young people when you give up using your power
> to control them...and the more you use power to try to control people, the less real
> influence you'll have on their lives. (p. 7)

Precisely how teachers acquire influence with students, and how they can best use that influence, is the central focus of Gordon's work.

Gordon's Principal Teachings

- *Noncontrolling methods of behavior change are available for teachers to use in influencing students to behave properly.* It is counterproductive for teachers to use authoritative power or rewards and punishments to control students.
- *A problem is a condition, event, or situation that troubles someone.* A problem exists only when someone is troubled.
- *When an individual is troubled by a condition, event, or situation, that individual is said to "own" the problem.* How problems are resolved depends in part upon who owns the problem.
- *I-messages are statements in which people tell how they personally think or feel about another's behavior and its consequences. They should be used when attempting to influence others.* For example, the teacher is using an I-message when saying, "I am having trouble concentrating because there is so much noise in the room."
- *You-messages are statements of blame leveled at someone's behavior. They should NOT be used when attempting to influence others.* For example, the teacher is using a you-message when saying, "You girls are making too much noise."

- *Confrontive I-messages are messages that attempt to influence another to cease an unacceptable behavior.* The teacher is using a confrontive I-message when saying, "I'm pleased so many of you have something to share about this, but when everyone tries to talk at once, I can't hear what anyone has to say."
- *Preventive I-messages attempt to forestall future actions that may later constitute a problem.* For example, the teacher might say, "I really hope we can have a quiet room when the principal visits. Can you help us all remember things we can do to help keep the room quiet?"
- *Preventive you-messages (to be avoided) are used to scold students for past behavior.* For example, the teacher might say, "You were very rude the last time our principal visited. You made me feel ashamed. I certainly hope you do better this time."
- *Shifting gears is a tactic that involves changing from a confrontive to a listening posture.* This strategy is helpful when students resist the teacher's I-messages or defend themselves.
- *Students' coping mechanisms are strategies that students use when confronted with coercive power.* The three coping mechanisms are: *fighting* (combating the person with whom they have the conflict); *taking flight* (trying to escape the situation); and *submitting* (giving in to the other person).
- *Win–lose conflict resolution is a way of ending disputes (temporarily) by producing a "winner" and a "loser."* This strategy usually has a detrimental effect on the loser. For example, Samuel and Justin scuffle and Samuel is made to apologize to Justin, which supposedly resolves the conflict. However, Samuel feels wronged and humiliated and therefore declines to cooperate with Justin or the teacher.
- *No-lose conflict resolution is a way of ending disputes by enabling both sides to emerge as "winners."* For example, when Samuel and Justin get in a scuffle, the teacher takes them aside and asks sincerely, "I wonder what we might do, so that you boys won't feel like fighting any more?" There is no winner or loser, and neither boy feels he has been unjustly treated.
- *Door openers are words and actions that invite others to speak about whatever is on their minds.* The teacher is using a door opener when asking Sheri, who appears to be upset, "Do you feel like telling me if anything is troubling you?"
- *Active listening involves carefully attending to and demonstrating understanding of what another person says.* The teacher is using active listening when nodding and reflecting back what Bobby is saying.
- *Communication roadblocks are comments by well-meaning teachers that shut down student willingness to communicate.* Examples of roadblocks include moralizing and telling the student what he or she ought to do.
- *Participative classroom management permits students to share in problem solving and decision making concerning the classroom and class rules.* This participation makes students more inclined to abide by rules they have helped formulate.
- *Problem solving is a process that should be taught and practiced in all classrooms.* In problem solving, students help clarify problems, put forth possible

solutions, select solutions that are acceptable to all, implement the solutions, and evaluate the solutions in practice.

Analysis of Gordon's *Discipline as Self-Control*

As you have seen, Gordon believes that classroom discipline occurs best when students are able to use their inner sense of self control. The techniques he advocates are designed to help teachers promote self-control in students. He rejects as counterproductive the traditional intervention techniques of power-based authority, reward and punishment, and win-lose conflict resolution. In order to understand Gordon's overall position more fully, let us examine what he has to say about authority, rewards and punishment, misbehavior, problem ownership, the behavior window, and teacher skills, including confrontive skills, helping skills, and preventive skills.

Authority

Authority is a condition that allows one to exert influence or control over others. Gordon says there are four different kinds of authority: (1) *Expertise* inherent in a person's special knowledge, experience, training, skill, wisdom, and education; (2) *Job description;* (3) *Commitments, agreements,* or *contracts;* and (4) *Power*—the ability to control others against their wishes as opposed to influencing them. For example, because of the power you have to give students low grades, you can make them do assignments they would not otherwise do.

Teachers who rely on expertise, job description, or contract can exert positive influence on students. But when they use power to control students rather than influence them, their effectiveness is diminished. Gordon urges teachers to use **noncontrolling methods** to promote behavior change that are derived from expertise, job description, and contracts.

Rewards and Punishment

Gordon (1989) is very much opposed to discipline that is based on **rewards.** He summarizes his concerns as follows:

> Using rewards to try to control children's behavior is so common that its effectiveness is rarely questioned...the fact that rewards are used so often and unsuccessfully by so many teachers and parents proves they don't work very well.... The ineffectiveness of using rewards to control children is due in part to the fact that the method requires such a high level of technical competence on the part of the controller—a level few parents or teachers can ever attain. (pp. 34–35).

> Considering all of the precise conditions that must be met to make this complex method work and the inordinate amount of time it takes, I am convinced that behavior modification with rewards could never be a method of any practical use for either parents or teachers. (pp. 37–38).

What does Gordon see as negative effects of behavior modification with rewards? He says the following are likely to occur when rewards are used to influence behavior:

- Students become concerned only with getting the rewards, not with learning or behaving desirably.
- When rewards are removed, students tend to revert quickly to undesirable behavior.
- When students accustomed to receiving rewards are not rewarded, they may equate the lack of reward with punishment.
- Students may receive stronger rewards from classmates for behaving improperly than from the teacher for behaving properly.

And why is **punishment** ineffective in producing self-discipline? According to Gordon, punishment's long-term negative effects include the following:

- Punished students experience feelings of belittlement, rage, and hostility.
- Punished students lose their desire to cooperate willingly with the teacher.
- There is an increased likelihood that punished students will lie and cheat in order to avoid punishment.
- Punishment engenders a false notion that might makes right.

What Is Misbehavior, and Who Owns the Problem?

Gordon (1976) sees **misbehavior** as an *adult concept* in which "a specific action of the child is seen by the adult as producing an *undesirable consequence for the adult*" (p. 107, italics added). It is the teacher, he says, not the student, who experiences the sense of "badness" in student behavior.

If students are to develop self-control, teachers must shift away from their traditional concept of misbehavior. Gordon says that teachers should begin by learning to identify correctly who owns a particular problem, the teacher or the student. The following example illustrates what Gordon means by **problem ownership:** When Kyla becomes morose because she feels other girls have slighted her, she sulks but doesn't bother anyone else. Because no one else is affected, Kyla "owns" the problem; it bothers her but causes no difficulty for her teacher or classmates. Her behavior may in fact be entirely acceptable to the teacher, since the class work continues normally. But if Kyla decides to confront the other girls angrily, the resultant squabble causes difficulties for the teacher. Because the teacher is now troubled by the situation (students become inattentive and the lesson is disrupted), the teacher is said to own the problem. When owning a problem of this sort, the teacher feels obliged to deal with it and may take corrective action against Kyla in order to stop the disruption that has ensued.

The Behavior Window

Gordon created a graphic device called the **behavior window** to help clarify the concept of problem ownership. Teachers are taught to visualize student behavior through the behavior window, which indicates who owns the problem, depending on whether teachers see the behavior as acceptable or unacceptable. The behavior window is shown in Table 6.1.

The behaviors found in the top section of the behavior window in Table 6.1 are acceptable to the teacher, though they are troublesome for the student. The student's needs are not being met, or the student is unhappy or frustrated or in trouble, but these behaviors do not have much effect on the teacher or other students in the class. For example, Mark's failure to appear for his scheduled drama audition (because he is overly self-conscious) affects only Mark, so Mark owns the problem. The drama teacher, Ms. Aldrice, will take no action against Mark, but if she is aware of his feelings, she may decide to speak with him using a helping skill such as active listening.

Behaviors found in the bottom section of the behavior window are unacceptable to the teacher; that is, they cause a problem for the teacher. At the drama auditions Mark heckles when others read for their parts. His behavior interferes with the tryouts. This bothers Ms. Aldrice, who now owns the problem, and it is up to her to try to change Mark's problem-causing behavior.

In the middle section of the behavior window in Table 6.1 are student behaviors that are problem-free. Here the teacher and student work together pleasantly. Mark does not want to try out for the play but does want to help with set construction and lighting, which leaves him on good terms with Ms. Aldrice.

The behavior window helps teachers understand problem ownership, but it should be understood that the window is not static. As Gordon (1976) explains, "You inevitably will be inconsistent from day to day, with your different moods, with different children, and in different environments" (p. 18). The window lines that demarcate behavior move in accordance with teacher mood (teacher is rested or upset), student behavior (student is quiet or careful, or aggressive or noisy), and the environment (indoors or outdoors, quiet time or group activity).

By understanding the behavior window and correctly identifying problem ownership, teachers can increase the likelihood of having effective interactions with students. Gordon describes three groups of skills that teachers can use when working

Behavior Window	Acceptability to Teacher
Student's behavior causes a problem for the student only **Student owns the problem**	Acceptable behavior
Student's behavior does not cause a problem for either the student or teacher. **No problem.**	Acceptable behavior
Student's behavior causes a problem for the teacher. **Teacher owns the problem**	Unacceptable behavior

TABLE 6.1
Source: Adapted from *P.E.T. in Action* (pp. 27, 174, 251) by T. Gordon, 1976. New York: Random House.

with students—skills that apply not only to problem behaviors but to ongoing communication and interactions. Those skills are clustered into three groups.

1. **Confrontive skills** are used when the teacher owns the problem. They include modifying the environment, sending I-messages that do not set off the coping mechanisms students use in response to power, shifting gears, and practicing the no-lose method of conflict resolution—tactics explained in the skill clusters that follow.

2. **Helping skills** are used when the student owns the problem, include passive listening, acknowledgment, door openers, active listening, and avoiding communication roadblocks.

3. **Preventive skills** are used to forestall future problems for teacher or students, include rule setting, preventive I-messages, and participative problem solving and decision making. In short, confrontive skills help teachers meet their own needs; helping skills assist students in meeting their needs; and preventive skills help ensure future satisfaction for both teacher and student. Let us turn now to the relationship between the three sections of the behavior window and their pertinent skill clusters.

Skill Cluster 1: Confrontive Skills

This skill cluster pertains to the bottom section of the behavior window, as shown in Table 6.2. Gordon explains that teachers are most likely to take action first at the point where they own the problem.

In this instance, teachers can meet their needs by confronting the misbehavior, provided they do so in a positive, nonadversarial manner. The following skills comprise this cluster: (1) modifying the environment, (2) sending I-messages that do not trigger the student's coping mechanisms, (3) shifting gears, and (4) using a no-lose method of conflict resolution.

1. *Modifying the environment (rather than the student).* By **modifying the environment** through enriching it or by limiting its distractions, teachers may be able to eliminate or minimize problem behavior. To encourage student curiosity and learning, teachers can enrich the room with learning centers and colorful posters,

Behavior Window	Skill Clusters
Student's behavior causes a problem for the student only. **Student owns the problem.**	Helping skills
Student's behavior does not cause a problem for either student or teacher. **No problem.**	Preventive skills
Student's behavior causes a problem for the teacher. **Teacher owns the problem.**	*Confrontive skills*

TABLE 6.2

Source: Adapted from *P.E.T. in Action* (pp. 27, 174, 251) by T. Gordon, 1976. New York: Random House.

student murals, and displays on the topic being studied. If these effects are too distracting for some students, teachers can provide an area without displays or have study carrels for students who occasionally need a more subdued atmosphere. Teachers can play quiet background music during certain activities and set up areas in the classroom where students study independently or in groups. If the teacher is bothered by the amount of student movement around the room during an art project, sets of supplies can be placed on the students' desks.

2. *Sending I-messages regularly.* When teachers own a problem because student behavior interferes with their needs or rights, instead of scolding students they should express their feelings through I-messages. Complete **I-messages** communicate three things: (1) the behavior that is presenting a problem for the teacher, (2) what the teacher is feeling about the behavior, and (3) why the behavior is causing a problem. Mrs. Watson's I-message is clear: "When class rules are broken as they are now, I feel upset because that keeps us from getting our work done and shows lack of consideration for others."

   I-messages contrast with you-messages. I-messages describe situations and teacher feelings and are therefore relatively nonhurtful to students. **You-messages,** on the other hand, carry heavy judgments and put-downs, evident in statements such as "You've been very careless with this work" or "Shame on you for tattling" or "Can't you follow simple directions?"

   A special kind of I-message—the **confrontive I-message**—is used to ask students for help and suggestions. The teacher may say, "When I have to wait too long for quiet and readiness, I have to rush through the directions, and then I have to spend more time repeating myself because the directions are not clear. Do you have any suggestions that might help me with this problem?"

3. *Shifting gears.* Sometimes the teacher's I-messages provoke defensive responses from students. When teachers see this happen, it is important that they listen sensitively to the resistance and change from a sending/assertive posture to a listening/understanding posture, a change that prompts students to react more positively. Gordon calls this change from assertion to listening **shifting gears.** The change usually improves the likelihood of reaching an acceptable solution, because students feel their needs are being considered and that the teacher understands how they feel. When Mr. Johnson sends a confrontive I-message to Marcos about his irregular attendance, such as "I am very bothered, Marcos, when any of my students miss class," Marcos heatedly responds, "School is not the only thing. I have responsibilities at home. I can't help missing class sometimes." Shifting gears, Mr. Johnson replies, "It sounds like you have some difficult things to deal with outside of school. Is there anything I can do to help?"

   Sometimes when I-messages do not work, teachers resort to power to change the student's behavior. This is not likely to be effective because students will in turn resist the controlling power, using **coping mechanisms,** which Gordon identifies as fighting, taking flight, and submitting. For some individuals, the first inclination is one of *fighting* the person with whom they are in conflict. If, however, they see they are unlikely to win the fight, or if they perceive the consequences of fighting as too severe (i.e., harsh punishment or physical or psychological hurt), they will tend to avoid the conflict by *taking flight* from it altogether. If unwilling to fight and unable to escape (as is the case when teachers impose punitive discipline), students generally respond by *submitting*. But they do not do so acceptingly. Indeed, most students would rather lie, cheat, or place blame elsewhere than to accept punishment and loss of dignity.

4. *Using the no-lose method of conflict resolution.* When conflict occurs in the classroom, Gordon urges teachers to defuse the situation and bring about a solution acceptable to everyone. This can be done, Gordon says, by using a no-lose method. To see how the **no-lose method of conflict resolution** works, let us first consider the result of **win–lose conflict resolution**. There, ego is on the line, and ultimately one person emerges as "winner" and the other as "loser." Suppose Mrs. Penny insists that Marta complete her assigned work before leaving the classroom. Marta complains that she cannot work fast enough to complete it and that it is unfair to make her stay longer than the other students. Mrs. Penny, who thinks Marta procrastinates, says, "You can either complete your work or take a grade of F on the assignment. It is your choice." Marta stays until she finishes but is seething with resentment. In this conflict, Mrs. Penny emerges as winner and Marta as loser, or so it would seem. In reality both may have lost, because their working relationship may have been ruined.

   Instead of win–lose conflict resolution, Gordon advocates what he calls the no-lose method. This approach enables both sides to find a mutually acceptable solution to their disagreement. By avoiding use of power, egos are preserved, work continues, and personal relations are undamaged. In this approach, Marta and Mrs. Penny talk about their feelings and about what is causing them to get upset with each other. Then they seek a solution acceptable to both, such as allowing Marta extra time to complete her work in class. This same procedure works well when teachers mediate conflicts between students.

Skill Cluster 2: Helping Skills

This skill cluster applies to the top section of the behavior window, as shown in Table 6.3, where the student owns the problem. Gordon's helping skills include (1) listening skills and (2) methods for avoiding communication roadblocks.

1. *Using listening skills.* When students voice a problem, teachers should listen to them carefully, but should not attempt to solve students' problems for them. Instead of telling students what they ought to do, teachers should make use of four *listening skills,* which Gordon calls passive listening, acknowledgment responses, door openers, and active listening.

   Passive listening usually consists of nothing more than attentive silence, but it is enough to encourage students to talk about what is bothering them. With passive listening, the teacher shows attention through posture, proximity, eye contact, and alertness as the student speaks. Mr. Aragon demonstrates

Behavior Window	Skill Clusters
Student's behavior causes a problem for the student only. **Student owns the problem.**	*Helping skills*
Student's behavior does not cause a problem for either student or teacher. **No problem.**	Preventive skills
Student's behavior causes a problem for the teacher. **Teacher owns the problem.**	Confrontive skills

TABLE 6.3
Source: Adapted from *P.E.T. in Action* (pp. 27, 174, 251) by T. Gordon, 1976. New York: Random House.

this skill when he sits down beside Julian as the boy begins to speak of difficulties at home.

Acknowledgment responses can be verbal ("uh-huh", "I see") or nonverbal (nods, smiles and frowns, and other body movements). They demonstrate the teacher's interest and attention. Mrs. Beck nods as Chris tells her about difficulties he is having at home.

Door openers invite students to discuss their problems. When the student needs encouragement, the teacher may say, "Would you like to talk about it?" or "It sounds like you have something to say about that." These comments are nonjudgmental and open-ended, and because they are nonthreatening, they invite the student to talk. Sensing that Eduardo is distressed about the math assignment, Mr. Sutton invites him to discuss his concerns: "I think there might be something bothering you about this assignment, Eduardo. Would you like to talk about it?"

Active listening is a process of mirroring back what students are saying. It confirms that the teacher is attentive and understands the student's message. No judgment or evaluation is made. The teacher might say, "You've been late to class this week because you've been working the closing shift at the restaurant, and that makes you so tired you sleep through your alarm."

2. *Avoiding communication roadblocks.* Gordon points out that when teachers try to communicate with students, they often set up inadvertent roadblocks that stifle student willingness to talk. He goes to some lengths to help teachers learn to recognize and avoid these **roadblocks to communication,** which are: giving orders, warning, preaching, advising, lecturing, criticizing, name-calling, analyzing, praising, reassuring, questioning, and withdrawing. The following examples involving the roadblocks show how a teacher might respond ineffectively or effectively. At student Del's middle school, all students are required to take physical education. Del, who is very self-conscious about his weight, detests physical education and has been offering various excuses in hopes that he won't be forced to participate.

When *giving orders*, the teacher tries to help by directing Del on what to do: "You might as well stop complaining about things you can't control. Go ahead and get ready now." A more effective response might be "Do you see any way I might be able to make this easier for you?"

When *warning*, the teacher threatens Del: "That's enough. Change into your PE clothes now, or I'll have you running laps." A more effective response might be "I can see this matter is bothering you a great deal. Would you like to discuss it after school?"

When *preaching*, the teacher reminds Del of "shoulds" and "oughts": "You ought to know that exercise is important. You should try to get yourself in shape." A more effective response might be "Some people like to exercise and others don't, but everyone needs it. How do you think we might help you get the exercise you need?"

When *advising,* the teacher tries to help by offering Del suggestions or giving solutions: "If you feel you can't keep up with the others, try setting your own personal goal and work to meet it." A more effective response might be "Sometimes even good athletes don't like PE classes. Have you heard any of them discuss their feelings?"

When *lecturing,* the teacher presents logical facts to counter Del's resistance: "I can assure you that if you develop a habit for exercise now, you will be pleased and will carry it with you for the rest of your life." A more effective response might be "Sometimes it is certainly tempting to stop exercising and just sit out the class. If you do, what effect do you think it might have on your health?"

When *criticizing,* the teacher points out Del's faults and inadequacies: "I can't believe you just said that. That kind of excuse-making is beneath your dignity." A more effective response might be "I think I'm beginning to understand what you are saying. Could you tell me a bit more about that?"

When *name-calling,* the teacher labels or makes fun of Del: "I might expect third graders to argue about dressing out for PE. Aren't you a bit large for third grade?" A more effective response might be "Frankly, I haven't understood exactly why you are reluctant. Can you help me understand a bit better?"

When *analyzing,* the teacher diagnoses or interprets Del's behavior: "What you are really saying is that you are afraid others will laugh about your weight." A more effective response might be "Go ahead with that thought. Can you explain it further?"

When *praising,* the teacher uses positive statements and praise to encourage Del: "You have above-average coordination. You'll handle yourself real well out there." A more effective response might be "I understand your concern. What might I do to make physical education more enjoyable for you?"

When *reassuring,* the teacher tries to make Del feel better by offering sympathy and support: "I know how you feel. Remember, there are a lot of boys just like you. You will forget your concerns after a little while." A more effective response might be "Have you known other students with concerns like yours? How did they deal with them?"

When *questioning,* the teacher probes and questions Del for more facts: "What exactly are you afraid of? What do you think is going to happen?" A more effective response might be "We often anticipate the worst, don't we? Have you had other experiences like this that troubled you?"

When *withdrawing*, the teacher changes the subject in order to avoid Del's concerns: "Come on, now. Enough of that kind of talk. It's time to get ready and get out there." A more effective response might be "Do you think this matter might be bothering others, too? Do you think I should talk to the class about it, or would you rather keep it between us?"

Skill Cluster 3: Preventive Skills

This skill cluster is used in connection with the middle section of the behavior window, which indicates no problems as shown in Table 6.4. Specific preventive skills addressed by Gordon include (1) preventive I-messages, (2) collaborative rule setting, and (3) participative classroom management, all of which contribute to maintaining harmonious relationships within the classroom.

1. *Using preventive I-messages.* **Preventive I-messages** influence students' future actions and thus help prevent problems. The teacher might say, "Next week we're going on our field trip. I need to make sure we all have a good time and don't have any problems. I'd like everyone to be sure to stay together so no one gets lost." By contrast, **preventive you-messages** place blame and should be avoided: "You behaved very badly on our last field trip, so I hope you can do better this time."
2. *Setting rules collaboratively.* Gordon believes rules of conduct are necessary in order to make classrooms safe, efficient, and harmonious. He says those rules should be formulated collaboratively by teacher and students through discussions of what each wants and needs. In a democratic manner, everyone agrees to the rules mutually. **Collaborative rule setting** is similar to the no-lose method of conflict resolution in that students and teachers both win because everyone's needs receive attention.
3. *Using participative classroom management.* Gordon believes that the most effective classrooms are those in which teachers share power and decision making with their students. He suggests **participative classroom management** in which teachers and students make joint decisions about class rules, room

Behavior Window	Skill Clusters
Student's behavior causes a problem for the students only. **Student owns the problem.**	Helping skills
Student's behavior does not cause a problem for either student or teacher. **No problem.**	*Preventive skills*
Student's behavior causes a problem for the teacher. **Teacher owns the problem.**	Confrontive skills

TABLE 6.4

Source: Adapted from *P.E.T. in Action* (pp. 27, 174, 251) by T. Gordon, 1976. New York: Random House.

arrangement, seating, and preferred activities. That style of management motivates students, gives them greater confidence and self-esteem, and encourages them to take risks and behave more responsibly.

As part of participative management, Gordon (1989) recommends a process of **problem solving** through which teachers show students how to solve problems and make good decisions. The steps in the problem-solving process are as follows:

Step 1. Identify and define the problem or situation. Good solutions depend on accurate identification of the problem at hand. Questions that should be asked at the beginning include "What is really going on here?" "What problems are we having?" "What exactly do we need to solve or do?" and "Is there another deeper problem here?"

Step 2. Generate alternatives. Once the problem is clarified, a number of possible solutions should be generated. To help bring forth ideas, questions and statements such as the following are usually helpful: "What can we do differently to make our work easier or better?" "What rules or procedures do we need to follow?" "Let's see how many ideas we can come up with," and "Are there still more solutions we can think of?"

Step 3. Evaluate the alternative suggestions. When alternatives have been specified, participants are asked to comment on them. The goal is to choose a solution that is agreeable to all. Thus it is appropriate to ask for each proposal, "What do you think of this suggestion?" "What are its advantages and disadvantages?" "What problems does it leave unsolved?" and "If we try this idea, what do you think will happen?"

Step 4. Make the decision. Alternatives are examined. The one that seems to suit most people best is selected for trial.

Step 5. Implement the solution or decision. The trial solution is put into place with the understanding that it may or may not work as anticipated and that it can be changed if necessary.

Step 6. Conduct a follow-up evaluation. The results of the trial solution or decision are analyzed and evaluated. Helpful questions include "Was this a good decision?" "Did it solve the problem?" "Is everyone happy with the decision?" and "How effective was our decision?" If the solution or decision is judged to be satisfactory, it is kept in place. If unsatisfactory, a modified or new solution is proposed and put to the test.

Strengths of Gordon's *Discipline as Self-Control*

Gordon envisions discipline not as forcing students to comply with rules, but rather as a process that promotes student self-control. By identifying specific alternatives and strategies to meet this goal, Gordon gives teachers many new tactics for helping students become self-reliant decision makers who exercise control over their own behavior. He moves away from the punitive/permissive extremes of discipline. He shuns behavior management based on reward and punishment and in its place proposes noncontrolling alternatives for influencing, not forcing, student behavior. The skills he advocates can be learned fairly easily, though they must be practiced in order to appear natural. One of the great skills taught by Gordon is teacher ability to listen to students and respond effectively. As teachers acquire further skills, they become able to avoid roadblocks to communication, use clear I-messages that reveal their feelings in reaction to behavior, and shift gears from sending I-messages to listening in order to support successful problem solving.

Initiating Gordon's *Discipline as Self-Control*

Suppose it is the beginning of the school year. You like Gordon's ideas and want to use them in your discipline system. What exactly do you do during the first days to put the Gordon model into place? Using language and demonstrations appropriate for your students, you might properly do the following:

Step 1. *Identify student behaviors that will help, and those that will hinder, learning in your classroom.* Are these behaviors most likely to occur during large group, small group, or individual activities? When is silence desirable? When is quiet talking helpful? When is group discussion and interaction needed? When is movement in the room necessary?

It is also important to think about your own needs concerning student behavior. How much noise can you tolerate? What degree of formal respect do you want students to show to you and to each other? To what extent do you need to structure students' behavior? May they speak out, or should they raise their hands first? How do you expect them to enter and exit the classroom? How much neatness and order do you require?

Step 2. *Discuss your concerns with the class.* On the first day, describe the curriculum and general expectations concerning work and behavior, but make a point also of asking for student input, to which you give serious consideration as suggested in participative management. In this process, you involve students in clarifying the conditions and working relationships that will make the class profitable and enjoyable. It is important that you use active listening and keep communication open. When students disagree over certain points, you can implement the problem-solving process to help them reach agreement. To culminate this phase, make a written summary of class agreements and post a copy in the classroom.

Step 3. *Help students learn to function in keeping with the class agreements.* This requires frequent reminders and perhaps practice and role playing. You will need to use preventive, helping, and confrontive skills as indicated by problem ownership. As the weeks pass, you will help students become increasingly self-disciplined as you demonstrate, in daily practice, your own self-discipline, flexibility, and ability to communicate and solve problems.

Review of Selected Terminology

The following terms are central to understanding Gordon's model of discipline:

Misbehavior: meaning of

Communication guidance: behavior window, problem ownership, communication roadblocks

Communication techniques: passive listening, acknowledgment responses, active listening, door openers, shifting gears, I-messages, preventive skills, preventive I-messages, preventive you-messages, confrontive skills, confrontive I-messages, you-messages, rewards

Discipline: authority, noncontrolling methods, participative management, collaborative rule setting, helping skills, modifying the environment

Conflict resolution: win–lose conflict resolution, no-lose conflict resolution

Application Exercises

Concept Cases

Case 1: Kristina Will Not Work ■ Kristina, in Mr. Jake's class, is quite docile. She never disrupts class and does little socializing with other students. But despite Mr. Jake's best efforts, Kristina rarely completes an assignment. She doesn't seem to care. She is simply there, putting forth virtually no effort. *How would Gordon deal with Kristina?*

If you were the teacher, Gordon would suggest the following: First, recognize that it is you who owns the problem, not Kristina. Don't try to force Kristina to complete the assignments, but use I-messages to convey your concern to Kristina. Encourage her to communicate about the assignments. Use active listening skills as she does so. Ask her how you can help. Invite her into a collaborative problem-solving exploration of why she doesn't work, and see if she has suggestions she wishes to make. Use I-messages to convey to the entire class how important it is that everyone, teacher and students alike, completes the work expected of them in school. But don't single out Kristina.

Case 2: Sara Cannot Stop Talking ■ Sara is a pleasant girl who participates in class activities and does most, though not all, of her assigned work. She cannot seem to refrain from talking to classmates, however. Her teacher, Mr. Gonzales, has to speak to her repeatedly during lessons, to the point that he often becomes exasperated and loses his temper. *What suggestions would Gordon give Mr. Gonzales to help with Sara's misbehavior?*

Case 3: Joshua Clowns and Intimidates ■ Joshua, larger and louder than his classmates, always wants to be the center of attention, which he accomplishes through a combination of clowning and intimidation. He makes wise remarks, talks back (smilingly) to the teacher, utters a variety of sound-effect noises such as automobile crashes and gunshots, and makes limitless sarcastic comments and put-downs of his classmates. Other students will not stand up to him, apparently fearing his verbal and physical aggression. His teacher, Miss Pearl, has come to her wit's end. *What do you find in Gordon's work that might help Miss Pearl deal with Joshua?*

Case 4: Tom is Hostile and Defiant ■ Tom has appeared to be in his usual foul mood ever since arriving in class. On his way to sharpen his pencil, he bumps into Frank, who complains. Tom tells him loudly to shut up. Miss Baines, the teacher, says, "Tom, go back to your seat." Tom wheels around and says heatedly, "I'll go when I'm damned good and ready!" *How would Gordon have Miss Baines deal with Tom?*

Questions and Activities

1. Describe how you would use the problem-solving process with your English class if they expressed concern about having too many projects, papers, and other assignments due at about the same time.

2. Refer to Scenario 2 in Appendix A. Which of Gordon's ideas do you think could best be used to improve Mr. Platt's interactions with student Arlene?

3. Refer to Scenario 4 in Appendix A. Explain how Gordon's ideas might be used to improve conditions in Mrs. Desmond's second-grade class.

4. Decide which of the following statements reflects (1) modifying the environment, (2) participative management, (3) confrontive I-message, or (4) preventive I-message.

   a. "Before we start our art project, let's talk about what we will need to do with the paints and brushes so we have enough time for cleanup before the bell rings."
   b. "Let's sit in our Jungle Hut today, and I'll turn down the lights while I read this story."
   c. "I am feeling tired, so let's all stand up. Is everyone ready? Good. Simon says..."
   d. "I feel so disappointed when I see one of my students being disrespectful to another."

Primary References

Gordon, T. 1970. *Parent effectiveness training: A tested new way to raise responsible children.* New York: New American Library. Gordon's classic book on parenting out of which grew *Teacher Effectiveness Training, Discipline as Self-Control, Leadership Training,* and other important works on interpersonal relations.

———. 1987. *T.E.T.: Teacher effectiveness training.* New York: David McKay. Gordon's highly influential book on helping teachers relate better with students, emphasizing the importance of communication and factors that inhibit and facilitate teachers' ability to talk productively with students.

———. 1989. *Discipline that works: Promoting self-discipline in children.* New York: Random House. The book that sets forth Gordon's views on discipline in school and in the family, in which he explains the importance of inner self-discipline. He points out the dangers of coercion and reward and punishment and indicates how teachers can replace them with joint decision making that brings cooperation and helps students become more self-disciplined.

Recommended Reading

Gordon, T. 1976. *P.E.T. in action.* New York: Bantam Books.

Jane Nelsen, Lynn Lott, and H. Stephen Glenn's *Positive Discipline in the Classroom*

PREVIEW OF NELSEN, LOTT, AND GLENN'S WORK

Focus

- Student joy for learning together with responsible behavior that results from acceptance of self and others.
- Humane, dignified regard for self and others.
- Involvement in looking for solutions to misbehavior rather than punishment.
- A learning environment that encourages rather than discourages and humiliates.

Logic

- Students can and will learn to behave with dignity, self-control, and concern for others.
- These traits develop in classrooms that are accepting, encouraging, and supportive.
- The process that serves best is cooperative planning infused with humane concern.

Contributions

- A strategic approach to positive classroom interaction, rather than a packaged system.
- Explanation of how teachers can stop directing students and begin working with them.

Nelsen, Lott, and Glenn's Suggestions

- Help students see themselves as capable, significant, and able to control their own lives.
- Help students develop intrapersonal, interpersonal, strategic, and judgmental skills.
- Learn to be a caring teacher who emphasizes these traits and skills throughout teaching.
- Replace barriers to communication with builders of communication.

Jane Nelsen

Lynn Lott

H. Stephen Glenn

About Jane Nelsen, Lynn Lott, and H. Stephen Glenn

Jane Nelsen, Lynn Lott, and H. Stephen Glenn are educators who promote their concepts through lectures, workshops, and private practice to help adults and children learn to accept themselves and others, behave responsibly, and contribute to the betterment of the groups of which they are members. Nelsen, Lott, and Glenn have among them almost 100 years of experience in teaching, lecturing, counseling, and writing. Their book *Positive Discipline in the Classroom* (2000) helps teachers establish learning climates that foster responsibility, mutual respect, and cooperation. They believe that such climates do away with most of the discipline problems teachers otherwise encounter, since students learn the value, for themselves, of respect, and of helpfulness toward others.

Nelsen, Lott, and Glenn have authored or coauthored a number of books, including *Raising Self-Reliant Children in a Self-Indulgent World* (Nelsen and Glenn, 1989), *Positive Discipline* (Nelsen, 1998), *Positive Discipline: A Teacher's A–Z Guide* (Nelsen, Duffy, Owen-Sohocki, Escobar, and Ortolano, 1996), *Positive Discipline for Parenting in Recovery* (Nelsen and Lott, 1996), *Positive Discipline for Preschoolers* (Nelsen, Erwin, and Duffy, 1999), *Positive Discipline: The First Three Years, from Infant to Toddler—Laying the Foundation for Raising a Capable, Confident Child* (Nelsen, Erwin, and Duffy, 1999), *Positive Discipline for Teenagers* (Nelsen and Lott, 2000), and *Positive Discipline in the Classroom* (Nelsen, Lott, and Glenn, 2000). Jane Nelsen and H. Stephen Glenn can be contacted at Empowering People, P.O. Box 1926, Orem, UT 84059-1926; telephone 1-800-456-7770; website www.empoweringpeople.com. Lynn Lott can be reached at 707-526-3141, ext. 3# or email Maxlynski@aol.com

Nelsen, Lott, and Glenn's Contributions to Discipline

Nelsen, Lott, and Glenn's main contribution is an approach to discipline that puts faith in students' ability to control themselves, cooperate, assume responsibility, and behave in a dignified manner. They believe that these desirable traits grow especially well in groups where positive discipline concepts are discussed and practiced in regular class meetings. They suggest that concerns of students or teacher be written into a notebook and be made agenda items for class meetings. In those meetings, everyone participates in attempting to resolve problems in a manner satisfactory to all concerned. Involvement in that process teaches students important life skills.

Nelsen, Lott, and Glenn's Central Focus

Nelsen, Lott, and Glenn help teachers develop classrooms where students are treated respectfully and taught the skills needed for working with others. These are classrooms where students (1) never experience humiliation when they fail, but instead learn how to turn mistakes into successes, (2) learn how to cooperate with teachers and fellow students to find joint solutions to problems, and (3) are provided an environment that instills excitement for life and learning in place of fear, discouragement, and feelings of inadequacy.

Nelsen, Lott, and Glenn's Principal Teachings

- *Discipline problems gradually become insignificant* in classrooms where there is a climate of acceptance, dignity, respect, and encouragement.
- *Students need to perceive themselves as capable, significant, and in control of their own lives.* These perceptions grow best in classes that hold regular class meetings that employ the principles of positive discipline.
- *It is crucial for students to develop skills of self-control, adaptability, cooperation, and judgment.* These skills are also best developed in class meetings.
- *Teachers must show that they truly care about their students.* This is necessary if the desired perceptions and skills are to develop properly.
- *Teachers demonstrate caring by showing personal interest, talking with students, offering encouragement, and providing opportunities to learn important life skills.*
- *Teachers can greatly facilitate desirable student behavior by removing barriers to good relationships with students and replacing them with builders of good relationships.* By simply avoiding certain barriers, teachers quickly bring about great improvement in student behavior.
- *Class meetings should emphasize participation by everyone, group resolution of problems, and win/win solutions.* They should also be a place where everyone, teacher and students alike, practices communication, respect, support, encouragement, and cooperation.

Analysis of Nelsen, Lott, and Glenn's *Positive Discipline in the Classroom*

Positive Discipline in the Classroom is intended to empower students at all levels to become more successful, not only in the classroom, but in all walks of life. The belief that underlies this approach is that behavior problems can be greatly diminished as students acquire the skills of accepting others, communicating effectively, showing respect, and maintaining a positive attitude. These outcomes are most likely to occur within a class atmosphere of kindness and firmness, with dignity and mutual respect. There, the mistaken goals of behavior are clarified. Positive discipline management tools are used, including encouragement and positive feedback. Collaboration occurs with other faculty, and parent/teacher/student conferences are held to communicate progress and find better ways to encourage students.

The authors say that class meetings are uniquely suited to implementing *Positive Discipline in the Classroom*. Although the meetings do not ensure all the desired outcomes, they do promote social skills such as listening, taking turns, hearing different points of view, negotiating, communicating, helping one another, and taking responsibility for their own behavior. Academic skills are strengthened in the process, as well, because students must practice language skills, attentiveness, critical thinking, decision making, and problem solving, all of which enhance academic performance.

Class meetings also alter students' perception of teachers by helping students see that teachers and other adults need nurturing and encouragement just as much as they do. When teachers involve themselves as partners with students in class meetings, a climate of mutual respect is encouraged. Teachers and students listen to one another, take each other seriously, and work together to solve problems for the benefit of all. Antagonisms so often seen in most classrooms tend to fade away.

The Significant Seven

Nelsen, Lott, and Glenn have identified three perceptions and four skills that contribute to the special benefits of *Positive Discipline in the Classroom*. They call these perceptions and skills the **significant seven,** which they describe as follows:

The Three Empowering Perceptions

Class meetings help students develop **three perceptions** about themselves that lead to success in life. Those three perceptions are:

1. Perception of *personal capabilities* (I have ability; I can do this.)
2. Perception of *significance in primary relationships* (I am needed; I belong.)
3. Perception of *personal power* to influence one's life (I have control over what happens to me.)

Four Essential Skills

Class meetings help students develop **four essential skills** that contribute significantly to success in life:

1. Intrapersonal skill (I understand my emotions and can control myself.)
2. Interpersonal skill (I can communicate, cooperate, and work with others.)
3. Strategic skill (I am flexible, adaptable, and responsible.)
4. Judgmental skill (I can use my wisdom to evaluate situations.)

Developing the Significant Seven

Nelsen, Lott, and Glenn have a number of things to say concerning how students can be helped to develop the significant seven (the three perceptions and the four skills). They include the following attributes:

Perception of Personal Capability

Being listened to and acknowledged for contributions builds a sense of personal capability. Class meetings provide a safe climate where students can express themselves and be listened to without concern about success or failure.

Perception of Significance in Primary Relationships

Primary relationships in the classroom refer to those between student and teacher and student and student. The perception of personal significance develops when others listen to one's feelings, thoughts, and ideas and take them seriously. This occurs naturally in class meetings, where everyone has the opportunity to voice opinions and give suggestions.

Perception of Power and Influence over One's Own Life

Class meetings emphasize encouragement coupled with accountability. They permit students to make mistakes in a safe atmosphere, take responsibility for the mistakes, and learn from them without being judged negatively for what they say. This helps students give up a **victim mentality** in which they blame others ("The teacher has it in for me.") and accept an **accountability mentality** in which they accept personal responsibility ("I received an F because I didn't do the work."). They also learn that even when they can't control what happens, they *can* control their own responses and their resultant actions.

Intrapersonal Skills

Young people seem more willing to listen to one another than to adults. They gain understanding of their personal emotions and behavior by hearing feedback from classmates. In a nonthreatening climate, young people are willing to be accountable for their actions. They learn to distinguish between their feelings and their actions, that is, that what they feel (anger) is separate from what they do (hit someone), and that while feelings are always acceptable, some actions are not.

Interpersonal Skills

Class meetings encourage students to develop interpersonal skills by means of dialogue, sharing, listening, empathizing, cooperating, negotiating, and resolving conflicts. Teachers, instead of stepping in and resolving problems for students, can suggest putting the problem on the class meeting agenda, where everyone can work to solve it together.

Strategic Skills

Students develop **strategic skills,** the ability to adapt to problems, by responding to the limits and consequences imposed by everyday life. Through the problem-solving process, they learn alternative ways to express or deal with their thoughts or feelings.

Judgmental Skills

Young people develop **judgmental skills,** the ability to evaluate situations and make good choices, when they have opportunity and encouragement to practice doing so. This process is fostered in class meetings which acknowledge effort rather than success or failure. There, students find themselves in a setting that allows them to make mistakes safely, learn, and try again.

The Importance of Caring

The approach to discipline advocated by Nelsen, Lott, and Glenn requires that teachers truly care about students' welfare and that such caring be made evident. Teachers show they care when they go out of their way to learn about students as individuals, encourage them to see mistakes as opportunities to learn and grow, and have faith in their ability to make meaningful contributions. Students know teachers care when they feel listened to and their thoughts and feelings are taken seriously.

Barriers to Relationships

Certain teacher behaviors act as barriers to developing caring relationships with students, while other behaviors help build such relationships. Nelsen, Lott, and Glenn identify five pairs of contrasting behaviors, which they call barriers and builders. **Barriers** are behaviors that are disrespectful and discouraging to students, whereas **builders** are behaviors that are respectful and encouraging, as explained in the following paragraphs.

Barriers versus Builders

1. *Assuming versus Checking*—All too often teachers *assume,* without checking with students, that they know what students think and feel, what they can and cannot do, and how they should or shouldn't respond. Teachers then deal with students on the basis of those assumptions. When they do so, however, they often prevent students' unique capabilities from becoming evident. It is greatly preferable that teachers verify what students actually think and feel, which is done by *checking* with them instead of assuming.
2. *Rescuing/Explaining versus Exploring*—Teachers wish to be helpful to students. They usually think they are helpful when they explain things, rescue students from difficulties, or do some of their work for them. Students progress better, however, when allowed to perceive situations for themselves and proceed on the basis of personal perceptions. Elementary teachers explain and rescue, for example, when they say, "It's cold outside, so don't forget your jackets." They help explore when they say, "Take a look outside. What do you need to remember in order to take care of yourself?"
3. *Directing versus Inviting/Encouraging*—Teachers do not realize they are being disrespectful to students when they say, "Pick that up." "Put that away." "Straighten up your desk before the bell rings." But such commands have many negative effects: They build dependency, eliminate initiative and cooperation, and suggest to students it is all right to do as little as possible on their own. Directives of this type stand in contrast to *inviting and encouraging* students to become self-directed. Instead of commanding, the teacher might say, "The bell will ring soon. I would appreciate anything you might do to help get the room straightened up for the next class."

4. *Expecting versus Celebrating*—It is important that teachers hold high expectations of students and believe in their potential. However, when students are judged for falling short of expectations, they become easily discouraged, as when teachers say, "I really thought you could do that," or "I thought you were more responsible than that." Students respond far better when teachers look for improvements to which they can call attention. Drawing attention to improvement is quite motivating to students.

5. *"Adult-isms" versus Respecting*—Nelsen, Lott, and Glenn use the term *adult-ism* for teacher statements that suggest what students *ought to do,* such as: "How come you never...?" "Why can't you ever...?" "I can't believe you would do such a thing!" These adult-isms produce guilt and shame rather than support and encouragement. Instead of handing an unacceptable paper back and saying, "You knew what I wanted on this project!" a teacher could say, "What is your understanding of the requirements for this project?" Nelsen, Lott, and Glenn (1993) flatly state:

> We guarantee 100% improvement in student–teacher relationships when teachers simply learn to recognize barrier behaviors and stop demonstrating them. Where else can you get such a generous return for ceasing a behavior? And when the builders are added, the payoff is even greater. (p. 18)

In addition to concentrating on builders in lieu of barriers, teachers can do a number of other things to show that they care about their students, such as:

Using a supportive tone of voice

Listening to students and taking them seriously

Acting as though they enjoy their jobs

Appreciating the uniqueness of individual students

Developing an appropriate attitude (e.g., eagerly looking forward to helping students)

Showing a sense of humor

Showing interest in and respect for students' outside interests

Involving students in making decisions about the class and curriculum

Looking for improvement, not perfection in student work and behavior

Eight Building Blocks to Effective Class Meetings

As you have seen, class meetings are the primary venue for identifying and implementing the caring, supportive, and cooperative climate that is the goal of *Positive Discipline in the Classroom.* Nelsen, Lott, and Glenn maintain that training in eight building blocks for effective class meetings is the surest route to the kind of classroom climate desired by both students and teachers. Each of the building blocks focuses on a particular skill. According to Nelsen, Lott, and Glenn, it takes about two hours to introduce the eight building blocks to students. After that, about four additional class meetings will be needed to give adequate attention to what they entail. Here's how they suggest proceeding:

1. Before beginning to explore the eight building blocks, introduce the concept of class meetings and get students to buy into the idea. This can be done by explaining that you would like to begin holding class meetings where students can express concerns and use their power and skills to help make decisions. Elementary students are usually eager to try class meetings, but middle school and high school students may need some persuading. A way to begin is to use language appropriate for your grade level and to initiate a discussion about power, how problems are usually handled in school, and how that method results in teachers telling students what to do. The students then comply or rebel, without being brought into the decision-making process.

2. Next, ask students questions such as: Who has an example they would like to share about what happens when someone tries to control you? What do you feel? What do you do? What do you learn? Students will usually say that they feel angry or scared and manipulated. What they learn is to rebel, comply, or withdraw. Ask them also, How do you try to control or manipulate others, including teachers?

3. Ask them if they would like to be more involved in the decisions that affect their lives. Would they be willing to do the work required to come up with solutions they like? Point out that some students actually *prefer* having adults boss them around, so that they can rebel, or so they don't have to take responsibility themselves. It takes time and personal responsibility from everyone to use class meetings effectively. Make it clear that you don't intend to waste time teaching and learning a respectful method if they prefer continuing with the usual way, where the teacher is in control and students' only options are to comply, rebel, and/or spend time in detention. This kind of discussion is especially helpful and effective in classrooms where students have been taught with authoritarian methods.

    Once students indicate support for classroom meetings, the next step is to decide when the meetings will be held. Preferences vary from weekly half-hour meetings to three shorter meetings per week. A meeting every day is advisable for the first week, as students learn the eight building blocks.

Building Block 1: Form a Circle

The first step in implementing class meetings is to establish an atmosphere that allows everyone an equal right to speak and be heard and where **win-win solutions** can take place. A circular seating arrangement serves best. Ask students for suggestions about forming the circle, listen to them, and write their ideas on the board. Make decisions based on their suggestions.

Building Block 2: Practice Compliments and Appreciation

It is important to begin class meetings on a positive note, which can be accomplished by having students and teacher say complimentary things to each other. Many students at first have difficulty giving and receiving compliments. Practice helps. Ask them to recall when someone said something that made them feel good about themselves. Let them share their examples with the group. Then ask them to think about something they would like to thank others for, such as thanking a classmate for lending a pencil or eating lunch together. See if they can put their feelings into words.

Receiving compliments is often as difficult as giving them. Probably the best response to a compliment is a simple "Thank you." The notion of giving and receiving compliments seems embarrassing to some middle school students. When that is the case, use the term *show appreciation* instead of compliment.

Building Block 3: Create an Agenda

All class meetings should begin with a specific agenda. When students and teachers experience concerns, they can jot them down in a special notebook, at a designated time such as when leaving the room. The class meeting will address only the concerns that appear in the notebook.

Building Block 4: Develop Communication Skills

Nelsen, Lott, and Glenn suggest a number of activities for developing communication skills such as taking turns speaking (begin by going around the circle and letting each person speak), listening attentively to what others say, learning to use **I-statements** (saying I think, I feel, and so forth), seeking solutions to problems rather than placing blame on others, showing respect for others by never humiliating or speaking judgmentally about them, learning how to seek and find win-win solutions to problems, and framing conclusions in the form of "we decided," showing it was a group effort and conclusion.

Building Block 5: Learn about Separate Realities

In this building block, teachers focus on helping students understand that not everyone is the same or thinks the same way. Nelsen, Lott, and Glenn describe an approach to this skill segment that poses situations involving turtles, lions, eagles, and chameleons, showing that each has special talents as well as limitations. This activity should be made appropriate to the age level of students.

Building Block 6: Recognize the Four Reasons People Do What They Do

Ask students if they have ever wondered why people do what they do. Ask for their ideas, acknowledge them, and then ask if they have ever heard of the four mistaken goals of misbehavior. Proceed by using examples to illustrate the mistaken goals of undue attention, power, revenge, and giving up.

Building Block 7: Practice Role Playing and Brainstorming

By the third class meeting, students are usually ready to begin considering problems and seeking solutions to them. Suggestions for exploring problems in a tactful manner involve discussions about the problem, role playing in which students act out roles involved in the problem, brainstorming in which a number of possible solutions are sought for the difficulty, and allowing students to select a solution that will work to solve the problem.

Building Block 8: Focus on Nonpunitive Solutions

Ask students the following and write their answers on the board: "What do you want to do when someone bosses you? What do you want to do when someone calls you names or puts you down? When others do these things to you, does it help you behave better?" Then ask them how their behavior is affected when someone is kind to them, helps them, or provides stimulation and encouragement. Have them compare their answers, which you have written on the board. Use the comparison to draw attention to the value of encouragement versus punishment.

Tell the students that you intend never to punish them, and that when they do something wrong you will try to help them behave more appropriately. Explain that what you will do to help will always be *related* to what they have done wrong, *respectful* of them as people, and *reasonable*. These are what Nelsen, Lott, and Glenn call the **Three R's of Solutions**. They explain the concept this way: If students don't do their homework, sending them to the office is not related to missed homework. A *related* solution might be to have them make up the homework or not get points for that assignment. *Respectful* means supporting the solution with dignity and respect: "Would you like to make up the homework assignment at home or right after school?" *Reasonable* means you don't add punishment such as, "Now you'll have to do twice as much."

Beyond Consequences

Nelsen, Lott, and Glenn caution that it is easy to misuse logical consequences, pointing out that well-meaning teachers often perpetuate the use of punishment despite giving it the new label of logical consequences. They urge teachers always to think in terms of solutions rather than consequences. The following illustrates their point.

During a class meeting, students in a fifth-grade class were asked to brainstorm logical consequences for two students who didn't hear the recess bell and were late for class. Following is their list of consequences:

1. Make them write their names on the board.
2. Make them stay after school that many minutes.
3. Take away that many minutes from tomorrow's recess.
4. No recess tomorrow.
5. The teacher could yell at them.

The students were then asked to forget about consequences and brainstorm for solutions that would help the students be on time. The following is their list of solutions:

1. Someone could tap them on the shoulder when the bell rings.
2. Everyone could yell together, "Bell!"
3. They could play closer to the bell.
4. They could watch others to see when they are going in.
5. Adjust the bell so it is louder.
6. They could choose a buddy to remind them that it is time to come in.

Notice the difference between these two lists. The first looks and sounds like punishment. It focuses on the past and making kids "pay" for their mistake. The second list looks and sounds like solutions that help students do better in the future. It focuses on seeing problems as opportunities for learning. The first list is likely to hurt; the second is likely to help.

Among Nelsen, Lott, and Glenn's other suggestions for moving beyond consequences are:

Involve students in the solutions. When students participate in finding solutions to behavioral problems, they strengthen communication and problem-solving skills. They are also more likely to abide by agreements they have helped plan. Because they are made to feel part of the classroom community, they have less reason to misbehave and are more willing to work on solutions to problems.

Focus on the future instead of the past. When teachers apply logical consequences, they are often likely to be focusing on the past, on the behavior the student has already committed. Rather than that, teachers should ask students to look to the future, thinking of solutions that will improve conditions in days to come.

Make connections between opportunity, responsibility, and consequence. Nelsen, Lott, and Glenn do not say that students should never experience logical consequences. Students need to learn that every new opportunity they encounter brings with it a related responsibility. If students are unwilling to take on the responsibility, they should not be allowed the opportunity. Nelsen, Lott, and Glenn illustrate this point as follows: Elementary students have the opportunity to use the playground during recess. Their related responsibility is to treat the equipment and other people with respect. If they treat things or people disrespectfully, the logical consequence is losing the opportunity of using the playground. A way to instill a sense of responsibility in students who have been given a consequence is to say, "You decide how much time you think you need to cool off and calm down. Let me know when you are ready to use the playground respectfully." Nelsen, Lott, and Glenn remind us that consequences are effective only if they are enforced respectfully and students are given another opportunity as soon as they are ready for the responsibility.

Be sure you don't piggyback. To piggyback is to add something to a consequence that isn't necessary and may actually be hurtful, such as, "Maybe this will teach you!" or, "You can just sit there and think about what you did!" Teachers who use piggybacking make punishment out of what would otherwise be a solution, or even a respectful consequence.

Plan solutions carefully in advance. A good way to prevent punishment's creeping into solutions is to plan out the solution in advance, with student collaboration. During a class meeting, ask students to think about what sort of solutions would actually help them learn. Make the questions specific, such as, "What kind of solution do you think would help any of us to remember to use the school equipment respectfully?" "What do you think a helpful solution would be when we return books late to the library?"

Standard Format for Class Meetings

Nelsen, Lott, and Glenn suggest that teachers use the following format for class meetings. The teacher normally initiates the meeting and makes sure everyone abides by the rules, but everyone has an equal right to speak:

1. *Express compliments and appreciation.* Each session begins in this way as a means of setting a positive tone.
2. *Follow up on earlier solutions applied to problems.* Any suggested solution is to be tried only for a week, so it is important to determine if the solution has been working. If it hasn't, the class may wish to put the issue back on the agenda for future problem solving.
3. *Go through agenda items.* When an agenda item is read, ask the person (student or teacher) with the issue if he or she still wants help with it. If so, ask that person what a satisfactory solution could be. If he or she can't think of any, go around the circle giving every student an opportunity to offer a suggestion. Ask each student to select the most helpful solution from the suggestions offered.
4. *Make future plans for class activities.* End the class meeting by discussing a fun activity for the entire class at a future date. For example, the class might decide to set aside some time on Friday to discuss an upcoming event, view a videotape, or complete homework assignments with a friend.

Remember That the Process Takes Time

When new procedures are implemented, it often takes some time before they begin to function smoothly. Nelsen, Lott, and Glenn say that if students do not respond to class meetings with the enthusiasm hoped for, don't be discouraged. You wouldn't stop teaching math or reading if students didn't grasp the concepts in a week or a month. Trust in the procedure; it will eventually come together. Although class meetings seem difficult at first, they will get better with practice, just like any academic skill.

Respectful Classroom Management

Nelsen, Lott, and Glenn continually emphasize mutual respect among all members of the class. They make suggestions such as the following.

Give students choices, but make the choices appropriate and limit their number. **Appropriate choices** are those that further the educational program. Instead of saying, "What do you want to do first this morning?" say "We can begin with our directed work or our group discussion—which do you prefer?" An **acceptable choice** is one that you, the teacher, deem worthwhile. Do not provide unacceptable choice options to students.

Ask students to use a problem-solving process to settle disputes. A **four-step problem-solving process** should be introduced for this purpose and its steps posted in the room:

1. Ignore the situation.
2. Talk it over respectfully with the other student.
3. Find a win-win solution.
4. (If no solution is agreed to) Put it on the class meeting agenda.

Nelsen, Lott, and Glenn (1993) explain the steps as follows:

> Step 1 encourages students either to avoid involvement or else leave the area of conflict for a cooling-off period.
>
> Step 2 is an opportunity for students to tell each other how they feel, to listen to and respect their own feelings, to figure out what they did to contribute to the problem, and to tell the other person what they are willing to do differently.
>
> Step 3 could involve brainstorming for solutions or simply apologizing.
>
> Step 4 lets students know it's okay to ask for help. (p. 111)

When students come to you with a problem, refer them to the Four Problem-Solving Steps chart, and ask if they have tried any of the steps. If they haven't tried any, ask which one they would like to try. This keeps you out of the role of perpetual problem solver.

When you cannot wait for a class meeting, follow through immediately. At times, kind and firm action is called for. In ten words or less, identify the issue and redirect the student's behavior. "I need your help to keep the noise down."

When conflict occurs, ask students about it rather than telling them what to do. Teachers tend to tell students what happened, why it happened, how they should feel about it, and what they should do. Instead of telling, they should ask students their perception of why it happened, how they feel about it, and how they could use that information next time. This encourages students to use judgment and be accountable for their actions. Nelsen, Lott, and Glenn say whenever you feel like telling students, stop yourself and *ask*. This is usually enough to get students to think about their behavior and decide what ought to be done.

Use questions that redirect behavior. Certain questions cause students to think about what they are doing and decide on better behavior. For example, the teacher might say, "How many of you think it is too noisy in here for people to concentrate? How many do not?"

Be willing to say no with dignity and respect. It is all right to say no. Many teachers don't think they have the right to say no without giving a lengthy explanation, but often a kind and succinct No is all that is required.

Act more, but talk less. Most teachers would be amazed if they could hear the number of useless words they speak. It is better to let one's behavior do the talking. Use hand signals, body posture, and facial expressions.

Put everyone in the same boat. It is almost impossible to identify the culprit and judge behavior correctly in every situation that arises. When some students are talking and others are not, say, "It is too noisy in here." If someone says, "It wasn't me; I wasn't doing anything wrong," simply say, "I'm not interested in finding fault or pointing fingers but in getting the problem resolved."

Putting It All Together

Teachers who wish to replace authoritarian methods with democratic ones must realize that it will take some time for the process to begin running efficiently. These efforts are for long-term quality, not short-term convenience. Have faith that students and teachers can cooperate happily with each other. When putting class meetings into practice, be willing to give up *control over* students in favor of gaining *cooperation with* students. Forego lecturing in favor of asking questions about students' thoughts and opinions. When students are encouraged to express themselves and are given choices, they become better able to cooperate, collaborate, and solve their problems.

Strengths of *Positive Discipline in the Classroom*

Nelsen, Lott, and Glenn provide a discipline program they believe will help students behave responsibly and take positive control over their own lives. They say that neither punishment, rewards, nor praise help develop self-directed people. They believe that each problem is an opportunity for learning and that students learn important life skills when they help each other find positive solutions to problems. To implement their suggestions, they advocate regular and frequent use of class meetings, which they believe afford the best opportunity for group discussions, identification of problems, and pursuit of solutions. They give many suggestions for making the meetings work effectively within the daily class program.

Although Nelsen, Lott, and Glenn provide lists of suggestions and cautions, the approach to discipline they advocate is not highly structured. Teachers who use it can adapt it to their needs and realities. This will be seen as a strength by teachers who like the ideas but want to adapt them to their style of teaching. It may be seen as a weakness by other teachers who are looking for a structure they can put into place quickly and that will bring immediate results. The Nelsen, Lott, and Glenn system will require some time for organizing and for student acclimatization. Therefore, its results may be somewhat slow in coming, but in the long run will be more effective and lasting than those achieved in discipline systems based on reward and punishment.

Initiating *Positive Discipline in the Classroom*

The Nelsen, Lott, and Glynn model of discipline depends on successful implementation of class meetings as an integral part of the instructional program. These meetings make it possible to involve students in discussions about curriculum and behavior and obtain their input in making decisions. They also furnish a venue for practicing many of the skills of communication, problem solving, and conflict resolution that Nelsen, Lott, and Glynn advocate. Therefore, a teacher wishing to implement *Positive Discipline in the Classroom* should set up class meetings and use the agenda suggested for them. They are best introduced at the beginning of the year or semester. It will take time to get this approach functioning fully, but once under way will help students develop skills that will last their entire lives. Any lost academic time will be regained once students begin behaving helpfully so that instruction is not disrupted.

Review of Selected Terminology

The following terms are central to understanding the Nelsen, Lott, and Glenn model of discipline. Check yourself to make sure you understand them:

Three self-perceptions in discipline: personal capabilities, significance in primary relationships, personal power to influence

Four personal skills for self-discipline: interpersonal skills, intrapersonal skills, judgmental skills, strategic skills

Mentalities: victim, accountability

Relationships: barriers, builders

Choices: acceptable, appropriate

Class meetings: eight building blocks — circle, practice complimenting, agenda, communication skills, separate realities, four reasons for behavior, role playing, non-punitive solutions

Solutions: win-win, three R's of related, respectful, reasonable

Four-step problem solving: ignore, respectful discussion, win-win solution, class meeting agenda

Application Exercises

Concept Cases

Case 1: Kristina Will Not Work ■ Kristina, a student in Mr. Jake's class, is quite docile. She socializes little with other students and never disrupts lessons. However, despite Mr. Jake's best efforts, Kristina will not do her work. She rarely completes an assignment. She is simply there, putting forth no effort at all. *How would Nelsen, Lott, and Glenn deal with Kristina?*

They would advise Mr. Jake to do the following: In a regular class meeting, discuss why students do what they do and make guesses as to what Kristina's unconscious goal of behavior may be. Ask for a show of hands to each of the following questions, "How many think a student might not do her work to get others to pay attention or do the work for her? How many think a student might not do her work to show that no one can

make her? How many think that a student might not do her work because she is upset and wants to upset others? How many think a student might not do her work because she thinks that no matter what she does, it won't be good enough, so why try? Then ask students to go around the circle and brainstorm solutions to help students who do not complete their work. Write down every suggestion. When finished, ask a volunteer to read the suggestions. Allow students to choose the best solution, such as working with a buddy. Ask Kristina to try the solution for a week and report back in a class meeting how it is working. If she begins to do her work, give her a compliment in the class meeting. If she does not, ask her at the end of the week if she would like to put the problem on the agenda again to receive more suggestions from the class. It is rare that students do not follow through on suggestions they choose.

Case 2: Sara Cannot Stop Talking ■ Sara is a pleasant girl who participates in class activities and does most, though not all, of her assigned work. She cannot seem to refrain from talking to classmates, however. Her teacher, Mr. Gonzales, has to speak to her repeatedly during lessons, to the point that he often becomes exasperated and loses his temper. *What suggestions would Nelsen, Lott, and Glenn give Mr. Gonzales for dealing with Sara?*

Case 3: Joshua Clowns and Intimidates ■ Joshua, larger and louder than his classmates, always wants to be the center of attention, which he accomplishes through a combination of clowning and intimidation. He makes wise remarks, talks back (smilingly) to the teacher, utters a variety of sound-effect noises such as automobile crashes and gunshots, and makes limitless sarcastic com-ments and put-downs of his classmates. Other students will not stand up to him, apparently fearing his size and verbal aggression. His teacher, Miss Pearl, has come to her wit's end. *Would Joshua's behavior be likely to improve if Nelsen, Lott, and Glenn's techniques were used in Miss Pearl's classroom? Explain.*

Case 4: Tom Is Hostile and Defiant ■ Tom has appeared to be in his usual foul mood ever since arriving in class. On his way to sharpen his pencil, he bumps into Frank, who complains. Tom tells him loudly to shut up. Miss Baines, the teacher, says, "Tom, go back to your seat." Tom wheels around, swears loudly, and says heatedly, "I'll go when I'm damned good and ready!" *How would Nelsen, Lott, and Glenn have Miss Baines deal with Tom?*

Questions and Activities

1. Each of the following exemplifies an important point in the Nelsen, Lott, and Glenn model of discipline. Identify the point illustrated by each.

   a. Miss Sterling, when Jacob interrupts her for the fifth time, says angrily, "Jacob, you go sit at the back table by yourself and stay there until you figure out how to act like a gentleman!"

   b. "If I catch you talking again during the class, you will have to stay an extra five minutes."

   c. "I am concerned about the lack of neatness in the work being turned in. I'd like to know your thoughts about neatness and what we might want to do, if anything, to improve."

   d. Teacher: "You are simply not working up to the standards I have for this class. You will need to put in more effort, or else I will have to increase the homework assignments."

2. Examine Scenarios 4 and 9 in Appendix A. How could *Positive Discipline in the Classroom* be used to improve behavior in (1) Mrs. Desmond's second grade? (2) Mr. Wong's American literature class?

3. For a grade level and/or subject you select, outline in one page what you would do if you wished to implement Nelsen, Lott, and Glenn's ideas in your classroom.

Primary References

Glenn, H., J. Nelsen, R. Duffy, L. Escobar, K. Ortolano, and D. Owen-Sohocki. 1996. *Positive discipline: A teacher's A–Z guide.* Rocklin, CA: Prima. Nonpunitive suggestions for dealing with over 100 typical classroom problem behaviors.

Nelsen, J. 1987. *Positive discipline.* New York: Ballantine. Revised edition 1996. Nelsen's basic book that explains the theory and application of positive discipline for parents and teachers.

Nelsen, J., L. Lott, and H. Glenn. 1993. *Positive discipline in the classroom.* Rocklin, CA: Prima. Revised editions 1997, 2000. Nelsen, Lott, and Glenn's basic book for helping teachers understand and apply positive discipline in their classrooms.

Recommended Reading and Viewing

Glenn, H. 1989. *Empowering others: Ten keys to affirming and validating people.* (Videotape). Fair Oaks, CA: Sunshine Press.

———. 1989. *Six steps to developing responsibility.* (Videotape). Orem, UT: Empowering People Productions. (1-800-456-7770).

———. 1989. *Teachers who make a difference.* (Videotape). Orem, UT: Empowering People Productions. (1-800-456-7770).

Glenn, H., and J. Nelsen. 1988. *Positive discipline video.* (Videotape) Fair Oaks, CA: Sunshine Press.

———. 1997. No more logical consequences—At least hardly ever! Focus on solutions. *Empowering People Catalog.* Winter/Spring, 8.

———. 1999. *Positive time-out: And over 50 ways to avoid power struggles in the home and the classroom.* Rocklin, CA: Prima.

Scott, B. 1997. *Positive discipline in the classroom.* (18-minute video featuring principal Bill Scott with teachers sharing why they like *Positive Discipline in the Classroom,* and students demonstrating the Eight Building Blocks for Effective Class Meetings.) Orem, UT: Empowering People Productions. (1-800-456-7770).

William Glasser's
Noncoercive Discipline

**PREVIEW OF
GLASSER'S
WORK**

Focus

■ Improving student satisfaction with school, which promotes
motivation and learning.
■ Teachers' reorienting themselves from boss teachers to lead
teachers.
■ Emphasizing quality in curriculum, teaching, and learning.

Logic

■ Most misbehavior occurs when students are bored or frustrated
by school expectations.
■ Students whose basic needs are being met show relatively little
misbehavior.
■ The most effective curriculum deals with what students consider
important in their lives.
■ The most effective teaching is done in a leading manner rather than a bossing manner.

William Glasser

Contributions

■ The concept and practice of classroom meetings as a regular part of the curriculum.
■ The focus on meeting students' basic needs as the key element in teaching and discipline.
■ The concepts and practices of quality curriculum, quality teaching, and quality learning.

Glasser's Suggestions

■ Do your best to meet students' needs for belonging, freedom, power, and fun.
■ Make quality the prime ingredient in all aspects of teaching, learning, and curriculum.
■ Work with students in the manner called "lead teaching," rather than "boss teaching."
■ Use nonpunitive, noncoercive techniques for motivating students to work and participate.

About William Glasser

William Glasser, a psychiatrist and educational consultant, has for many years written and spoken extensively on issues related to education and discipline. Born in
Cleveland, Ohio, in 1925, he was first trained as a chemical engineer but later turned

to psychology and then to psychiatry. He achieved national acclaim in psychiatry for the theories expressed in his book *Reality Therapy: A New Approach to Psychiatry* (1965), which shifted the focus in treating behavior problems from past events to present reality. Glasser later extended reality therapy to the school arena. His work with juvenile offenders convinced him that teachers could help students make better choices concerning how they behaved in school. He explained how to do so in his book *Schools without Failure* (1969), acclaimed as one of the century's most influential books in education. In 1986, Glasser published *Control Theory in the Classroom,* which gave a new and different emphasis to his contentions concerning discipline, as encapsulated in his pronouncement that if students are to continue working and behaving properly, they must "believe that if they do some work, they will be able to satisfy their needs enough so that it makes sense to keep working" (p. 15). Since the publication of that book, Glasser has emphasized the school's role in meeting basic needs as the primary means of encouraging participation and desirable behavior. This theme is furthered in his books *The Quality School: Managing Students without Coercion* (1998), *Choice Theory in the Classroom* (with Karen L. Dotson, 1998), and *The Quality School Teacher* (1998). Glasser's earlier work, prior to 1985, had great influence on subsequent thought and practice regarding discipline. That portion of his work was summarized in Chapter 2 and is briefly reviewed here. Major emphasis in this chapter is given to Glasser's more recent work. Glasser can be contacted through the William Glasser Institute, 22024 Lassen Street, Suite 118, Chatsworth, CA 91311; telephone 800-899-0688; 818-700-8000; fax 818-700-0555; e-mail wginst@earthlink.net; website www.wglasserinst.com

Glasser's Contributions to Discipline

Glasser has greatly influenced thought and practice in school discipline. He was the first to insist that students are in control of their behavior, that no unseen factors are forcing them to do this or that, and that they actually choose to behave as they do. He claimed that misbehavior was simply bad behavior choice, while good behavior was good behavior choice. He insisted, further, that teachers have the power and the obligation to help students make better behavioral choices, and he provided numerous suggestions about how to interact with students to help them succeed. He set forth the concept of **classroom meetings,** now universally acclaimed, in which teacher and students jointly discuss, and find solutions to, problems of behavior and other class matters. These contributions were all made in Glasser's earlier work.

Since 1985, Glasser has made many new contributions to thought and practice in discipline. His most revolutionary contention is that discipline depends upon meeting students' basic needs for belonging, freedom, fun, and power. In further developing that theme, he contributed the concepts of quality curriculum, quality learning, and quality teaching, maintaining that all of them are essential to good discipline.

Glasser's Central Focus

Prior to 1985, Glasser's main focus, as we have seen, was on helping students make good behavior choices that would lead to personal success in the classroom and elsewhere. That early work had great impact on school discipline and many of his ideas were incorporated into other systems of discipline. Since 1985, Glasser's views on discipline have changed markedly. Previously he depicted the school as a benevolent place that provides unbounded opportunities for students, and he placed responsibility on students for taking advantage of those opportunities. Now, given the fact that student effort has declined and behavior has steadily grown worse, Glasser has concluded that improvement in education and student behavior can only be accomplished by changing the way classrooms function. Consequently, his present work focuses on strategies that motivate students to participate willingly in the school program. He says this approach is essential because it is now evident that trying to force students to behave properly will not succeed.

Glasser also maintains that if schools are to survive, they must be redesigned to emphasize quality in all student work. They must no longer attempt to coerce students, a tactic that is clearly ineffective. Instead, they must lead students deeply into learning that addresses what is important in students' lives. Glasser therefore urges teachers to make sure that curricular activities satisfy students' **basic needs** for survival, belonging, power, fun, and freedom. Glasser has moved away from tactics he advocated in earlier work for confronting student misbehavior, feeling that if students cannot be enticed willingly into learning, it is fruitless to try to make them behave in an orderly manner. They will simply drop out of learning, figuratively if not literally.

Glasser's Principal Teachings

Prior to 1985

In 1969, Glasser published *Schools without Failure,* one of the most important education books of the Twentieth Century. There he put forth the contentions that students are rational beings in control of their behavior, and therefore choose to act as they do. Good choices equal good behavior, while bad choices equal bad behavior. In school, teachers should continually help students make good choices. Teachers who do so, showing they really care about their students, accept no student excuses for bad behavior. Instead, they help offending students make better choices. This is done by seeing to it that reasonable consequences always follow student behavior, good or bad. When students choose to behave properly, they should be acknowledged for doing so. When they choose to misbehave, they should suffer reasonable consequences. In order for this plan to work, it is necessary that every class have a workable list of rules to govern behavior and that those rules be consistently enforced. Teachers should involve students in formulating rules and consequences, but it is the teacher's responsibility to enforce compliance with the rules. The best place for discussing behavior, class rules, and consequences is in the classroom meeting. These are meetings of the entire class, conducted regularly with teacher and students sitting together in a closed circle, an arrangement that has come to be known as the *Glasser circle*. In classroom meetings one never finds fault or assigns blame, but only seeks to establish agreements or find solutions to problems that concern the class.

Since 1985

In 1986, Glasser published *Control Theory in the Classroom*, in which he set forth a new vision of what is needed to correct learning and behavior problems in school. Since that time his contentions have been as follows:

- *All of our behavior is our best attempt to control ourselves to meet five basic needs: survival, belonging, power, fun, and freedom.* The school experience is intimately associated with all but survival, and not infrequently with survival as well.
- *Students feel pleasure when their basic needs are met and frustration when they are not.* Students are usually contented and well-behaved when their needs are being met, but discontented and often misbehaving when their needs are not being met.
- *At least half of today's students will not commit themselves to learning if they find their school experience boring, frustrating, or otherwise dissatisfying.* Furthermore, there is no way that teachers can make students commit to learning, though they can usually force compliance temporarily.
- *Few students in today's schools do their best work.* The overwhelming majority is apathetic about schoolwork. Many students do no schoolwork at all.
- *Today's schools must create quality conditions in which fewer students and teachers are frustrated.* Students must feel they belong, enjoy a certain amount of power, have some fun in learning, and experience a sense of freedom in the process.
- *What schools require is a new commitment to quality education.* Quality education occurs where students are encouraged, supported, and helped by the teacher, traits of a quality school.
- *The school curriculum should be limited to learnings that have usefulness or other relevance in students' lives.* This usefulness or relevance is the hallmark of quality curriculum, which is delivered through activities that attract student interest, involve students actively, provide enjoyment, and lead to meaningful accomplishments.
- *Students should be allowed to acquire in-depth information about topics they recognize as being useful or relevant in their lives.* This increases the likelihood of quality learning.
- *Students show that quality learning has occurred when able to demonstrate or explain how, why, and where their learnings are valuable.* The opportunity for making such explanations should be made a part of daily classroom activities.

- *Teachers, instead of scolding, coercing, or punishing, should try to befriend their students, provide encouragement and stimulation, and show an unending willingness to help.* Their ability to do so is a mark of quality teaching.
- *Teachers who dictate procedures, order students to work, and berate them when they do not, are increasingly ineffective with today's students.* They are "boss teachers."
- *Teachers who provide a stimulating learning environment, encourage students, and help them as much as possible are most effective with today's learners.* They are "lead teachers."

Analysis of Glasser's *Noncoercive Discipline*

What School Offers

In his earlier views on discipline, Glasser contended that school offered students an excellent opportunity to encounter success and be recognized. Indeed, he said, for many students school afforded the only real possibility for meeting those needs. Success in school produced a sense of self-worth and an ability to cope, which reduces the likelihood of deviant behavior. The road to this self-identity begins with good relationships with people who care. For students who come from atrocious backgrounds, school may be the only place where they will find adults who are genuinely interested in their well-being.

In most ways, what Glasser said about schools in 1969 is true today. They remain one of the few places where a great many students can associate with successful adults who care about their future. But since 1985 Glasser has moved his focus to a new arena. He remains concerned about student behavior in the classroom, but has seen the futility of attempting to force students to behave against their will. For example, when a student is not paying attention because the lesson is boring, it is a losing battle to try to force the student's attention. On the other hand, when lessons are interesting, students pay attention naturally and don't have to be continually cajoled. Recognizing this fact, Glasser has moved away from tactics for correcting misbehavior, and has focused instead on what he calls **quality education**, which entices students to engage willingly in the curriculum with little misbehavior. Glasser's new perspective has developed out of his realization that the majority of students today are content to do low-quality schoolwork or even none at all. It was his conclusion that "No more than half of our secondary school students are willing to make an effort to learn, and therefore cannot be taught" (1986, p. 3) and that "...no more than 15 percent of high school students do quality work" (1990, p. 5). He concluded that, in light of student apathy, we have gotten about as much as we can out of the traditional secondary school. His solution to the problem is to offer instruction in a different manner—one in which a substantial majority of students willingly do high-quality schoolwork. Nothing less, he says, will suffice.

Glasser has spent the last decade refining how the quality learning he envisions can be accomplished. What must be done, he says, is to provide instruction, support, and other conditions in the classroom that meet students' basic needs. This requires only modest changes in curricula, materials, and physical facilities but a significant change in the way teachers work with students. Glasser says effective teaching is the hardest job in the world. He expresses sympathy for beleaguered secondary teachers who yearn to work with dedicated, high-achieving students but are continually frustrated by the majority who make little effort to learn. Those teachers report that their main discipline problems are not defiance or disruption but, rather, students' overwhelming apathy, resignation, and unwillingness to participate in class activities or assignments. Students, for their part, tell Glasser that the problem with schoolwork is not its difficulty; the problem is that it is too boring. For Glasser, this is another way of saying that schoolwork does not meet students' psychological needs. He has a remedy for this problem, which he puts forth in three fundamental propositions:

1. The school curriculum must be organized to meet **students' needs** for survival, belonging, power, fun, and freedom.
2. **Quality schoolwork** and **self-evaluation** (of quality) by students must replace the fragmented and boring requirements on which students are typically tested and evaluated.
3. Teachers must abandon traditional teaching practices and move toward **quality teaching.** Let us examine what Glasser means by these three points.

Students' Needs

All human beings have genetic needs for

- **Survival** (food, shelter, freedom from harm)
- **Belonging** (security, comfort, legitimate membership in the group)
- **Power** (sense of importance, of stature, of being considered by others)
- **Fun** (having a good time, emotionally and intellectually)
- **Freedom** (exercise of choice, self-direction, and responsibility)

Glasser is adamant that education which does not give priority to these needs is bound to fail. Teachers do not have to be psychologists in order to meet students' needs. Glasser points out that students sense **belonging** when they are involved in class matters, receive attention from the teacher and others, and are brought into discussions of matters that concern the class. Students sense **power** when the teacher asks them to participate in decisions about topics to be studied and procedures for working in the class. A sense of power also comes from being assigned responsibility for class duties, such as helping take attendance, caring for class animals, helping distribute and take care of materials, being in charge of audiovisual equipment, and so forth. Students experience **fun** when they are able to work and talk with others, engage in interesting activities, and share their accomplishments. And they sense **freedom** when the teacher allows them to make responsible choices concerning what they will study, how they will do so, and how they will demonstrate their accomplishments. Glasser frequently mentions the value of cooperative learning groups and **learning teams** in helping students meet their basic needs (Glasser and Dotson, 1998).

Curriculum and Quality Work

Glasser finds much fault with the present school curriculum, the way it is presented, and how student learning is evaluated. He claims that present-day education consists too much of memorizing facts irrelevant to students' lives, and that its quality is judged by how many fragments of information students can retain long enough to be measured on standardized achievement tests. Students agree. Glasser says school should be a place where students learn useful information and learn it well. To make that possible, a **quality curriculum** is necessary. The old curriculum should be revised so that it consists only of learnings that students find enjoyable and useful; the rest should be discarded as "nonsense" (Glasser 1992). When teachers introduce new segments of learning, they should hold discussions with students and, if the students are old enough, ask them to identify what they would like to explore in depth. Adequate time should then be spent so that the topics they identify can be learned well. Learning a smaller number of topics very well is always preferable to learning many topics superficially, says Glasser. Indeed, quality learning requires depth of understanding together with a good grasp of its usefulness. Evaluation of learning should call upon students to explain why the material they have learned is valuable and how and where it can be used. When a quality curriculum is provided, it is reasonable to ask students regularly to assess the quality of their own efforts as well.

Quality Teaching

Even teachers who are committed intellectually to quality teaching may find it difficult to identify the needed changes and put them into effect. It is not easy to change one's teaching style, but Glasser (1993, p. 22ff) says it can be done by striving for the following, which lead toward **quality teaching** and **quality learning**.

1. *Provide a warm, supportive classroom climate.* This is done by helping students know and like you. Use natural occasions over time to tell students who you are, what you stand for, what you will ask them to do, what you will not ask them to do, what you will do for them, and what you will not do for them. Show that you are always willing to help.

2. *Ask students to do only work that is useful.* **Useful work** consists of skills, as distinct from information, that students see as valuable in their lives. At times, teachers may have to point out the value of new skills, but that value must become quickly apparent to students before they will make a sustained effort to learn. Students should be required to memorize no information except that which is essential to the skill being learned. However, information should be taught and learned provided it meets one or more of the following criteria (1993, p. 48):

   - The information is directly related to an important skill.
   - The information is something that students express a desire to learn.
   - The information is something the teacher believes especially useful.
   - The information is required for college entrance exams.

3. *Always ask students to do the best they can.* Quality work by students must be nurtured slowly. Glasser (1998a) suggests that a focus on quality can be initiated as follows:

- Discuss quality work enough so that students understand what you mean.
- Begin with an assignment that is clearly important enough to do well.
- Ask students to do their best work on the assignment; do not grade it, because grades suggest to students that the work is finished. Then,

4. *Ask students to evaluate work they have done and improve it.* Quality comes from improvements that result from continued effort. Glasser suggests that when students have done a piece of work on a topic they consider important, the teacher should help them make **value judgments** about it, as follows:

- Ask students how they think they might improve their work further.
- Ask students to explain why they feel their work has high quality. As students see the value of improving their work, higher quality will result naturally.
- Progressively help students begin to use **SIR,** a process of self-evaluation, improvement, and repetition, until quality is achieved.

5. *Help students see that quality work makes them feel good.* This effect will occur naturally as students learn to do quality work. As Glasser (1993) says,

> There is no better human feeling than that which comes from the satisfaction of doing something useful that you believe is the very best you can do and finding that others agree. As students begin to sense this feeling, they will want more of it. (p. 25)

6. *Help students see that quality work is never destructive to oneself, others, or the environment.* Teachers should help students realize that it is not possible to achieve the good feeling of quality work by harming people, property, the environment, or other creatures.

Boss Teachers and Lead Teachers

Glasser has much to say about the style of teaching required for quality education. In order to attain the quality Glasser advocates, teachers must move away from what he calls *boss teaching* and toward what he calls *lead teaching.* Teachers typically function as bosses, Glasser contends, because they do not realize that motivation cannot be furnished to students but must come from within. **Boss teachers,** as Glasser describes them, do the following:

- Set the tasks and standards for student learning.
- Talk rather than demonstrate and rarely ask for student input.
- Grade the work without involving students in the evaluation.
- Use coercion when students resist.

To illustrate how a boss teacher functions, consider the example of Mr. Márquez, who introduces his unit of study on South American geography in the following way:

> Class, today we are going to begin our study of the geography of South America. You will be expected to do the following things:
>
> 1. Learn the names of the South American countries.
> 2. Locate those countries on a blank map.
> 3. Describe the types of terrain typical of each country.
> 4. Name two products associated with each country.
> 5. Describe the population of each country in terms of ethnic origin and economic well-being.
> 6. Name and locate the three most important rivers in each country.
>
> We will learn this information from our textbooks and encyclopedias. You will have two tests, one at....

Mr. Márquez's boss approach limits both productivity and quality of work. It is unlikely that students will pursue the work eagerly and most will do only enough, and only well enough, to get by.

Glasser would have teachers forgo Mr. Márquez's style and function not as boss teachers but as **lead teachers.** Lead teachers realize that genuine motivation to learn must arise within students and will arise from their needs and interests. They also realize that their task in teaching is to use any tactic they can to help students learn. Glasser says teachers should spend most of their time on two things: organizing interesting activities and providing assistance to students. Such lead teachers would do the following:

- Discuss the curriculum with the class in such a way that many topics of interest are identified.
- Encourage students to identify topics they would like to explore in depth.
- Discuss with students the nature of the schoolwork that might ensue, emphasizing quality and asking for input on criteria of quality.
- Explore with students resources that might be needed for quality work and the amount of time such work might require.
- Demonstrate ways in which the work can be done, using models that reflect quality.
- Emphasize the importance of students' continually inspecting and evaluating their own work in terms of quality.
- Make evident to students that everything possible will be done to provide them with good tools and a good workplace that is noncoercive and nonadversarial.

To illustrate how lead teaching might proceed, consider the example of Mr. Garcia's introduction to a unit of study on the geography of South America.

> Class, have any of you ever lived in South America? You did, Samuel? Which country? Peru? Fantastic! What an interesting country! I used to live in Brazil. I traveled in the Amazon quite a bit and spent some time with jungle Indians. Supposedly they were headhunters at one time. But not now. At least so they say. Tomorrow I'll show you a bow and arrow I brought from that tribe. Samuel, did you ever eat monkey when you were in Peru? I think Peru and Brazil are very alike in some ways but very different in others. What was Peru like compared to here? Did you get up into the Andes? They have fabulous ruins all over Peru, I hear, and

those fantastic Chariots of the Gods lines and drawings on the landscape. Do you have any photographs or slides you could bring for us to see? What a resource you could be for us! You could teach us a lot!

Class, Samuel lived in Peru and traveled in the Andes. If we could get him to teach us about that country, what do you think you would most like to learn? (The class discusses this option and identifies topics.)

We have the opportunity in our class to learn a great deal about South America, its mountains and grasslands, its dense rain forests and huge rivers, and its interesting people and strange animals. Did you know there are groups of English, Welsh, Italians, and Germans living in many parts of South America, especially in Argentina? Did you know there are still thought to be tribes of Indians in the jungles that have no contact with the outside world? Did you know that almost half of all the river water in the world is in the Amazon basin, and that in some places the Amazon River is so wide that from the middle you can't see either shore?

Speaking of the Amazon, I swam in a lake there that contained piranhas, and look, I still have my legs and arms. Surprised about that? If you wanted to learn more about living in the Amazon jungle, what would you be interested in knowing? (Discussion ensues.)

How about people of the high Andes? Those Incas, for example, who in some mysterious way cut and placed enormous boulders into gigantic, perfectly fitting fortress walls? Samuel knows about them. The Incas were very civilized and powerful, with an empire that stretched for three thousand miles. Yet they were conquered by a few Spaniards on horseback. How in the world could that have happened? If you could learn more about those amazing people, what would you like to know? (Discussion continues in this manner. Students identify topics about which they would be willing to make an effort to learn.) Now let me see what you think of this idea: I have written down the topics you said you were interested in, and I can help you with resources and materials. I have lots of my own, including slides, South American music, and many artifacts I have collected. I know two other people who lived in Argentina and Colombia that we could invite to talk with us. We can concentrate on what you have said you would like to learn about. But if we decide to do so, I want to see if we can make this deal: We explore what interests you; I help you all I can; and you, for your part, agree to do the best work you are capable of. We would need to discuss that to get some ideas of what you might do that would show the quality of your learning. In addition, I hope I can persuade each of you regularly to evaluate yourselves as to how well you believe you are doing. Understand, this would not be me evaluating you, it would be you evaluating yourself—not for a grade but for you to decide what you are doing very well and what you think you might be able to do better. What do you think of that idea? Want to give it a try?

The Relation of Quality Teaching to Discipline

Glasser believes that teachers who learn to function as leaders of quality classrooms avoid the trap of becoming adversaries of their students, a trap that destroys incentive for students to learn as well as pleasure in teaching. When teachers stay out of that trap, they not only foster quality learning but at the same time reduce discipline problems to a minimum.

Glasser acknowledges that no approach can eliminate all behavior problems. He urges teachers to work with students to establish standards of conduct in the classroom. Toward that end, he makes the following suggestions: Begin with a discussion of the importance of quality work, which is to be given priority in the class, and explain that you will do everything possible to help students learn and enjoy themselves without forcing them. That discussion should lead naturally to asking students about class rules they believe will help them get their work done and truly help them learn. Glasser says that if teachers can get students to see the importance of courtesy, no other rules may be necessary. Teachers should also solicit student advice on what should happen when rules are broken. Glasser says students will suggest punishment, though they know punishment is not effective. If asked further, they will agree that behavior problems are best solved by looking for ways to remedy whatever is causing the rule to be broken. Glasser urges teachers to ask, "What could I do to help?" and to hold classroom meetings to explore alternatives to inappropriate behavior. Once the rules and consequences are agreed to, they should be written down. All students sign, attesting that they understand the rules and that, if they break those rules, they will try—with the teacher's help—to correct the underlying problem. Rules established and dealt with in this way, says Glasser, show that the teacher's main concern lies in quality, not power, and that the teacher recognizes that power struggles are the main enemy of quality education.

When Rules Are Broken

Glasser reminds teachers that, when class rules are broken, their interventions should be nonpunitive acts that stop the misbehavior and get the student's mind back on class work. Suppose that Jonathan has come into the room obviously upset. As the lesson begins, he turns heatedly and throws something at Michael. Glasser would suggest that the teacher do the following:

> *Teacher:* It looks like you have a problem, Jonathan. How can I help you solve it? [Jonathan frowns, still obviously upset.]

> *Teacher:* If you will calm down, I will discuss it with you in a little while. I think we can work something out.

Glasser says you should make it clear that you are unable to help Jonathan unless he calms down. You say this without emotion in your voice, recognizing that your anger will only put Jonathan on the defensive. If Jonathan doesn't calm down, there is no good way to deal with the problem. Glasser (1990) says to allow him 20 seconds, and if he isn't calm by then, admit that there is no way to solve the problem at that time. Give Jonathan time out from the lesson, but don't threaten or warn him. Say something like the following: "Jonathan, I want to help you work this out. I am not interested in punishing you. Whatever the problem is, let's solve it. But for now you must go sit at the table. When you are calm, come back to your seat." Later, at an opportune time, discuss the situation with Jonathan, approximately as follows:

> *Teacher:* What were you doing when the problem started? Was it against the rules? Can we work things out so it won't happen again? What could you and I do to keep it from happening?

If the problem involves hostilities between Jonathan and Michael, the discussion should involve both boys and proceed along these lines:

> *Teacher:* What were you doing, Jonathan? What were you doing, Michael? How can the three of us work things out so this won't happen anymore?

It is important to note that no blame is assigned to either Jonathan or Michael. No time is spent trying to find out whose fault it was. You remind the boys that all you are looking for is a solution so that the problem won't occur again. Glasser contends that if you treat Jonathan and Michael with respect and courtesy, if you show you don't want to punish them or throw your weight around, and if you talk to them as a problem solver, both their classroom behavior and the quality of their work will gradually improve.

Strengths of Glasser's *Noncoercive Discipline*

Glasser has provided a great service by pointing out that schools traditionally expect students to do boring work while sitting and waiting, which goes strongly against students' nature. He asks teachers to consider that expecting students to do boring work in school "is like asking someone who is sitting on a hot stove to sit still and stop complaining" (1986, p. 53) and that "Teachers should not depend on any discipline program that demands that they do something to or for students to get them to stop behaving badly in unsatisfying classes. Only a discipline program that is also concerned with classroom satisfaction will work." (1986, p. 56)

Glasser has also given us much to think about regarding quality in teaching and learning. He has shown how teachers can function more effectively as lead teachers who provide great support and encouragement but do not coerce, intimidate, or punish. In so doing, they meet students' needs sufficiently that students stay in school and do better quality work. Glasser maintains that if schools and classes are conducted in keeping with his quality concept, discipline problems will be few and relatively easily resolved.

Glasser's approach does not have to be taken as a total system and set into place lock, stock, and barrel. His suggestions for teachers' acting as problem solvers without arguing or punishing should be seriously considered by all teachers. His procedures for increasing quality in teaching and learning can be put into practice, thus allowing teachers to evaluate for themselves the effect on classroom climate and morale. Glasser's suggestions, though they take time to implement, help bring about what all teachers desire—for their students to learn well and enjoy school while becoming more self-directing and responsible.

Initiating Glasser's *Noncoercive Discipline*

Suppose you find Glasser's current views on schooling and discipline persuasive and want to use them in your classroom. How do you go about putting them into practice? The general framework suggested by Glasser for moving toward quality teaching was presented earlier in the chapter. You would begin with class discussions about how students think school could be made more interesting. In doing so, you would go into the following:

- Involve students in discussions about topics to be pursued, ways of working, procedures for reporting or demonstrating accomplishment, establishment of class rules, and decisions about steps to be taken when misbehavior occurs. You would offer your opinions but give serious attention to student suggestions as well.
- Make plain to students that you will try to arrange activities they might have suggested and that you will do all in your power to help them learn and succeed.

Meanwhile, you would also take the following steps:

- Learn how to function as a lead teacher rather than a boss teacher. (The scenario given earlier showing Mr. Garcia's introduction of his unit on South America illustrates lead teaching.)
- Hold regular class meetings to discuss curriculum, procedures, behavior, and other educational topics. These meetings should always be conducted with an eye to improving learning conditions for students, never as a venue for finding fault, blaming, or criticizing.
- When students misbehave, discuss their behavior and why it was inappropriate for the class. Ask them what they feel you could do in order to be more helpful to them. If the misbehavior is serious or chronic, talk with the involved student privately at an appropriate time.

Review of Selected Terminology

The following terms are central to Glasser's suggestions regarding education, teaching, learning, and discipline. Check yourself for understanding:

Student: behavior as choice, responsibility, excuses, self-evaluation, useful work, value judgments

Basic needs: survival, belonging, power, fun, freedom

Quality: education, curriculum, learning, schoolwork, teaching, SIR

Types of teachers: boss teacher, lead teacher

Class: rules, meetings

■Application Exercises

Concept Cases

Case 1: Kristina Will Not Work ■ Kristina, a student in Mr. Jake's class, is quite docile. She socializes little with other students and never disrupts class. However, despite Mr. Jake's best efforts, Kristina never does her work. She rarely completes an assignment. She is simply there, putting forth no effort. *How would Glasser deal with Kristina?*

Glasser would first suggest that Mr. Jake think carefully about the classroom and the program to try to determine whether they contain obstacles that prevent Kristina from meeting her needs for belonging, power, fun, and freedom. He would then have Mr. Jake discuss the matter with Kristina, not blaming her but noting the problem of nonproductivity and asking what the problem is and what he might be able to do to help. In that discussion, Mr. Jake might ask Kristina questions such as the following:

1. You have a problem with this work, don't you? Is there anything I can do to help you with it?
2. Is there anything I could do to make the class more interesting for you?
3. Is there anything in this class that you especially enjoy doing?
4. Do you think that, for a while, you might like to do only those things?
5. Is there anything we have discussed in class that you would like to learn very, very well?
6. How could I help you do that?
7. What could I do differently that would help you want to learn?

Glasser would not want Mr. Jake to punish Kristina or use a disapproving tone of voice, but every day to make a point of talking with her in a friendly and courteous way about nonschool matters such as trips, pets, and movies. He would do this casually, showing he is interested in her and willing to be her friend. Glasser would remind Mr. Jake that there is no magic formula for success with all students. Mr. Jake can only encourage and support Kristina. Scolding and coercion are likely to make matters worse, but as Mr. Jake befriends Kristina she is likely to begin to do more work and of better quality.

Case 2: Sara Cannot Stop Talking ■ Sara is a pleasant girl who participates in class activities and does most, though not all, of her assigned work. She cannot seem to refrain from talking to classmates, however. Her teacher, Mr. Gonzales, has to speak to her repeatedly during lessons, to the point that he often becomes exasperated and loses his temper. *What suggestions would Glasser give Mr. Gonzales for dealing with Sara?*

Case 3: Joshua Clowns and Intimidates ■ Joshua, larger and louder than his classmates, always wants to be the center of attention, which he accomplishes through a combination of clowning and intimidation. He makes wise remarks, talks back (smilingly) to the teacher, utters a variety of sound-effect noises such as automobile crashes and gunshots, and makes limitless sarcastic comments and put-downs of his classmates. Other students will not stand up to him, apparently fearing his size and verbal aggression. His teacher, Miss Pearl, has come to her wit's end. *How do you think Glasser would have Miss Pearl deal with Joshua?*

Case 4: Tom Is Hostile and Defiant ■ Tom has appeared to be in his usual foul mood ever since arriving in class. On his way to sharpen his pencil, he bumps into Frank, who complains. Tom tells him loudly to shut up. Miss Baines, the teacher, says, "Tom, go back to your seat." Tom wheels around, swears loudly, and says heatedly, "I'll go when I'm damned good and ready!" *How would Glasser have Miss Baines deal with Tom?*

■Questions and Activities

1. Select a grade level and/or subject you enjoy teaching. Outline what you would consider and do, along the lines of Glasser's suggestions, concerning the following:

a. Organizing the classroom, class, curriculum, and activities to better meet your students' needs for belonging, fun, power, and freedom

b. Your continual efforts to help students improve the quality of their work.

2. Do a comparative analysis of Glasser's system with that of either the Canters, Jones, Albert, Gordon, or Nelsen, Lott, and Glenn. Explain your conclusions concerning the following:

a. Effectiveness in suppressing inappropriate behavior

b. Effectiveness in improving long-term behavior

c. Ease of implementation

d. Effect on student self-concept

e. Effect on bonds of trust between teacher and student

f. The degree to which each model accurately depicts realities of student attitude and behavior.

3. Examine Scenario 9 or 10 in Appendix A. What advice would Glasser give Mr. Wong or Miss Thorpe to help improve learning conditions in the classroom?

Primary References

Glasser, W. 1969. *Schools without failure.* New York: Harper & Row. Glasser's monumental book that broke new ground on several fronts, including the damaging effects of failure, student behavior as conscious choice, and classroom meetings, all powerful concepts that still exert great influence on education.

———. 1977. 10 steps to good discipline. *Today's Education, 66,* 60–63. An article that briefly outlines Glasser's earlier notions about discipline and how it should be applied in the classroom.

———. 1978. Disorders in our schools. Causes and remedies. *Phi Delta Kappan, 59,* 331–333. A short article that explains how to correct classroom disorder through helping students make better behavior decisions.

———. 1986. *Control theory in the classroom.* New York: Harper & Row. A book that marks Glasser's change of view concerning discipline, in which he contends that every person's behavior represents their attempts to control

events to meet their needs for survival, belonging, fun, power, and freedom, and that if we are to reverse the downward trend in quality of education, we must adjust instruction and treatment of students to attend to those primary needs.

———. 1992. The quality school curriculum. *Phi Delta Kappan, 73*(9), 690–694. An article describing what the school curriculum should be if we are truly to achieve high quality learning.

———. 1998a. *The quality school: Managing students without coercion.* New York: Harper & Row. First edition 1990. Revised editions 1992, 1998a. A series of revisions that show progressive refinement in Glasser's suggestions for making quality the main goal of student achievement and how that goal is to be attained.

———. 1998b. *The quality school teacher.* New York: HarperCollins. Glasser's progressive ideas on how teachers should work with students when quality is their primary goal.

Recommended Readings

Glasser, W. 1965. *Reality therapy: A new approach to psychiatry.* New York: Harper and Row.

———. 1996. Then and now. The theory of choice. *Learning, 25*(3), 20–22.

Glasser, W., and K. Dotson. 1998. *Choice theory in the classroom.* New York: HarperCollins.

Richard Curwin and Allen Mendler's *Discipline with Dignity*

PREVIEW OF
CURWIN
AND
MENDLER'S
*DISCIPLINE
WITH
DIGNITY*

Focus

■ Establishing classroom discipline upon a basis of dignity and hope.
■ Reclaiming students destined to fail in school because of their misbehavior.
■ Finding long term solutions to problems of misbehavior, including violence.

Richard Curwin

Logic

■ By solving misbehavior problems, we can save students who otherwise fail in school.
■ Many students misbehave when their sense of personal dignity is threatened.
■ It is essential to restore a sense of hope in students who chronically misbehave.
■ Violence and aggression, which teachers fear, can be dealt with effectively.

Contributions

■ The concept of student dignity as the cornerstone of effective classroom discipline.
■ The understanding that most chronically misbehaving students have no sense of hope.
■ A systematic approach to discipline based on preserving dignity and restoring hope.
■ Concrete suggestions for dealing with violence, hostility, and aggression.

Allen Mendler

Curwin and Mendler's Suggestions

■ Recognize that helping students learn to behave acceptably is an integral part of teaching.
■ In all circumstances, interact with students in a manner that preserves their dignity.
■ Do all you can to reinstill hope of success in students who chronically misbehave.
■ Make sure that the discipline techniques you use never interfere with motivation to learn.

About Richard Curwin and Allen Mendler

Richard Curwin, born in 1944, began his teaching career in a seventh-grade class of boys whose behavior was seriously out of control. This experience led him to a career specialization in school discipline, first as a classroom teacher and later as a university professor and private consultant and writer. He earned a doctorate in education from the University of Massachusetts in 1972. Allen Mendler, born in 1949, earned a doctorate in psychology at Union Institute in 1981. His career has been devoted to serving as school psychologist and psychoeducational consultant. He has worked extensively with students and teachers at all levels.

Curwin and Mendler attracted national attention through their 1983 book, *Taking Charge in the Classroom.* They revised and republished that work in 1988 with the title *Discipline with Dignity,* which more accurately reflects the central concept of their approach. In 1992 Curwin published *Rediscovering Hope: Our Greatest Teaching Strategy,* a book devoted to helping teachers improve the behavior of difficult-to-control students who are otherwise likely to fail in school. In 1997 Curwin and Mendler published *As Tough as Necessary: Countering Violence, Aggression, and Hostility in Our Schools,* in which they provide suggestions for working with hostile, aggressive students. Curwin and Mendler regularly conduct training seminars in a wide variety of locations. They can be contacted through Discipline Associates, P.O. Box 20481, Rochester, NY 14602; telephone 800-772-5227, or through their website www.disciplineassociates.com

Curwin and Mendler's Contributions to Discipline

Curwin and Mendler's major contributions to school discipline have been (1) strategies for improving classroom behavior through maximizing student dignity and hope, and (2) strategies for interacting effectively with students who are hostile, aggressive, or violent. Their ideas have been especially useful to teachers who work with chronically misbehaving students. Those students—about five percent of the student population, Curwin and Mendler say—are the ones who disrupt instruction, interfere with learning, and make life miserable for teachers. Described by Curwin and Mendler as "without hope," such students deal misery to teachers and will almost certainly fail unless treated with special consideration and care. Curwin and Mendler explain what without-hope students need if they are to have a chance for success in school, and they provide strategies to help teachers reclaim those students.

Curwin and Mendler's Central Focus

The central focus of Curwin and Mendler's work is on helping all students have a better opportunity for success in school through building a sense of dignity and providing a sense of hope. They describe techniques that, in a dignified manner, encourage students to behave acceptably in school, and they provide a number of explicit suggestions for interacting productively with students, motivating them, ensuring success, and developing responsible behavior. In recent years they have given strong attention to working with students whose behavior is hostile and aggressive.

Curwin and Mendler's Principal Teachings

- *The number of students whose chronic classroom misbehavior puts them in imminent danger of failing in school is on the increase.* These students are referred to as behaviorally at risk.
- *Most of these chronically misbehaving students have lost all hope of encountering anything worthwhile in school.* A crucial responsibility of teachers is to help those students believe that school can be of benefit and that they have some control over their lives.
- *Students do all they can to prevent damage to their dignity, that is, to their sense of self-worth.* Students' attempts to protect themselves against such damage frequently transgress class rules and are justifiably considered misbehavior.
- *Five underlying principles of effective discipline should always be kept in mind.* Those principles are that (1) discipline is a very important part of teaching, (2) short-term solutions are rarely effective, (3) students must always be treated with dignity, (4) discipline must not interfere with motivation to learn, and (5) responsibility is more important than obedience.
- *Responsibility, not obedience, is the goal of discipline.* Responsibility, which involves making enlightened decisions, almost always produces better long-term behavior changes than does obedience to teacher demands.
- *Consequences, which are preplanned results that are invoked when class rules are broken, are necessary in discipline.* Consequences are best when planned by teacher and students working together.
- *Wise teachers de-escalate potential confrontations by actively listening to the student, using I-messages, and keeping the discussion private.* What is wrong with most confrontations between teacher and student is that both try to "win" the argument. The resulting struggle often escalates to a more serious level.
- *The behavior of difficult-to-manage students can be improved by providing interesting lessons on topics of personal relevance that permit active involvement and lead to competencies students value.* Students who are very difficult to manage usually have little or no motivation to learn what is ordinarily taught in school, and they have little compassion or concern for others.

Analysis of Curwin and Mendler's *Discipline with Dignity*

Why Students Misbehave

All students misbehave at times. They talk without permission, call each other sarcastic names, and laugh when they shouldn't. Some do this out of boredom, some because they find certain misbehaviors (such as talking) irresistible. Some break rules simply for expedience's sake. These kinds of misbehavior are relatively benign. They irritate teachers, but do not place students in danger of failing. In contrast, other students who are behaviorally at risk break rules for more malicious reasons, such as "gaining a measure of control over a system that has damaged their sense of dignity" (Curwin 1992, p. 49). They exert their control by refusing to comply with teacher requests, arguing and talking back to the teacher, tapping pencils and dropping books, withdrawing from class activities, and increasingly through overt acts of hostility and aggression. These students have found they can't be good at learning but can be very good at being bad and, by doing so, can meet their needs for attention and power. Although such students are relatively few in number, they are not isolated. They find others like themselves with whom to bond, which motivates further misbehavior.

Dignity

Dignity refers to respect for life and for oneself. It has long been at the center of Curwin and Mendler's approach to discipline. In their book *Discipline with Dignity* (1988a), they point out that students with chronic behavior problems see themselves as losers and have stopped trying to gain acceptance in normal ways. In order to maintain a sense of dignity, they tell themselves it is better to stop trying than to keep on failing, and that it is better to be recognized as a troublemaker than to be seen as stupid.

The importance of this sense of dignity can hardly be overstated. Students try to protect their dignity at all costs, even with their lives when pushed hard enough (Curwin and Mendler 1988a). Teachers must take pains, therefore, to keep dignity intact and bolster it when possible. Curwin (1992) advises:

> We must…welcome high risk students as human beings. They come to school as whole people, not simply as brains waiting to be trained. Our assumptions about their social behavior need to include the understanding that their negative behaviors are based on protection and escape. They do the best they can with the skills they have under the adverse conditions they face…. When they are malicious, they believe, rightly or wrongly, that they are justified in defending themselves from attacks on their dignity. (p. 27)

It is very difficult for most teachers to remain understanding and helpful when students behave callously toward them. A steady diet of defiant hostility makes many teachers become cynical and give up trying to help students. Many leave teaching because they don't feel its rewards are commensurate with the turmoil they must endure.

Students Who Are Behaviorally At-Risk

Behaviorally at-risk is a label given to students whose behavior prevents their learning and puts them in serious danger of failing in school. Like most labels, *at-risk* is often misinterpreted and misapplied—while helpful for communication it provides no guidance for remediating their behavior. Curwin and Mendler therefore make plain that they use the term to refer solely to behavior, not to the nature of the student: "It is what students do under the conditions they are in, not who they are, that puts them at risk" (Curwin 1992, p. xiii).

The students Curwin and Mendler refer to are those whom teachers consider to be out of control—students often referred to as lazy, turned off, angry, hostile, irresponsible, disruptive, or withdrawn. They are commonly said to have "attitude problems." They make little effort to learn, disregard teacher requests and directions, and provoke trouble in the classroom. Because they behave in these ways, they are unlikely to be successful in school. Curwin and Mendler (1992) describe them as follows:

- They are failing
- They have received, and do not respond to, most of the punishments and/or consequences offered by the school.
- They have low self-concepts in relation to school.
- They have little or no hope of finding success in school.
- They associate with and are reinforced by similar students.

The number of behaviorally at-risk students is increasing steadily. Many can see no role for themselves in the mainstream. Increasingly, they experience depression and contemplate suicide, which accounts for almost one quarter of all adolescent deaths (Curwin 1992). Students without hope do not care how they behave in the classroom. It does not worry them if they fail, bother the teacher, or disrupt the class.

Why Behaviorally At-Risk Students Are Difficult to Control

Behaviorally at-risk students are difficult to control for several reasons. They usually, though not always, have a history of academic failure. Unable to maintain dignity through achievement, they protect themselves by withdrawing or acting as if they don't care. They have learned that it feels better to misbehave than to follow rules that provide no payoff. Curwin (1992) illustrates this point.

> Ask yourself, if you got a 56 on an important test, what would make you feel better about failing? Telling your friends, "I studied hard and was just too stupid to pass." Or, "It was a stupid test anyway, and besides I hate that dumb class and that boring teacher." (p. 49)

When students' dignity has been repeatedly damaged in school, it makes them feel good to lash back at others. As they continue to misbehave, they find themselves systematically removed from opportunities to act responsibly. When they break rules, they are made to sit by themselves in isolation. When they fight, they are told to apologize and shake hands. In such cases they are taken out of the very situations in which they might learn to behave responsibly. Curwin (1992) makes the point as follows:

> No one would tell a batter who was struggling at the plate that he could not participate in batting practice until he improved. No one would tell a poor reader that he could not look at any books until his reading improved. In the same way, no student can learn how to play in a playground by being removed from the playground, or how to learn time management skills by being told when to schedule everything. Learning responsibility requires participation. (p. 50)

Students who are behaviorally at-risk know and accept that they are labeled "discipline problems." They know that they can't do academic work as expected and that they are considered bothersome and irritating. Wherever they turn, they receive negative messages about themselves. They have become, in their own eyes, bad persons. How can teachers help students who see themselves as bad persons and whose only gratification in school comes from causing trouble?

Helping Students Regain Hope

Teachers can do little about the depressing conditions in society, but they can do a good deal to help students regain a **sense of hope.** Hope is the belief that things will be better for us in the future. It inspires us and helps us live meaningfully. It provides courage and the incentive to overcome barriers. When hope is lost, no longer is there reason to try. Students who are behaviorally at-risk have, for the most part, lost hope that education will serve them. Curwin and Mendler contend that such students can be helped to regain hope and, further, that as they do so their behavior will improve. This can be accomplished, they say, by making learning much more interesting and worthwhile. If students are to get involved in the learning process, they need something to hope for, something that will make their efforts seem worthwhile. Learning activities can succeed when they promise students competence in doing what is important to them. (Curwin 1992, p. 25)

Learning must not only be made attractive but, as mentioned, must also bring success as well. At-risk students will not persevere unless successful, despite the initial attractiveness of the topic. To ensure success, teachers can explore ways to redesign the curriculum, encourage different ways of thinking, provide for various learning styles and sensory modalities, allow for creativity and artistic expression, and use grading systems that provide encouraging feedback without damaging the students' willingness to try.

Disciplining Difficult-to-Control Students

It should be recognized that traditional methods of discipline are ineffective with students who are behaviorally at-risk. These students have grown immune to scolding, lecturing, sarcasm, detention, extra writing assignments, isolation, names on the chalkboard, or trips to the principal's office. It does no good to tell them what they did wrong; they already know. Nor does it help to grill them about their failure to do class work or follow rules. They already doubt their ability, and they know they don't want to follow rules. Sarcastic teacher remarks, because they attack students' dignity, almost always make matters worse. At-risk students need no further humiliation. Punishment destroys their motivation to cooperate. They see no reason to commit to better ways of behaving and therefore cannot achieve the results teachers hope for.

How, then, should teachers work with these students? Curwin and Mendler set forth principles and approaches they believe work significantly better than the discipline approaches normally used. They acknowledge that dealing with the chronic rule breaker is never easy and admit that the success rate is far from perfect, but they claim it is possible to produce positive changes in 25 to 50 percent of students considered to be out of control (Curwin and Mendler 1992). Curwin (1992) would have teachers base their discipline efforts upon the following principles:

1. *Dealing with student behavior is an important part of teaching.* Most teachers do not want to deal with behavior problems, but their attitude can change when they realize that being a professional means doing whatever they can to help each individual student. Teachers can look upon misbehavior as an ideal opportunity for teaching responsibility. They should put as much effort into teaching good behavior as they put into teaching content.

2. *Always treat students with dignity.* Dignity is a basic need that is essential for a healthy life; its importance cannot be overrated. To treat students with dignity is to respect them as individuals, to be concerned about their needs and understanding of their viewpoints. Effective discipline does not attack student dignity but instead offers hope. Curwin and Mendler advise teachers to ask themselves this question when reacting to student misbehavior: "How would this strategy affect my dignity if a teacher did it to me?"

3. *Good discipline must not interfere with student motivation.* Any discipline technique is self-defeating if it reduces motivation to learn. Students who become involved in lessons cause few discipline problems. Poorly behaved students usually lack motivation to learn what is being offered them. They need encouragement and a reason to learn. Curwin suggests that teachers, when about to deal with misbehavior, ask themselves this question: "What will this technique do to motivation?"

4. *Responsibility is more important than obedience.* Curwin differentiates between obedience and responsibility as follows: **Obedience** means "do as you are told." Responsibility means "make the best decision possible." Obedience is desirable in matters of health and safety, but when applied to most misbehavior, it is a short-term solution against which students rebel. Responsibility grows, albeit slowly, as students have the opportunity to sort out facts and make decisions. Teachers should regularly provide such opportunities.

Consequences

Consequences are the actions teachers take when students transgress class rules. Curwin and Mendler differentiate among four types of consequences: logical, conventional, generic, and instructional. **Logical consequences** are those in which students must make right what they have done wrong. The consequence is logically related to the behavior. If they make a mess, they must clean it up. If they willfully damage material, they must replace it. If they speak hurtfully to others, they must practice speaking in ways that are not hurtful.

Conventional consequences are those that are commonly in practice, such as time out, removal from the room, and suspension from school. They are rarely logically related to the behavior. Curwin and Mendler suggest modifying conventional consequences so as to increase student commitment. For time out, they suggest that instead of banning the student for a specified length of time, teachers should say something like "You have chosen time out. You may return to the group when you are ready to learn."

Generic consequences are reminders, warnings, choosing, and planning that are invoked when misbehavior is noted. Often, simple reminders are enough to stop misbehavior: "We need to get this work completed." Warnings are very firm reminders: "This is the second time I have asked you to get to work. If I have to ask you again, you will need time out." Choosing allows students to select from three or four options a plan for improving their behavior. Planning, which Curwin (1992) calls "the most effective consequence that can be used for all rule violations" (p. 78), requires that students plan their own solution to a recurring behavior problem. Planning conveys that the teacher has faith in the student's competence. That faith often engenders a degree of commitment. The plan should name specific steps the student will follow and should be written, dated, and signed.

Instructional consequences teach students how to behave properly. Simply knowing what one ought to do does not ensure correct behavior. Some behaviors, such as raising one's hand or speaking courteously, are learned more easily when taught and practiced.

Curwin (1992) makes a number of suggestions concerning how teachers should use consequences, such as the following:

- Always implement a consequence when a rule is broken.
- Select the most appropriate consequence from the list of alternatives, taking into account the offense, situation, student involved, and the best means of helping that student.
- State the rule and consequence to the offending student. Nothing more need be said.
- Be private. Only the student(s) involved should hear.
- Do not embarrass the student.
- Do not think of the situation as win-lose. This is not a contest. Do not get involved in a power struggle.
- Control your anger. Be calm and speak quietly, but accept no excuses from the student.
- Sometimes it is best to let the student choose the consequence.
- The professional always looks for ways to help the client. (pp. 79–80)

Preventing Escalation

When teachers respond to student misbehavior, students often dig in their heels and a contest of wills ensues, with neither side willing to back down. Curwin and Mendler remind teachers that their duty is not to win such contests but to do what they can to help the student. This requires keeping the channels open for rational discussion of problem behavior. That cannot be done if the teacher humiliates, angers, embarrasses, or demeans the student. This point is critical for high-risk students, who are predisposed to responding negatively. Curwin (1992) suggests that teachers do the following toward **preventing escalation of conflicts:**

- Use active listening. Acknowledge and/or paraphrase what students say without agreeing, disagreeing, or expressing value judgment.
- Arrange to speak with the student later. Allow a time for cooling off. It is much easier to have positive discussions after anger has dissipated.
- Keep all communication as private as possible. Students do not want to lose face in front of their peers and so are unlikely to comply with public demands. Nor do teachers like to appear weak in front of the class. When communication is kept private, the chances for productive discussion are much better because egos are not so strongly on the line.
- If a student refuses to accept a consequence, invoke the insubordination rule. Don't use this provision until it is clear the student will not accept the consequence.

Motivating Difficult-to-Manage Students

Rules, consequences, and enforcement are necessary in all classrooms, but the key to better student behavior lies elsewhere—in motivation. Most students are somewhat motivated to learn and behave properly in school, whether because they find school interesting, like to please the teacher, or simply want to avoid failure. Such is not the case for behaviorally at-risk students. It would be foolish to suggest that a magical set of techniques exists for helping such students. But teachers do know what motivates students in general. Students who are behaviorally at-risk have the same general needs and interests as other students, but they have encountered so much failure that they have turned to resistance and misbehavior to bolster their egos. Curwin (1992) makes the following suggestions for increasing motivation among students who are behaviorally at-risk:

- Select for your lessons as many topics as you can that have personal importance and relevance to the students.
- Set up authentic learning goals—goals that lead to genuine competence that students can display and be proud of.
- Help students interact with the topics in ways that are congruent with their interests and values.
- Involve students actively in lessons. Allow them to use their senses, move about, and talk. Make the lessons as much fun as possible. Lessons needn't be easy if they are important and enjoyable.
- Give students numerous opportunities to take risks and make decisions without fear of failure.
- Show your own genuine energy and interest in the topics being studied. Show that you enjoy working with students. Try to connect personally with them as individuals.
- Each day, do at least one activity that you love. Show pride in your knowledge and ability to convey it to your students. Don't be reluctant to ham it up.
- Make your class activities events that students look forward to. Make them wonder what might happen next. (pp. 130–144)

Dealing with Aggression, Hostility, and Violence

Curwin and Mendler have concluded that students are becoming more aggressive, hostile, and violent than ever before, and they are doing so at an earlier age. Teenagers are especially prone to violence, two and a half times more likely to experience violence than people over age 20. Curwin and Mendler say the progressive increase in violence has occurred in part because of rewarding and punishing students in school (and in the home and community) rather than teaching them values—such as that it is wrong to intimidate others, hurt them physically, or destroy their property. A large proportion of students who use violence in these forms lack any sense of compassion or remorse and thus do not respond to normal discipline techniques. This makes it especially difficult for teachers to work productively with these students.

Curwin and Mendler have addressed this growing problem in their 1997 book *As Tough as Necessary: Countering Violence, Aggression, and Hostility in Our Schools.* They point out that by "As Tough As Necessary" they do not mean the zero-tolerance tactic now used in many schools. Instead, they mean using "a variety of ways to help aggressive, hostile, and violent children learn alternatives to hurting others" (p. ix). They contend that "behavior change among hardened, antisocial, and angry students cannot occur simply by offering more love, caring, and opportunities for decision making" (p. 16). They say that if schools are to deal with violence, they must adopt schoolwide approaches that (1) teach students how, when threatened or frustrated, to make nonviolent choices that serve them more effectively than do violent choices, (2) model for students nonhostile methods of expressing anger, frustration, and impatience, and (3) emphasize the teaching of values that relate to cooperation, safety, altruism, and remorse.

A Four-Phase Plan for Schools and Educators

Curwin and Mendler suggest a four-phase plan for schools and educators to help students move toward value-guided behavior. The four phases are: (1) Identify the core values that the school wishes to emphasize; (2) Create rules and consequences based on the core values identified; (3) Model the values during interactions with students and staff; and (4) Eliminate interventions that violate the core values. The following are some suggestions they offer within each of the four phases.

Identify the Core Values of the School

Curwin and Mendler suggest that each school have faculty, staff, students, and parents work together to specify a set of core values that shows how they want individuals in the school to conduct themselves and relate to each other. A set of core values might include statements such as the following. (1997)

- School is a place where we solve our problems peacefully.
- School is a place where we protect and look out for one another, rather than attack or hurt one another.

- School is a place where we learn we are responsible for what we do.
- School is a place where we learn that my way is not the only way. (p. 24)

Create Rules and Consequences Based on the Core Values

Rules are needed to govern classroom behavior, and those rules should be based on the school's stated values. While the values state broad intentions, rules say exactly what one should and should not do. This can be seen in the following examples. (1997, p. 31)

Value	Rule
School is a place where we protect and look out for one another, rather than hurt or attack one another.	No put-downs allowed.
School is a place where we solve our problems peacefully.	Keep your hands and feet to yourselves.

Model Values with Students and Staff Members

It is essential that teachers and administrators continually model behaviors that correspond with the school values. Teachers must express their emotions nonviolently, use positive strategies to resolve conflict with students, and walk away when they receive put-downs from students. Curwin and Mendler (1997, p. 32) suggest the following as helpful to teachers. Individually or in staff meetings write on paper how you want students to express their anger toward you and how you want them to resolve classroom conflicts with you and other students. Then teach your students these techniques and use them yourself in practice.

Eliminate Interventions that Violate Core Values

Teachers everywhere tend to rely on their past experiences when responding to student misbehavior. Their responses often take the form of threats, intimidation, and using students as examples for others. Responses of these types fail to model behavior consistent with school values and tend to produce further conflict with students. Threats, for example, destroy student comfort in the classroom. If carried out vengefully, they produce a backlash of resentment. If made but not carried out, student behavior worsens, which calls for still more dire threats that cannot be carried out. Students in turn conclude that it is all right to threaten others, since the teacher does so. That cycle is broken by showing students the dangers of threat and teaching them alternative behaviors.

The same applies to intimidation and using students as examples. Those were mainstay tactics of a majority of teachers years ago and are still evident in classrooms. When teachers intimidate students, students may cower (or may not), but the students in turn become more likely to treat others in the same way. It is also self-defeating to reprimand one student as an example for others. The resultant humiliation felt by the disciplined student produces a negativity that will never die. The primary goal of interventions is to help students learn more responsible behavior. We cannot accomplish this through hurtful tactics. The real way to help students is to model positive, nonviolent behavior, use it when intervening in student behavior, and help students to use it in their interactions with others.

Techniques for Dealing with Violence in the Classroom

Curwin and Mendler suggest several strategies to help teachers and students when they encounter violence. These strategies are designed first to help everyone calm down and decide how to proceed. Teachers should teach the procedures to students and model them in practice. The following are a few of the many techniques suggested. (1997, pp. 94–118)

Use the Six-Step Solution

1. Stop and calm down—wait a moment, take a deep breath, relax.
2. Think—quickly explore options and foresee what will happen if you use them.
3. Decide what you want to have happen.
4. Decide on a second solution in case the first doesn't work.
5. Carry out the solution you deem best.
6. Evaluate the results—have you accomplished what you hoped? Will you use the tactic again in similar circumstances?

Solving My Problems

First, name the problem, indicating specifically what somebody has said or done. Second, say what you would like to have happen. Third, say what you will do to make things happen as you would like. Fourth, make a backup plan to use in case the first doesn't work. Fifth, carry out the plan.

Learning to Have Patience

As we grow up we learn that our needs can't always be met when we'd like, that often we will have to wait. If we don't learn to have patience, we will feel frustrated and angry because we are not getting what we want when we want it. Learning to be patient requires practice on actions such as walking away from a fight, waiting in line with a smile, and remaining calm when somebody cuts in line.

Wearing an Invisible Shield

You pretend you are wearing an invisible shield that deflects all bad thoughts and unkind words. It makes you immune to them. You cannot be hurt as long as you are wearing it.

Using Words That Work

Instead of being provoked into retaliation, you can practice saying things that will stop almost all attacks, such as (1) being polite, using words such as please and thank you, (2) asking if you have done something that has upset the other person, and (3) apologizing if you have offended the person.

Planning for Confrontations

Name five situations you recall where people got into a dispute. Next to each, write down strategies you think would bring the situation to a calm close. Practice what you would say and do should you find yourself in one of the situations.

Suggestions to Help Teachers Retrain Themselves

It is helpful for teachers to prepare themselves for situations they might encounter. Curwin and Mendler suggest doing the following: (1997)

1. Write down things students do or say that you find irritating.
2. Determine why students do those things. What basic needs are they trying to meet? What motivates them?
3. What do you now do when students say or do irritating things?
4. Are your current tactics effective in solving the problem?
5. What response strategies can you think of that address the reasons for the irritating behavior while at the same time modeling behavior consistent with school values?
6. Practice the strategies beforehand and then put them into practice at the next opportunity. (p. 71)

Specific Suggestions for Dealing with Conflict

Teachers who agree with approaches to deter violence still ask the legitimate question, "What specifically do I do when...?" To answer that question, Curwin and Mendler provide many concrete suggestions, such as: (1997)

- Use privacy, eye contact, and proximity when possible. Speak privately and quietly with the students. This preserves their dignity and takes away the likelihood of their fighting back.
- Indicate to the student politely but clearly what you want. Use the words "please" and "thank you" (e.g., "Bill, please go to Mr. Keene's room. There's a seat there for you. Come back when you are ready to learn. I hope that doesn't take very long. Thank you, Bill.")
- Tell the student that you see a power struggle brewing that will do no one good. Defer discussion to a later time. (e.g., "Juan, you are angry and so am I. Rather than have a dispute now, let's calm down and talk later. I'm sure we can help each other out after we cool off. Thanks a lot.") (p. 66)

Strengths of Curwin and Mendler's *Discipline with Dignity*

All teachers experience misbehavior in their classrooms. Most have found ways to deal with minor infractions such as talking, speaking out, chewing gum, and failing to complete homework. But all teachers dread dealing with students whose behavior is so chronically unacceptable they not only disrupt learning but are likely to fail in school. Such behaviors make teachers feel trapped and overwhelmed. Curwin and Mendler have provided realistic help for working with chronically misbehaving students and have given teachers and students workable strategies for reducing behavior that is hostile, aggressive, and violent.

Initiating Curwin and Mendler's *Discipline with Dignity*

Suppose you teach a class that contains several chronically misbehaving students, and you feel the Curwin and Mendler model can help you deal with them more effectively. How do you get it installed and running?

Principles You Must Accept

Before using the approaches Curwin and Mendler propose, you must subscribe to certain principles that support their model. Foremost among these principles is that student dignity must be preserved. Students will do all in their power to protect their dignity. They don't want to appear stupid, feel incapable, or be denigrated, especially in front of their peers. When faced with threat, students, especially the chronically misbehaved, use antisocial behavior to counter it. You must be willing to guard against threatening students' dignity, even when they threaten yours.

A second principle is that dealing with misbehavior is an important part of teaching. You are in the classroom to help your students. Those whose behavior puts them at risk of failure especially need your help, though their behavior may suggest that they want nothing to do with you. The best thing you can do for them is to find ways to encourage prosocial behavior.

A third principle is that lasting results are achieved only over time. There are no quick-fix solutions to chronic misbehavior, but by finding ways to motivate students and help them learn, you will enable many to make genuine improvement.

A fourth principle is that responsibility is more important than obedience. The ability to weigh facts and make good decisions is far more valuable in students' lives than is obedience to demands. You must be willing to put students into situations where they can make decisions about matters that concern them, be willing to allow them to fail, and then help them try again. Progressively, they will learn to behave in ways that are best for themselves and others.

Establishing the Social Contract

You will have given much thought to the kind of classroom you want and how you want your students to behave. When you first meet the students, spend as much time as necessary discussing goals for the class, activities that might be helpful, and class behavior that will improve enjoyment and accomplishment for everyone. In those discussions, class rules and consequences should be agreed to. It is important that students contribute significantly to those decisions and clearly indicate their agreement to abide by them. The rules and consequences should be written out, dated, and signed by teacher and students. The document should be posted in the room and copies sent to parents and administrators.

Providing Motivation and Helpfulness

From the outset you must seek to structure lessons to help students be active and successful. It is far better that students engage in activities they find interesting than be dragged perfunctorily through the standard curriculum. Your own energy, enjoyment of learning, and pride in teaching will affect students positively, while your willingness to help without confrontation will slowly win them over.

Review of Selected Terminology

The following terms are central to the Curwin and Mendler model of discipline. Check yourself concerning their meanings:

Principles of discipline: Discipline an important part of teaching; always based on dignity, hope, responsibility, motivation; no short-term solutions

Consequences: instructional, conventional, generic, logical, social contract, invoking

Teachers as professionals: nature and responsibilities of

Students and needs: behaviorally at-risk, sense of hope, dignity, responsibility

Application Exercises

Concept Cases

Case 1: Kristina Will Not Work ■ Kristina, in Mr. Jake's class, is quite docile. She never disrupts class and does little socializing with other students. But despite Mr. Jake's best efforts, Kristina rarely completes an assignment. She doesn't seem to care. She is simply there, putting forth virtually no effort. *How would Curwin and Mendler deal with Kristina?*

They would suggest the following sequence of interventions: Consider that Kristina's behavior might be due to severe feelings of incapability. She may be protecting herself by not trying. Relate to Kristina as an individual. Chat with her informally about her life and interests. Find topics that interest Kristina and build some class lessons around them. Assign Kristina individual work that helps her become more competent in her areas of special interest. Have a private conversation with Kristina. Ask for her thoughts about how you could make school more interesting for her. Show her you are interested and willing to help. As Kristina begins to work and participate, continue private chats that help her see herself as successful.

Case 2: Sara Cannot Stop Talking ■ Sara is a pleasant girl who participates in class activities and does most, though not all, of her assigned work. She cannot seem to refrain from talking to classmates, however. Her teacher, Mr. Gonzales, has to speak to her repeatedly during lessons, to the point that he often becomes exasperated and loses his temper. *What suggestions would Curwin and Mendler give Mr. Gonzales to help with Sara's misbehavior?*

Case 3: Joshua Clowns and Intimidates ■ Joshua, larger and louder than his classmates, always wants to be the center of attention, which he accomplishes through a combination of clowning and intimidation. He makes wise remarks, talks back (smilingly) to the teacher, utters a variety of sound-effect noises such as automobile crashes and gunshots, and makes limitless sarcastic comments and put-downs of his classmates. Other students will not stand up to him, apparently fearing his verbal and physical aggression. His teacher, Miss Pearl, has come to her wit's end. *What do you find in Curwin and Mendler's work that might help Miss Pearl deal with Joshua?*

Case 4: Tom is Hostile and Defiant ■ Tom has appeared to be in his usual foul mood ever since arriving in class. On his way to sharpen his pencil, he bumps into Frank, who complains. Tom tells him loudly to shut up. Miss Baines, the teacher, says, "Tom, go back to your seat." Tom wheels around and says heatedly, "I'll go when I'm damned good and ready!" *How would Curwin and Mendler have Miss Baines deal with Tom?*

Questions and Activities

1. In small groups, conduct practice situations in which classmates act as students who make hurtful comments to you, the teacher. Begin with the examples given here and explore new ones you have seen or think might occur. Take turns being the teacher and responding to the comments in some of the ways Curwin and Mendler suggest.

   Example 1
   Teacher: "Jonathan, I'd like to see that work finished before the period ends today."
   Jonathan: [Sourly] "Fine. Why don't you take it and finish it yourself if that's what you want?"
   Teacher:

   Example 2
   Teacher: "Desirée, that's the second time you've broken our rule about profanity. I'd like to speak with you after class."
   Desirée: "No thanks. I've seen enough of your scrawny butt for one day."
   Teacher:

   Example 3
   Teacher: "Marshall, I'd like for you to get back to work, please."

   Marshall: [Says nothing but nonchalantly makes a finger signal at the teacher. Other students see it and snicker.]
   Teacher:

   Compose additional occurrences. Practice de-escalating the confrontations without becoming defensive, fighting back, or withdrawing your request.

2. Explore Scenario 1 or 2 in Appendix A. Discuss how Curwin and Mendler would have Mrs. Miller or Mr. Platt respond to the situation encountered.

3. One of the suggestions given for motivating reluctant students was "Make your class activities events that students look forward to. Make them wonder what might happen next." For a selected grade level, brainstorm ways of complying with this suggestion.

4. Many suggestions were made for anticipating and dealing with violent, aggressive, or hostile behavior. What would you do to prepare yourself for situations involving such behavior?

Primary References

Curwin, R. 1992. *Rediscovering hope: Our greatest teaching strategy*. Bloomington, IN: National Educational Service. Makes the points that many students have no hope that school will provide anything of value for them, that misbehavior is associated with loss of hope, and that students without hope are often at-risk of failing because of poor behavior. Tells why and how to restore vitally important hope for these students.

Curwin, R., and A. Mendler. 1988a. *Discipline with dignity*. Alexandria, VA: Association for Supervision and Curriculum Development. Describes how to improve student behavior through responsible thinking, cooperation, mutual respect, and shared decision making.

Strongly emphasizes the importance of preserving student dignity and shows that responsibility is far more important to students' future lives than merely following rules.

———. 1997. *As tough as necessary. Countering violence, aggression, and hostility in our schools.*

Alexandria, VA: Association for Supervision and Curriculum Development. Curwin and Mendler's suggestions for working productively with hostile or violent students who have little sense of compassion or remorse and who do not respond to ordinary discipline techniques.

Recommended Readings

Curwin, R. 1980. Are your students addicted to praise? *Instructor, 90,* 61–62.

———. 1995. A humane approach to reducing violence in schools. *Educational Leadership, 52*(5), 72–75.

Curwin, R. and A. Mendler. 1988b. Packaged discipline programs: Let the buyer beware. *Educational Leadership, 46*(2), 68–71.

Barbara Coloroso's
Inner Discipline

Focus

■ Treating students with respect, giving them power and responsibility to make decisions.

■ Providing guidance and support to help students manage their own discipline.

■ Differentiating between punishment and discipline and responding accordingly.

Logic

■ Teachers can help students develop inner discipline.

■ Students become good decision makers by making decisions and learning from the results.

■ Consequences should not be punitive; they should invite constructive student responses.

Barbara Coloroso

Contributions

■ Depicted classrooms as places to learn problem solving and develop inner discipline.

■ Clarified the differential effects of consequences, rewards, bribes, and punishment.

■ Delineated three types of misbehavior: mischief, mistakes, and mayhem.

Coloroso's Suggestions

■ Truly believe students are worth every effort, then treat them as adults want to be treated.

■ Make unconditional commitment to help your students develop, as best you can.

■ Give students opportunity to solve their problems. Ask them how they plan to do so.

■ Use reasonable consequences for behavior, rather than bribes, rewards, or threats.

■ Apply the RSVP checklist to test the value and practicality of consequences.

About Barbara Coloroso

Barbara Coloroso, a former Franciscan nun, is now a parent, teacher, workshop leader, author, and affiliate instructor at the University of Northern Colorado. She contends that schools have a major duty to develop responsibility in students, and that the climate for a responsibility-oriented school is based upon trust cultivated by teachers and administrators. Her ideas are set forth in her books *Kids Are Worth It!: Giving Your Child the Gift of Inner Discipline* (1994)and *Parenting with Wit and Wisdom in Times of Chaos and Confusion* (1999). She has also made numerous contributions to educational publications on topics such as strategies for working with troubled students, creative media for students with special needs and talents, and assertive confrontations and negotiations. Her 1994 "Kids are worth it!" series includes videos, audiotapes, and workbooks to assist educators in developing a discipline system that creates trust, respect, and success in school. The materials are available from Kids Are Worth It!, Post Office Box 621108, Littleton, CO 80162; telephone 800-729-1588; fax 303-972-1204; website www.kidsareworthit.com

Coloroso's Contributions to Discipline

Coloroso helps teachers distinguish between punishment and discipline, which allows them to deal with students more effectively. She explains three different categories of student misbehavior, which she calls *mistakes, mischief,* and *mayhem.* Each is dealt with in its own way. She describes how to use discipline rather than punishment in a manner that enables students to take charge of their lives. She contends that good discipline shows students what they have done wrong, has them assume ownership of the problem that is created, gives them ways to solve the problem, and leaves their dignity intact. She also stresses that children develop inner discipline by learning how to think, not just what to think. She shows how to ensure that students experience either natural or reasonable consequences for their behavioral choices, and she provides the RSVP test, described later, for use when deciding on consequences.

Coloroso's Central Focus

Coloroso puts major emphasis on helping students make their own decisions, while providing guidance and allowing students to take responsibility for their choices. She believes that in order to have good discipline, teachers must do three things: (1) treat students with respect and dignity, (2) give them a sense of positive power over their own lives, and (3) give them opportunities to make decisions, take responsibility for their actions, and learn from their successes and mistakes. She believes that children, given adult help, have the ability to develop inner discipline and manage problems they encounter. She says that under these conditions students can grow to like themselves, think for themselves, and believe there is no problem so great it can't be solved.

Coloroso's Principal Teachings

- *Students are worth all the effort teachers can expend on them.* They are worth it not just when they are bright, good looking, or well behaved, but always.

- *School should be neither adult-dominated nor student-controlled.* Rather, it should be a place where joint efforts are made to learn, relate, grow, and create community.
- *Teachers should never treat students in ways they, the teachers, wouldn't want to be treated.* Children have dignity and innate worth, and they deserve to be treated accordingly.
- *If a discipline tactic works, and leaves student and teacher's dignity intact, use it.* Self-worth and dignity are to be maintained; anything that damages them is to be avoided.
- *Proper discipline does four things that punishment cannot do:* (1) shows students what they have done wrong, (2) gives them ownership of the problems created, (2) provides them ways to solve the resultant problems, and (4) leaves their dignity intact.
- *In order to develop inner discipline, children must learn how to think, not just what to think.* To this end, teachers must give students responsibility and allow them to make mistakes.
- *Students have the right to be in school, but they have the responsibility to respect the rights of those around them.* Rights and responsibility go hand in hand.
- *Disputes and problems are best resolved with win-win solutions.* Rather than rescuing students or lecturing them, teachers can give students opportunities to solve their problems, but in ways that do not depict any disputants as "losers."
- *Consequences, natural and reasonable, are associated with rules, and are to be allowed or invoked consistently when rules are violated.*
- *Natural consequences are events that happen naturally in the real world.* You kick a chair and the consequence is that you hurt your toe. Teachers should allow students to experience natural consequences so long as the consequences are not physically dangerous, immoral, or unhealthy.
- *Reasonable consequences are events imposed by the teacher that are related to a violation of rules.* If you damage material on loan from a museum, you need to write a letter of apology to the museum indicating how you will repair or otherwise fix the damage and avoid a similar accident in the future.
- *Misbehavior falls into three categories: mistakes, mischief, and mayhem.* Mistakes are simple errors that provide opportunity for learning better choices. Mischief, although not necessarily serious, is intentional misbehavior. It provides opportunity to help students find ways to fix what was done and learn how to avoid doing it again, while retaining their dignity. Mayhem, willfully serious misbehavior, calls for application of the Three R's.
- *The Three R's provide guidance in helping students take responsibility and accept consequences.* The first R, *restitution*, means to somehow repair whatever damage was done. The second R, *resolution*, involves identifying and correcting whatever caused the misbehavior so it won't happen again. The third R, *reconciliation*, entails the process of healing the relationships with people who were hurt by the misbehavior.

- *The RSVP test is used to check on consequences the teacher imposes.* It reminds teachers that consequences must be reasonable, simple, valuable, and practical.
- *Students who experience consistent, logical, realistic consequences learn that they themselves have positive control over their lives.* On the other hand, students who are constantly bribed, rewarded, and punished become dependent on others for approval, work only to please the teacher, and figure out how to avoid getting caught.
- *When reasonable consequences are invoked, students frequently try to get teachers to change their minds, but teachers must not give in.* Students may cry, beg, argue angrily and aggressively, and sulk. They should not get their way by doing so.

Analysis of Coloroso's *Inner Discipline*

Coloroso's views on discipline are consistent with recent trends that assign students a more active role in taking responsibility for their behavior. She believes that educators should work with students to help them develop **inner discipline,** which she defines as the ability to behave creatively, constructively, cooperatively, and responsibly.

Coloroso firmly contends that teachers must believe that their students have innate value, that those students are worth all effort expended in their behalf, and that the students can learn to be responsible for their own behavior, make their own decisions, and resolve their own problems. Students do not easily develop these qualities naturally. Most require help to do so. The best way for teachers to help is to allow students to make decisions and grow from the results of those decisions, whatever they may be. Teachers have the responsibility to make sure that student decisions do not lead to situations that are physically dangerous, morally threatening, or unhealthy. Otherwise, the role of teachers is to bring students to situations that require decisions and, without making judgments, let them proceed through the process.

What students then do will sometimes make teachers and students uncomfortable. The discomfort disappears when students resolve the problem constructively. This experience builds the power to deal with problem situations and keeps students' self-esteem intact because it leaves responsibility and power to them. Teachers must trust students with this responsibility and power.

Three Types of Schools and Teachers

Coloroso says she sees three basic types of schools and teachers, which have very different effects on students. She calls the types *brickwalls, jellyfish,* and *backbones.*

Brickwall schools and **teachers** are strict and rigid. They use power and coercion to control. They demand that students follow rules and use punishment, humiliation, threats, and bribes to make them do so.

Jellyfish schools and **teachers** are wishy-washy, with little recognizable structure, consistency, or guidelines. Teachers are lax in discipline, set few limits, and more or less let students have their way, but when sufficiently provoked turn to lecturing, put-downs, threats, and bribes. Some jellyfish teachers have little faith in students and believe that if anything is to get done they must do it themselves.

Backbone schools and **teachers** provide support and structure necessary for students to reason through problems and behave responsibly. Students get opportunities to make decisions and correct mistakes they make, with full support from the teacher. Because the teacher neither tells them what to do nor does the work for them, they learn how to think and act on their own.

Tenets of Inner Discipline

Coloroso bases her work on two fundamental tenets. The first is that students are worth all the time, energy, and effort it takes to help them become resourceful, responsible, resilient, compassionate human beings. The second tenet reflects the Golden Rule and is worded this way: "I will not treat a student in a way I myself would not want to be treated." (Coloroso 1994, p. 11) Discipline based on this proposition places limits on power and control, while making paramount the preservation of dignity and self-worth.

Discipline, Not Punishment

In order to deal successfully with today's discipline problems, teachers must abandon punishment and rely on what Coloroso calls "discipline." She describes **punishment** as treatment that is psychologically hurtful to students and likely to provoke anger, resentment, and additional conflict. She calls it adult-oriented imposed power. Students typically respond to punishment with the "**three F's**"—*fear, fighting back*, or *fleeing*. They become afraid to make a mistake. Students rarely know for sure that a given act will bring punishment. They see it as depending on who the student is, which teacher catches the student, and how the teacher feels at the time.

Discipline, on the other hand, helps students see what they have done wrong and gives them ownership of the problem. It provides options and opportunities to solve problems and in so doing leaves students' dignity intact. It uses **RSVP of consequences** (reasonable, simple, valuable, and practical) to help students see that they are responsible for and in control of themselves. Those consequences either occur naturally or are provided by the teacher, but are always related to decisions students have made. By making clear the connections between behavior and consequence, teachers help students better understand whether their behavior has been responsible or irresponsible. Discomfort that arises from irresponsible behavior only goes away after teacher and students work together to resolve the problem constructively.

Three Types of Misbehavior

Coloroso illustrates these points further in relation to three types of student misbehavior—mistakes, mischief, and mayhem—that are usually handled with either punishment or discipline. **Mistakes** are simply errors in behavior, made without intent to break rules. They provide opportunity to learn how to behave more acceptably.

Mischief goes beyond mistakes. It is intentional misbehavior, though not necessarily serious, and presents an opportunity for teaching students that all actions have consequences, sometimes pleasant and sometimes not. It also provides opportunity for showing students ways to solve their problem with dignity.

Mayhem usually involves intentional misbehavior, and when it does it calls for application of the **Three R's of reconciliatory justice**—*restitution,* which means repairing or otherwise fixing whatever damage has been done; *resolution,* which involves identifying and correcting whatever caused the misbehavior so it won't occur again; and *reconciliation,* which is the process of establishing healing relationships with people who were hurt by the misbehavior. The Three R's are described in more detail later in this chapter.

The choice teachers make between discipline and punishment in response to misbehavior is vitally important because it can later determine how students will solve problems and deal with traumas. Discipline helps children grow up to be responsible, resourceful, resilient, compassionate humans, who feel empowered to act with integrity and a strong sense of self. Punishment, on the other hand, causes children to become adept at making excuses, blaming, and denying, while feeling powerless, manipulated, and not in control (1999, 223).

Coloroso goes on to explain why this difference occurs. She says

> Punishment removes vital opportunities to learn integrity, wisdom, compassion, and mercy, all of which contribute to inner discipline. Discipline, on the other hand, helps children learn how to handle problems they will encounter througout life. It does so by providing four things:
>
> 1. It helps make students fully aware of what they have done.
> 2. It gives students as much ownership of the problem as they are able to handle.
> 3. It provides options for solving the problem in which students are involved.
> 4. It leaves student dignity intact. (p. 227)

Let's see how these ideas apply to real situations:

> *Anna in kindergarten.* Anna is very enthusiastic about the coloring lesson, so enthusiastic that she colors beyond the paper and onto her desk with the permanent marker she is using. Anna never intended to damage her desk. It was an accident, but the marks remain. Her teacher, Mrs. Alvarez, hopes to get the marks off the desk and also prevent the accident from happening again. She believes in giving Anna partial responsibility for resolving the problem, so she asks Anna to use a special cleaner to remove as much as possible. Mrs. Alvarez also realizes that such accidents could be prevented if she would cover the desks with paper and make sure Anna and the others use washable pen or chalk for their art projects.

> *Fifth-grader Aaron.* Aaron has shown little interest in the lessons Mr. Flynn is presenting about the Civil War. Aaron is very interested in rockets and so while Mr. Flynn tells about battles that happened someplace far away and long ago, Aaron uses the clip from his marker to scratch a rocket on the surface of his desk. At recess Mr. Flynn notices the damage. Mr. Flynn, though distressed, knows that Aaron needs discipline, not punishment. He talks with Aaron and points out that the desk requires refinishing. He mentions various possibilities including contacting a professional refinisher, asking Aaron's father to come help, or allowing Aaron

to do the job under Mr. Flynn's guidance. Aaron opts for doing it himself. He makes arrangements to remain after school. Mr. Flynn gets materials from the school custodian and shows Aaron how to remove the finish from the affected area and then apply a matching finish. Mr. Flynn's strategy of invoking reasonable consequences allows Aaron to take ownership of the problem, show responsibility for his actions, and maintain his personal dignity.

Alexis in high school. Alexis is a starting player on the high-school basketball team, but because she received a detention from her chemistry teacher for several tardies, Coach Stein informs her she will have to sit out the next game. Even though this is school policy, Alexis thinks the chemistry teacher harbors a grudge against her and is upset that Coach Stein doesn't back her up. While angry, Alexis writes some unacceptable comments on the locker room wall. When Coach Stein finds the damage, she knows other girls have seen it and she feels hurt, disappointed, and angry. Her first reaction is to call Alexis in and suspend her for another game, but when she has time to reconsider she realizes punishment of that sort would be unproductive and might not help Alexis make better choices in the future. Coach Stein decides to encourage Alexis to accept ownership of the problem and the attendant mayhem she has created. Coach Stein realizes this can happen only in an atmosphere of compassion, kindness, gentleness, and patience. Somehow Alexis must repair the damage she did to the locker room, make a plan to ensure it won't happen again, and also mend fences with her coach, teammates, and the chemistry teacher. Coach Stein resolves to meet with Alexis and help her acknowledge what she has done wrong, help her assume ownership of the problem, and help her identify options for dealing with the problem. Coach Stein will then help Alexis plan for accomplishing the "Three R's" of discipline. Coach Stein knows all this must be done in a way that preserves Alexis's dignity.

Earlier we noted that Coloroso stresses that students involved in discipline situations, particularly mayhem, must be helped to accomplish three things, which she calls the *Three R's of reconciliatory justice.* These are *restitution, resolution,* and *reconciliation.* **Restitution** means fixing the damage that has been done. While cleaning, refinishing, or paying for work done can accomplish the physical repairs in the Anna, Aaron, and Alexis cases, restitution does not necessarily involve repentance. Only if she is repentant can Alexis begin to reconcile matters with those she harmed. Making excuses, citing "buts" or "if only's" and shifting blame are far removed from true repentance. Having her apologize does not make Alexis repentant either. Honest repentance involves admitting the error, expressing assurance it will not be repeated, taking responsibility for the harm done, and making efforts to mend torn relationships. Students cannot be forced to repent, but they will often do so as they work through the reconciliation process. Coach Stein can provide structure, support, and the permission Alexis needs to begin the process.

Resolution involves identifying and correcting the causative factors so the improper behavior will not occur again. Alexis knows that as much as she might regret her actions, she cannot go back and change things. She must clarify in her mind what she did, why she did it, and what she can learn from the experience. It is not enough for her to say, "I won't do this again." She must come up with a plan to make sure she does not repeat her mistakes. Her plan might include talking with the chemistry teacher, apologizing to her teammates and Coach Stein, and involving herself in an anger-control program in order to find constructive ways of expressing her emotions.

Reconciliation is the process of bringing about healing with the people who are hurt by one's actions. It involves a genuine commitment to make restitution and live up to resolutions. It also involves trying to regain the trust of those who were hurt. It will be helpful if Alexis finds a way to give of her time and talents to those she has offended. Coach Stein knows this is something young people seldom think of, but she wants to suggest it to Alexis because she believes it is key to the entire process. She thinks it essential if those affected by Alexis's actions are to open themselves to Alexis's attempts at reconciliation.

Effective Classroom Discipline Leads to Inner Discipline

The ultimate purpose of discipline, illustrated in the Anna, Aaron, and Alexis cases, is to enable students to make intelligent decisions, accept the consequences of their decisions, and use the consequences to make better decisions in the future. Recognizing the relationship between decisions and their consequences teaches students that they have control over their lives, a requisite for the development of inner discipline.

Coloroso assigns teachers a key role in bringing about inner discipline. She believes teachers can best help by bringing students face to face with their problems and providing them tactics for resolution. She says that before teachers can see themselves in this role, rather than the role to which they are traditionally accustomed, they must ask themselves two questions and answer them honestly: "What is my goal in teaching?" and "What is my teaching philosophy?" The first has to do with what teachers hope to achieve with learners, and the second with how they think they should accomplish the task. Coloroso says that because teachers act in accordance with their beliefs, it is important for them to clarify those beliefs: "Do I want to empower students to take care of themselves, or do I want to make them wait for teachers and other adults to tell them what to do and think?" Teachers who feel they must control students turn to bribes, rewards, threats, and punishment to restrict and coerce behavior. Teachers who want to empower students to make decisions and resolve their own problems give students opportunities to think, act, and take responsibility.

When given this opportunity, students will not always make the best choices. For that reason they must be provided a safe and nurturing environment in which to learn and to deal with consequences. Teachers should allow and respect student decisions, even when those decisions are clearly in error, and must let students experience the consequences of their decisions. Even when consequences are unpleasant, students learn from them and at the same time learn that they have control over their lives through the decisions they make. When teachers recognize this fact, they see that it is counterproductive to nag, warn, and constantly remind students of what they ought to be doing.

Teaching Decision Making

Coloroso says that the best way to teach students how to make good decisions is to bring them to situations that call for decisions, ask them to make the decision (while the teacher provides guidance without judgment), and let them experience the results of their decision. This may seem inefficient, but it produces rapid growth in the ability to solve one's own problems. Mistakes and poor choices become the students' responsibility. If they experience discomfort, they have the power to correct the situation in the future.

Coloroso believes that teachers should never rescue students by solving thorny problems for them. Doing so sends the message that students don't have power in their own lives and that some other person must take care of them. When students make mistakes, as they will do, teachers must not lecture them: "If you had studied more, you wouldn't have failed the test." Students already know this. What they now need is opportunity to correct the situation they have created. Coloroso suggests saying the following to them: "You have a problem…What is your plan for dealing with it?"

When students are given ownership of problems and situations, they know it is up to them to make matters better. There is no one else to blame. Teachers are there to offer advice and support, but not provide solutions. This may entail only a subtle difference in reaction. Rather than telling a student, "You can't go to the library during choice time until you finish your math assignment" (punishment), a teacher should say, "You can go to the library during choice time when you finish your math assignment" (discipline). This simple response difference better allows students to take responsibility for their mistakes, rather than rationalizing them away.

The Three Cons

When students violate class rules, they should know that consequences will come into play. But even when the consequences are expected and reasonable, students will try to get out of them. Coloroso describes three ploys you can expect students to use in hopes of escaping consequences. She calls them the **three cons** and describes them as follows:

Con 1: Students beg, bribe, weep, and wail, trying to get teachers to let them by ("Oh, please, oh, please"). Some teachers give in and admonish students, saying "All right this once, but you better never do that again." Coloroso says that when teachers do this, the message they are really sending is: "I don't believe in you or trust in you…. I'll have to take care of you." This attitude works against students' developing a sense of inner discipline. If Con 1 fails, students often follow with….

Con 2: Students respond with anger and aggression: "I hate this stupid class." Because Con 2 affects teachers' emotions, they tend either to become passive or to lash back. Passivity invites aggression, and lashing back tends to produce counter-attack. Teachers must do neither. They must remain calm and say, "I'm sorry you do, but this is the consequence we have agreed to."

Con 3: Students sulk. Sulking is the most powerful of the three cons: Students' actions say, "I'm not gonna do what you say. You can't make me." It is true that teachers cannot force students to do anything they choose not to do. But it only makes matters worse to say something like "That's right! Go ahead and pout!" Students are virtually certain to follow that suggestion. The best course is calmly to invoke the consequence in a matter-of-fact way. Coloroso says that teachers lose positive power in students' lives when they give in to pleas or bribes, become angry at students in response to students' anger, and reinforce sulking. To retain their positive power, teachers should encourage students to own both the problem and the solution.

Problem Solving

Problem solving is one of the most important skills students can learn. They will learn better and more quickly if they know that it is all right to make mistakes. They must also learn to distinguish between reality and problem, with *reality* being an accurate appraisal of what has occurred in a situation and *problem* being the discomfort being caused by the reality. Coloroso says that in learning to solve problems, "We first accept (the) realities; (then) we solve the problems that come from them" (1994, p. 31). Coloroso contends that, as students make the distinction between reality and problem, they begin to see that there is no problem so great it cannot be solved. But when faced with a problem, students need a way of attacking it. The approach they use should become embodied in a plan, not an excuse. Coloroso suggests a problem-solving strategy that consists of six steps:

1. Identify and define the problem. Accurate identification of the problem is necessary if students are to resolve it effectively. Josh asks for the book he lent Melissa. He needs it for a report due on Friday. Melissa can't find the book, but remembers she left it on the kitchen table near the books her mother was donating to the library. Both Josh and Melissa experience a problem— discomfort for Josh regarding the assigned report, and pressure on Melissa for not returning the book. Let us look at the problem from Melissa's perspective. How is it to be resolved?

2. List possible solutions. Melissa's first thoughts about dealing with the problem are to say she left the book on Josh's desk or else avoid Josh. After she thinks about it a bit, she identifies three more options: see if she can find the book at the library, buy a new book for Josh, or borrow Randy's book for Josh to use.

3. Evaluate the options. Melissa considers the options and finds one that might work for her. The option she first identified isn't satisfactory. Though the thought crossed her mind, Melissa decides she is unwilling to lie. The second cannot work either: Josh is her neighbor and they usually do homework together after school. The third is a possibility: The book may have been delivered to the library and can be found there. The fourth is an option but not a desirable one: Melissa borrowed the book in the first place because she didn't want to pay what a new book cost. The fifth would be only a temporary solution and, besides, Randy needs his book for himself.

   Melissa's teacher has taught her to ask herself four questions about each of the options she has identified. They are:

   • Is it unkind?
   • Is it hurtful?
   • Is it unfair?
   • Is it dishonest?

Melissa recognizes that the first option would be dishonest, the second hurtful, and the fifth unfair to both Randy and Josh. She is in the process of learning that negative qualities only lead to further trouble. That leaves her two possible options: Check the library again or buy a replacement book.

4. Select the option that seems most promising. Melissa decides that she must go to the public library and see if the book can be found. If the book is located, she will explain the circumstances and get the book back.

5. Make a plan and carry it out. Admitting to and owning a problem, making a plan, and following through are difficult things to do, for adults as well as children. It means that excuses are not acceptable, and it means one must accept responsibility for mistakes and consequences. If the plan does not work, then a new option must be tried. If Melissa cannot find the book at the library, she will have to borrow money from her parents to replace the book. That will mean taking on extra chores to repay them, but it is a responsibility she knows she must accept.

6. In retrospect, re-evaluate the problem and the solution. Most people skip this step, but it is important for learning. Three questions should be asked:

> What caused the problem in the first place?
> How can a similar problem be avoided in the future?
> Was the problem solution satisfactory?

In this instance, the problem was probably caused accidentally. However, if Melissa is often careless in misplacing things she needs, a change in her behavior is called for. She might improve by designating a special place in which to put borrowed items. In this process of solving the problem, Melissa's self-esteem has remained intact and her sense of ability to solve problems has been reinforced. No one told her what to do. She maintained positive control over her own decisions.

Natural Consequences

When students are allowed to solve their own problems, their decisions will lead to consequences they may or may not anticipate. Coloroso believes in allowing consequences to occur without adult intervention, provided the consequences are not harmful. For example, if Jacob walks to the gym without his coat, he will get cold. Being cold is a natural consequence of dressing improperly for weather and temperature. If Fazilat borrows crayons but returns them broken, her table mates will stop lending her their crayons.

But when consequences are harmful to students, the teacher should intervene to prevent them. If Jose and Zachary are fighting on the playground, it is no time for the teacher to stand aside so the boys can work out the situation between them. The teacher must intervene and the boys will have to experience logical consequences that have been established for fighting. The teacher must also intervene when students make decisions that are unlawful or unethical. When a student steals from another or spreads lies or engages in sexual harassment, the resultant problem may be outside the students' power to resolve. The teacher will need to step in to stop the behavior, but they can use it as the basis for discussions about behavior that is right and wrong.

Reasonable Consequences and RSVP

Sometimes natural consequences do not produce discomfort and thus cannot help students learn. This is especially the case when students decide to break rules that have been established for the good of the class, as when they shout out during instruction. To deal with cases such as this, teacher and students should jointly agree to a set of reasonable logical consequences that will be invoked when rules are broken. Coloroso proposes a checklist she calls RSVP to use in assessing the quality of such consequences. **RSVP** stands for reasonable, simple, valuable, and practical—qualities that all logical consequences should have. Reasonable logical consequences do not punish, but instead call upon the student to take positive steps to improve behavior. They do this by making the student uncomfortable enough to realize there is a problem. Then, in order to solve the problem the student will be helped to see what has been done wrong, understand that ownership of the problem must be accepted, and accept that a good way must be found to resolve the situation.

Strengths of Coloroso's *Inner Discipline*

Coloroso believes in students' ability to accept ownership of their problems, resolve those problems, and live by the consequences of their decisions. She believes this process helps students take charge of their lives.

Coloroso sees discipline as a schoolwide concern and would have schools establish an overarching positive climate that permits students and teachers to make mistakes, resolve problems, and profit from the mistakes.

Within this broad climate, students would understand that they have a rightful place in school, but that they also have the responsibilities to respect the rights of others and to be actively involved in their own behavior and learning. They would learn they must take ownership of their decisions and not try to rationalize mistakes. In so doing, students can maintain their personal dignity.

Coloroso provides teachers a manageable approach to effective discipline. Her beliefs are humanistic and focused on preserving dignity and a sense of self-worth. It is through experiences with these qualities that Coloroso believes students develop inner discipline.

Initiating Coloroso's *Inner Discipline*

To begin using Coloroso's *Inner Discipline,* you must genuinely make the following tenets part of your beliefs about teaching.

1. All students are worth all I am capable of contributing to them.
2. I will not treat a student in a way I myself would not want to be treated.

With those tenets firmly in mind, you should formalize a plan for how you will work with the class. If you follow Coloroso's suggestions, the plan will be similar to the following:

1. Develop rules to guide the class. Involve students in helping compose them. Restrict the rules to what you can see or hear students do. Make them specific and be sure they have meaningful consequences. Both rules and consequences should be reasonable, simple, valuable, and practical.
2. Hold class discussions on the rules, their implications, and their consequences. This step is extremely important. Students need to hear and understand each rule, the reasons for the rule, and the consequences for violating the rule. Students need to believe they are capable of following the rules and able to make reasonable choices. Rules and consequences must be presented in such a way that students believe choice and responsible behavior are truly available to them.
3. If a rule is broken, the teacher should concentrate immediately on the behavior and consequences. (If a rule must be bent, it is because of the situation, not because of who the student is.) Applying consequences should include these steps:

   - Help students see what they did wrong.
   - Make sure students differentiate between the reality and the problem.
   - Give students ownership of the problems they have created.
   - Help them find ways to solve those problems.
   - Do all of this in a way that leaves their dignity, and yours, intact.

   For more serious infractions, students will need to go a step beyond the preceding five, to the Three R's of reconciliatory justice: restitution, resolution, and reconciliation. That means they need to fix what was done wrong, figure out how to keep it from happening again, and heal with the people they have harmed.
4. Get across to students that it is OK, even beneficial, to make mistakes, and that no problem is so great that it can't be solved.
5. Help students understand that when they have a problem, they need a plan, not an excuse. The teacher's role is to encourage students to solve problems in constructive ways, while experiencing the real-world consequences of their choices.
6. Take into account the fact that discipline problems are likely to result when rules are unclear and enforcement is inconsistent. This is often the case in areas of schools such as halls, playgrounds, lunchroom, and restrooms, where different people are on duty. When setting up a discipline procedure, it is best that the entire school be involved in the same program, including faculty, staff, aides, and others. When everyone is on the same page, students know the rules and consequences wherever they might be in the school.

Review of Selected Terminology

The following terms are central to understanding Coloroso's *Inner Discipline*. Check yourself to make sure you understand them:

Discipline: versus punishment, what discipline provides (awareness of wrong doing, ownership of problem, options for resolution, intact dignity)

Inner discipline: meaning of, value of

Types of misbehavior: mayhem, mischief, mistakes

Three types of schools and students: brickwall, jellyfish, and backbone

Consequences: logical, natural, RSVP (reasonable, simple, valuable, practical)

Problem: resolution, steps in solving (resolution, restitution, reconciliation)

The three cons: imploring, complaining, sulking

Application Exercises

Concept Cases

Case 1: Kristina Will Not Work ■ Kristina, a student in Mr. Jake's class, is quite docile. She socializes little with other students and never disrupts lessons. However, despite Mr. Jake's best efforts, Kristina will not do her work. She rarely completes an assignment. She is simply there, putting forth no effort at all. *How would Coloroso deal with Kristina?*

In order to convey that she believes and trusts in Kristina's ability, Coloroso might quietly say "Kristina, I see the work is not getting done. This is not in keeping with our class agreement. It seems this might be a problem. I wonder what we can do to resolve it? Perhaps we can think of some possible solutions and come up with a plan to help you finish your work. I'd like you to see if you can do that." Kristina then might identify some options: She might ask for extra help, work with another student, copy the answers during review, or do extra problems from another assignment to make up for the ones she misses. Guiding her through the problem solving and decision making process, Coloroso listens to Kristina without making judgments and helps her evaluate the options. Suppose Kristina decides to work with another student. She has taken responsibility for the problem and selected an option to help her solve it. Later that week

Coloroso may say to Kristina, "Now that you have been studying with Saundra, how is this working for you? Is this a satisfactory solution for you? I appreciate that you solved this problem and now are finishing your work." If Kristina's response indicates that this option was not successful, Coloroso can support her again through the decision-making process.

Case 2: Sara Cannot Stop Talking ■ Sara is a pleasant girl who participates in class activities and does most, though not all, of her assigned work. She cannot seem to refrain from talking to classmates, however. Her teacher, Mr. Gonzales, has to speak to her repeatedly during lessons, to the point that he often becomes exasperated and loses his temper. *What suggestions would Coloroso give Mr. Gonzales for dealing with Sara?*

Case 3: Joshua Clowns and Intimidates ■ Joshua, larger and louder than his classmates, always wants to be the center of attention, which he accomplishes through a combination of clowning and intimidation. He makes wise remarks, talks back (smilingly) to the teacher, utters a variety of sound-effect noises such as automobile crashes and gunshots, and makes limitless sarcastic comments and put-downs of his classmates. Other students will not stand up to him, apparently fearing his size and verbal aggression. His teacher, Miss Pearl, has come to her wit's end. *Would Joshua's behavior be likely to improve if Coloroso's techniques were used in Miss Pearl's classroom? Explain.*

Case 4: Tom Is Hostile and Defiant ■ Tom has appeared to be in his usual foul mood ever since arriving in class. On his way to sharpen his pencil, he bumps into Frank, who complains. Tom tells him loudly to shut up. Miss Baines, the teacher, says, "Tom, go back to your seat." Tom wheels around, swears loudly, and says heatedly, "I'll go when I'm damned good and ready!" *How would Coloroso deal with Tom?*

Questions and Activities

1. Each of the following exemplifies or relates to an important point in the Coloroso model of discipline. Identify the point illustrated by each.

   A. When Miles joined his friends to play basketball, he wore his new sneakers rather than his play shoes. When it began to rain, his new shoes got muddy and wet, which made Miles quite unhappy. His teacher and parents allow Miles to experience this natural consequence without nagging, lecturing, or rescuing him from his choice.

   B. Ms. Benedict is very angry and hurt that Alejo tore pages from one of her favorite read-aloud books. However, she wants to help him find a way to fix the damage, understand what he did, and make a plan so he won't do it again. Also, she wants to help him mend fences, both with her and with his classmates.

   C. When the children at Table 3 forgot to recap all the glue tubes, the glue dried up. However, with Mrs. Nguyen's help the children realized that the problem was something they could solve by remembering always to check their art supplies when they put things away.

   D. When third-grader Beth continued to misplace her work and supplies in her messy desk, the teacher asked her to straighten it out during choice time. This is reasonable, simple, a valuable experience, and practical.

   E. Brian's father is a respected member of the school board and his mother is active in the PTA. David's mother is a single parent and does not have much time to participate in school activities. When the boys are found playing recklessly with the tools in woodshop class, Brian is given a verbal reprimand while David is made to watch a film on proper tool handling and safety.

   F. When Angeline continued to be tardy to fifth-period algebra, Mrs. Wayne asked her to identify some options and come up with a plan so she could arrive to class on time. When Angeline presented her plan to Mrs. Wayne, they agreed to reevaluate the problem and solution in two weeks.

2. Examine Scenarios 1 and 2 in Appendix A. How could *Inner Discipline* be used to improve behavior in those two cases?

3. For a grade level and/or subject you select, outline in one page what you would do if you wished to implement Coloroso's ideas in your classroom.

4. According to Coloroso, teaching children how to think instead of what to think builds self-confidence. Also, she says that proper discipline does four things that punishment does not do: (1) shows students their mistake, (2) lets them own the problem it created, (3) gives them options for solving the problem, and (4) leaves their dignity intact. Describe a situation from your experience that exemplifies what she says.

5. Discipline problems seem to occur frequently in common school areas, such as the hallways and lunchroom. How do you think a school might set up a discipline procedure so these areas don't present a problem?

Primary References

Coloroso, B. 1990. *Discipline: Creating a positive school climate.* (Booklet; video; audio.) Littleton, CO: Kids are worth it! Coloroso's suggestions for establishing and maintaining a positive climate in the classroom and school.

———. 1990. *Winning at teaching...without beating your kids.* (Booklet; video; audio.) Littleton, CO: Kids are worth it! An early Coloroso work on how best to interact with students.

——— . 1994. *Kids are worth it!: Giving your child the gift of inner discipline.* New York: Avon Books. Coloroso's fundamental suggestions for helping teachers build a sense of inner discipline in their students.

———. 1999. *Parenting with wit and wisdom in times of chaos and loss.* New York: Harper-Collins. Coloroso's latest book in which she offers her basic principles and suggestions for helping children become responsible, self-directing individuals.

CHAPTER 11

Patricia Kyle, Spencer Kagan, and Sally Scott's *Win-Win Discipline*

PREVIEW OF KYLE, KAGAN, AND SCOTT'S WIN-WIN DISCIPLINE

Focus

- Teachers and students working together and sharing responsibility for proper behavior.
- Helping students toward self-management and autonomous life skills.
- Discipline structures to use for the moment of disruption, follow-up, and long-term solution.

Logic

- The ultimate goal of discipline is long-term self-managed responsibility.
- Irresponsible, self-defeating behavior can be replaced with useful alternatives.
- Discipline is a shared responsibility—a "we" approach involving student and teacher.
- Responsible behavior is closely linked to curriculum, instruction, and management.

Kyle, Kagan, and Scott's Contributions

- Identification of student "positions" to help teachers better select discipline structures.
- A framework that uses a "we" approach to produce long-term learned responsibility.
- A process to deal with the moment of disruption, follow-up, and long-term solutions.
- Ways to analyze individual and whole-class patterns of behavior.
- Differentiated step-by-step discipline structures for various disruptions and student positions.

Kyle, Kagan, and Scott's Suggestions

- Create a positive environment, with students and teacher working toward the same end.

Patricia Kyle

Spencer Kagan

Sally Scott

■ Share responsibility by actively involving students in both learning and discipline.
■ Work toward making students independent and self-managing.
■ Develop parent and community alliances to make win-win solutions work for everyone.

About Patricia Kyle, Spencer Kagan, and Sally Scott

Patricia Kyle, an experienced classroom teacher, school counselor, school psychologist, and now professor at Boise State University, has taught, researched, and written about classroom discipline for more than fifteen years. *Win-Win Discipline* shows her conviction that effective discipline is intertwined with effective teaching, and that active student involvement is essential in both. Kyle can be contacted by e-mail at pkyle@rmci.net

Spencer Kagan, a clinical psychologist, former professor of psychology and education at the University of California, and educational consultant, has researched, written about, and now specializes in training teachers to be more effective in their classrooms. He has published widely and heads his own company, Kagan Publishing and Professional Development. Kagan can be contacted through Kagan Publishing and Professional Development, P.O. Box 72008, San Clemente, CA 92674-9208; telephone 1-800-933-2667 (WEE-COOP); fax 949-369-6599; website www.KaganOnline.com; e-mail Win-Win@KaganOnline.com

Sally Scott is a teacher trainer and school administrator. She has been the main Win-Win trainer since its inception. Scott and her school have been featured nationally, and her school is considered a "must-see school" by national and international educators. Scott can be contacted by e-mail at sscott@washoe.k12.nv.us

Kyle, Kagan, and Scott's Contributions to Discipline

Kyle, Kagan, and Scott have shown that every discipline problem presents an opportunity to teach students how to make better behavior choices. They have provided the acronyms ABCD and AAA-BCDE to help teachers understand their approach. ABCD indicates the four main types of disruptive behavior—Aggression, Breaking rules, Confrontation, and Disengagement. AAA-BCDE refers to "student positions," which Kyle, Kagan, and Scott define as a mix of feelings, cognitions, and physical states that predispose students to act in certain ways, or as they say, position can be thought of as "where the student is coming from." Students sometimes disrupt when they come from a position of being Angry, seeking Attention, attempting to Avoid failure, Bored, seeking Control, Don't know, or Energetic. Kyle, Kagan, and Scott present concrete step-by-step structures with associated tactics for use at the moment of disruption, in follow-up, and for long-term solutions. *Win-Win Discipline* emphasizes to all concerned that teachers and students are on the same side in helping students learn to control their own behavior through responsible choices. The disruptive student's position always is considered valid: *Win-Win Discipline* helps students find nondisruptive ways to meet the needs associated with their position.

Kyle, Kagan, and Scott's Central Focus

Kyle, Kagan, and Scott focus on helping students meet their needs in nondisruptive ways. They begin by emphasizing that teachers and students are on the same side when it comes to discipline—both are trying to find ways for students to meet their needs in nondisruptive ways. They treat discipline as a joint responsibility of teachers and students. When disruptive behavior occurs, teachers intervene to help students recognize the position they occupy, and from that basis find responsible ways of fulfilling their needs. This is done by employing practical structures tailored to the student's position and then applying follow-up and long-term solutions to prevent problem recurrence. Kyle, Kagan, and Scott emphasize the linkage between discipline and curriculum, instruction, and management, maintaining that students who are actively involved in the learning process are seldom inclined to behave disruptively.

Kyle, Kagan, and Scott's Principal Teachings

- *Any disruptive behavior that interrupts the learning process can be used as a learning opportunity.* The aim is to help students meet their needs in a nondisruptive manner.
- *When working with disruptive students, Win-Win teachers use solutions based on the Three Pillars of Win-Win, which are: Same Side, Shared Responsibility, and Learned Responsibility.* Teacher and student are on the same side, working toward the same end. They share responsibility for creating a discipline solution that will help the student act more responsibly in the future.
- *Win-Win identifies four types of disruptive behavior: aggression, breaking rules, confrontation, and disengagement (the ABCD's of Disruptive Behavior).* By identifying the disruptive behavior, teachers are better able to supply the help students need.
- *Disruptive students occupy one or more of seven student positions (AAA-BCDE).* The seven positions are: attention-seeking, angry, avoiding failure, bored, control-seeking, don't know, and energetic.
- *Understanding a student's position does not mean allowing or affirming the disruption or trying to change the position.* It does mean dealing with the disruption, validating the position, maintaining the student's dignity, and helping the student toward responsible behavior.
- *Teachers must work together with students to show they are on the same side.* This involves openly expressing genuine caring for students, validating the position they are coming from, and providing support in establishing responsible behaviors.

- *Shared responsibility between teacher and students should be emphasized.* Students who participate in the learning process and help create their own discipline solutions are more likely to make responsible choices.
- *The ultimate goal of Win-Win Discipline is for students to become able to manage themselves and meet their needs through responsible choices.* When these new skills are learned properly, students can use them in many walks of life.
- *For the moment of disruption, Win-Win Discipline provides teachers a number of different discipline structures, depending on student positions.* Teachers must match strategies to students' needs.
- *After the moment of disruption has passed, teachers employ follow-up structures and long-term solutions.* This further encourages responsible behavior and sustained results.
- *When individual disruptive behavior occurs, the teacher also looks for whole class disruptive patterns.* Classes sometimes disrupt as a group, but these disruptions can be minimized through attention to curriculum, instruction, and management.
- *Teachers should recognize the importance of parent and community alliances and creating schoolwide programs for dealing with disruptive behavior.* When parents, teacher, and students collaborate in creating a solution—when they see themselves on the same side—students are more likely to make responsible choices. Schoolwide programs ensure win-win for all.
- *Consequences for responsible and irresponsible behavior are made known ahead of time, involve student input, and are instructional.* They follow the 3 R's of logical consequences—related, reasonable, and respectful.

Analysis of Kyle, Kagan, and Scott's *Win-Win Discipline*

The name *Win-Win Discipline* indicates that this is a discipline system in which teachers, students, administrators, and parents all emerge as "winners." Students are winners because they learn to choose responsible behavior that helps them learn better and relate better with others, while having their needs met in the classroom. Teachers and administrators are winners because *Win-Win Discipline* reduces disruptive behavior, making teaching more effective, relationships with students more positive, and satisfaction greater for everyone concerned. Parents are winners because they know their children are being helped in a humane manner to be more successful in school and life.

The general operating procedure of *Win-Win Discipline* is revealed in what Kyle, Kagan, and Scott call the **Three Pillars of Win-Win Discipline**: teacher, students, and parents are (1) working together on the same side, (2) sharing responsibility, and (3) learning to make more responsible choices. These pillars provide the philosophical underpinning for *Win-Win Discipline*, and each is associated with a critical question. *Same Side* encourages teachers to ask, "Can I relate to where the student is coming from?" *Shared Responsibility* encourages teachers to ask, "Did we create the solution together?" Teachers do not impose solutions on students with disruptive behavior but involve students equally in working toward more responsible choices. *Learned Responsibility* relates to the critical question, "Is it more likely that the student will act responsibly in the future?" Responsibility is built through follow-up structures and long-term solutions, discussed later in this section.

In *Win-Win Discipline*, each behavior problem is considered to be an opportunity for teaching and learning. Almost all behavior problems fall into four types, ABCD: Aggression, Breaking rules, Confrontation, and Disengagement. Disruptive students are said to be in "student positions" that can be identified and dealt with positively. There are seven such positions, coded AAA-BCDE: Attention-seeking, Angry, Avoiding failure, Bored, Control-seeking, Don't know, and Energetic. *Win-Win Discipline* provides step-by-step suggestions for identifying a disruptive student's position, applying positive solutions at the moment of disruption, following-up, and working toward long-term solutions.

Win-Win Discipline does not condemn student positions. To the contrary, it validates them as natural to everyone. What *Win-Win* does is to help teachers work with students so the needs that prompt the disruptive behavior can be met in nondisruptive ways. The teacher is asked to take the side of the disruptive student, making comments such as, "It's OK to need attention; from birth on, we all need attention." The teacher uses disruptive behavior as an opportunity to help students realize and accept their needs and then to find nondisruptive ways of meeting them.

Applying the *Win-Win Discipline* Process

Win-Win Discipline is applied as a five-phase process, beginning with the moment of disruption and extending through to long-term solutions. The phases converge into a natural process that converts disruptions into learning opportunities.

> Phase 1. The teacher identifies the disruptive behavior as A, B, C, or D—aggression, breaking rules, confrontations, or disengagement.
>
> Phase 2. The teacher identifies the position the student is coming from: AAA-BCDE—attention-seeking, angry, avoiding failure, bored, control-seeking, don't know, energetic.
>
> Phase 3. The teacher responds in the moment by validating the student position and then, together with the student, seeking a nondisruptive means of satisfying the needs associated with the position.
>
> Phase 4. The teacher initiates follow-up to help the student further, emphasizing the Three Pillars of *Win-Win Discipline*—same side, shared responsibility, and learned responsibility.
>
> Phase 5. The teacher and student collaborate to seek long-term ability to select nondisruptive behavior to meet one's needs.

Let's explore components of these phases a bit further.

Identifying the Type of Disruptive Behavior—ABCD

Kyle, Kagan, and Scott believe that when students are disruptive, they almost always display one of four types of behavior. Students may be *aggressive*. They may *break rules*. They may be *confrontational*. Or they may be *disengaged*. The type of behavior suggests the type of intervention the teacher should use.

Aggression

Aggressive behavior creates an unsafe atmosphere in the classroom. Physical aggressive acts include hitting, kicking, biting, and slapping. Verbal and behavioral aggression includes verbal put-downs, swearing, throwing, or destroying things. Aggressive behavior may escalate in response to the reactions of others: Therefore, at the moment of aggressive disruption, teachers must control their own reactions and, when possible, have everyone take time to cool down. Teachers should ask themselves these three behavior-specific questions:

1. Have I controlled my reaction?
2. Have I worked on relationship building with this student?
3. Does this student have structures to help him/her control aggression?

Breaking Rules

Students may break the rules for a variety of reasons: because they are angry, bored, or overly energetic; because they want attention or want to avoid failure; because they want to control; or simply because they do not understand, know enough, or have the skill to follow the rule. Common examples of breaking-the-rules behavior include talking without permission, making weird noises, chewing gum, passing notes, being out of seat, and not turning in work.

At the moment a rule is broken, the teacher wants to be sure of three behavior-specific concerns:

1. Does the student recall the rule?
2. Does the student understand the rule?
3. Can the student apply the rule?

A student may not remember the rule, in which case the rule might be retaught. The student may remember the rule, but not really understand it, in which case the teacher reteaches for understanding. Finally, the student may understand the rule but not be able or willing, at the moment, to follow it.

Confrontation

Students who disrupt in a confrontive manner usually are adept at provoking reactions from the teacher. Examples of confrontational behaviors include "You can't make me," complaining and arguing a myriad of reasons why things should be done differently, and putting down the teacher or the task.

When a student is confrontational, Kyle, Kagan, and Scott advise that teachers first must handle their own reactions and not push back. They should keep calm and be aware of their language and nonverbal messages. When teachers see confrontive behavior, they should ask themselves these behavior-specific questions:

1. Am I using a win-win leadership style?
2. Have I involved students in the class decision-making process?
3. Have I given students choices?

Disengagement

Students may disengage from lessons for several reasons. They may feel incapable of performing the task or they may consider the task to be boring or unworthy of their effort and attention. Passive disengaged behavior includes the student not listening, working off task, not finishing work, acting helpless, or saying "I can't." Active disengaged behavior includes put-downs, excessive requests for help, and comments such as "I've got better things to do" or "It would be better if..."

Teachers can do several things at the moment of disruption to assist students who are disengaged. They can begin by asking themselves these three behavior-specific questions:

1. Have I made the learning relevant for the students?
2. Have I used a variety of teaching strategies?
3. Have I been clear in my directions and expectations?

Identifying the Student's Position

Before teachers can formulate discipline structures to help a student make more responsible behavior choices, they need to know the reasons for the inappropriate behavior. This requires understanding the position of the disruptive student.

A "position" is explained as "an interaction of attitudes, cognitions, and physiology which influences the type of behavior students are likely to choose." More simply, position can be thought of as "where the student is coming from." The student is disruptive because some need manifest in his or her position is not being met. Working together, teacher and student must identify that need and determine how it can be satisfied in a nondisruptive manner. Student positions can be remembered using the acronym AAA-BCDE: Attention-seeking, Angry, Avoiding failure, Bored, Control-seeking, Don't know, and Energetic. The nature of these positions, together with the discipline structures they call for, are described later. *Win-Win Discipline* holds the following views of student positions:

- Student positions are not to be considered negative; they simply reflect the student's needs at the time he or she acts out.
- Disruptive behavior springs from unmet needs associated with student positions.
- Effective teachers try to gain the student's perspective in order to understand where the student is coming from.
- Every disruption is an opportunity for teaching and learning.

Understanding a student's position does not imply that the teacher approves of the disruptive behavior, nor does it mean that the teacher wishes to change the student's position. Positions are identified simply in order to help students make more responsible choices in meeting the need associated with the position, and to see the long-term benefits of doing so.

Discipline Structures for the Moment, Follow-Up, and Long-Term

Kyle, Kagan, and Scott identify three propitious times for teachers to help students choose better behavior by meeting the needs of their particular positions. The first intervention is at the *moment of disruption;* the second is with *planned follow-up;* and the third is joint planning of *long-term solutions.* The authors present a number of **discipline structures** and show how they are applied at these three prime phases. Four examples of the many structures they provide are presented to illustrate their suggestions—Spot the Signs, Language of Choice, Table the Matter, and Student Conference. Each structure is implemented through a series of steps.

Spot the Signs is a structure in which teachers help students recognize the early warning signs of disruptive behavior, correct themselves, and choose responsible behavior. This structure is applied as follows:

1. *Teacher offers support.* ("Mark, I'd like to help you spot the signs of disruptive behavior so you can show responsibility by choosing not to disrupt.")
2. *Explore student reactions to consequences.* Teacher asks Mark directly about his reaction to various consequences. For example, if Mark has previously forfeited computer time because he was banging on the keys, the teacher can say, "Mark, do you like it when you lose computer time?" Teacher continues to ask similar questions until the student responds with a "No." Teacher then asks, "Would you like to learn how to keep your computer time?" Again, the teacher persists until Mark responds with a "Yes."
3. *Generate alternatives.* Teacher explains that Mark is the only one who can make the change. Together they explore what triggers the disruptive behavior, and together they generate alternatives. "Mark, the person who can help you the most is you. I care about you and I know that if we work together we can solve this. What happened right before you lost your temper and began pounding on the computer keys? What are some responsible choices that you can make to avoid losing your temper again?"
4. *Practice selected alternative.* Mark and teacher select an alternative and practice it together. This allows Mark to learn what to say and how to act in situations that in the past have led to disruption.
5. *Plan follow-up.* Mark and teacher set a time to follow-up on Mark's progress.

Language of Choice helps control and direct the teacher's reaction while at the same time emphasizing responsible behavior and helping students understand the consequences of their actions. When disruptive behavior occurs, Language of Choice is applied in five steps.

1. *State a responsible behavior.* Teacher states a specific responsible behavior, ending this statement with the word "or." ("Franzi, you must put away your drawing tablet and markers, and open your history book now or...")
2. *State the consequence.* The teacher states the logical consequence that will be invoked should Franzi choose an irresponsible behavior. ("...you will not be allowed to sketch during project time today.")
3. *Indicate that the student must choose.* ("Franzi, it is your choice to put away your art materials or lose art time later.")
4. *Use encouragement.* Teacher encourages Franzi to choose the responsible behavior. ("I believe in you to make a responsible choice, Franzi.")
5. *Conduct follow-up conference.* Teacher schedules a follow-up conference with Franzi which focuses on working together to help create solutions for future disruptive situations. This follow-up conference is a way for Franzi to share responsibility.

Table the Matter is intended to give students and teacher opportunity to discuss an issue at a more appropriate time. Table the Matter is applied in four steps.

1. *Acknowledge or ask about the student's feelings.* ("Greg, you seem angry. Is that the way you feel? We all get angry sometimes. That's OK. It's what we do about our anger that makes us responsible or irresponsible.").
2. *Indicate inappropriate timing.* Teacher makes a clear statement that this is not an appropriate time to discuss the problem ("Greg, I can't stop the lesson to discuss this with you right now" or, "Greg, let's talk about this after our feelings have cooled down a bit.")
3. *Suggest an appropriate time.* ("Greg, let's talk about this after class. Can you meet then?").
4. *Meet with the student.* Teacher meets with Greg in a follow-up conference after class to discuss the problem calmly.

Conferences help produce closer student involvement in the discipline process. Follow-up conferences are conducted in the following sequence:

1. *Express caring.* Teacher begins by saying that she or he cares for the student and wants to support the student in choosing responsible behavior.
2. *Describe disruptive behavior.* Teacher clearly describes the specific disruptive behavior. For example, Pia continually calls out answers in class. Teacher may say, "Pia, I really care about you. I can understand how you are eager to be called upon. We all have been in the position of wanting to contribute so badly that we interrupt. I'm happy you want to be called on and make contributions and have me see what you know. But in our class we can't have students calling out answers without waiting to be called on. I wonder if together we can figure out a more responsible way for you to participate?"
3. *Explore the student position.* The teacher identifies the position that the student seems to be coming from and checks it out with the student. The teacher may say, "Pia, it seems you want me and the others to know you have worked

really hard. We all need attention of that sort. An actor or rock star would feel terrible if no one paid attention during a concert; an author would feel like a failure if no one read her book. I like attention too; everyone does sometimes. What are some times when you would like attention? Who would you like attention from?"

4. *Generate solutions.* Teacher encourages the student to come up with possible solutions, and together they evaluate the ideas. "Pia, let's think together. Students have different ways of getting attention, some of which are responsible while others aren't. What have you seen students do that you think are responsible ways to get attention? How would any of those things work for you?"

5. *Agree and plan.* Teacher and student agree on a solution and a time to conference again.

Matching Discipline Structures to Student Positions

Kyle, Kagan, and Scott make the following suggestions for matching intervention strategies to student positions when disruptive behavior occurs.

Position: Attention-Seeking

Most individuals want to know that others care about them, and when they feel they are not cared about, they seek attention. Students wanting attention may interrupt, annoy others, work slower than others, ask for extra help, or simply goof off. Instead of bringing the positive results the student is hoping for, attention-seeking behavior tends to annoy the teacher and disrupt the class. Teachers usually react by nagging or scolding. Students may cease to disrupt temporarily, but they usually fall back to attention-seeking fairly quickly.

Positive interventions teachers can use at the *moment of disruption* for attention-seeking include physical proximity, hand signals, and "I" messages. They can also give students attention, appreciation, and affirmation. But if attention-seeking is chronic, teachers will need to meet with students, first, to help them understand and accept their need for attention, and second, to look for positive, responsible ways to meet the need. Suggested structures for *long-term solutions* include focusing on the interests of the student and building self-concept and self-validation skills.

Position: Angry

Everyone wants to be able to express displeasure. Angry students may go to the extreme because they are unable—or don't know how—to do so in socially acceptable ways. Teachers don't like to deal with angry students and when doing so may experience feelings of hurt or indignation. Their immediate reaction often is to isolate the student or retaliate in some manner. However, this does nothing to help students better manage their anger. Kyle, Kagan, and Scott provide several *moment of disruption* structures to help teachers handle angry disruption, including cool down and think time and tabling the matter. *Long-term interventions* include conflict resolution conferences, spot the sign, and practice in skills of self-control.

Position: Avoiding Failure

We all have been in situations where we rationalize our inadequacies in order to avoid pain or embarrassment. The student who says, "I don't care about the stupid math quiz, so I won't study for it" knows that it is more painfully embarrassing to fail in front of others, than not to try at all. She might say, "I'm not stupid; I just didn't study." Win-Win teachers accept that none of us wants to appear stupid. They seek to help students find ways to work and perform without feeling bad if they aren't first or best. For *moment of disruption,* teachers can encourage students to try, reorganize and present the information in smaller instructional pieces, and assign partners or helpers. *Follow-up* and *long-term structures* include peer support, peer tutoring, personal affirmation, developing skills of independence, showing how mistakes can lead to excellent learning, and team pair solo, in which students practice first as a team, then in pairs, before doing activities alone.

Position: Bored

Students who act bored send messages to teachers that they do not enjoy and do not want to participate in the curriculum, instruction, and activities in the class. These students display their boredom in their body language, their lack of participation, and by being off-task. To help bored students at the *moment of disruption,* teachers can restructure the learning task or involve students more actively. As *follow-up,* they may conference with the students and assign them helping roles such as gatekeeper, recorder, or coach. For *long-term solutions,* teachers can provide a rich and relevant curriculum that actively involves students in the learning process and emphasizes cooperative learning and attention to multiple intelligences.

Position: Control-Seeking

Control-seeking students engage in power struggles with the teacher, and when challenged, argue or justify their actions. Teachers do not usually respond well to such behavior. Their reaction is to fight back, to show their dominance. For *moment of disruption* interventions, Kyle, Kagan, and Scott suggest that teachers acknowledge the student's power or use Language of Choice. For *follow-up* they may need to schedule a later conference to discuss the situation. There they would solicit student input concerning what causes students to struggle against the teacher and how the struggle can be avoided. *Long-term strategies* include involving students in the decision-making process and working with them to establish class agreements concerning challenge to teacher.

Position: Don't Know

Sometimes students respond or react disruptively because they simply don't know how to behave responsibly. If students don't know what is expected, the teacher *at the moment of disruption* should gently ask them and, if necessary, teach them at the time. If they need support, they can work with a buddy. *Follow-up* structures include reteaching, modeling, and practicing the responsible behavior. *Long-term solutions* include encouragement and focusing on the student's strengths.

Position: Energetic

All of us have experienced moments when we have so much energy we cannot concentrate or sit still. Some students are this way a good deal of the time, moving and talking incessantly. If energetic behavior becomes troublesome, teachers can *at the moment of disruption* move close to the disruptive student, remove any distracting elements or objects, and channel energy back into productive work. *Follow-up structures* include providing activities for students to work off energy in a positive manner, while *long-term* solutions include managing energy levels during instruction and connecting student interests to the instruction.

The Role of Logical Consequences

Logical consequences are conditions, either pleasant or unpleasant, that teacher and students have agreed should occur following student behavior. In *Win-Win Discipline*, logical consequences help teachers manage disruptions. These consequences are agreed to ahead of time. They are made plain to everyone, they involve student input, and they are instructional in nature. Additionally, they are *related* to the situation, *reasonable*, and *respectful* in both delivery and intent.

Identifying and Dealing with Whole Class Patterns

Sometimes disruptions involve more than individual students. When teachers take time to look beyond the individuals in their class, they also may discover patterns of disruptive behaviors in the whole class. Kyle, Kagan, and Scott encourage teachers to analyze behaviors and disruptions at the class level. For example, an unappealing curriculum may lead to a class pattern of disengagement; ineffective instruction may lead to a class pattern of avoiding failure; and poor management may be associated with a class pattern of rule-breaking. Once teachers determine class patterns, they can implement appropriate structures to minimize the moment of disruption and also to obtain good long-range results.

A variety of structures help teachers respond effectively to disruptive class patterns. For *aggressive class disruption,* structures for immediate application include think time or cool-down time, calm Language of Choice, and implementation of class-created logical consequences. Follow-up structures include class meetings and instruction in controlling aggression. Long-term solutions include activities in impulse control, conflict resolution skills, building mutual concern for class members, and the use of peer mediation.

For *breaking-rules class disruption,* it is appropriate to remind, clarify, model, and reinforce the rule, give verbal cues, and refocus attention. Follow-up structures include having the students restate or rewrite the rule as they understand it, reteaching the rule or the procedure, class meetings with the students, and expressing appreciation for responsible behavior. Long-term solutions include involving the students in creating the rules, instructing and reteaching the rules and procedures, and class community-building activities.

For *confrontational class disruption,* it is important first to use a "we" rather than "you versus me" approach, ask redirecting questions, or use class-created logical consequences. Follow-up structures might include class meetings, class contracts, student input, an appreciation box, and character-building activities. In addition to working on the student-teacher relation, other long-term solutions might involve students in decision making, situations involving choice and responsibility, and conflict management.

When the class displays *disengaged disruptive behaviors,* teachers can change instruction to make it more appealing, present the content in smaller bits, allow students to work in pairs, and assign students roles such as encourager and leader. Follow-up structures include class and team-building activities and a continuing effort to capitalize on student interests. For long-term structures, Kyle, Kagan, and Scott advise teachers to examine the Big Three (curriculum, instruction, and management); use varied teaching structures; and cooperative learning and multiple intelligences structures. They also advise teachers to involve students in curriculum choices.

The Big Three

The *Big Three*—curriculum, instruction, and management—are the primary elements that help teachers prevent behavior problems and reap the benefits of *Win-Win Discipline.* Students enjoy curriculum that is interesting and sufficiently challenging. They like to participate in the learning activities, so they appreciate cooperative learning and other interactive teaching strategies that deal with applying information, solving problems, and discovery. Students who understand expectations and procedures, and who have choices in what they learn and how they learn it, are more likely to participate, cooperate, and do their work. Teacher enthusiasm and willingness to vary and adapt instruction to the needs and various intelligences of the students help ensure that students remain engaged in learning.

Parent and Community Alliances and Schoolwide Programs

Partnerships with parents and community assist greatly in helping students make responsible behavior choices. Parents are more likely to support teachers who handle disruptive behavior in a positive manner and guide their child toward responsible behavior. The parents' input, support, follow-through, and backup strengthen the likelihood of responsible behavior. Ongoing teacher-parent communication builds positive parent attitudes toward teacher, school, and the educational program. Admittedly, not all parents will choose to cooperate in the discipline program. The degree of cooperation depends largely on how teachers reach out to parents. Rather than give up when parents won't work with them, teachers will profit by continuing to invite them to be actively involved in the process.

Win-Win Discipline provides many helpful suggestions for teacher-parent communication and interaction, suggesting that contact be made during the first week of school. Letters sent home, class newsletters, and e-mails are efficient ways to connect with parents. Phone calls can be used as well, though they take considerable time.

Parent nights and open houses offer person-to-person communication opportunities. Conferences can be used to show parents they are valued as allies. This can lead to some parents serving as mentors and tutors. Creating schoolwide programs, such as assemblies and incentive programs, encourage whole school involvement. The broader community can become involved through field trips, guest speakers, apprenticeships, and adopting and working with day-care and senior centers.

Strengths of Kyle, Kagan, and Scott's *Win-Win Discipline*

Kyle, Kagan, and Scott have given teachers a system of discipline that removes the adversarial relationship between teachers and students evident in many systems of discipline. They place teacher, students, and parents on the same side and attempt to get all working toward the same goal, which is enabling students to make responsible choices that serve them well in the classroom and life. They emphasize that every disruption is a fertile moment for teaching students how to make responsible choices. They help teachers identify the type of disruptive behavior being exhibited and the student position at the time. They show teachers how to validate the student's position and then implement the appropriate discipline structure. They provide an extensive set of such structures designed for application at the moment of disruption, for follow-up, and for long-term benefits, and they clearly indicate how the structures should be applied.

Initiating Kyle, Kagan, and Scott's *Win-Win Discipline*

Ideally, implementation of *Win-Win Discipline* should begin on the first day of school, but if that is not possible, it can be put in place at any time. It should then receive major attention for a few weeks. Maintenance of the program continues through the school year. In keeping with Kyle, Kagan, and Scott's suggestions, here is how you can introduce *Win-Win Discipline* to your students.

Begin by setting the tone for a win-win climate in the classroom. Let the students know that this will be a class built on the Three Pillars of *Win-Win Discipline*—same side, shared responsibility, and learned responsibility. You might say something like this: "This is our class, and with all of us working together we will create a place where each person feels comfortable and where we all can enjoy the process of learning. As your teacher, I have a responsibility to create an environment where this can happen, but I need your help to make it work. Each of you must know that you are an important member of this class with important responsibilities, and that you can help make the class a pleasant place to be. One of your important responsibilities is to help us create a positive learning atmosphere, one where everybody's needs are met. To accomplish this, we all must work together. I suggest that we begin by creating a class agreement."

Kyle, Kagan, and Scott describe a structure to use in creating a class agreement. Write Win-Win Class on the left side of a chart paper and ask the class: "Let's name some behaviors we all could choose that would make all of us happy to be in this class and able to get our work done." Record student responses, guiding the process so the behaviors are stated positively and are ones everyone could use. For example, if someone suggests "No put-downs," ask questions such as, "If we were not going to use put-downs in this class, what would we be using instead?" List responsible behaviors on the left and behaviors such as put-downs on the right, under a column labeled Win-Lose Class.

When you have a reasonable list, ask students, "How do you feel about this list? Would you be willing to adopt the Win-Win list of behaviors as our class agreement? Can we agree to avoid the behaviors on the Win-Lose list?

It is important that students believe their opinions and cooperation are valued. Tell them, "You and I need to be on the same side, and work together to create a classroom we all enjoy where everyone can learn. You will always be included in the decision-making process. You will be able to have your say. We will learn and practice skills that are important for being citizens in a democratic society. Choosing responsible behavior will be one of the most important things we will learn."

During the first weeks, use activities that strengthen the concept of Three Pillars—same side, shared responsibility, and learned responsibility. This reassures students that discipline will not be done "to" them, but will happen "with" them. In collaboration with the class you might decide on preferred classroom procedures, discuss discipline structures and their purposes, develop logical consequences to be used for encouraging responsible behavior, and solicit student input on some curriculum decisions. You can do all this in a series of class meetings. You also can show students how you will help them turn irresponsible choices into good learning situations. That is where follow-up and long-term structures come into play. Remember that during the first weeks you will need to begin establishing alliances with parents. Letters home, class newsletters, and e-mails are the most effective methods. Also be ready to use parent nights, open houses, and parent conferences as times to build those alliances.

Review of Selected Terminology

The following terms are central to understanding Kyle, Kagan, and Scott's *Win-Win Discipline*. Check yourself to make sure you understand them.

Win-Win Discipline

ABCD of disruptive behavior: aggression, breaking rules, confrontations, disengagement

AAA-BCDE of student positions: attention-seeking, angry, avoiding failure, bored, control-seeking, don't know, energetic

Three Pillars of Win-Win Discipline: same side, shared responsibility, learned responsibility

Big Three: curriculum, instruction, management

Application of Discipline Structures: moment of disruption, follow-up, long-term

Types of Discipline Structures: spot the signs, language of choice, table the matter, and student conference

Win-Win Discipline Process: steps in applying

■Application Exercises

Concept Cases

Case 1. Kristina Will Not Work ■ Kristina, a student in Mr. Jake's class, is quite docile. She socializes little with other students and never disrupts lessons. However, despite Mr. Jake's best efforts, Kristina will not do her work. She rarely completes an assignment. She is simply there, putting forth no effort at all. *How would Kyle, Kagan, and Scott deal with Kristina?*

Kyle, Kagan, and Scott would advise Mr. Jake to do the following: First, Mr. Jake quickly determines Kristina's disruptive behavior and asks behavior-specific questions. Next he attempts to identify, validate, and help Kristina accept her position. Because one of the best ways to determine a student's position is simply to ask, Mr. Jake might well ask Kristina how she feels about the work, determining if it is too hard (leading to avoidance of failure), or not interesting (leading to boredom.) If Mr. Jake determines that the work is too difficult, and that Kristina's position is one of trying to avoid failure or that she doesn't know how to do the work, he might say quietly, "I really care about you, Kristina, and I want to help you be successful. I see this work is not getting finished. None of us wants to tackle something we know will be too hard for us. The best thing to do if something is too hard is to break it into smaller pieces, mastering a part at a time. Another good strategy is to work on the difficult pieces with others. Two heads are smarter than one. What suggestions do you have that will help you be successful?" Together they come up with possible solutions and then, if they agree that Kristina could benefit by working with a partner on smaller steps, Mr. Jake may ask, "Would you like to work on this section with Danielle before moving on?" Throughout this interaction, Mr. Jake is attempting to help Kristina meet her needs through responsible behavior. As follow-up, Mr. Jake might focus on her success by saying something like "Kristina, I knew you could

do this if we tried making the steps smaller." His long-term solutions will include further encouragement and individual attention to Kristina's strengths.

Case 2: Sara Cannot Stop Talking ■ Sara is a pleasant girl who participates in class activities and does most, though not all, of her assigned work. She cannot seem to refrain from talking to classmates, however. Her teacher, Mr. Gonzales, has to speak to her repeatedly during lessons, to the point that he often becomes exasperated and loses his temper. *What suggestions would Kyle, Kagan, and Scott give Mr. Gonzales for dealing with Sara?*

Case 3. Joshua Clowns and Intimidates ■ Joshua, larger and louder than his classmates, always wants to be the center of attention, which he accomplishes through a combination of clowning and intimidation. He makes wise remarks, talks back (smilingly) to the teacher, utters a variety of sound-effect noises such as automobile crashes and gunshots, and makes limitless sarcastic comments and put-downs of his classmates. Other students will not stand up to him, apparently fearing his size and verbal aggression. His teacher, Miss Pearl, has come to her wit's end. *Would Joshua's behavior be likely to improve if win-win discipline were used in Miss Pearl's classroom? Explain.*

Case 4: Tom Is Hostile and Defiant ■ Tom has appeared to be in his usual foul mood ever since arriving in class. On his way to sharpen his pencil, he bumps into Frank, who complains. Torn tells him loudly to shut up. Miss Baines, the teacher, says, "Tom, go back to your seat. Tom wheels around, swears loudly, and says heatedly, "I'll go when I'm damned good and ready!" *How would Tom's behavior be handled in a win-win classroom?*

Questions and Activities

1. To what extent do you feel you could put *Win-Win Discipline* into effect in your classroom? What portions do you believe you could implement easily? What portions do you believe might present a difficulty?

2. *Win-Win Discipline* rests on Three Pillars called same side, shared responsibility for solutions, and learned responsibility. To what extent do you believe teachers will be able to convey these perspectives to students? What would be appropriate statements to help them do so?

3. In what ways are curriculum, instruction, and management linked to preventing discipline problems? How might each help with the moment of disruption, follow-up, and long-term solutions?

4. Kyle, Kagan, and Scott believe that parent and community alliances are important for *Win-Win Discipline* to succeed. Indicate how you would obtain support from parents and community.

5. Examine either Scenario 1 or 8 in Appendix A. To what extent do you think behavior might improve in those classes if *Win-Win Discipline* were used?

Primary Reference

Kyle, P., S. Kagan, and S. Scott. 2001. *Win-win discipline: Structures for all discipline problems*. San Clemente, CA: Kagan Publishing.

Suggested Readings

Kagan, L., M. Kagan, and S. Kagan. 1998. *Teambuilding*. San Clemente, CA: Kagan Publishing.

Kagan, M., L. Robertson, and S. Kagan. 1998. *Classbuilding*. San Clemente, CA: Kagan Publishing.

Kyle, P., S. Scott, and S. Kagan. 2001. *Win-win discipline course workbook*. San Clemente, CA: Kagan Publishing.

Alfie Kohns's *Beyond Discipline*

Focus

■ Teaching that promotes thinking, decision making, and consideration for others.
■ Developing a sense of community in the classroom, with shared responsibility.
■ Involving students in resolving classroom problems, thus eliminating aversive control.

Alfie Kohns

Logic

■ Coercive discipline has no place in enlightened teaching: It harms rather than helps.
■ Students develop self-control and responsibility when trusted and allowed initiative.
■ Effective teachers use collaborative problem-solving instead of coercive control.

Contributions

■ Urged "constructivist teaching" as the best approach to education.
■ Showed how coercive discipline works against the development of caring human beings.
■ Popularized the concept of classroom as community, where everyone participates equally.
■ Provided guidance to help teachers transform their classrooms into communities.

Kohn's Suggestions

■ Involve students seriously in discussing curriculum, procedures, and class problems.
■ Organize the curriculum to attend to student interests and promote in-depth thinking.
■ Always ask the question: How can I bring my students into helping to decide on this matter?
■ Use participative classroom management to resolve problems that occur in the class.

About Alfie Kohn

Formerly a teacher, Alfie Kohn is now a full-time writer and lecturer. He has several influential books to his credit, including *The Brighter Side of Human Nature: Altruism and Empathy in Everyday Life* (1990); *No Contest: The Case against Competition* (1986, 1992); *Punished by Rewards: The Trouble with Gold Stars, Incentive Plans, A's, Praise, and Other Bribes* (1993, 1999); *Beyond Discipline: From Compliance to Community* (1996); *What to Look for in a Classroom: And Other Essays* (1998); and *The Schools Our Children Deserve: Moving Beyond Traditional Classrooms and "Tougher Standards"* (1999). He has also published numerous journal articles related to motivation, grading, discipline, and developing caring people. Now recognized as one of the most original thinkers in education, Kohn has appeared on over 200 radio and television programs, including "Oprah" and "The Today Show," and his work has received mention in scores of national newspapers and magazines. He speaks frequently at major conferences and conducts workshops across the nation. He can be reached at his website www.alfiekohn.org

Kohn's Central Focus

Kohn's critical analyses of schooling and teaching have focused mainly on helping teachers develop caring, supportive classrooms in which students pursue in depth topics of interest to them and participate fully in solving class problems, including problems of behavior. He has roundly criticized teaching (and discipline approaches) that do things *to* students rather than *involving* students as partners in the process. Particularly scathing have been his attacks on discipline schemes that involve reward and punishment, which most do. He says that nothing valuable comes from reward and punishment—that the process is actually counterproductive, not only because it produces side effects such as mistrust, avoidance, and working for rewards only, but also because it causes students to mistrust their own judgment and thwarts their becoming caring and self-reliant. He advises teachers to forget all the popular systems of discipline and work instead toward developing a **sense of community** in their classes, where students feel safe and are continually brought into making judgments, expressing their opinions, and working cooperatively toward solutions that affect themselves and the class.

Kohn's Contributions to Discipline

Kohn has made two significant contributions to discourse on classroom discipline. The first is his proposition that instruction should be based on **constructivist theory,** which holds that students cannot receive knowledge directly from teachers but must construct it from experience. A corollary of this view is that for instruction to be effective students must be involved deeply in topics they consider important, and when they do so there is little need for discipline controls of any sort. The second contribution is his rationale and prescription for developing a sense of community in the classroom, which he judges essential for developing caring, responsible students. This sense of community would more effectively bring about purposeful activity and concern for others, which is what teachers normally hope to achieve through discipline techniques.

Kohn's Principal Teachings

- *Educators must abandon teaching that "does things to" students and replace it with teaching that takes students seriously, involves them in decisions, and helps them explore in depth topics they consider important.* Students quickly forget most of what they learn in traditional teaching because the learning is superficial and of little importance from the students' point of view.
- *Educators must look beyond the techniques of discipline and ask the question: What are we attempting to accomplish with discipline?* Doing this, he says, will make evident that most teachers are thinking in terms of making students compliant and quiet, conditions that do not develop the kinds of people we'd like students ultimately to become.
- *Virtually all popular discipline programs are based on threat, reward, and punishment, used to gain student compliance.* Essentially, discipline programs differ only in how kindly and respectfully the teacher speaks to students while using threat, reward, and punishment.
- *When students are rewarded (or punished) into compliance, they usually feel no commitment to what they are doing.* They have no real understanding of why they are doing the act and are not becoming people who *want* to act this way in the future.
- *Teacher-made rules are of no practical value in the classroom.* This is because students learn how best to behave not from being told, but from having the opportunity to behave responsibly.
- *Some teachers—and most authorities in discipline—have an unrealistically negative view of students' basic motives.* They consider students to be predisposed to disobedience and trouble-making. They seem also to ignore that the curriculum powerfully influences student interest and involvement.
- *Student growth toward kindness, happiness, and self-fulfillment occurs as they work closely with fellow students.* This includes students' disagreeing and arguing with each other, which can have positive benefits.
- When concerns arise, the teacher should always ask students "What do you think we can do to solve this problem?"
- Class meetings offer the best forum for addressing questions that affect the class.
- *Education must be reformed so that classrooms take on the nature of communities.* A classroom community is a place where students are cared about

and care about others, are valued and respected, and think in terms of *we* instead of *I*.

- *Teachers who wish to move beyond discipline must do three things:* provide an engaging curriculum based on student interests, develop a sense of community, and draw students into meaningful decision-making.

Analysis of Kohn's *Beyond Discipline*

Discipline *per se* makes no sense except in relation to what the teacher is attempting to accomplish in the classroom. If the teacher is primarily concerned with keeping order and maintaining quiet, there are a number of effective discipline systems they can use. If on the other hand, the teacher is primarily concerned with developing self-directed, responsible, caring students who explore in depth topics they consider interesting and relevant, then an entirely different approach is required. Before we can properly understand what discipline means to Kohn, we need to examine his views concerning education and teaching.

The Trouble with Today's Teaching

Kohn thinks "traditional instruction" is falling well short of the expectations we hold for it. When he says traditional instruction, he means the type, seen in classrooms everywhere, in which the teacher selects the curriculum, does the planning, delivers the lessons through lecture, demonstration, guided discussion, reading assignments, worksheets and homework, and tests students to assess their progress. Emphasis in that kind of instruction is placed on helping students reach certain specific objectives—information and skills that students can demonstrate behaviorally. Little attention is giving to exploring ideas, seeking new solutions, looking for meaning or connections, or attempting to gain deeper understanding of the phenomena involved. Students remain relatively passive during traditional instruction. They listen, read assignments, answer questions when called on, and complete worksheets. There is little give and take. Instruction and learning are deemed "successful" in the extent to which students show on tests they have reached most of the stated objectives.

What is wrong with this kind of teaching? After all, it has been the predominant method of teaching for many years. Kohn (1999, p. 28) says that it counterproductively puts emphasis on *how well* students are doing rather than *on what* they are doing. Instruction concerned with *how well* tends to focus on outcomes that are shallow, relatively insignificant, and of little interest or relevance to learners. Students come to think of correct answers and good grades as the major goals of learning. They rarely experience the satisfaction of exploring in depth a topic of interest and exchanging their views and insights with others. Kohn says an impressive and growing body of research shows that the traditional approach produces several undesirable outcomes, such as:

- Undermines student interest in learning
- Makes failure seem overwhelming

- Does not lead students to challenge themselves
- Reduces the quality of learning (that is, it has little depth or relevance)
- Causes students to think of how smart they are instead of how hard they are trying

He goes on to say that students taught in this way develop a poor attitude toward learning. They think of learning as getting the work done rather than something they could be excited about exploring. Once they have done the "stuff," they quickly forget much of it as they move on to learn more new stuff. They strive to get the right answer, and when they do not, or if they don't make top scores on the test, they experience a sense of failure that is out of place in genuine learning where making mistakes is the rule rather than the exception. They never have reason to challenge themselves intellectually. Their learning is superficial and their desire to learn for its own sake nonexistent. The overall result is that while students seem to be learning well, they are actually doing poorly because they are not thinking widely and exploring ideas thoughtfully.

How Instruction Should Be Done

Kohn argues for instruction that is very different from the traditional. He says, first, that kids should be taken seriously. By that he means teachers must honor them as individuals and seek to determine what they need and enjoy. Good teachers, he says, use a constructivist approach, knowing that students must construct knowledge and skills out of the experiences provided in school. These teachers look for where students' interests lie, continually trying to imagine how things look from the child's point of view and figuring out what lies behind the child's questions and mistakes. These teachers know knowledge cannot be absorbed from the teacher. They therefore lead students to explore topics, grapple with them, make sense of them. They provide challenges and emphasize that making mistakes is an important part of learning. Kohn has much to say about the role of mistakes in learning. He gives an example (1999, pp. 138–139) in which the teacher asks the class how many legs an insect has. A boy answers, "twelve or fifteen or more." The teacher is tempted to say "No…" but instead decides to try to get a feeling for what the boy is thinking. She asks if he can give an example, and he replies, "a caterpillar." This unexpected answer opens up a good discussion about adult insects, larvae, and the possibility of mutations.

How do teachers help students move into "deeper levels of thinking?" Kohn says the best way is by asking them for examples or asking the question "How do we know that?" This helps students maintain a critical mind, a healthy skepticism, a need for evidence, a willingness to hear different points of view, and a desire to see how things are connected. It encourages them to appraise the importance of what they are learning and to explore how it can be useful in their lives.

From his constructivist position, Kohn argues for a curriculum that allows students to be purposefully active most of the time, rather than passive. He says the way to bring that about is to "…*start* not *with facts to be learned or disciplines to be mastered, but with questions to be answered*" (1999, p. 145). He says these questions should not lead students to correct answers, but make students pause, wonder, and reflect. Kohn gives examples of what he means in questions such as, "How could you improve the human hand?" and "Why were the founding fathers so afraid of democracy?" (1999, p. 146).

Kohn urges educators to remember three key facts about teaching: (1) Students learn most avidly and have their best ideas when they get to choose which questions they want to explore, (2) all of us tend to be happiest and most effective when we have some say about what we are doing, and (3) when student choice and control over learning is not allowed, achievement drops. Given these facts and the difference they make in learning, it is astonishing that present-day instruction tends systematically to ignore them. It is unnerving to most teachers, to say the least, to try to organize instruction in accordance with these facts. However, says Kohn, it is breathtaking to be involved in learning where students have a say in the curriculum and can decide what they will do, when, where, with whom, and toward what end. Although Kohn points out that this approach must be adjusted to the maturity levels of students, he says it is a rule of thumb that "the more students' questions and decisions drive the lesson, the more likely (it is) that real learning will occur" (1999, p. 151). The best teachers, he insists, are those who ask themselves "Is this a decision I must make on my own, or can I involve students in it?"

To summarize, Kohn's description of good teaching includes the following:

- Teachers must take students seriously by treating them as individuals with needs to be met, including the opportunity to delve deeply into topics of interest.
- Students should be brought into making decisions about what is to be learned and how progress will be demonstrated.
- Curriculum and instruction should be organized in large part around questions students want to explore.
- Questions should be explored in depth, rather than superficially, and opinion, evidence, relevance, and interconnectedness examined critically.
- Students work actively, purposefully, and often cooperatively, with give and take.
- The teacher assists students by helping obtain needed resources, listening, urging and encouraging, exploring mistakes and showing students how to use mistakes productively, and helping students make sense of what they are learning.
- Progress is demonstrated not in test results, but in productivity, insight, and ability to explain and analyze critically.

Where Discipline Fits in Kohn's Views on Teaching

It is time, Kohn says (1996, p. 54), to decide just what it is we hope to accomplish with discipline. We should take a serious look beyond the *methods* of discipline and give careful consideration to the *goals* of discipline. This statement gives pause. Most people have taken for granted that the goal of discipline is to control student behavior (or enable students to control their own behavior in accordance with adult expectations) so that teaching and learning may proceed as intended. But Kohn persists in putting the question: "Just what is it we are trying to do here?"

This question presents an issue, he says, that people who write about and do research in discipline never address. They expound on "effective discipline," but effective in regard to what? The obvious answer is that discipline is effective when it causes students to behave as teachers wish them to. Therein lies the rub, in Kohn's view. All approaches to discipline, when analyzed, reveal a clear set of assumptions about students, learning, and the role of the teacher. While these assumptions are never made explicit, even in the writings of the most respected authorities, they directly suggest that (1) students are by nature predisposed to disrupt the learning program and deal misery to teachers, (2) learning occurs best in an atmosphere of structure, quiet, and order, and (3) the teacher's role in discipline is to make students obedient, compliant, and above all, quiet.

Kohn contends that all three assumptions are ill-founded, and he therefore finds fault with virtually all the popular approaches to classroom discipline. He points, for example, to the work of Jacob Kounin (see Chapter 2), one of the first writers to attempt a scientific analysis of classroom behavior related to discipline. Preeminent among several teacher traits that Kounin found helpful in discipline is one called "withitness." Teachers display this trait when they are attentive to what all students are doing in the classroom at all times and when they make sure the students are aware of it. Such teachers are more effective than their "withoutit" colleagues, to use Kohn's words. But to what does the word "effective" refer? Kohn points out that Kounin used it to mean getting student conformity and obedience. In other words, it means that students keep busy at their assigned work and don't do anything the teacher considers inappropriate. Kohn (1996) says:

> Now, if a good classroom is one where students simply do what they're told, we shouldn't be surprised that a teacher is more likely to have such a classroom when students are aware that she can quickly spot noncompliance. (p. 55)

Kohn levels some of his sharpest criticisms against the Canters' *Assertive Discipline* but is also troubled by contentions in the works of Dreikurs (see Chapter 2), Albert (see Chapter 5), and Curwin and Mendler (see Chapter 9). He alludes (1996) to what he calls the rhetoric that accompanies the newer, supposedly more humane discipline systems, but says:

> ...I have reluctantly concluded...that the New Disciplines are just as much about getting compliance as is the more traditional approach. The overriding goal is to get students to do what they are supposed to be doing...(and) to learn what's acceptable to the teacher and what's not. (p. 59)

The Trouble with Compliance

Kohn is deeply troubled by the notion that schooling is usually structured to force, or at least entice, *compliant behavior* from students. Most teachers are delighted when students comply with their expectations, so what is wrong with compliance? Kohn (1996) describes how he often begins workshops with teachers by asking the question: "What are your long-terms goals for the students you work with? What would you like them to be—to be like—long after they've left you?" (p. 60). Teachers say they want their students to be caring, happy, responsible, curious, and creative, a conclusion that

> …is unsettling because it exposes a yawning chasm between what we want and what we are doing, between how we would like students to turn out and how our classrooms and schools actually work. We want children to continue reading and thinking after school has ended, yet we focus their attention on grades, which have been shown to reduce interest in learning. We want them to be critical thinkers, yet we feed them predigested facts and discrete skills—partly because of pressure from various constituencies to pump up standardized test scores. We act as though our goal is short-term retention of right answers rather than genuine understanding. (p. 61)

Many teachers rely heavily on class rules and rewarding students who behave or respond as teachers want. But Kohn points out that even when students are rewarded into compliance, they usually feel no commitment to what they are doing, no genuine understanding of the act or why they are doing it, and no sense that they are becoming people who *want* to act this way in the future. Moreover, classroom rules are self-defeating because they cause students to look for ways of subverting rules and cast teachers as policemen who feel obliged to take action when students break the rules. Kohn (1996) concludes that the entire process of behavior management works against what we hope to achieve because

> The more we "manage" students' behavior and try to make them do what we say, the more difficult it is for them to become morally sophisticated people who think for themselves and care about others. (p. 62)

Kohn says that if compliance is *not* what teachers are looking for in the long run, then we are faced with a basic conflict between our ultimate goals for learners and the methods we are using to achieve those goals. One or the other, Kohn asserts, has got to give.

The Changes That Are Needed

If we give up reward and punishment as means of ensuring desired behavior, indeed, if we move away from compliance entirely as the goal of discipline, then what are we left with? Most people ask, "Aren't there times when we simply need students to do what we tell them?" Kohn begins his reply to that question with the suggestion that teachers think carefully about how often "students need to do what the teacher tells them." He notes that the number of such occasions varies widely from one teacher to another, which suggests that the need for student compliance is seated in the teacher's personality and background. Teachers ought to examine their preferences and bring them to a conscious level: If one teacher needs students to be more compliant than another, is that teacher then entitled to use a coercive discipline program to meet his or her particular needs?

When reflecting on this point, many teachers are inclined to ask whether this means that anything goes, whether students don't have to comply with expectations that they participate and learn, and whether they can ignore assignments, shout obscenities, and create havoc.

This concern, Kohn explains, misses the point. The question isn't whether it's all right for students to act in those ways, but rather, are they likely to do so if their teacher does not demand control and compliance, but instead emphasizes a curriculum that appeals to students. Teachers do not have to choose between chaos on the one hand and being a strong boss on the other. There is another, and better, approach for teachers, which is to work with students in creating a democratic community where the teacher is not much concerned with personal status and only rarely with demanding compliance.

Kohn contends that students in such classrooms are likely to comply with teacher expectations when it is truly necessary for them to do so, and he admits that there will be such times. But students are more apt to comply willingly when bonds of trust have been built between teacher and students. Just as the teacher has made a habit of trusting students, students come to trust and respect the teacher in return.

The Value of Conflict

Student growth toward kindness, happiness, and self-fulfillment depends more on working closely with fellow students, including disagreeing and arguing with them, than with following rules and learning discrete bits of information. Kohn says that it is more important for students to wrestle with dilemmas, clash with others' ideas, and take others' needs into account than to follow sets of rules. The sound of children arguing (at least in many circumstances) should be music to teachers' ears. True, conflict can become destructive, in which case it must be stopped and ironed out. But disagreement presents golden opportunities for learning and, therefore, should not be suppressed. Even hurtful conflict needs to be resolved rather than pushed aside. Kohn notes that teachers should be wary of various versions of "conflict resolution" that do not examine the deeper issues involved, including people's motives and the possibility that something valuable may be gained from dealing with the conflict. Kohn expresses suspicion about classrooms that operate too smoothly and cleanly. To him, they suggest that conflict may have been conveniently suppressed by the teacher. Teachers question the practicality of stopping planned lessons in favor of lessons about resolving conflict. Certainly many situations do not permit an extended discussion at the time they occur. When that is the case, the teacher may wish to ask for a conversation about the matter later on. The enlightened point of view, hard though it may be to accept at first, is that teachers should expect and welcome students' arguments about the rules. Students become thinkers when they try to make sense of things in their own minds. Students who cannot voice their opinions find ways of expressing them in ways far less productive than rational argument. Kohn says that discipline writers are wrong in suggesting that teachers should do everything possible to keep classroom misbehavior from occurring. He suggests (1996) instead that

> ...the real quantum leap in thinking is not from after-the-fact to prevention, where problems are concerned. It involves getting to the point that we ask, "What exactly is

construed as a problem here—and why?" It means shifting from eliciting conformity and ending conflict to helping students become active participants in their own social and ethical development. (p. 77)

Regarding Structure and Limits

Most teachers feel it is necessary to place structure and limits on student behavior if the class is to function efficiently. Is their belief justified? Kohn presents criteria for determining how defensible a structure or limit is, that is, how much it resembles plain teacher control. Here are some of his criteria:

- *Purpose.* A restriction is legitimate to the extent its objective is to protect students from harm, as opposed to imposing order for its own sake.
- *Restrictiveness.* The less restrictive a structure or limit, the better. Kohn says that it is harder, for example, to justify a demand for silence than for quiet voices.
- *Flexibility.* While some structure is helpful, one must always be ready to modify the structure in accordance with student needs.
- *Developmental appropriateness.* Kohn uses the example that while we need to make sure that young children are dressed for winter weather, it is better to let older students decide on such matters for themselves.
- *Presentation style.* The way in which restrictions are presented makes a big difference in how students accept them. Kohn cites a study that found no negative effects when guidelines for using art supplies were presented respectfully to students. But when the identical rules were presented to another group in a tone that ordered them to comply, the students showed less interest and did less creative work.
- *Student involvement.* Most importantly, it is student input that makes structure acceptable. When concerns arise, the teacher can ask students "What do you think we can do to solve this problem?"

Class Meetings

Kohn agrees with many other authorities that class meetings offer the best forum for addressing questions that affect the class. He makes the following points about class meetings.

- *Sharing.* Class meetings are a place to talk about interesting events. Students decide whether or not they want to speak up.
- *Deciding.* Class meetings are ideal places for deciding on matters that affect the class, such as furniture arrangement and procedures for working on projects.
- *Planning.* Class meetings are places where planning should be done for field trips, raising money, inviting chaperons, and so forth. Teachers should always be asking themselves "Wait a minute: How can I bring the students in on this?"
- *Reflecting.* Class meetings are good places to think about progress, what has been learned, what might have worked better, and what changes might help the class.

Holding good class meetings is not as easy as it sounds. Sometimes participants can't agree on a solution. Some don't participate. Some behave in an unkindly manner to someone's idea, or don't pay attention. Sometimes one or two students dominate the meeting. Kohn reminds us that these are not problems for the teacher to solve alone. They are to be brought up for consideration and dealt with by the group.

Many teachers say they like the idea of class meetings, but can't find time in their schedules to include them. Kohn gives a simple response to that concern: Make the time. Class meetings are too important to leave by the wayside. They bring social and ethical benefits, foster intellectual development, motivate students to become more effective learners, and greatly cut down on the need to deal with discipline problems. Kohn tells of a secondary math teacher who regularly devotes time to class meetings even though the class is limited to a total of 45 minutes per day. In their meetings the students reflect on how the class is going, exchange ideas on their independent projects, decide when the next test should be scheduled, and decide when it would be appropriate to work in small groups.

Making Decisions

The process of making decisions produces many benefits for students, such as helping them become more self-reliant, causing them to think issues through, and encouraging them to buy-in to the school program. This is not a matter to be reserved for older students alone. As Kohn says, it is experience with decisions that helps children become capable of handling them. But students long accustomed to being told what to do may need time to get used to deciding on things for themselves. Kohn cautions that students may respond to increased freedom in several different ways—ways that can be discouraging to educators who aren't prepared for reactions such as:

- *Acting out.* As students adjust to greater freedom, teachers may see a lot more behavior of every kind, including negative behavior. This is not especially pleasant, Kohn says, but he urges teachers to keep thinking, "Bring the kids in on it." In class meetings, ask them if they can figure out what's going on and what to do about it.
- *Testing the teacher.* Students may test teachers in several ways in order to see whether the teacher means what he or she says about wanting students to express themselves. They may be trying to see whether the teacher really means it when saying "This is *our* classroom!"
- *Outright resistance.* Students may simply refuse to do what the teacher asks. That is a good time to discuss with them questions such as "What is the teacher's job? And what about yours? Are you old enough to participate in such decisions? Do you learn better in a classroom where someone is always telling you what to do?"
- *Silence.* Some students will not participate in class discussions, even when asked for their opinion. The teacher should reflect on why this is happening. It might be that the student has nothing to say for the moment, or doesn't

feel safe with the teacher or classmates, or is chronically shy, or has trouble handling new responsibility.

- *Parroting*. Some students will make glib remarks in discussions, hoping to say what the teacher wants to hear. When that occurs, the teacher might want to invite deeper reflection rather than taking that response at face value. In so doing, one should be careful not to criticize the individual student.

School as a Community

Kohn writes at length about the importance of transforming schools and classrooms into **communities.** By *community* Kohn (1996) means

> ...a place in which students feel cared about and are encouraged to care about each other. They experience a sense of being valued and respected; the children matter to one another and to the teacher. They have come to think in the plural: they feel connected to each other; they are part of an "us." And, as a result of all this, they feel safe in their classes, not only physically but emotionally. (pp. 101–102)

Kohn suggests various strategies that will help teachers and schools move toward a greater sense of community. Among them are the following:

Building Relationships between Teachers and Students

Students come to behave more respectfully when important adults in their lives behave respectfully toward *them*. They are more likely to care about others if they know *they* are cared about. If their emotional needs are met, they show a tendency to help meet other people's needs rather than remaining preoccupied with themselves.

Enhancing Connections among Students

Connections among students are established and enhanced through activities that involve interdependence. Familiar activities for accomplishing this objective include cooperative learning, getting-to-know-you activities such as interviewing fellow students and introducing them to the class, and finding a partner to check opinions with on whatever is being discussed at the moment. Kohn also suggests using activities that promote **perspective taking,** in which students try to see situations from another person's point of view.

Undertaking Classwide and Schoolwide Activities

To develop a sense of community, students need plenty of opportunity for the whole class to collaborate on group endeavors. This might involve producing a class mural, producing a class newsletter or magazine, staging a verse choir performance, or doing some community service activity as a class. Kohn contends that the overall best activity for involving the entire group is a class meeting, as discussed earlier. Such meetings at the beginning of the year can be particularly helpful in establishing a sense of community. Kohn suggests posing questions at these first meetings, such as: "What makes school awful sometimes? Try to remember an experience during a previous year when you hated school, when you felt bad about yourself, or about everyone else, and you couldn't wait for it to be over. What exactly was going on when you were feeling that way? How was the class set up?"

Kohn says that not enough teachers encourage this sort of reflection, particularly in elementary schools where an aggressively sunny outlook pervades. Students' feelings of anger or self-doubt do not vanish just because their expression is forbidden.

Using Academic Instruction

The quest for community is not separate from academic learning. Class meetings can be devoted to talking about how the next unit in history might be approached, or what the students thought was best and worst about the math test. Academic study pursued in cooperative groups enables students to make connections while learning from each other. And units in language arts and literature can be organized to promote reflection on helpfulness, fairness, and compassion.

Strengths of Kohn's Views

Kohn brings into public debate intriguing ideas about how education can be done to produce people who lead full lives and contribute to society. He is very critical of traditional education for being shallow and unattractive to learners. But he doesn't stop with criticism—he sets forth compelling alternatives that he believes will make education the dynamic force it should be. His suggestions have to do mostly with curriculum and teaching, and have little to do directly with discipline. This is understandable because he advocates building curriculum around topics students find interesting and relevant, while eschewing topics that have no appeal or relevance to real life. When students are afforded the opportunity to delve into such topics, and when their progress is not driven by getting answers right on tests, they will eagerly explore learning in depth, enjoy give and take with other students, and seek out connections that help them make sense of things. When thus engaged in learning, students have little reason to misbehave. Should personal problems arise, they are sorted out by those involved or, if necessary, addressed by the class as a whole. Yet, Kohn does make suggestions to strengthen relationships among members of the class, as seen in the next section on implementing his ideas.

Implementing Kohn's *Beyond Discipline*

Teachers who wish to move beyond discipline must do three things: provide an engaging curriculum, develop a caring community, and provide students latitude in making choices. When this is accomplished, Kohn says, the result can be properly called a *democracy*. In this kind of classroom, the teacher's point of departure when problems occur is to ask: *How can I work with students to solve this problem? How can I turn this into a chance to help them learn?*

Kohn offers ten suggestions that he believes will be helpful to teachers who wish to move beyond discipline but find that their efforts do not produce the desired results.

1. Work on establishing a trusting, caring relationship with your students. It's hard to work with a student to solve a problem unless the two of you already have a relationship on which to build.

2. Work diligently toward acquiring in yourself, and developing in your students, skills of listening carefully, remaining calm, generating suggestions, and imagining someone else's point of view.

3. When an unpleasant situation occurs, your first effort should be to diagnose what has happened and why. If you have a trusting relationship with students, you can gently ask them to speculate about why they hurt someone else's feelings, or why they keep coming to class late.

4. To figure out what is really going on, be willing to look beyond the concrete situation. Do not immediately identify the student as the sole source of the problem while letting one's self off the hook. We should ask ourselves, or the student or the class, what is really going on here? Can we do anything to help? Try sitting down in a friendly way and see if a plan can be made that will resolve the problem.

5. Maximize student involvement in making decisions and resolving problems. Individual students should be asked, "What do you think we can do to solve this problem?" Involving students is far more likely to lead to a meaningful, lasting solution than having the teacher decide unilaterally what must be done.

6. Work with students on coming up with authentic solutions to problems. This requires not easy responses but an open-ended exploration of possibilities and reflections on motive.

7. When students do something cruel, our first priority is to help them understand that what they did is wrong, why it is wrong, and how to deter it from happening again. Then, an examination should be made of ways to make restitution or reparation, such as trying to restore, replace, repair, clean up, or apologize. Making amends is important and should be viewed as an essential part of the process, but more importantly, students must construct meaning for themselves around concepts of fairness and responsibility, just as they would around concepts in mathematics and literature.

8. When new plans or strategies are put into effect, be sure to review them later to see how they have worked.

9. Remain flexible and use judgment concerning when you need to talk with a student about a problem. Sometimes it is better to delay the talk for a while so the student will feel more inclined to discuss it.

10. On the rare occasions when you must use control, do so in a way that minimizes its punitive impact. Sometimes, despite your every effort, you will have to control misbehavior. A student may be disrupting the class, despite repeated requests not to do so. In that case, you may have to isolate the student or send him or her from the room. But even then your tone should be warm and regret-

ful and you should express confidence that the two of you will eventually solve the problem together.

Review of Selected Terminology

The following terms are used with special meaning in Kohn's model of discipline:

compliant behavior	perspective taking
constructivist theory	sense of community
democracy	traditional teaching
goals of discipline versus methods of discipline	

Application Exercises

Concept Cases

Case 1: Kristina Will Not Work ■ Kristina, a student in Mr. Jake's class, is quite docile. She socializes little with other students and never disrupts lessons. However, despite Mr. Jake's best efforts, Kristina will not do her work. She rarely completes an assignment. She is simply there, putting forth no effort at all. *How would Kohn deal with Kristina?*

From the first day Kristina was in his class, Kohn would have begun establishing a trusting, caring relationship with her and all other students. He would try to put himself in her place and imagine her situation, hoping thereby to understand her reluctance to participate. He would examine the class situation and himself to see if the problem lay there. He would chat with Kristina and gently sound her out. He would ask why she didn't feel like participating, if she could suggest a solution, and if there was a way he might help her. He would see if the two of them could devise a plan to resolve the problem. He would ask her opinions and involve her fully. After deciding on a possible solution, he would remain flexible, talk with her, and be ready to alter the plan if the need were indicated.

Case 2: Sara Cannot Stop Talking ■ Sara is a pleasant girl who participates in class activities and does most, though not all, of her assigned

work. She cannot seem to refrain from talking to classmates, however. Her teacher, Mr. Gonzales, has to speak to her repeatedly during lessons, to the point that he often becomes exasperated and loses his temper. *What suggestions would Kohn give Mr. Gonzales for dealing with Sara?*

Case 3: Joshua Clowns and Intimidates ■ Joshua, larger and louder than his classmates, always wants to be the center of attention, which he accomplishes through a combination of clowning and intimidation. He makes wise remarks, talks back (smilingly) to the teacher, utters a variety of sound-effect noises such as automobile crashes and gunshots, and makes limitless sarcastic comments and put-downs of his classmates. Other students will not stand up to him, apparently fearing his size and verbal aggression. His teacher, Miss Pearl, has come to her wit's end. *Would Joshua's behavior be likely to improve if Kohn's techniques were used in Miss Pearl's classroom? Explain.*

Case 4: Tom Is Hostile and Defiant ■ Tom has appeared to be in his usual foul mood ever since arriving in class. On his way to sharpen his pencil, he bumps into Frank, who complains. Tom tells him loudly to shut up. Miss Baines, the teacher, says, "Tom, go back to your seat." Tom wheels around, swears loudly, and says heatedly, "I'll go when I'm damned good and ready!" *How would Kohn deal with Tom?*

Questions and Activities

1. Kohn advises abandoning class rules and all traditional means of trying to make students behave in particular ways. To what extent do you agree with his suggestions? To what extent do you presently feel capable of teaching in the way he suggests?

2. Compare Kohn's views on discipline with those of Canter (Chapter 3) and Curwin and Mendler (Chapter 9). Of the three, who do you feel has the best grasp of classroom realities and the best way to help students?

3. Examine Scenario 1 in Appendix A. How do you believe Kohn would advise dealing with the situation in Mrs. Miller's room?

4. With a fellow student or in small groups, discuss (a) what you think of Kohn's views, (b) the extent to which you feel his views are grounded in the realities of classrooms and students, (c) whether you yourself would consider implementing his plan, and why, and (d) the changes you would have to make in your views of discipline before you could enthusiastically endorse his suggestions.

Primary References

Kohn, A. 1993. *Punished by rewards: The trouble with gold stars, incentive plans, A's, praise, and other bribes.* Boston: Houghton Mifflin.

———. 1996. *Beyond discipline: From compliance to community.* Alexandria, VA: Association for Supervision and Curriculum Development.

———. 1999. *The Schools Our Children Deserve: Moving beyond Traditional Classrooms and "Tougher Standards."* Boston: Houghton Mifflin.

Recommended Reading

———. 1992. *No contest: The case against competition.* Boston: Houghton Mifflin.

———. 1994. Bribes for behaving: Why behaviorism doesn't help children become good people. *NAMTA Journal, 19*(2), 71–94.

———. 1995. Discipline is the problem—not the solution. *Learning 1995, 24*(2): 34.

C. M. Charles's
Synergetic Discipline

Focus

- Establishing classroom conditions that increase energy and motivation.
- Augmenting pleasure and satisfaction in teaching, learning, and associating with others.
- Implementing gentle yet effective means of helping students behave advantageously.

C. M. Charles

Logic

- Learning occurs best when schoolwork is enjoyable and compatible with student needs.
- Synergetic teaching produces active student involvement with little misbehavior.
- Misbehavior is best corrected by dealing with its causes, in a dignified, helpful manner.

Charles's Contributions

- A way of teaching that produces high energy and satisfaction for teachers and students.
- A unified approach to teaching and discipline that helps students function at their best.
- A strategy of discipline that prevents and redirects misbehavior by attending to its causes.

Charles's Suggestions

- Strive for a positively energized class by putting in place known elements of synergy.
- Work with students from a basis of trust, built on ethics, dignity, and helpfulness.
- Prevent misbehavior by limiting its causes; correct misbehavior by attending to its causes.

About C. M. Charles

C. M. Charles, born in 1931, grew up in New Mexico and began his teaching career there in 1953. In 1961, he earned a Ph.D. in curriculum and educational psychology at the University of New Mexico and thereafter was on the faculty of education at San Diego State University, where he is now professor emeritus. Charles directed innovative programs in teacher education and five times received coveted outstanding professor and distinguished teaching awards. He also served on several occasions as advisor in teacher education and curriculum to the governments of Peru and Brazil, living in those countries for periods of time. Charles has authored a number of books that have attracted wide audiences in the United States and abroad, with translations into several foreign languages. Those having to do most directly with school discipline are *Teachers' Petit Piaget* (1972); *The Synergetic Classroom: Joyful Teaching and Gentle Discipline* (2000); and *Building Classroom Discipline* (2002). Charles can be contacted via e-mail at cmcsdsu2@aol.com or through the Allyn and Bacon Publishing Company.

Charles's Contributions to Discipline

Charles describes a way of teaching and working with students that produces quality results while obviating the trauma that comes from dealing continually with misbehavior. He calls his approaches **synergetic teaching** and **synergetic discipline,** which he says cannot be separated in practice. They require the installation of specific elements of teaching that energize the class while eliminating or limiting the usual causes of misbehavior. This allows teachers to interact with students in ways that are motivational and helpful. Teaching becomes much more satisfying because it concentrates on providing quality instruction, with little distraction from misbehavior. Learning is improved because motivation is increased and activities are seldom disrupted by misbehavior. Students enjoy themselves, learn more, and maintain a positive attitude toward school.

Charles's Central Focus

Charles focuses on a more effective way of teaching, one that motivates students, produces energy and excitement, and removes or reduces the causes of classroom misbehavior. When using this approach, teachers do not make demands on students, do not struggle against them, and do not use coercive measures to force students to behave. Instead, they energize the class and obtain the willing cooperation of students by putting in place elements that contribute to class synergy. In so doing, they meet student needs and limit the causes of misbehavior. When misbehavior does occur, teachers identify and deal with the cause, maintaining an attitude of gentle helpfulness.

Charles's Principal Teachings

- *Classroom misbehavior is the bane of most teachers everywhere, but it need not be so and can be reduced dramatically.* The cure is to work with students in ways that complement their needs and interests.
- *Discipline at its best occurs as a natural, functional, ongoing part of teaching.* It is not something separate from teaching that teachers do when students misbehave.
- *Students have seven predominant needs that motivate their behavior in school.* Those needs are for security, hope, acceptance, dignity, power, enjoyment, and competence. Wise teachers try always to help students meet those needs.
- *It is natural for students to resist what teachers attempt to make them do.* Teachers who are most effective do not use force but instead entice cooperation.
- *Students almost always cooperate with teachers they trust.* Trust is a main component of discipline. Establishing it is the teacher's responsibility.
- *In the most successful classes, students and teachers often experience synergy, a condition characterized by heightened enthusiasm and a sense of purpose.* When synergy is evident, very little misbehavior occurs.
- *The essential elements needed for synergy include teacher ethics, trust, charisma, communication, and interest. Also helpful are coopetition (a combination of cooperation and competition), class agreements, and procedures for problem resolution.* Teachers who are able to activate these components in the classroom encounter very little misbehavior.
- *When they first have contact with students, teachers should begin working out agreements with the class concerning instruction, learning activities, and personal behavior.* From that point forward they should always help students abide by the agreements and accept responsibility for their actions and for the well-being of the class.
- *When misbehavior occurs, which is normal until a trusting, supportive atmosphere is fully in place, teachers should deal with it in a helpful, nonconfrontive manner.* Teachers should never argue with students, put them down, or back them into a corner. Instead, they should show continual willingness to try to correct whatever is troubling the students.
- *To deal with misbehavior, the teacher should look for the cause and attempt to correct it.* Most student misbehavior is caused by one or more of the following: probing boundaries, mimicking others, strong curiosity or interest in something outside the lesson, desire for attention, desire for power, boredom or frustration, residual emotion from an outside event, threat to dignity, disagreements that escalate, or an egocentric personality.
- *The way to approach misbehaving students is to ask them "Is there a problem I can help you with?" or "Can you help me understand why this is happening? I'd like to help fix the problem."* Show you are not interested in punishing, but only in helping.

- *Should a conflict arise between you and a student, remain calm and resist the urge to fight back*. Drop your defenses. Be positive and helpful. Your challenge is to win the student over, not show that you can dominate.
- *Don't take misbehavior personally*. Accept that it is being caused by something outside yourself, and that you can possibly help correct the cause.

Analysis of Charles's *Synergetic Discipline*

Charles contends that the best way to deal with misbehavior is to change the way we work with students—in particular the way we adapt instruction to students' natural capabilities, inclinations, and motivations. Too often we fail to take into account three very important facts: (1) that students are continually trying to satisfy needs for security, hope, acceptance, dignity, power, enjoyment, and competence; (2) that they will immerse themselves wholeheartedly in topics they find interesting; and (3) that they have a built-in resistance to being forced but a ready willingness to cooperate.

Instead of capitalizing on those realities, we too often teach in ways contrary to them. For example, we know students need to enjoy school activities if they are to persevere, yet students often find classwork boring and meaningless. We know that students will do almost anything to protect themselves against loss of dignity, yet we often treat them offhandedly or even disrespectfully and allow them to treat each other the same way. When students are thwarted in trying to meet their needs, they become uncooperative. They may complain and comply grudgingly, or they may look for more interesting things to do, quit trying altogether, or even lash back at us. We blame students for these reactions and try to force them to shape up. As always, force only makes matters worse.

Students do misbehave, in greater or lesser degree, in almost all classrooms. To stifle their misbehavior we often use verbal warnings and reprimands, which we repeat dozens of times each day, and sometimes we impose harsh penalties. We do these things trying to squelch misbehavior and keep it under wraps, but at best the results are short-lived. To our distress, the same students continue to misbehave and many develop a bad attitude toward school and teachers. We keep hoping to find a way to reform students, preferably instantly, but that hope remains idle, and over time we grow frustrated and embittered.

Charles contends that the solution to discipline lies not in a system that squelches misbehavior, but rather in teaching in a manner that keeps students happily engaged. Should misbehavior occur despite good teaching, the teacher should identify and correct its cause. The place where we can best help students and ourselves is at the point where our curriculum, instruction, and expectations interact with students' capabilities, inclinations, and needs. The best curriculum is one that meshes with students' needs and abilities while maintaining educational integrity—that is, the curriculum should be pleasing to students but should remain educationally sound.

Elements of the Synergetic Approach

Synergy is a condition characterized by heightened energy, creativity, and productivity. It occurs, typically unexpectedly, when members of the class feed psychic energy to each other. When the energy level reaches a certain point, teachers and students are suddenly swept up in the exhilaration of learning. Many teachers report sporadic occurrence of such episodes in their classes, but usually can't explain its nature or what caused it. They say that at those times discipline is never a problem.

Synergetic teaching refers to working with students in a way that brings about classroom synergy. Later in the chapter we will see how that is accomplished. **Synergetic discipline** is that part of synergetic teaching that helps students behave responsibly. Synergetic discipline concentrates on two things: (1) removing the causes of misbehavior, and (2) correcting misbehavior that does occur by dealing with its cause. In no case must one resort to reprimand, force, or negative consequences, as will be described later.

Synergetic teaching attempts to put in place nine elements that when used in conjunction produce class synergy. Four of these nine elements—*ethics, trust, charisma,* and *communication*—are dependent upon the teacher as a person, while the other five elements—*interest, class agreements, coopetition, human relations,* and *problem resolution*—are more closely related to class life and work. As teachers become adept in activating these elements, they become able to bring synergy into effect when desired. Here is how Charles describes the nine elements.

1. *Ethics.* Ethics means doing the right thing, given the circumstances. Ethical teacher behavior is essential for building trust in the class. Teachers are seen as ethical if they continually display the following *ethical qualities: kindness, consideration, faith in students, helpfulness, fairness, honesty,* and *patience.* (Charles, p. 23)

2. *Trust.* To trust people means we believe we can count on them, that they will come through for us if they possibly can, and that they will support and not harm us. Trust is the centerpiece of the synergetic classroom. Everything else revolves around it. Students will not work closely with teachers they do not trust. Teachers can earn and maintain students' trust by consistently reflecting the ethical principles just listed. They can lose student trust very quickly if they behave unethically.

3. *Charisma.* Charisma is the quality people have that attracts others to them. It stems from what we say and do. Students greatly enjoy charismatic teachers and flock to them, eager to follow their lead. Most people think of charisma as static, that each of us has a certain fixed amount of it. In fact, charisma is not fixed and can certainly be increased. It is comprised of talent, experience, knowledge, and understanding of others, and is dependent on how these qualities are displayed. Smiles, bodily carriage, gestures, and friendliness play parts in charisma, as do enthusiasm and sensitivity.

4. *Communication.* With the exception of trust, no element of synergy is more important than communication. The type of communication that contributes the most to synergy is verbal give-and-take between teacher and students. It involves listening sensitively, showing genuine interest, and speaking encouragingly rather than arguing, moralizing, or giving unsolicited advice.

5. *Interest.* A great many of our students don't like school but attend because they have to. They enjoy being with their friends but care little for the usual

lessons, activities, and assignments. Teachers complain that these students are apathetic and do not like working with them. Thus we face dual problems: students don't like school and teachers don't like working with reluctant learners. These problems have bogged education down, but there is an amazingly simple solution. All we have to do is make school interesting for students. Then they will be pleased to be there and we will be pleased to teach them.

We know students like activities that are fun, interesting, or challenging, while they detest activities that are boring or meaningless. Synergetic teaching is dependent on making instruction as interesting as possible. That is accomplished as follows (Charles 2000):

- Inform yourself thoroughly about what your students are like—what they are capable of, incapable of, interested in, and predisposed to do.
- Adapt instruction and your ways of relating to students so they match students' capabilities, needs, and preferences.
- Allow students to have considerable say in selecting lesson topics and activities that interest them.
- Spice up topics that are clearly important though not inherently interesting, or else do a superb job of convincing students they genuinely need to know what you want to teach them. (p. 65)

Student needs, as noted before, are for security, acceptance, hope, dignity, power, enjoyment, and competence. None of those needs should be overlooked in teaching. Students also have a natural interest in movement, novelty, mystery, adventure, drama, storytelling, challenge, role-playing, music and rhythm, and guest speakers. They almost always respond well to them. On the other hand, students do *not* like sitting still for long, keeping quiet for long, working alone, memorizing facts for tests, long writing assignments, repetitive busy work, long reading assignments, and competition where the same few students win every time. To the extent possible, synergetic teachers build instruction around students' interests and needs while assiduously avoiding what students dislike.

6. *Class agreements.* When students are allowed to help make class decisions about behavior and instruction, they show greater cooperation and sense of responsibility. The process of reaching class agreements is described later in the chapter. Ultimately, a set of class agreements might, though not necessarily, look something like the following, which teachers would word appropriately for their class:

- Everyone will be respectful and helpful toward all others in the class.
- When disputes occur, they will be resolved peacefully.
- All lessons will be made interesting.
- All activities will have a clear purpose. There will be no busy work.
- Students can move and talk quietly except during designated quiet times.
- Everyone will work in ways they can be proud of.

7. *Coopetition.* Coopetition, pronounced co-opetition, refers to members of groups cooperating together in order to compete against other groups. Coopetition is not given a great deal of attention in teaching, but, in fact, it can contribute powerfully to synergy. Probably the greatest example of synergy in

education involves athletic teams competing against each other, often bringing not just the team but the entire school to a fever pitch. Coopetition can be incorporated into almost all areas of the curriculum. Students respond to it more enthusiastically, on the whole, than to any other kind of activity.

8. *Human relations skills.* Human relations have to do with the ways we treat each others in various situations. Synergy rarely occurs when group members are inconsiderate of each other. Charles describes several aspects of human relations and how they can be improved in the classroom, including conferring dignity, building trust, and reacting positively to others. He says the best way to improve relations is simply to treat others as we'd like them to treat us, an adage most people say they believe in but have trouble living up to.

9. *Resolving nondisciplinary problems and conflicts.* The word *problem* refers to a troublesome situation that affects the class seriously enough to require attention. The word *conflict* refers to strong disputes between students or between teacher and student. The next two sections describe how Charles says to address each of them.

How to Address Problems

Suppose students in a high-school geometry class are troubled by heavy loads of homework. Or suppose a middle-school teacher is greatly embarrassed when the principal visits and finds the room very untidy. When a problem such as these begins to hinder teaching or learning, or if it causes feelings to run high, it should be addressed immediately. In times past, the teacher would identify the problem and tell the class how to correct it. In synergetic teaching, the teacher, having sensed the problem and its nature, might say, "Class, something is going on that I think we need to talk about right now. Let's move our chairs into a circle." The problem is then clarified, possible solutions are sought, and a solution is selected and tried.

How to Address Conflicts

Conflicts are interpersonal situations characterized by strong disagreements, which may or may not involve misbehavior. Conflict threatens the dignity of individuals involved. If those individuals do not know how to find a peaceful solution, they will fight each other verbally, or sometimes physically. Examples of conflict situations include disputes over who won a contest, who is entitled to play with a toy, whether work was turned in on time, and whether work has met the standards expected. The best way to resolve conflict is to use a win-win approach in which both sides get most of what they want. Often, teachers must act as mediators between students in the win-win process. When you find yourself in this situation, you can facilitate the process by doing the following (Charles 2000):

- Make sure each person has a chance to express himself or herself.
- Try to make sure all ideas are presented in a friendly manner.
- Encourage both sides to be open and honest, but tactful.
- Encourage each person to try to see things from the other's point of view.
- Keep bringing attention back to areas of agreement between the disputants.
- Help disputants formulate conclusions as if they are joint agreements.
- Don't allow arguing back and forth, defending oneself, or debating. (p. 134)

Discipline in the Synergetic Classroom

Synergetic discipline is first and foremost preventive in nature. It is part of synergetic teaching which increases student motivation, attention, and active involvement, thereby greatly reducing the amount of misbehavior that would otherwise occur. However, synergetic discipline also has the power to deal effectively with misbehavior that has occurred, by identifying the cause of misbehavior and then removing it or limiting its effects. Charles (2000, pp. 149–151) provides the following advice:

When misbehavior occurs, try immediately to identify its cause. (Charles lists the causes of misbehavior as desire to probe boundaries, strong curiosity or interest in a matter unrelated to the lesson, failure to sense belongingness, boredom or frustration, threats to personal dignity, and egocentric personality.) The cause may be apparent, as when students seem to find the lesson boring and therefore disengage from it, or it may be obscure, as when Jason and Nathan continue an emotional dispute outside the classroom. Charles says that even if you think you know the cause, you should check with students before proceeding because mistaking the cause of misbehavior can lead to errors in dealing with it. Teachers can ask students, "Are you feeling bored?" or "Boys, is there a problem I can help you with?" If the cause is more obscure you can say, "Something is causing us to violate our class agreement about always being considerate of others. Can you help me understand what is causing that?" Tell students you want to do the proper thing while treating everyone fairly, but that it is difficult unless all the facts are brought out in the open.

When the cause is identified, correct or limit it to the extent possible. You may or may not be able to change what is causing students to misbehave. You can usually remove the cause easily if it has to do with boredom, frustration, or probing limits. You can lessen its effects when it involves lack of belonging or threat to personal dignity—you do this by helping students receive what they need. When misbehavior is occasioned by strong curiosity or emotion or disputes that have boiled over, you can make accommodations in schedule or lesson topic, perhaps discussing the matter in a class meeting. It is more difficult to limit causes that have to do with egocentric personalities. You can say, "Jason, something is causing you to call out and disrupt the lesson. That makes it difficult for me to teach and for other students to learn, and violates our class agreement. Can you help me understand what is causing you to do that?"

If the misbehavior involves, or leads to, a confrontational dispute, help those involved identify the cause of the disagreement and find a solution to it. If Jason and Nathan are speaking angrily to each other, the teacher can take the following steps:

1. Ask, "Boys, this is disturbing the class. Can you work the problem out between yourselves, or do you need my help?" (If they say they can work it out between themselves, ask them if they can keep their dispute from affecting the class. Ask them if they would mind telling you later what they have decided.)

2. If the conflict is such that they can't resolve it themselves, consider trying the following. At a suitable time, get together with the boys and in a nonthreatening manner:

- Ask each to tell you calmly what is troubling them. (Explain that you need to hear each clearly, so please no interrupting or arguing while each is talking.)
- Ask Jason what he would like for Nathan to do differently. Nathan listens carefully.
- Ask Nathan what he would like for Jason to do differently. Jason listens carefully.
- Ask each of the boys if he feels he could do part, or most, of what the other wants.
- If they agree on a possible solution, thank them and leave it at that. If they cannot reach a resolution, ask them if they'd mind the class discussing the matter in order to learn more about resolving disputes considerately.
- If they agree, bring up the matter at the next class meeting. If they decline permission, say, "Boys, it is not good for any of us in the class when bad feelings exist. How can we resolve this matter so both of you feel all right? What ideas do you have?" If they reach a settlement, thank them. If they can't, say, "I'm disappointed we can't settle this matter so both of you feel all right. But since we can't, I need to ask you to control yourselves, for the sake of the class." It is unlikely that the conflict negotiations will ever reach this point; the boys will agree to a solution earlier in the process.

When you are helping a misbehaving student, your efforts will seldom lead to conflict provided you treat the student with consideration. But if conflict should occur, you need to deal with it in a way that brings resolution while preserving good feelings. Suppose Melissa has once again failed to do her homework. You ask her kindly if there is a problem that is preventing her from complying with the class agreement. For some reason your question strikes a nerve and Melissa retorts, "There wouldn't be a problem if you didn't assign this stupid stuff!" What do you do? Charles (2000) suggests:

> Say, "Melissa, can you help me understand why you think the homework is stupid? I'd like your opinion because I wanted it to be helpful to your progress. What can you suggest that would help me make it better?" Melissa may apologize, say nothing, come back with another snide remark, or give you an explanation for her feelings. If she says nothing or remains uncooperative, consider saying:
>
> "Now is not a good time for us to discuss the matter. Perhaps we can do so later, just the two of us. Could you meet with me for a minute or two at (name a time and place)?" When you meet, tell her you are willing to listen if she has something she needs to talk about. If she declines, assure her you are interested in her views about the homework and are ready to help if she has further problems with it. (p. 151)

If Melissa apologizes or explains her feelings or talks about some other problem in her life that is probably her real cause of concern, consider saying:

> "Thank you, Melissa, for being open and honest with me. If I can make good changes in the homework or otherwise help with your situation, I'd like to do so. Do you have suggestions?"

Strengths of Charles's *Synergetic Discipline*

Synergetic discipline offers several strategies that teachers find helpful. It has the ability to cut down markedly on misbehavior by removing or limiting its causes. This alone contributes much to the quality of teaching and learning. Synergetic discipline also offers a calm yet effective intervention strategy to deal with misbehavior that does occur. This intervention is always done in a way that is helpful, never punitive, and is directed at the cause of the misbehavior rather than the student's personality. There is no struggle of wills between teacher and student. In fact, teachers are able to enlist the cooperation of students in correcting the cause of misbehavior. This leaves dignity intact for everyone.

One of the greatest strengths of synergetic discipline is that it is closely entwined with synergetic teaching. Traditional approaches to discipline make a rather clear distinction between teaching (what the teacher does to impart information) and discipline (what the teacher does to correct student misbehavior). In the synergetic approach, teaching itself is done in a way that, first, prevents misbehavior, and second, draws on student cooperation to correct misbehavior. The synergetic approach enlivens classes. Students participate eagerly and cooperate willingly. They are given a stake in planning the class and responsibility in maintaining a productive learning environment. They have little reason to misbehave wantonly. Teachers appreciate the synergetic approach that integrates teaching and discipline. They move into it easily, find it pleasant to use, and appreciate students' positive reactions.

Initiating Charles's *Synergetic Discipline*

Charles emphasizes that synergetic discipline is used only to *help* students—to be more successful in accomplishing their work, to get along and work well with others, and to develop self-discipline. In response to misbehavior, synergetic teachers take care to acknowledge students' feelings, support their interests, and show respect, while providing assistance needed for success. They do this in a dignified manner.

For introducing synergetic discipline to the class, Charles (2000, pp. 148–149) makes the following suggestions:

On the first day of class begin putting in place the conditions that foster synergetic teaching and discipline. The procedure is accomplished with three emphases. The first emphasis is to establish a set of agreements about how the class is to function, as concerns teaching, learning, and behavior. The second emphasis is to begin developing a sense of family in the class, where everyone is alert to the well-being of individuals and the class as a whole. This phase takes time and students should be reminded of its importance regularly. The third emphasis is to begin putting into practice the nine elements of synergetic teaching—ethics, trust, charisma, communication, interest, class agreements, coopetition, human relations, and problem resolution. It will take a few weeks to bring all nine elements into full function.

Charles (2000, pp. 159–160) goes into some detail describing how these three tasks are accomplished. He says approximately *seven sessions* are needed initially to install synergetic teaching and discipline. For young children the sessions should be scheduled for 15 minutes, while for older students the sessions will require 20 minutes or a bit more.

For all sessions, students should be seated in a tight circle. Explain that these class meetings, used for student input and discussion, will occur regularly and that the circular seating arrangement allows eye contact and encourages discussion.

In Session #1, open yourself to students, and students to you. Smile. Look into their faces. Tell them you are pleased to see them and are looking forward to working with them. Tell them you have some ideas for making the class enjoyable and useful, which you'd like to discuss with them, but first you want to know them better. Call their names and ask if you have pronounced them correctly. For three or four minutes tell students a bit about yourself—family, hobbies, travel, pets, special interests and skills, why you became a teacher, and your views on education, as might be appropriate. Then tell the students you'd like to learn more about them. Using the class roster, call on individual students. As appropriate to their age, ask about siblings, pets, hobbies, and special interests. Call on as many as time allows and end the session by saying you want to learn about each of them as quickly as possible.

In Session #2, draw the students out concerning how they'd like the class to function. Tell them the purpose is always to learn but you want the class to be very enjoyable for them, too. Ask them the following and make notes on the left side of a chart:

- What are some of the things you like best about school? List their comments, which will probably include playing, being with friends, sports, art, and music. Some may mention plays, concerts, and athletics.
- Ask what they like, specifically, about each of the things you've written on the chart. Make notes on the right side of the chart.
- Ask if they think any of the things they've mentioned might be possible in this class. Circle things they indicate.

Thank them for their contributions and tell them you want the class to be as they'd like it, insofar as possible. Assure them you will consider their suggestions carefully and make use of as many as possible.

In Session #3, give feedback concerning the suggestions they made in session #2. Beforehand, re-do the chart and indicate the suggestions you think you can incorporate into the class. Ask if they have further thoughts or suggestions. Turn to a fresh page on the chart and elicit comments about the kind of teacher they prefer.

- Ask if they have had a teacher they really enjoyed or respected. Ask them not to mention names but to indicate what that teacher did that made such a good impression. They will say things such as nice, interesting, helpful, fair, and sense of humor. They may also mention favorite activities and special teacher talents. Make note of the preferred traits on the left side of the chart.

- Review the traits with the class. Ask for examples or further details, such as what they mean by "helpful" or "really fun." Make notes on the right side of the chart.
- Tell students that all teachers are different but you hope to be the kind of teacher they prefer, to the extent you are able. Tell them you want time to study the notes and that you will give them feedback at the next session. Thank them for their helpfulness.

In Session #4, show students a clean copy of the traits they have identified in teachers they like. Ask if they have additional comments. Tell them you will do your best to be the kind of teacher they appreciate. If you can't do so in every respect, tell them so, and why. Next, draw students out about how they feel they should behave in the class.

- Ask students to think of a classmate who has behaved in ways they admired or appreciated. Without giving names, have them tell what the student was like or what he or she did. List the descriptions on the left side of a clean page.
- When several behaviors have been listed, go back and ask students *why* they appreciated those behaviors. Make notes of the comments on the right side of the chart.
- Now ask students how they would like for other members of a class to treat them. On a clean page make notes on the lefthand side. Go back and once more ask *why*.
- Next, ask what kind of behavior they most appreciate from other students when they are working together on assignments. Ask why.
- Finally, ask students if they think it would be possible to have the kinds of behavior in this classroom that are listed on the chart. Thank them for their input and tell them you'll have their suggestions ready for review at the next session.

In Session #5, give students feedback on behaviors they have indicated they like and appreciate. Ask if they have further comments.

- Move on to asking what they *dislike* fellow students doing in class. Make notes as usual.
- When that is done, ask if they have ideas about how to keep those unwanted behaviors from occurring. Tell the students you are interested in preventing them from occurring rather than correcting them later.
- Ask students if they feel they have control over how they behave in the class. Follow with "What makes you decide whether to behave properly or improperly?" Ask them if they feel they could almost always behave properly, for their own sake and for the good of the class.
- Say: Suppose despite everything we do, someone decides to misbehave, to do something the class has agreed not to do. What should we do then? How should we deal with that person? Students will typically suggest punishment or removal of privileges. If they do, say:
- I would want the person to understand that the behavior is hurtful to the class. I wouldn't be interested in punishing the person. If I fight against that person, or perhaps you, it doesn't do any of us good. When there is a problem,

what we need to do is fix it. Now put yourself in the place of a student who has misbehaved. How would you like for me to treat you? Would you prefer punishment or a kind attitude where I try to help you behave better?

Thank the students for their input and indicate you will provide feedback at the next session.

In Session #6, ask students to respond to a summary you have made of their suggestions so far. Show them a chart you have prepared that lists (1) things students said they liked best in school, (2) traits they said they liked best in teachers, (3) behaviors they said they appreciated in their classmates, (4) behaviors they said they disliked in classmates, and (5) a plan you have made for helping students want to behave properly in the classroom. Review the first four items and ask if you have understood correctly. Then move to item 5, your plan for behavior, which includes:

(a) Why you think misbehavior won't often occur if class is interesting, the teacher is helpful, and students treat each other nicely
(b) How students can resolve most of their disputes in a friendly manner
(c) How you will talk with students who misbehave to try to correct whatever is causing their misbehavior

Ask the class to comment on the plan and make suggestions. Thank them and indicate that you hope the group can formalize some agreements to live by in class.

In Session #7, work toward a set of class agreements. Bring back the chart used in the previous session. Put it to the side, in view. Using a blank chart, tell the students you hope they can finalize statements about the following:

(a) Class activities that are valuable and enjoyable
(b) The teacher's way of teaching and treating students
(c) The students' ways of treating each other and the teacher
(d) How students will work at assigned tasks

When satisfactory statements have been made, tell the class you feel sure everyone can abide by the agreements and that you hope they will remember them and do their best. Tell them you will do your best to follow them yourself and will help students do so. Indicate that you will prepare a chart showing the agreements and post it in the room for everyone to see.

Review of Selected Terminology

The following terms and concepts are central to your understanding of *Synergetic Discipline*. Check yourself to make sure you understand them:

Misbehavior: nature of (breaking agreements); usual causes of (probing boundaries, strong distraction, no sense of belongingness, boredom or frustration, threats to personal dignity, egocentric personality)

Student needs: security, hope, acceptance, dignity, power, enjoyment, competence

Student interests: movement, novelty, mystery, adventure, drama, storytelling, challenge, role-playing, music, rhythm, guests

Classroom synergy: nature of, production of

Elements of classroom synergy: ethics, trust, charisma, communication, interest, coopetition, class agreements, human relations, problem resolution

Ethical qualities: kindness, consideration, faith in students, helpfulness, fairness, honesty, patience

Synergetic discipline: nature of, steps in (identify cause, correct or limit, resolve problems)

Conflict or problem: disciplinary, non-disciplinary, pointers for resolving

■ Application Exercises

Concept Cases

Case 1: Kristina Will Not Work ■ Kristina, a student in Mr. Jake's class, is quite docile. She socializes little with other students and never disrupts lessons. However, despite Mr. Jake's best efforts, Kristina will not do her work. She rarely completes an assignment. She is simply there, putting forth no effort at all. *How would Charles deal with Kristina?*

Charles would advise Mr. Jake to do the following: First, Mr. Jake should quickly appraise Kristina's efforts and general demeanor, to see if he can ascertain why Kristina is not working. Then in a quiet, friendly tone, he might say, "Kristina, I see this work is not getting done. Our class agreement is that we will always try to do our best. Is there something about the assignment that bothers you?" If she indicates a difficulty, such as the work is too hard or she doesn't understand it, Mr. Jake could reply, "What do you think might help?" or "Is there something I could do to help you get started?" Probably Kristina will begin working. If she does not, Mr. Jake could say, "Kristina, I think this work is important and I want to help you get it done. Would you like to try…" Mr. Jake lists two options, such as work with another student to complete the assignment or do an alternative assignment which he names. In the unlikely possibility this still doesn't get Kristina started, Mr. Jake might say, "Kristina, I want to do everything possible to help you enjoy the class and learn successfully. Frankly, I'm not sure what to suggest now. Can you think of anything?" If she cannot, ask if she would allow the class to discuss the situation in their next class meeting, as a way to learn better how to help each student learn.

Case 2: Sara Cannot Stop Talking ■ Sara is a pleasant girl who participates in class activities and does most, though not all, of her assigned work. She cannot seem to refrain from talking to classmates, however. Her teacher, Mr. Gonzales, has to speak to her repeatedly during lessons, to the point that he often becomes exasperated and loses his temper. *What suggestions would Charles give Mr. Gonzales for dealing with Sara?*

Case 3: Joshua Clowns and Intimidates ■ Joshua, larger and louder than his classmates, always wants to be the center of attention, which he accomplishes through a combination of clowning and intimidation. He makes wise remarks, talks back (smilingly) to the teacher, utters a variety of sound-effect noises such as automobile crashes and gunshots, and makes limitless sarcastic comments and put-downs of his classmates. Other students will not stand up to him, apparently fearing his size and verbal aggression. His teacher, Miss Pearl, has come to her wit's end. *Would Joshua's behavior be likely to improve if synergetic discipline were used in Miss Pearl's classroom? Explain.*

Case 4: Tom Is Hostile and Defiant ■ Tom has appeared to be in his usual foul mood ever since arriving in class. On his way to sharpen his pencil, he bumps into Frank, who complains. Torn tells him loudly to shut up. Miss Baines, the teacher, says, "Tom, go back to your seat." Tom wheels around, swears loudly, and says heatedly, "I'll go when I'm damned good and ready!" *How would Tom's behavior be handled in a synergetic classroom?*

Questions and Activities

1. To what extent do you feel you could put synergetic teaching and discipline into effect in your classroom? What portions do you believe you could implement easily? What portions do you believe might be difficult?

2. Synergetic discipline does not punish students for misbehavior nor does it apply penalties or other measures to try to force student compliance. Do you think students will take advantage of synergetic discipline's softer nature—that is, that they will disregard the teacher because they have no fear of the consequences? Is there anything in syn

ergetic discipline that would prevent their doing so?

3. According to Charles's plan for implementing synergetic teaching and discipline, a few days might pass before students understand there are class rules they are to abide by. Can you think of four or five things you might do to keep students from misbehaving while the program is taking effect?

4. Examine either Scenario 1 or 8 in Appendix A. To what extent do you think behavior might improve in those classes if synergetic teaching and discipline were used?

Primary Reference

Charles, C. 2000. *The synergetic classroom: Joyful teaching and gentle discipline*. New York: Longman. Describes the nature and value of class synergy, shows that synergetic teaching

and discipline are inextricably intertwined, and explains how teachers can achieve synergy in the classroom, thereby improving their professional lives and that of their students.

Recommended Readings

Carnegie, D. 1981. *How to win friends and influence people*. Revised edition. New York: Pocket Books.

Charles, C. 1974. *Teachers' Petit Piaget*. Belmont, CA: Fearon.

Collis, J. 1998. *When your customer wins, you can't lose*. Sydney, Australia: HarperBusiness.

Slavin, R. 1991. Synthesis of research on cooperative learning. *Educational Leadership*, 48, 71–82.

Spence, G. 1995. *How to argue and win every time*. New York: St. Martin's Press.

CHAPTER 14

Clarifying Your Philosophy and Theory of Discipline

In previous chapters, we explored a number of highly regarded approaches to classroom discipline. The authors of those approaches in some cases emphasized the prevention of misbehavior while in other cases they focused more on how to correct misbehavior once it occurs. Most suggested a balance between prevention and correction, but made different suggestions concerning precisely what to do. Some presented their plans without making clear what they considered to be the ultimate purpose of discipline—readers would infer that it was simply to prevent or suppress misbehavior. Now that you have considered what those authorities had to say, what conclusions have you reached regarding the following questions? Just read through the questions now for orientation. We will come back momentarily to consider them one by one.

1. What is classroom misbehavior and why does it require attention?
2. To what extent can teachers bring about desired changes in student behavior?
3. What is the purpose of discipline? What sorts of results does one hope for?
4. In your view, what are the essential components of an effective discipline system?
5. How do those components relate to or influence each other?
6. What makes you believe those components will produce the results you desire?
7. What can teachers do to limit the occurrence of misbehavior?
8. How can teachers react most effectively when students misbehave?
9. How can teachers help students actually want to behave more responsibly?

The answers you give to the first three questions reveal much about your **philosophy of discipline**—what you believe discipline to be, how important you think it is, how well you think it can serve you, and what you believe it will help you accomplish. When you compose your personal system of discipline, your philosophy will guide your thinking.

Questions 4, 5, and 6 help you clarify your **theory of discipline.** A theory is a tentative explanation of a large-scale phenomenon. It is based on information that is factual but insufficient to provide complete understanding. A theory typically includes the components that seem to play important roles in the phenomenon and an explanation of how those components interact with each other. An example of a familiar theory is Charles Darwin's speculations about the origin of new species through the process of natural selection. Darwin's theory is based on factual information, yet the supporting facts are not sufficient to remove all doubt as to whether or not new species originate as he suggested.

Questions 7, 8, and 9 help clarify your views concerning the **practice of discipline,** that is, how discipline should be implemented in the classroom. Ideally, practice should be guided by philosophy and theory, but most teachers skip them when organizing discipline, moving ahead to stipulating what they will do in practice. They are understandably eager to get down to what they will actually do and say when students misbehave, but they would do better to begin by clarifying their philosophy and theory. By doing so, they can more effectively compose a system that is attuned to student needs and focused on the goals identified for their students.

Philosophy of Discipline

Edward Savage, a high school math teacher who recently retired, was asked about the views he had on discipline when he first began teaching in 1961, and in particular if at that time he had clarified for himself a philosophy or theory of discipline. He shook his head and said, "No, I don't think I ever thought much about a philosophy or theory of discipline. If you are asking how I approached discipline, well…my methods changed over the years, but I knew when students were behaving improperly and so did they, and I stopped them from doing it. I don't think I was tyrannical. They knew how they were supposed to act in class. Everybody had students who liked to see what they could get away with. When my students were out of line I asked them to stop, and they usually did. Sometimes if they kept at it I gave them detention or made them do extra work. I had confrontations with students occasionally, which left me feeling pretty bad afterward." Prompted again about philosophy and theory of discipline, Mr. Savage said, "No, I really am not sure what that means. What do you mean by that?"

Mr. Savage gave a candid description of his views on discipline during his career. Those same views are evident in teachers today. Mr. Savage was considered to be a good disciplinarian, but he relied mainly on strength of personality to make students behave properly. Most of us aren't as successful as he was, and to be honest about it, our students today aren't as compliant as his were. We are well-advised to prepare ourselves better than did Mr. Savage for working with students, and that necessitates our looking into matters philosophical and theoretical.

Your *philosophy* about any matter—life, education, politics, teaching, what have you—summarizes what you believe to be true, good, and correct about that matter, and conversely, what is false, bad, and incorrect about it. Philosophy encapsulates meaning and gives direction to how you think and what you do. Humans (including Mr. Savage) philosophize every day, and yet we rarely organize our conclusions to make full use of them. For example, we are all keenly interested in human nature and behavior, but few of us can explain what we actually believe about them, that is, what they are like, what is good and bad about them, whether or not they can be changed, and if so, for what purpose, to what extent, and under what conditions. Those of us in teaching would profit from organizing our thoughts along those lines in order that we might better understand and work with students. Consider the questions that were listed earlier:

1. *What is classroom misbehavior and why does it require attention?* For a long time, philosophers argued about whether humans are born evil, good, or neutral. *Evil* was rooted in original sin; people were bound to go wrong but could, given stern morality and plenty of religion, keep their sinful qualities in check. *Good* meant we are born with admirable qualities and remained that way unless corrupted by society. That view held that we need to keep the young away from bad influences until they grow up and take charge of their own minds. *Neutral* depicted newborns as blank slates to be filled in with experience—their behavior could be perfected or debauched, made good or evil. In the past, those three different notions of human nature very strongly affected educational practice. Educators who saw students as inherently sinful kept them under short rein, made them toe the line, and not infrequently beat the devil out of them, or tried to. Educators who saw students as inherently good gave them free rein to do pretty much as they pleased, in a clean wholesome environment rich with learning opportunities. Educators who saw students as blank slates tried to imprint good on them and help them steer clear of the darker aspects of human experience.

For teachers in today's world, there is a more useful way of looking at human nature. Instead of focusing on good and evil, think instead about actions that serve individuals well or poorly. Earlier we said that human behavior includes all the things humans do. *Misbehavior* refers to behavior that someone disapproves of—that someone is the teacher when we speak of classroom misbehavior. For the most part, teachers should not think of misbehavior as something immoral, but simply as breaking class rules. That may take some change of thought because most people feel that certain acts, such as talking back sassily to one's elders, are bad in any circumstance. But we step into uncomfortable waters when we judge student behavior in terms of our personal morality. We remain on firmer ground when we think of student behavior in terms of desirable outcomes of education, or whether or not students have abided by class agreements, or whether the behavior serves the student poorly or well.

As to why student misbehavior requires your intervention, consider the following: Class agreements specify the kinds of behavior that permit students to learn more easily and enjoyably. They allow you to teach more effectively and help students become more self-directing, responsible, and concerned about the well-being of others. When students break an agreement, you should never consider it a personal affront. Rather, you should help them see they are doing damage to themselves or to others in the group and then see if you can help them choose behavior that serves everyone better. If you truly want to do the best you can for all your students, you must help them learn to choose responsible behavior that serves them well. When they make mistakes, you must help them learn from those mistakes. To make all this possible, help the class formulate clear agreements about how they will work and conduct themselves. Help them see how violations of those agreements are detrimental to the class, why intervention is required when agreements are transgressed, and how mistakes can be turned into valuable learning experiences.

2. *To what extent can teachers bring about desirable changes in student behavior?* There is no doubt you can help students behave in ways that serve them better. Teachers frequently report success with the most hard-bitten and resistant students, though they admit they are unsuccessful at times, too. Many of your students won't cause any trouble at all. They will be relatively self-directing, make an effort to learn, accept responsibility, and behave in accordance with class agreements. A few others might be different. Having found little satisfaction in school, they disengage from what they find uninteresting, are continually on guard against threat, and are sometimes so self-centered they won't listen to you or anyone else—at first. These students often break class rules despite agreeing to abide by them.

And yet over time, skilled teachers can establish communication and trust with the majority of those students. As they do so, behavior improves. You have learned that it is much easier and more effective to work with student nature than against it. Students never respond well to argument, demands, threat, or punishment, which at best can only make them temporarily compliant. But they do respond well to teachers they find interesting, helpful, and trustworthy. If you show them consideration and continual helpfulness, they will begin to seek you out, emulate your behavior, and even try to please you.

3. *What is the purpose of discipline? What sorts of results does one hope for?* The purpose of discipline is not simply to squelch misbehavior. The purpose is broader and much more helpful: It helps students learn more; it helps them relate better with others; and it helps them become self-directed and responsible. Discipline is not put to good use when it forces students to comply with teacher demands and punishes them when they do not. Students accept discipline if they know it is intended to help them be successful, but they resist it when it is forceful and punitive.

You will now see the first of a series of exercises for you to complete in this chapter. By completing the exercises, you will establish a framework for finalizing your personal system of discipline, a task that will be completed in Chapter 15.

> *Exercise 1.* At this point, take a couple of minutes to jot down thoughts on your philosophy of discipline. Perhaps you might begin with your views on "natural" student behavior, that is, what students prefer to do in the classroom, as concerns learning and socialization and how that behavior helps or hinders them in school. Then you might describe what you hope your students will eventually become, ethically, socially, and intellectually, and indicate how discipline can help achieve those goals.

Theory of Discipline

We noted earlier that theory helps us understand larger events and processes when there is not enough factual information to provide certainty. We have theories in abundance— theories of gravitation, atomic structure, intellectual development, learning, chaos, and on and on. And, of course, there are theories of teaching and education and discipline. Such theories provide a framework, comprised of knowledge and speculation, that gives us better insights into working with the young.

All educators, students, parents, and other adults have concepts and notions of discipline which they have never had reason to articulate. For example, Mr. Savage had never thought about a theory of discipline, yet we can get a good picture of his operating theory must have been from what he said about his discipline techniques—he thought kids would naturally misbehave, which would interfere with teaching and learning, and so they should be kept from doing so. When you mention class discipline, many, if not most, people envision a beleaguered teacher meting out punishment, justly or unjustly, to an abashed child. If a group of people were asked to explain fully the nature of discipline, what it's for and how it works, probably all would mention that discipline is tied up with right and wrong and involves things teachers or parents do to misbehaving kids. Beyond that, most couldn't think of much to say. But teachers require a more encompassing view of discipline. They need to know what it's for, which we explored in the philosophy of discipline. In addition, they need to identify major components of discipline and their presumed effects. To help us explore further, let's return to questions posed earlier in the chapter.

4. *What seem to be the essential components of an effective system of discipline?* The answer to this question is dependent on your philosophy of discipline. As you have seen, philosophies of discipline vary and, in turn, lead to different theories of discipline. For clarification's sake, we will contrast four different philosophical views and the theories that emerge from them. Please remember that these are only four of a number of different possibilities and those presented here make no mention of self-control, responsible self-direction, and learning from mistakes, which most teachers would want to emphasize.

Philosophy 1. Discipline is for making students behave. If you believe, as did Mr. Savage, that the be-all and end-all of discipline is to make students behave themselves in class, you have only two main elements to be concerned about—misbehavior and enforcement. Teachers who adhere to this theory—and many still do—sometimes tell their students exactly what kinds of misbehavior they will not tolerate. Others simply react to whatever displeases them at the moment, assuming that their students "know better." Both, once students misbehave, take actions that make students so uncomfortable they stop misbehaving. Favorite tactics include scowls, scoldings, stern moralizing, and punishment.

Philosophy 2. Discipline is for shaping desired behavior. If your philosophy of discipline emphasizes shaping desired behavior, the elements in your theory are still two in number. On the one hand, you have student behavior which you'd like to improve and on the other hand, you have a set of reinforcers you dispense to students who behave nicely, causing them progressively to behave even better. In this theory, one disregards behavior that is inappropriate, in the belief (or perhaps hope) that students will gradually abandon misbehavior if they are not rewarded for it.

Philosophy 3. Discipline is for helping students get along together and sense they belong. If your philosophy holds that the goal of discipline is to help students get along with each other and that they misbehave mainly when they cannot satisfy their desire to belong in the group, class, or school, your theory of discipline will include four main elements—(1) what "getting along well" and a "sense of belonging" mean, and how they affect each other, (2) the types of misbehavior students engage in when they have no sense of belonging, (3) tactics that positively redirect misbehavior when it goes awry, and (4) what can be done to provide the belonging students crave.

Philosophy 4. Discipline is for identifying and correcting causes of misbehavior. If your philosophy holds that misbehavior has many identifiable causes, that students misbehave when a range of needs goes unmet, and that student behavior improves when those causes of misbehavior are limited or removed, your theory of discipline will contain a number of elements. First there is a list of student needs that discipline should help meet. Second, there are the agreements, formulated jointly by teacher and students, that indicate the behavior that best serves individuals and the group. Third, there is a list of factors that often cause students to violate class agreements. Fourth, there are the preventive procedures done in advance to remove or limit the causes of misbehavior. Fifth, there are steps taken to build trust among teacher and students. And sixth, there are the dignified interventions the teacher uses to remove causes of misbehavior and redirect students who have transgressed agreements.

5. How do the components in your theory relate to or influence each other? The elements in discipline interact in ways we call *cause-effect* and *means-end.* The **cause-effect relationship** occurs in two significant ways, illustrated in these examples: First example: Jon is in class. He becomes bored (cause) and to relieve his boredom begins to talk to his neighbor (effect). Here, a factor (boredom) has caused Jon to misbehave. Second example: Jon misbehaves by talking to his neighbor. Mrs. Abel moves closer to him (cause) and Jon stops talking (effect). In this example, Mrs. Abel has caused Jon to stop misbehaving—she has used what is called *corrective discipline.*

The **means-end relationship** is illustrated as follows: We want Jon to behave properly (the end result) so in advance we take actions (means) that will encourage him to do so. In other words, we remove or reduce the potential causes of misbehavior. Means-end is central to *preventive discipline,* a prominent feature of many discipline systems.

Although prevention is greatly preferable to correction—a stitch in time saves nine, and so on—all teachers, novice and experienced, express more interest in how to stop Jon's misbehavior than how to prevent it. The question you hear everywhere is: When Jon is disrespectful, or doesn't do his homework, or bothers others, or sits and does nothing, what do I do? The question is asked as though there is a single answer. But as we have seen, there can be a number of acceptable answers as well as lots of poor ones.

Suppose Jon gets up and wanders around the room bothering others when he is supposed to be working. What do we really want for Jon, both for now and for the longer picture? Could it be one or more of the following, which we could consider desirable ends?

- Stop wandering around bothering others, period
- Stop misbehaving, but maintain a good attitude
- Learn how to behave more appropriately

- Show more self-control, self-direction, and responsibility
- Show consideration for the well-being of the class

When we decide what we want for Jon, we need an idea of how to get there. Ideally, in keeping with conditions and agreements reached in the class, Jon would never have gotten up and wandered around in the first place. But given the fact he has done so, what do we do in response? Consider the following possibilities:

- We can work on the cause of Jon's misbehavior. To do this, we must first identify it. Why is Jon misbehaving? What is causing him to break class agreements? We have previously noted a number of causes of misbehavior, such as boredom, frustration, desire for attention, self-centeredness, threat to personal dignity, and strong curiosity. We can usually find misbehavior rooted in one of those causes. Once we have identified the cause, we can remove or limit it. The various models of discipline analyzed earlier suggest tactics for preventing boredom and fatigue, teaching in charismatic ways, managing lessons to hold student attention, and holding students accountable for learning. These tactics obviate certain known causes of misbehavior.
- We can provide direct help to Jon. We might talk to him and see if he is experiencing a problem we might assist with. If he identifies a problem, we need to show willingness to deal with it if possible. If he says there is no problem, we might want to ask for his cooperation so the lesson can continue without further disruption. We might also consider arranging for him to work with another student or altering the lesson by shortening it or changing activities.
- We should make sure the intervention has a positive effect on Jon. A good intervention should stop the misbehavior and help Jon behave properly in the future, with a positive attitude. We can usually accomplish this by speaking to him in a kindly manner and showing respect without giving personal offense.

6. *What makes you believe the components in your theory of discipline will produce the results you desire?* Four sources can validate the effectiveness of the components in your theory of discipline. *First,* there is a body of research dealing with reinforcement, communication, lesson management, and other topics important in discipline. That information has been presented in earlier chapters. *Second,* there is the persuasive logic of authorities who have devoted much of their careers to improving class discipline. This too is provided in the models. *Third,* there is an abundance of teacher experience that helps us understand what works well with students and what does not. You may have some of this experience yourself, or you may glean it from other teachers. *Fourth,* and very important, is your own logical thought based on what you know about human nature and how you, yourself, react to guidance and intervention. Simply recognizing how students are likely to behave and knowing how you would like to be treated in those circumstances provides excellent guidance for establishing an approach to discipline. You almost never go wrong when you treat others as you would like them to treat you.

Your theory of discipline, including its elements and their relationships, will emerge as you clarify your philosophy of discipline. You will find that as you make your system more helpful to students, it will include more elements. That might suggest that helpful systems become overly complicated, but in fact they don't. The effort they require comes early, in the thinking and planning, much of which you are doing at the present time. Once your students buy into the plan, it becomes rather easy to use. After a time, you won't notice much difference between how you teach and how you work with student behavior.

> *Exercise 2:* Take a few minutes to outline your theory of discipline. Look back to how you phrased your philosophy of discipline. Identify the specific behaviors and attitudes you hope to develop in your students. When that is done, indicate the classroom conditions and general strategies that are likely to produce the outcomes you desire.

The Practice of Discipline

Here we move to a consideration of how, exactly, you intend to use your system of discipline. This should be derived logically from your philosophy and theory of discipline. Once more we will refer back to questions listed at the beginning of the chapter.

7. *What will you do to limit the occurrence of misbehavior?* This question takes us back into the arena of preventive discipline, where your efforts yield the greatest results. The more thought and energy you invest in this area, the more pleased you are likely to be with your discipline system. Every bit of misbehavior you are able to prevent can save you many minutes of instructional time. It will yield other important benefits as well, such as good interpersonal relations and positive attitudes toward school and learning.

The preventive aspect of discipline entails removing, in advance, the known causes of misbehavior or limiting their effects to the extent possible. To repeat: The principal causes of misbehavior include: students' mimicking and feeding off each other's behavior; desire for attention; desire for power; boredom; frustration; emotionality from outside factors; threats to personal dignity; disagreements that boil over; and egocentric personalities. These causes can all be minimized and some can be eliminated, resulting in a marked decrease in misbehavior.

Many of the models discussed earlier contain excellent suggestions for preventing or limiting causes of misbehavior. Jacob Kounin suggested efficient lesson management and showing students we know what is going on everywhere in the room. Haim Ginott urged us to use congruent communication and show continual willingness to help. Rudolf Dreikurs wanted us to forego authoritarian tactics and bring students into the decision-making process. The Canters stressed cooperatively-planned rules of behavior, combined with pre-planned consequences. Fredric Jones would like to see us use body language, keep students involved by using Say, See, Do teaching and providing help efficiently. Linda Albert asks us to give students personal attention and show them they are competent and valued. Jane Nelsen, Lynn Lott, and H. Stephen Glenn advise us to help students see themselves as significant and able to control their own lives. Thomas Gordon tells us to do all we can to help students develop inner discipline so they can direct themselves intelligently. William Glasser tells us teaching and learning will go better if we meet students' needs for belonging, freedom, power, and fun. Richard Curwin and Allen Mendler urge us to preserve students' dignity and restore a sense of hope, especially for students at risk of failure. Barbara Coloroso advises teachers to give students power and responsibility to make decisions. Alfie Kohn stresses the importance of building a sense of community in the classroom where everyone feels responsibility for everyone else. Patti Kyle, Spencer Kagan, and Sally Scott urge teachers to help students meet their needs in nondisruptive ways. C. M. Charles advocates building strong bridges of trust between teachers and students while energizing the class with teacher charisma and interesting, worthwhile activities.

The suggestions from these authorities are helpful in limiting the causes of misbehavior. We can conclude that most misbehavior can be prevented in advance when we do the following:

Treatment of Students
- Show students that each and every one is a valued member of the class.
- Give personal attention to each individual student as often as possible.
- Never threaten students or back them into a corner.

Trust and Responsibility
- Develop bonds of trust with students, through helpfulness and fair treatment.
- Give students responsibility to make decisions and allow them to make mistakes.
- Use mistakes as excellent opportunities for learning.

Communication
- Learn students' names quickly and chat with each as often as feasible.
- Always speak respectfully; don't preach to students or use sarcasm.
- Use I-messages rather than you-messages when discussing problem situations.

Instruction
- Make instructional activities as interesting and worthwhile as possible.
- Give constant attention to students' needs for security, hope, and competence.
- Always ask yourself how you can be of most help to your students right now.

Teacher Personality
- Present yourself as enthusiastic, energetic, and eager.
- Tactfully share information about your life, aspirations, and interests.
- Always be a model of kindness, consideration, and good manners.

Class Agreements
- Involve your students in making class agreements about instruction and behavior.
- Encourage students to accept the agreements as the code that guides the class.
- Think of misbehavior not just as violation of the code but as opportunity to learn.

8. *How can you react most effectively when students misbehave?* Despite your diligent efforts to prevent misbehavior, students will still misbehave, sometimes for reasons outside your control and sometimes as willful transgressions of class agreements. This brings us to the question all teachers ask: "What do I do when…?" There is no single correct answer to that question, of course. Let's examine some good possibilities for various occasions, such as when students first become restive, when they transgress class rules, and when they behave immorally or viciously.

When you see students becoming restive. Even the most accomplished teachers expect at some point to see their students begin to fidget, doodle, look out the window, smile or make gestures at each other, whisper, and otherwise indicate they are disengaging from the lesson. You can cut down considerably on this sort of behavior by making your instructional activities especially interesting. But it is difficult to do this under all circumstances, and, in truth, some important topics are so boring that your best ingenuity won't always see you through.

Let us suppose you have shown an awareness of what students are doing in all parts of the room at all times. Your students will realize this and will often glance at you to see if you are noticing their behavior. Your eye contact is often enough to get them going again. If not, you might move to the student involved and ask a question about the work in progress. All the while you are beginning to ask yourself if the lesson is interesting enough to hold student attention much longer. You may need to make a comment such as, "Class, I'll really appreciate it if you can stick with the lesson for five more minutes." If they like and trust you, they will probably comply with your request. If they don't comply, you might ask, "Class, I see that the lesson is not holding your attention. What is bothering you about it?" Later, you might make modifications that eliminate the problem.

When students mundanely break class agreements. Most of the time when students transgress class agreements they do so by talking, calling out, moving about, goofing off, or not completing work. What do you do? You have seen that different authorities offer different suggestions. Most prominent among those suggestions are:

- Invoke logical consequences and/or show appreciation when students behave appropriately.
- Use body language such as eye contact, physical proximity, and attention.
- Remind the students of the class agreements they have agreed to live by.
- Stop the class and say, "This lesson doesn't seem to be holding your attention. What might I do to help?"
- Stop the class and say, "We seem to have a problem here. What do you think we can do to resolve it?"
- In no case should you call offending students to task publicly.
- Conduct class meetings to discuss ongoing incidents and explore solutions. Here you must be careful not to single out individual students. You want their cooperation, not their enmity.

All of these tactics are effective. It is for you to decide which makes most sense to you personally and which you feel best about using on a daily basis. Just remember it is self-defeating to scold or deride the offending students. You and they will both be better off if you can help them abide by class rules willingly.

When students misbehave seriously. We have noted that the vast majority of student misbehavior is disruptive but benign. It interferes with learning, wastes time, and annoys the teacher and perhaps other students, but it can be dealt with fairly easily. Occasionally, however, students behave in ways considered immoral, outrageous, or violent. These behaviors range from lying and cheating to stealing, sexual immorality, bullying, cruelty, aggression, and violence. Although these behaviors occur only rarely, they affect everyone strongly. You should carefully think through how you will react to them. Before any matters of this type occur, hold a class meeting. Tell the class there are certain kinds of behaviors so serious they are bound to cause problems if they occur. Mention the kinds of behaviors you are concerned about. Indicate that while you don't expect the behaviors to occur in the class, you feel it will be helpful to bring them out in the open. That way, students will be mindful of them, perhaps can help determine how to react to them, and anticipate how they will be dealt with.

Then, should a serious transgression occur, conceal your distress and maintain your composure. If it is possible to speak with the students, say either privately to the individual or to the entire class if all are affected, "This is a serious problem. I'd like us to resolve it together. Let's try. But if we can't, I'll need to ask for help from the Vice Principal."

Meanwhile, begin working immediately toward positive solutions with the students involved. Show your willingness to help them choose behavior that serves them and the class productively. Later, bring the topic up for discussion in class meetings, provided it is not a private issue.

You can usually handle lying, cheating, stealing, and sexual innuendo or harrassment without having to call for expert assistance. Sexual innuendo or harrassment should be squelched immediately. Without singling out the individuals involved, point out what is occurring and why it is forbidden in the classroom. If the behavior continues, speak with the culpable individual privately and explain once more why those acts are not permitted in the class or school. Remind yourself that your goal is not to punish but to help. Ask the individual to meet with you privately and, without casting blame, explain your concern frankly. Some students will admit what they've done; others will deny it. Don't try to make students admit wrongdoing. Don't use logic or threat to persuade them, and never insist they apologize. That works against the relationship you hope to preserve. When you talk with the student, admit you might be wrong, then explain your perception of the situation. Ask students if they understand why, when they behave in those ways, others lose trust in them and don't want to associate with them. Assure offending students that you want to help them learn and be the best persons they can. Show them kind personal attention. Go out of your way to be helpful. This is as much as you can realistically do. If that does not resolve the problem, you should inform the school counselor or administrator and let that person take over from there.

For behavior that is threatening, dangerous, or wantonly cruel—such as severe bullying, intimidation, fighting, or possession of weapons or dangerous substances—be ready to call for help immediately. You are not expected to deal with those conditions. Some authorities suggest including a "severe clause" in class agreements, which makes clear to students that dangerous or threatening behavior will result in immediate notification of the school administrator and removal from the classroom. From that point, the matter moves out of your hands into those of persons with special training. To make sure what you are expected to do in those circumstances, discuss the matter with your school administrator.

9. *How can teachers help students actually want to behave more responsibly?* The dream of all teachers is to work with students who behave responsibly because they feel it is the best thing to do. These students do not require incentives or reward, but behave appropriately because they believe doing so is to their personal advantage or simply the right thing to do. Many years ago Rudolf Dreikurs made "social interest" a prime ingredient in his scheme of classroom discipline. He sought to help students see that they prospered individually when the class prospered as a whole. He pointed out that the best way for students to help themselves was to help the class function well. Social interest can be developed through joint decision-making, assumption of personal responsibility, developing a sense of community, and production of class synergy, as described in the following paragraphs.

Joint decision-making. Students like to have a sense of power in the classroom. Some students, when power is not allocated to them, try to seize it by rebelling against teacher authority and refusing to cooperate. Wise teachers give students power by involving them in helping to make decisions that affect the class. This helps put students' destiny in their own hands and gives them a feeling of being in control. When they help make decisions they become more likely to comply with them and to work in ways that improve learning and attitude toward school. When they see that what benefits the class also benefits them personally, they become predisposed to work toward the betterment of the class.

Responsibility. Students desire freedom and power, but often do not understand that responsibility is tied to them. Teachers are admonished to give students more responsibility, so they put students in charge of keeping the room tidy, managing the media or science equipment, helping take care of plants and pets, and so forth. This is one kind of responsibility, certainly, and it does contribute to a sense of concern about the class. There is, however, another kind of responsibility that of necessity is tied to freedom and power. This is responsibility in accepting the results of one's actions and learning from them. When students are allowed to make decisions about what goes on in the class, they must be helped to understand they must deal with the results of their decisions. If the class decides to forego preparation for an upcoming test, and then does poorly, they must accept that they are to blame, not the teacher. They need to see, too, that they can learn from the situation so that they can do better in the future. Mr. Abrams, the teacher, always stands ready to help the class overcome difficulties. He allows them to make decisions, but when they do poor work he does not excuse them. This same principle applies when students decide to work in groups, but find that some students are not doing their part. They must assume responsibility for working things out. Mr. Abrams will help them find ways to do so, but the working-through process is up to them. In this manner, the class begins to realize that they have a collective responsibility to make things run smoothly for the class. Given the opportunity, most students would rather be involved in this process than have the teacher make all decisions for them. They certainly learn more from working through problems than when only told what to do.

Sense of community. Joint decision-making combined with responsibility helps build a sense of community in the class. Alfie Kohn urges teachers to work toward establishing what he calls a sense of community, a place where students feel valued and connected to each other and think in terms of "we" instead of "I." Kohn believes sense of community grows when teachers consistently show they care about students and behave respectfully toward them. He says that when students' personal needs are met, they show increased tendency to help meet their classmates' needs rather than remaining preoccupied with their own. To facilitate this process, Kohn advises instructional activities that encourage students to work together and practice seeing things from other people's points of view.

Synergy. Teachers have long recognized the value of group spirit, where students reach high levels of energy and involvement. It is usually seen in connection with athletic contests and, to a lesser degree, in school plays, concerts, and other productions. It can also occur in the classroom. Most teachers have experienced it and know that it provides a time of happy learning, joyful teaching, and few or no discipline problems. However, teachers have not understood clearly what causes it or how they can make it occur.

C. M. Charles calls the phenomenon "class synergy" and says it occurs when members of a class begin, through interest or excitement, to feed psychic energy to each other. When the energy level becomes high enough, students work together eagerly with little thought for themselves as individuals. They communicate, cooperate, share resources, and find pleasure in the process. Learning occurs rapidly. Good will predominates, and misbehavior disappears.

Charles says the elements of synergy can be put in place by teachers and that with practice they can cause synergy to occur on demand. He lists elements of synergy such as trust, teacher charisma, communication, interest, class agreements, competition, human relations, and problem resolution. While synergy can occur without all the elements being in place, it cannot be made to occur reliably when certain of them are absent, especially trust, communication, charisma, and interest.

Exercise 3. Refer back to your notes concerning your philosophy and theory of discipline, then take a few minutes to list what you would like to include in your actual practice of discipline—that is, what you would do to help students behave in ways that serve them better, as individuals and as a class. No need to go into detail at this point, because the process will be continued in the next chapter. If you need a starting place, you might want to think in terms of what you would do to prevent discipline problems, to assist restive students, to redirect students who have broken class agreements, and to help students actually want to behave in ways that serve them better individually and collectively.

cted Terminology

were explained in the chapter. Check yourself to make sure you

cause-effect relationship
means-end relationship
philosophy of discipline

practice of discipline
theory of discipline

Finalizing a Personal System of Discipline

If you worked through the previous chapter, you have sketched out your philosophy and theory of discipline as well as some ideas for organizing your discipline system and putting it to work. As you know, the contention of this book is that your system of discipline, to be most effective, must be consonant with your well-considered views on how to work with the young as well as the realities of the community, school, and students where you teach. It is unlikely that any of the excellent discipline models described in previous chapters will provide a sufficient match to meet your needs optimally. In order to achieve the results you want, you or your school will need to work through what you want your discipline system to include and how you will use it. This chapter is organized to help you do that.

What You and Other Teachers Want

In your philosophy of discipline you indicated how you would like your students to conduct themselves, now and in the future. You are probably like other teachers in wanting students to show positive attitude, humane behavior, self-direction, initiative, strong effort to learn, and personal responsibility. You can rely on your curriculum and teaching methods to accomplish some of these goals. Others will be accomplished through your discipline system. At this point we won't reiterate the positive effects that curriculum and instruction can have on student behavior, a matter that has received attention elsewhere, especially in Chapters 8 and 13. With regard to discipline, the list presented here in Exercise 1 shows what most teachers hope discipline will do for them, in both the short and long term.

Exercise 1: Compare your list of desired outcomes of discipline with the following list. Note agreements and disagreements. From that basis, finalize your list of desired outcomes.

- Prevent most misbehavior
- Redirect misbehavior in a positive, helpful manner

- Promote trusting relationships between teacher and students
- Help students become responsible and self-controlled
- Help students meet their needs in nondisruptive ways
- Be effective and easy to use
- Merit support from administrators, parents, and students

Your Plan of Action

It is helpful to think of three groups of interventions teachers use in discipline: (1) those that prevent misbehavior; (2) those that support students who are wavering; and (3) those that correct misbehavior and rechannel it in positive directions. These groups of intervention techniques are often referred to as **preventive discipline, supportive discipline,** and **corrective discipline.** Let's examine the nature and purpose of each.

Preventive Discipline

You can prevent most misbehavior if you treat students sensitively, provide an interesting curriculum, and use a helpful teaching style. For this preventive aspect of discipline, think through what you will do concerning:

- Making curriculum topics and lessons enjoyable and worthwhile
- Being ever mindful of students' needs for security, hope, acceptance, dignity, power, enjoyment, and competence, and seeing that those needs are met, not thwarted
- Being pleasant, considerate, respectful, understanding, and helpful toward students, and teaching them to treat each other the same
- With student input, reaching joint understandings about behavior that serves, rather than harms, the class, and frequently discussing these understandings while providing a positive model for your students
- Teaching students about good manners, how to use them, and how they help the class function better for everyone
- Teaching students to meet their needs and react to situations, in ways that do not disrupt the class

Supportive Discipline

Despite your best efforts, students will at times become restive and can easily slip into misbehavior. This is the time for you to make use of supportive techniques, which are pleasant yet effective in keeping students engaged in their work. You should practice a number of these techniques so you can use them naturally when needed. Examples include:

- Showing interest in the student's work and asking cheerful questions or making favorable comments
- Learning to catch students' eyes and send private signals such as head shakes
- Using physical proximity—that is, taking a position closer to the student
- Helping students with suggestions and hints when they get stuck
- Providing a light challenge: "Can you get five more problems done before we stop?"
- If the work is too difficult, restructuring it or changing the activity

Corrective Discipline

We have to accept that while good discipline systems can prevent most misbehavior, your students will nevertheless break rules at times and you must deal with the transgressions. If you approach misbehaving students in a sensitive manner, you can help them return to proper behavior with no ill feelings. Here are some ways you can do this:

- Intervening in a positive manner when class agreements are broken
- Talking with offending students calmly and respectfully, without lecturing, threatening, impugning their dignity, or backing them into a corner
- Invoking the corrective measures that you and your students have agreed to, such as applying consequences, correcting causes, or carrying out other approaches you have formulated
- Doing all you can to remain pleasant, retain your composure, refuse to argue with students, and show you want to help them abide by class rules
- Applying your plan consistently, in very nearly the same way every day

Exercise 2. In the previous chapter, you indicated how you would structure and implement your system of discipline. Compare your ideas with the suggestions made in the previous paragraphs on preventive, supportive, and corrective discipline. Before adding the finishing touches to your plan, you might wish to examine the following discipline plans made by individual teachers and two school faculties, presented here with their permission.

Sample Discipline Plans

In recent decades, we have seen significant changes in the way teachers attempt to influence student behavior. The main change is that teachers have begun to relinquish authoritarian dominance in favor of humane approaches that emphasize student involvement, collaboration, and responsibility. Here are two approaches that embody the newer philosophy, presented for you to consider as examples. They are only that—examples. You might want to use either of them in your planning, modify either to make it more appropriate for your situation, or turn to another approach you like better.

Approach 1. A Plan That Emphasizes Rules and Consequences

Many teachers now use discipline plans that feature rules and consequences. Teachers who use plans of this type believe the teacher should exercise firm, but sensitive and fair control in the classroom. They believe students consciously choose to behave as they do, and that the teacher's responsibility is to help students make good behavioral choices. They feel their approach allows students to learn in a classroom free from worry and disruption, while cutting down disruptions that interfere with teaching. Discipline plans of this type usually contain the following:

- *Rules.* A set of rules that indicates what students are allowed and not allowed to do in class. Students help compose the rules.
- *Consequences.* Consequences (results that follow behavior) are attached to the rules and made plain to students. "Positive" consequences are pleasant experiences that students experience when they follow the rules. "Negative" consequences are unpleasant experiences that students experience when they break the rules. Students participate in selecting the consequences to be used.
- *Procedure.* A series of steps is established for applying the consequences. When students behave properly they receive something they like, such as compliments, bonus points, privileges, or a favorite activity. When they behave unacceptably, they receive negative consequences, which may grow progressively more severe if students continue to repeat the misbehavior. Parents are kept fully informed about the rules, consequences, and procedures of enforcement. Teachers ask parents for their support.

This approach has served tens of thousands of teachers for many years and continues to be widely popular. To see how a present-day teacher uses the rules-consequences-procedure protocol, adjusted to her needs, consider the following program developed by third-grade teacher Deborah Sund.

Deborah Sund's Third-Grade Discipline Program

Deborah Sund, who had been teaching for two years when she devised this program, was seeking a discipline approach that provided structure for herself and her students while at the same time meeting students' needs. She felt structure was important for helping everyone know exactly what was expected. Notice in the plan that Ms. Sund clarifies her students' needs, her own needs, and her special dislikes, then builds her discipline system so all are taken into account.

My Students' Needs

- To learn interesting and useful information, especially that which promotes skills in reading, math, and language
- A learning environment that is attractive, stimulating, free from threat, and conducive to productive work
- A teacher who is helpful, attentive, and kind
- The opportunity to interact and work cooperatively with other students

- To be accepted and feel part of the group
- To learn how to relate to others humanely and helpfully
- To have the opportunity to excel

My Own Needs

- Orderly classroom appearance; good room arrangement; materials neatly stored, interesting, well-thought-out displays
- Structure and routines: a set schedule that is flexible and allows for improvisation when needed
- Attention and participation: students pay attention to directions and speakers, and participate willingly in all instructional activities
- Situationally appropriate behaviors: quiet attention during instruction, considerate interaction during group activities
- Enthusiasm from me and my students
- Warmth as reflected in mutual regard among all members of the class
- Positive, relaxed classroom environment reflecting self control, mutual help fulness, and assumption of responsibility

My Dislikes

- Inattention to speaker, teacher, other adult, or class member
- Excessive noise: loud voices, inappropriate talking and laughing
- Distractions: toys, unnecessary movement, poking, teasing, and so on
- Abuse of property: misusing, wasting, or destroying instructional materials
- Unkind and rude conduct: ridicule, sarcasm, bad manners, and physical abuse

Class Rules

I ask students on the first day of school to tell me how they would like to be treated by others in the room. I ask them what they especially dislike. We discuss their contributions at length, making sure through examples that we have a clear understanding of their wishes. By the next day, I have written out some statements that summarize what they have said. I ask them if these ideas seem good ones to live by in the room. They invariably say yes and we call the statements our class rules. We spend some time practicing how we will behave and speak, in accordance with the rules. In the days that follow, I demonstrate to students the prompts, cues, hints, and other assistance I will give to help them abide by the behaviors we have agreed on.

The following are class rules that typically emerge from discussions with my students:

1. Be considerate of others at all times. (Speak kindly. Be helpful. Don't bother others.)
2. Do our best work. (Get as much done as possible. Do work neatly, to be proud of it. Don't waste time.)
3. Use quiet voices in the classroom. (Use regular speaking voices during class discussions. Speak quietly during cooperative work. Whisper at other times.)
4. Use signals to request permission or receive help. (I explain the signal systems for assistance, movement, restroom pass.)

Positive Consequences

I emphasize that I will always try to show how pleased I am when students follow the rules we have agreed to. I tell them:

- Mostly I will give them smiles, winks, nods, and pats when they are behaving well.
- Sometimes I will say out loud how pleased I am with the way they are working or behaving toward each other.
- Once in a while, when the whole class has behaved especially well, I will give them a special privilege (go early to recess, do one of their favorite activities, see a video).
- From time to time I will send a complimentary note to their parents, or call their parents and comment on how well they are doing.

Negative Consequences

When discussing the class rules, I ask students what they think should happen when someone breaks a rule. They usually suggest punishment. I tell them that because I want them always to be as happy as possible, I don't want to punish them. I say that instead of punishment, I will do the following:

- Give them "pirate eyes" or a stern glance with disappointed or puzzled expression.
- Remind them of what rule is being broken: "I hear noise." "Some people are not listening."
- Tell them exactly what they are doing wrong: "Gordon, you did not use the signal. Please use the signal."
- Separate them from the group until they can control themselves.
- Contact their parents to see how they can help.

To Prevent Misbehavior

I discuss with my students a number of things I will do to help them feel more like behaving properly, such as:

- Show respect for each student as entitled to the best education I can provide.
- Look for the positive and enjoyable qualities in each student.
- Take time to know each student better on a personal level.
- Each day assess students' feelings and discuss them if necessary.
- Talk with students in ways that imply their own competence, such as, "Okay, you know what to do next."
- Involve them in establishing rules and assuming responsibility for proper behavior.
- Keep a good room environment to prevent their feeling strained, tired, or inconvenienced. (Proper lighting, temperature, traffic patterns, attractiveness.)
- Emphasize, model, and hold practice sessions on good manners, courtesy, and responsibility.

- Provide a varied, active curriculum with opportunities for physical movement, singing, interaction, and times of quiet.
- Communicate with parents in the following ways:

  1. Send letters outlining expectations and the discipline system.
  2. Make short, positive phone calls to parents.
  3. Send home with children notes concerning good work and behavior.

  End each day on a positive note, with a fond goodbye and hope for a happy and productive tomorrow.

To Correct Misbehavior

When students begin to misbehave, I do the following:

- Move close to the student.
- Show interest in the student's work.
- Modify the lesson or activity if it seems to be causing difficulty.
- Invoke the negative consequences that we have agreed to.

Approach 2. A Plan That Emphasizes Prevention and Human Relationships

The following exemplifies an approach to discipline intended to prevent misbehavior through meeting student needs and building personal relationships. The rationale for this approach is, first, that it is difficult to confront misbehavior head-on without producing undesirable side effects such as student resentment, desire to retaliate, and reluctance to cooperate, and second, that working with students in this manner helps teachers find greater satisfaction and enjoyment in teaching. When needs are met rather than thwarted, students become more inclined to cooperate and less interested in outsmarting or disdaining their teachers. Moreover, when causes of misbehavior are addressed rather than the dignity of the student, positive feelings are kept intact. Plans of this sort emphasize the following:

- Attending continually to students' needs for security, hope, acceptance, dignity, power, enjoyment, and competence
- Communicating effectively and regularly with students and their parents
- Making sure to give all students attention, encouragement, and support
- Making class activities consistently enjoyable and worthwhile
- Ensuring that all students experience success regularly
- Establishing agreements about how everyone will interact and behave
- Discussing and practicing manners, courtesy, and responsibility
- Involving all students meaningfully in the operation of the class
- Dealing with misbehavior by attending to its causes

Teachers who select this discipline strategy feel it allows them to relate with students in a way that builds positive relationships and produces relatively little stress. An example of a discipline plan that incorporates many of these qualities is that of English teacher Gail Charles.

Gail Charles's Discipline Plan—Eighth-Grade English

The following narration is in Gail Charles's words:

> I have been teaching for more than 20 years. For most of that time my students misbehaved much more than I thought proper, and I tried to control their misbehavior with scowls, reprimands, lectures, threats, and detentions. My students grudgingly behaved themselves well enough to learn most of what I intended, but I'm sure they felt under seige. I know I did, and the effort it required left me continually frustrated and exhausted.
>
> Recently I have begun to understand that I am more effective and enjoy my work more when I organize the curriculum to accommodate, even embrace, the needs of my adolescent students. While I still provide a strong and challenging curriculum, I have switched from a coercive to a collaborative way of teaching. I now try to guide, encourage, and support my students' efforts rather than endlessly push and prod. The result has been fewer power struggles, more success, and happier students and teacher.

Winning My Students Over

> My students want to feel part of the group. They want to feel accepted and valued by each other and especially by me. They want to feel safe, so I forbid all ridicule and sarcasm. I've never ridiculed a student, but sorry to say, I have spoken sarcastically many times when struggling against students who defied my rules. I no longer use sarcasm or allow students to belittle each other in any way.
>
> I give my students a voice in class matters and listen to them sincerely. I allow them to make decisions about where they sit and with whom they wish to work. I do this as part of trying to make learning enjoyable. They like to work with each other, participate, talk, and cooperate.

Meeting My Needs

> We discuss the importance of making classwork enjoyable, and I tell my students that the class needs to be enjoyable for me, too. I tell them up front what I need in order to feel good about the class—that I want the tone to be positive, with everyone showing patience, tolerance, good manners, and mutual respect. I tell them that I want them to be enthusiastic and do the best work they can. I say I need their attention and that I want them to help care for materials and keep the room clean. I promise to treat them with respect, and they usually want to reciprocate.

Rules and Student Input

> My new approach to discipline has required me to make changes in my curriculum and ways of establishing rules. I have learned to request and make use of student input concerning expectations, operating procedures, and codes of conduct. Formerly, I greeted new students with a printed set of rules and consequences, but they always saw them as impositions rather than as cooperative agreements they wanted to support. Now when I meet a new class, I discuss their needs and mine and focus on how we can meet those needs and make our class productive. I give students power to make many decisions and show that I respect what they say.

Together we write a plan for how we will work and behave in the class. Because I want them to make thoughtful suggestions, I ask them, for their first homework assignment, to think back on previous years in school and write brief responses to the following:

1. When have you felt most successful in school?
2. What did the teacher do to help you feel successful?
3. What kinds of class activities have you found most helpful and enjoyable?
4. What suggestions do you have for creating a classroom in which all can work, learn, and do their best?

The next day I organize students into small groups to share and discuss what they have written. Volunteers present each group's responses, which I list on the overhead projector. Occasionally I may add a suggestion of my own. We then streamline, combine, reword, and sometimes negotiate until we reach a set of agreements we think best. Before the next class, I type up the agreements and ask each student and his or her parent to sign, indicating their support. I do this for each of my five classes. The agreements turn out to be quite similar from class to class.

Prevention

In classes of 35 students, there exists an endless supply of distractions. It is up to me to keep students successfully engaged in activities they enjoy and find rewarding. I have had considerable success using reading and writing activities in which students choose books to read and respond to them in writing. I present mini-lessons that address common needs I see in the class. Students evaluate their own work and make it the best possible for inclusion in their Showcase Portfolios, which are displayed for parents, teachers, administrators, and others at a Writers' Tea. In addition, students complete at least one project per quarter. They have choices on what they will pursue in their projects and how they will show what they have learned. Always there is a high emphasis on quality.

During these efforts, I try to interact personally with every student. It is not easy to forge relationships with 160+ students, but I try to do so in order to show I "see" and like them. At the beginning of the year, I write a letter to my students introducing myself and telling a bit about my family, hobbies, interests, and goals. I ask them to do the same so I can know them better. I keep a birthday calendar to remember student birthdays. I try to comment on new hairstyles, new outfits, or how great a now brace-free set of teeth looks. I chaperon field trips and dances, supervise the computer writing lab after school, and make myself available for conversation before and after school. These little things mean a lot to students.

For their part, many students like to involve themselves in the workings of the classroom. I assign them tasks such as classroom librarian, bulletin board designer, plant caretaker, and class secretary. Their involvement makes them feel important and useful.

More than anything else, I have found that if I want respect from my students, I must show them respect. I want them to enjoy writing, so I write along with them. I want them involved in learning, so I get involved with them. I want them to show good manners, humor, and kindness, so I exemplify those qualities the best I can in my behavior and dealings with them. I make mistakes in these efforts and lots of them, but the more sincerely I try, the more forgiving my students become.

Enforcement

With the collaborative plan in place, I have few discipline problems and little difficulty dealing with those that occur. Most often, a simple reminder is all that is needed to get students back on track. For the occasional student who repeatedly misbehaves despite our agreements, I ask the counselor to set up a meeting with the students' parents and, sometimes, with other teachers. We discuss the problem and how it can be resolved. Very occasionally, a student may behave in a dangerous manner or prevent my teaching. When that happens, I call the vice-principal for assistance.

Schoolwide Discipline Plans

Increasingly, groups of teachers and administrators are developing discipline plans for the entire school that provide consistency from one class to another. They often adopt and sometimes modify a commercial program such as *Assertive Discipline, Cooperative Discipline,* or *Positive Discipline in the Classroom.* But schools have other options as well. Many pick and choose from multiple sources and construct plans that suit their particular needs, just as individual teachers do. The following descriptions and examples are provided to assist groups interested in organizing a plan for their school.

Recommended Components of a Schoolwide System

The generic plan for a schoolwide system of discipline consists of four components— (1) a *policy statement* that shows the philosophy that supports the system, (2) *rules* and/or *agreements* about desirable student conduct, (3) efforts the school will make to *prevent misbehavior,* and (4) *procedures of enforcement* or follow-up that will be used to gain student cooperation. Parents and representatives of the community are usually invited to help plan the schoolwide system.

Component 1, the policy statement, communicates (1) the relationship between effective discipline and student attitude, cooperation, and learning, (2) the school's responsibility in providing a quality learning environment and helping students behave in ways that serve them best, (3) the students' responsibilities in helping make the program effective, (4) the role of the administration and counselors in setting standards and working with students and teachers, and (5) a list of prohibited behaviors having to do with disrespect, fighting, destruction of property, and possession of dangerous objects and banned substances.

Component 2, the rules and/or agreements pertaining to behavior, indicate how students are expected to behave, such as:

- Always be on time and ready to work.
- Treat all people and property with respect.
- Do nothing that prevents the teacher from teaching or students from learning.

Component 3, prevention of misbehavior, outlines what the school and individual teachers will do to limit causes of misbehavior, such as are listed in the following table:

Causes	Prevention
Boredom	All activities will be made as interesting as possible.
Frustration in learning	All activities will be made challenging but within the capabilities of all students.
Desire for attention	Each student will receive regular direct attention from the teacher and others in the school setting.
Lack of acceptance	Every student will be given responsibility and made to feel a valued part of the group.
Threat to personal dignity	Every student will be treated with respect and encouraged to take responsibility for the welfare of the class.
Egocentric personality	All school personnel will work to help individual students fit in and show normal consideration for others.

Component 4, enforcement and/or follow-through, indicates what school personnel will do to gain student cooperation and deal with causes of misbehavior, such as:

- Conduct discussions with students to get input on how their needs can best be met in the school and class
- Reach agreements about desirable behavior of teachers, students, and others
- Specify what will transpire should students transgress the agreements, such as invocation of specific consequences or follow-though with procedures to identify and correct the causes of misbehavior

In actual practice, schoolwide systems don't necessarily include the four elements just described. Schools select plans for specific purposes and organize them for convenience. This will be evident in the two schoolwide examples presented in the following pages, both organized to help attain a specific goal.

Two Examples of Schoolwide Systems of Discipline

Example 1. Dry Creek Elementary School

At the time this description was submitted, Dry Creek School was just completing a five-year program of restructuring the curriculum to make it compatible with brain-based education. One of their most important tasks was implementing a positive learning environment in which students felt safe yet excited about learning. Toward that end, the school decided to use Linda Albert's *Cooperative Discipline*. Specifically, the program focused on improving the behavior of all students by having teachers do the following whenever misbehavior was observed:

1. Identify the goal of (reason for) the misbehavior.
2. Select and apply appropriate intervention techniques.
3. Apply specific encouragement strategies to build student self-esteem.
4. Involve parents as partners in the process.

To help provide uniformity and continuity, the Dry Creek School staff developed what they called the Dry Creek Critter Code. This is a code of behavior based on the "Three C's" of Cooperative Discipline—*capable, connect,* and *contribute.* The staff designed a logo in the form of an umbrella with the words CAPABLE, CONNECT, CONTRIBUTE written on it. Just beneath the umbrella are these four statements:

> I will respect myself, others, and property.
>
> I will be responsible for my behavior.
>
> I will be punctual and prepared.
>
> I will be safe.

The overall intent of the Critter Code is to help students live by those statements.

In addition to, and in connection with the Critter Code and Cooperative Discipline, Dry Creek School includes two other components in its schoolwide program. These components are life skills and the citation program. The *Life Skills Program* provides systematic instruction in the skills of teamwork, perseverance, responsibility, caring, and cooperation. This is aimed at helping students become more effective citizens. A month is devoted to the development of each skill. At the end of each month, a ceremony is held to recognize students who have demonstrated the skill in exemplary fashion. The *Citation Program* involves giving citations to students for serious misbehavior. But rather than carry a punitive connotation, the citations provide a positive opportunity to help students understand why they are misbehaving, to assist them with problem-solving skills, and to support them as they learn to connect effectively with others in school. The following are some of the main elements of the citation program.

Manners and safety class. Students who receive citations must attend manners and safety class during the last recess of the day. There they make a problem-solving map in collaboration with a teacher. This allows the child to connect with a caring adult and to learn problem-solving skills that support better behavior choices.

Action plan meetings. These meetings are held once a week to help students take positive steps to correct chronic misbehavior. Student referrals are made by classroom teachers on the basis of accumulated citations or social, emotional, or academic needs. These meetings are attended by teacher, student, parent, principal, and action plan coordinator, and their purpose is to develop a plan to reconnect the student positively with the school.

Critter activities. On Friday afternoons, Critter Activities are provided for students who have lived in accordance with the school code of conduct. These activities, which students especially enjoy, are used as further incentives for good behavior. They are characterized by meaningful content, student choice, multiage groupings, and adequate time for goal accomplishment. Activity groups include landscape artists, dance troupes, newsletter editors, culinary academicians, artists in residence, clay masters, musicians, athletes, jewelers, math masters, and technologists.

Citation clinic. This is the weekly counterpart of Critter Activities. The clinic is conducted by the Student Success Team, comprised of sixth-grade students who have been trained to work, under adult supervision, with peers and younger students who have received citations for serious behavior such as fighting or disrespectful profanity. Problems are discussed and worked out, strategies that lead to good behavior are reviewed, and supportive connections are established between students. The Success Team also helps in leadership roles such as schoolwide decision making.

The newcomer club. This club of sixth-grade students creates and extends a warm welcoming environment to new students. New students are invited to a special luncheon to meet club members. There they receive folders containing supplies and welcoming correspondence.

These programs at Dry Creek School focus on making students feel they are capable, connected, and contributing members of the school. The staff and parents laud the program for helping to cultivate good citizenship, enhance self-esteem, and raise academic achievement.

Example 2. The Emerald Way

The Emerald Way is a schoolwide program for improving student behavior that has been used at Emerald Middle School in El Cajon, California, since 1996. Developed by the principal and teacher leaders, it is a way of presenting a theme and common language that help create a sense of community in the school. It emphasizes the development of 10 specific character traits that enable students to lead more effective lives. This increases civility while reducing misbehavior. When students do misbehave, teachers intervene with supportive techniques that are in keeping with the schoolwide plan.

The program is undergirded by counseling and parent contacts. A Student Success Team is in place to deal with more serious offenses and to support students who are at risk of failure. A Homework Club meets four afternoons a week to help students keep up in classes—the teachers at Emerald Middle School believe a main cause of misbehavior is students' dropping behind, leaving them feeling hopeless and disengaged. Supervised peer mediation is used to resolve conflicts between students and help them deal with personal problems. Should students fight or talk disrespectfully to teachers or other adults on campus, they face the possibility of detention or in-school suspension.

Goals of the Emerald Way

The Emerald Way sets forth the following goals for students:

- To interact more effectively and successfully with others
- To feel connected to the school
- To learn specific behaviors that demonstrate the 10 character traits specified in the program
- To develop students' positive feelings toward themselves, their school, and their community

The 10 Targeted Traits

A separate character trait is featured each month. It is emphasized by all teachers and administrators. A number of activities are built around the trait. The character traits are considered in the following sequence:

- *Courtesy*—Showing behavior that is gracious, kind, and thoughtful of others
- *Commitment*—Making and living up to pledges or agreements

- *Respect*—Showing high regard or strong consideration for something or someone
- *Appreciation*—Showing sensitive enjoyment, awareness, or grateful recognition
- *Initiative*—Taking the first step; thinking or acting without being urged
- *Responsibility*—Showing reliability and accountability in one's own actions
- *Self-Discipline*—Maintaining self-control; taking charge of one's own conduct
- *Honesty*—Behaving in a fair and straightforward manner, without intending to deceive
- *Cooperation*—Participating helpfully with others for the benefit of all
- *Success*—Experiencing a feeling of accomplishment and satisfaction

Schoolwide Procedures

The Emerald Way is put into effect through teacher teams, schoolwide reinforcement procedures, and daily support from school administrators.

Character trait posters are displayed in all classrooms, showing the 10 traits for the year. The trait being emphasized in a given month is highlighted.

Teacher teams and schedules are established. The teams each select one of their members to introduce the trait for the month and plan associated activities. The activities are discussed and approved by the team before being used and are reviewed during weekly team meetings.

Incentives and rewards are approved and applied by members of the team. They are given for demonstration of good character and for academic achievement. For example, all teachers and staff members have access to Emerald Way Knight Cards, which they can present to students who show exemplary behavior. Students use the cards to purchase items in the Student Store or to put in the Knight Card drawing in hopes of winning a school T-shirt.

Time commitment to the program is at least 55 minutes of instruction per month, divided into sessions as the team sees fit.

Scheduling of activities is as follows: In the first week of each month, the designated teachers introduce and explain to students the character trait being emphasized. They identify its objectives and preview instructional activities. Throughout the month teachers teach the trait using activities such as role-plays, readings, writing, and discussions. Each week, teachers nominate students who are exemplary or have shown great improvement. Three of those students from each grade level are recognized as Knights of the Week and their names are read during the morning bulletin. Their names go into a pool, from which faculty select the Knights of the Month.

At the end of each month, all faculty members vote for one Knight of the Month from each grade level, 6, 7, and 8. Student recipients are treated to lunch with the principal at a local restaurant. Teams also implement other incentive programs they have put in place, such as bonus points, assembly program, guest speaker, or field trip.

Suggested teaching activities are in keeping with the program guide, but teachers are allowed latitude in selecting activities they find effective. Examples include journal writing, skits, role-plays, cooperative learning tasks, debates, discussions, keeping daily logs, service projects, art projects, guest speakers, and inspirational sayings and readings.

Daily support from administrators is provided as follows: Each day on the closed circuit TV broadcast, a school administrator, usually the principal, presents special announcements, "Powerful Learners" statements, examples of character traits noted in action, and the principal's Thought for the Day related to the character trait. The TV is also used as an electronic bulletin board to display motivational information about the Emerald Way and showcase photos of Knights of the Month with their teachers and peers.

Examples of Monthly Plans and Lessons

To illustrate more clearly the activities teachers provide, here are the contents of the school plan for improving *courtesy*.

Target Behaviors

- Use the words "please" and "thank you."
- Extend friendly greetings (smile, make eye contact, say something considerate).
- Listen and wait (don't interrupt, wait your turn, say excuse me).
- Be aware of people and space around you (share space with others, don't crowd halls or doorways, show kindness, don't laugh at others' mistakes or embarrassment, no name calling).

Thoughts and Quotes   (only a few of many suggestions are shown here)

- Do unto others as you'd have them do unto you.
- All doors open to courtesy.
- Rudeness is the weak person's imitation of strength.

Suggested Classroom Activities

(only a few examples from many are shown here)

- Describe what school would be like if people were more courteous to each other.
- Describe the differences in norms of courtesy when you are with friends as contrasted with when you are with your parents, grandparents, teachers, or other people.
- Write or act a brief conversation for each of these types of language: formal (with adults in school or business), informal (with friends), and family (used with family and loved ones).
- In groups, write skits that demonstrate courtesy in various settings and present the skits to the class.
- Have a vocabulary enhancement lesson related to courtesy, including words such as polite, empathetic, faux pas, diplomacy, gracious, etiquette, chivalry, manners, gaffe.
- Learn about and practice communication door openers, roadblocks, active listening, and I-statements to take the place of you-statements.

Program Effectiveness

Teachers at Emerald Middle School are seldom able, given time restrictions, to do all the activities contained in the program guide. They report, however, that what they do accomplish is quite effective. There has been a marked decline in referrals to the Assistant Principal's office, and visitors to the campus invariably comment on how well-behaved, polite, and friendly the students are.

Implementing Your Personal System

The First Days

Once you have planned your system of discipline, whether individual or schoolwide, you must give thought to how you will introduce and implement it. Consider the following suggestions for individual plans. Similar approaches can be used for schoolwide plans.

Beginning on the first day of class, arrange class members into a circle and initiate discussion that obtains student input concerning their role in school, teachers, instruction, behavior of fellow students, and class climate.

Session 1. With language adjusted to the age of your students, ask questions such as the following:

- You probably have had some favorite teachers. What did you like best about those teachers?
- I'm sure you have some subjects and class activities you like better than others. What are your favorites and what do you like most about them?
- If you had your choice, what kind of classroom environment would you prefer: Neat and orderly? Warm and supportive? Organized and businesslike? Lots of materials? Bulletin boards?
- How do you like your fellow students to behave in class? What about manners, courtesy, laughter, talking, joking, working?

Share your personal preferences with students also, and point out areas where the two of you agree. Where there are disagreements, decide with student collaboration if a compromise can be reached.

Session 2. Work out agreements with the class concerning teacher demeanor, instructional activities, student work, and student and teacher behavior. Explore examples or scenarios that help clarify the agreements. As agreements are reached, put them in writing. Ask the class if they can support and live happily with the agreements. Give students your commitment to live by the agreements and ask for theirs in return. Write the agreements in abbreviated form and post them in the room.

Session 3. Together with the class, decide how misbehavior will be dealt with. Consider the following options as examples you might follow:

Option 1. If your program emphasizes dealing with causes of misbehavior. Tell the class that "misbehavior" simply means violating class agreements. Violations are always caused by something, usually boredom, frustration with assigned work, desire for attention, threats to personal dignity, emotions from incidents that occurred outside the class, or self-centeredness. Reassure the class of the following: (1) the class agreements everyone has pledged to support will remove or limit most causes of misbehavior and conflict, and (2) when misbehavior or conflict occurs, the situation is best handled by calmly correcting the cause. Therefore, when you see someone violate class rules, you will ask if together you can correct whatever is causing the violation. The problem may sometimes need the help of the class and will be addressed in class meetings. Tell the class that in the unexpected case of fighting or other severe behavior, the situation may require the help of the principal or vice principal, whom you will call if necessary.

Option 2. If your program emphasizes rules and consequences. You may decide you need a more systematic way of correcting misbehavior than is provided in the approach that focuses on causes. In this case, you and the class might consider establishing a hierarchy of consequences to accompany the class agreements, or rules. Begin with the least aversive, such as a look or reminder, and if the student continues to misbehave, progressively apply more stringent consequences, such as meeting with the teacher or going to in-school suspension. Plan the consequences jointly with the class, decide how they will be invoked, and discuss fully whether they are just and appropriate. Once the consequences are finalized, write out the procedure. Post a copy in the room and send copies home for parents to read, sign, and return.

Sessions Ongoing: Exemplify in your behavior the traits you want students to emulate. Endeavor consistently to show ethical qualities of kindness, consideration, helpfulness, fairness, honesty, and faith in students. This will help students trust you. Do your best to be interesting to students personally, as well as to make instruction interesting. Maintain good communication through personal attentiveness, listening, and encouragement. And display the best in human relations by conferring dignity and making students feel they are valued.

Keeping Your System Flexible

Emphasize to students that class agreements are not set in stone, nor will the same interventions always be used when violations occur. The purpose of agreements and interventions is always to make school life better for students, and for teachers. When a particular agreement no longer functions as intended, it should be changed. When interventions fail to resolve situations helpfully, they should be replaced with better ones. Those changes should not be made unilaterally, but in collaboration with students. Just how you communicate this flexibility depends on students' levels of understanding. From third grade upward, students understand well and can provide helpful insights and input. Younger students need to be involved, too, although they cannot collaborate so extensively.

Classroom Scenarios for Analysis and Practice

Presented here are descriptions of 10 classrooms exhibiting misbehaviors typical of those that teachers might encounter. The scenarios can be used for behavior analysis, application of concepts and strategies, and testing of personal systems of discipline. Each scenario consists of a general description of the class followed by one or more typical occurrences. It is suggested that when analyzing the scenarios, you ask yourself the following questions:

1. What is the problem behavior, if any, and why is it a problem?
2. If it is a genuine problem, what seems to be causing it?
3. What should the teacher do to stop the misbehavior—invoke consequences? Correct the cause? Talk with the student privately?
4. Should the teacher involve other students in resolving the situation, and if so, how?
5. How can the misbehaving students be put back on a positive course with good attitude?
6. What can be done when resolving the situation to maintain student dignity and good personal relations?

Scenario 1: Fifth Grade

The Class

Mrs. Miller's fifth grade enrolls students from a small, stable community. Because the transiency rate is low, many of her students have been together since first grade, and during those years they have developed certain patterns of interacting and role-playing. Unfortunately, many of those behaviors interfere with teaching and learning. During the first week of school Mrs. Miller noticed that four or five students enjoyed making smart-aleck remarks about most things she wanted them to do. When such remarks were made, the other students laughed and sometimes joined in. Even when Mrs. Miller attempts to hold class discussions about serious issues, many of the students make light of the problems and refuse to enter genuinely into a search for solutions. Instead of obtaining the productive discussion she had hoped for, Mrs. Miller finds the class degenerating into flippancy and horseplay.

Typical Occurrences

Mrs. Miller has begun a history lesson that contains a reference to Julius Caesar. She asks if anyone has ever heard of Julius Caesar. Ben shouts out, "Yeah, they named a salad after him!" The class laughs and calls out encouraging remarks such as "Good one, Ben!" Mrs. Miller tells Ben she does not appreciate such contributions. She waits for some semblance of order, then says, "Let us go on." "Lettuce, continue!" cries Jeremy from the back of the room. The class falls into a chaos of laughter and talk. After waiting a while, Mrs. Miller slams a book down on the desk and demands quiet. "Any more such comments and you will go straight to the office!" she says loudly. For the remainder of the lesson, no more students call out remarks, but most continue to smirk and whisper comments about Caesar salad. A great deal of giggling goes on. Mrs. Miller tries to ignore the display, but because of the disruptions she is not able to complete the lesson on time or to get the results she hoped for.

Scenario 2: High School Biology

The Class

Mr. Platt teaches advanced placement classes in biology to students from middle- to upper-income families. Most of the students have already made plans for attending college. When the students enter the classroom, they know they are to go to their assigned seats and write out answers to the questions of the day that Mr. Platt has written on the board. After that, Mr. Platt lectures on text material that he assigned students to read before coming to class. During the lecture, he calls randomly on students to answer questions and requires that they support their answers with reference to the assigned reading. Following the lecture, students engage in lab activity for the remainder of the period.

Typical Occurrences

Mr. Platt has begun his lecture on the process of photosynthesis. He asks Arlene what the word photosynthesis means. She pushes her long hair aside and replies, "I don't get it." This is a comment Mr. Platt hears frequently from Arlene. "What is it you don't understand?" "None of it," she says. Mr. Platt retorts, "Be more specific! I've only asked for the definition!" Arlene is not intimidated. "I mean, I don't get any of it. I don't understand why plants are green. Why aren't they blue or some other color? Why don't they grow on Mercury? The book says plants make food. How? Do they make Twinkies? That's ridiculous. I don't understand this business about photosynthesis." Mr. Platt stares at Arlene for a while, and she back at him. He asks, "Are you finished?" Arlene shrugs. "I guess so." She hears some of the boys whistle under their breath; she enjoys their obvious admiration. Mr. Platt says to her, "Arlene, I hope some day you will understand that this is not a place for you to show off." "I hope so, too," Arlene says. "I know I should be more serious." She stares out the window. For the remainder of the lecture, delivered in an icy tone of voice, Mr. Platt calls only on students he knows will give correct answers. His lecture completed, Mr. Platt begins to give instructions for lab activity. He notices that Nick is turning the valve of the gas jet on and off. He says to Nick, "Mr. Turner, would you please repeat the rule about the use of lab equipment?" Nick drops his head and mumbles something about waiting for directions. Arlene says calmly, "Knock it off, Nick. This is serious business." She smiles at Mr. Platt. Mr. Platt stares at the class for a moment, then completes his directions and tells them to begin. He walks around the room, monitoring their work. He stands behind lab partners Sherry and Dawn, who are having a difficult time. He does not offer them help, believing that advanced placement students should be able to work things out for themselves. But as they blunder through the activity, he shakes his head in disbelief, leaving the strong impression that he hopes the two girls will drop the class.

Scenario 3: Middle School Library

Setting and Students

Mrs. Daniels is a media specialist in charge of the middle school library. She sees her job as serving as resource person to students who are seeking information and is always eager to give help to those who request it. The students in her school would be characterized as lower middle class. About half are white, the remainder African American, Latino, and Southeast Asian. Each period of the day differs as to the number and type of students who come under Mrs. Daniels's direction. Usually, small groups have been sent there to do cooperative research. Always some unexpected students appear who have been excused from physical education for medical reasons but who hate to be sent to the library, or else they bear special passes from their teachers for a variety of purposes.

Typical Occurrences

Mrs. Daniels has succeeded in getting students settled and working when Tara appears at her side, needing a book to read as makeup work for missing class. Mrs. Daniels asks Tara what kinds of books interest her. Tara sullenly shrugs her shoulders. Mrs. Daniels takes her to a shelf of newly published books. "I read this one last night," she says. "I think you might like it. It's a good story and fast reading." Tara only glances at it. "That looks stupid," she says. "Don't you have any good books?" She glances down the shelf. "These are all stupid!" Another student, James, is tugging at Mrs. Daniels's elbow, with a note from his history teacher, who wants the source of a particular quotation. Mrs. Daniels asks Tara to look at the books for a moment while she takes James to the reference books. As Mrs. Daniels passes a table of students supposedly doing research, she notices that the group is watching Walter and Tim have a friendly pencil fight, hitting pencils together until one of them breaks. She admonishes Walter, who appears to be the more willing participant. Walter answers hotly, "Tim started it! It wasn't me!" "Well," Mrs. Daniels replies, "if you can't behave yourself, just go back to your class." The other students laugh at Walter, who feels he has been treated unjustly. He sits down and pouts. Meanwhile, Tara has gone to the large globe and is twirling it. Mrs. Daniels starts to speak to her but realizes that James is still waiting at her shoulder with the request for his teacher. Somehow, before the period ends, Tara leaves with a book she doesn't want and James takes a citation back to his teacher. The research groups have been too noisy. Mrs. Daniels knows they have done little work and wonders if she should speak to their teacher about the students' manners and courtesy. After the period finally ends, Mrs. Daniels notices that profane remarks have been written on the table where Walter was sitting.

Scenario 4: Second Grade

The Class

Mrs. Desmond teaches second graders in a highly transient neighborhood. She receives an average of one new student each week, and those students typically remain in her class for fairly short lengths of time before moving elsewhere. Most are from single-parent, dysfunctional homes, and their poor behavior, including aggression, boisterousness, and crying, seems to reflect many emotional problems.

Typical Occurrences

The morning bell rings, and students who have been lined up outside by an aide enter the classroom noisily. Mrs. Desmond is speaking with a parent who is complaining that her son is being picked on by others in the class. When finally able to give attention to the class, Mrs. Desmond sees that Ricky and Raymond have crawled underneath the reading table, while a group of excited children is clustered around Shawon who has brought his new hamster to share with the class. Two girls are pulling at Mrs. Desmond's sleeves, trying to give her a note and lunch money. Mrs. Desmond has to shout above the din before she can finally get everyone seated. Several minutes have passed since the bell rang. Mrs. Desmond, having lost much of her composure, finally gets the reading groups started when she realizes that the assembly scheduled for that morning has slipped her mind. She suddenly stands up from her reading group and exclaims, "We have an assembly this morning! Put down your books and get lined up quickly! We are almost late!" Thirty-one students make a burst for the door, pushing and arguing. Rachael, a big, strong girl, shoves Amy and shouts, "Hey, get out of the way, stupid!" Amy, meek and retiring, begins to cry. Mrs. Desmond tries to comfort Amy while Rachael pushes her way to the front of the line. During the assembly, Ricky and Raymond sit together. They have brought some baseball cards and are entertaining the students seated around them. When the first part of the assembly performance is over, they boo loudly and laugh instead of applaud. Under the school principal's disapproving eye, Mrs. Desmond separates Ricky and Raymond, but for the rest of the performance they make silly faces and gestures to each other, causing other students to laugh. Upon returning to the classroom, Mrs. Desmond, certain that the principal will speak to her about her class's behavior, tries to talk with them about the impropriety of their actions. She attempts to elicit positive comments about the assembly, but several students say it was dumb and boring. The discussion has made little progress before time for recess. Mrs. Desmond sighs and directs the students to line up, ordering them sternly to use their best manners. As they wait at the door, Rachael is once again shoving her way to the head of the line.

Scenario 5: High School Special Education

The Class

Mrs. Reed teaches special education English to high-school students, all of whom have a history of poor academic performance, though some seem to her to have at least average intelligence. Some of the students have been diagnosed as learning disabled. For others, no specific learning difficulties have been identified. Several live in foster homes. About one-third are Latinos bused from a distant neighborhood. Some of the students are known to be affiliated with gangs.

Typical Occurrences

The students enter the classroom lethargically, find their seats, and as directed, most of them begin copying an assignment from the board. Something is going on between Lisa and Jill, who shoot hateful glances at each other. Neither begins work. When the students are settled, Mrs. Reed reviews the previous day's lesson and then begins instruction on how to write a business letter. She asks the class to turn to an example in their textbooks. Five of the fourteen students do not have their books with them, though this is a requirement that is reemphasized almost daily. Students without books are penalized points that detract from their course grade. Mrs. Reed sees that Lisa has her book and asks her to open it to the correct page. Lisa shakes her head and puts her head down on the desk. Mrs. Reed gives her the option of time out. Lisa leaves the room and sits by herself at a table outside the door. Mrs. Reed goes on with the lesson. She asks the students to work in pairs to write a letter canceling a magazine subscription and requesting a refund. She lets them pick their own partners but finds after a while that several students have formed no partnerships. Lisa's absence leaves an odd number of students. Jill asks if she can work by herself. Mrs. Reed grants her request, but Jill spends most of her time glancing back at Lisa. Two other girls, Marcia and Connie, have taken out mirrors and are applying makeup instead of working on their assignment. Mrs. Reed informs them that she intends to call on them first to share their letter with the class. After the allotted work time, Mrs. Reed asks for volunteers to read their letters. With prodding, a pair of boys is first to share. Mrs. Reed then calls on Marcia and Connie. They complain that they didn't understand how to do the assignment. Mrs. Reed tells them they must complete the letter for homework. They agree, but Mrs. Reed knows they will not comply and expects them to be absent the next day. Other students read their letters. Some are good; others contain many mistakes. The students do not seem to differentiate between correct and incorrect business letter forms. Mrs. Reed tries to point out strengths and weaknesses in the work, but the class applauds and makes smart-aleck remarks impartially. At the end of the period, Mrs. Reed, intending that the students refine their work the next day, asks the students to turn in their letters. She finds that two papers are missing and that Juan and Marco have written on theirs numerous A+ symbols and gang-related graffiti.

Scenario 6: Continuation High School Photography Lab

The Class

Mr. Carnett teaches photography lab, an elective class, in a continuation high school attended by students who have been unsuccessful for behavioral reasons in regular high-school settings. Many of the students want to attend this particular school, as it is located in what they consider their turf. Some of the students are chemically dependent and/or come from dysfunctional homes. The photography lab class enrolls 18 students, all of whom are on individual study contracts.

Typical Occurrences

As students begin work, Mr. Carnett busies himself with a number of different tasks: setting out needed materials, giving advice on procedures, handing out quizzes for students who have completed contracts, examining photographs, and so forth. He sees Tony sitting and staring into space. He asks Tony if he needs help. Tony shrugs. Mr. Carnett asks if Tony has brought his materials to work on. Tony shakes his head. Mr. Carnett tells Tony he can start on a new part of his contract. Tony doesn't answer. Mr. Carnett asks what's the matter. When Tony doesn't respond, Mike mutters, "He's blasted out of his head, man." At that moment, Mr. Carnett hears heated words coming from the darkroom. He enters and finds two students squaring off, trying to stare each other down. He asks what the problem is but gets no reply. He tells the boys to leave the darkroom and go back to their seats. They ignore him. As tension grows, another student intervenes and says, "Come on, we can settle it later. Be cool." Mr. Carnett calls the office and informs the counselor of the incident. The boys involved hear him do so and gaze at him insolently. The class settles back to work, and for the remainder of the period Mr. Carnett circulates among them, providing assistance, stifling horseplay, urging that they move ahead in their contracts, and reminding everyone that they only have a limited amount of time in which to get their work done. From time to time he glances at Tony, who does no work during the period. He asks Tony if something is bothering him. Tony shakes his head. Mr. Carnett asks Tony if he wants to transfer out of the class, since it is an elective. Tony says, "No, man, I like it here."

"That's fine," Mr. Carnett says. "But this is not dream time. You do your work, or else we will find you another class. You understand?" "Sure, man. I understand." Mr. Carnett turns away, but from the corner of his eye he is sure that he sees Tony's middle finger aimed in his direction.

Scenario 7: Sheltered English Kindergarten

The Class

Mrs. Bates teaches a sheltered English kindergarten class comprised of 30 students, only seven of whom speak English at home. The ethnic/racial makeup of the class is a mixture of Vietnamese, Laotian, Chinese, Samoan, Iranian, Latino, Filipino, African American, and Caucasian. The emphasis of the class is rapid English language development. For the most part, the students work in small groups, each of which is directed by a teacher, aide, or parent volunteer. The groups rotate every half hour so as to have a variety of experiences.

Typical Occurrences

Shortly before school begins, a new girl, Mei, is brought into the class. She speaks very little English and is crying. She tries to run out of the classroom but is stopped by the aide. When Mrs. Bates rings her bell, the students know they are to sit on the rug, but those already at the play area do not want to do so. Mrs. Bates calls them three or four times, but finally she has to get up and physically bring two of them to the rug. As the opening activities proceed, Mrs. Bates repeatedly asks students to sit up. (They have begun rolling around on the floor.) Kinney is pestering the girl seated next to him. Twice Mrs. Bates asks him to stop. Finally, she sends him to sit in a chair outside the group. He has to sit there until the opening activities are finished, then he can rejoin his group for the first rotation at the art table. As soon as the groups get under way, Mrs. Bates hears a ruckus at the art table, which is under the guidance of Mrs. García, a parent volunteer. She sees that Kinney has scooped up finger paint and is making motions as if to paint one of the girls, who runs away from him. Mrs. García tells him to put the paint down. Kinney, who speaks English, replies, "Shut up, you big fat rat's ass!" Mrs. Bates leaves her group and goes to Kinney. She tells him, "You need time out in Mrs. Sayres's room (a first-grade next door to Mrs. Bates's kindergarten)." Kinney, his hand covered with blue paint, drops to the floor and refuses to move. He calls Mrs. Bates foul names. Mrs. Bates leaves him there, goes to the phone, and calls the office for assistance. Kinney gets up, wipes his hand first on a desk and then on himself, and runs out the door. He stops beside the entrance to Mrs. Sayres's room, and when Mrs. Bates follows he goes inside and sits at a designated table without further resistance. Mrs. Bates returns to her group, comprised mostly of Asian students. They sit quietly and attentively but do not speak. Mrs. Bates is using a big book on an easel, trying to get the students to repeat the words she says, but she has little success. When it is time for the next rotation, Mrs. Bates goes quickly to Mrs. Sayres's room and brings Kinney back to the class. He rejoins his group. As Mrs. Bates begins work with her new group, she sees Ryan and Duy at the measuring table pouring birdseed on each other's heads. Meanwhile, the new girl, Mei, continues sobbing audibly.

Scenario 8: Junior High World History

The Class

Mr. Jaramillo's third-period world history class is attended by students whose achievement levels are average to below average. He paces his work slowly and keeps it simple. For the most part he enjoys the class, finding the students interesting and energetic. Mr. Jaramillo's lessons follow a consistent pattern. For the first part of the period, students take turns reading aloud from the textbook. Mr. Jaramillo selects the student readers at random from cards with students' names on them. If a student who is called on has lost the place in the textbook or is unable to answer a question about material read by the previous reader, the student loses a point, which affects the final grade. For the second part of the period, the class is divided into work groups. Each group selects a portion from the text reading and uses the information it contains as the basis for making something creative, such as group posters, to be shared at the end of the class if time allows.

Typical Occurrences

During oral reading, Mr. Jaramillo calls on Hillary to read. Although she has been following along, she shakes her head. This has happened several times before. Mr. Jaramillo, not wanting to hurt Hillary's feelings, simply says, "That costs you a point, Hillary," and he calls on someone else. Unfortunately, Hillary's reluctance carries over into group work as well, in which she refuses to participate. The other students ignore her and complete the work without her involvement. Occasionally, Clarisse refuses to involve herself in group work as well. When Mr. Jaramillo speaks to her about it, she replies, "You don't make Hillary do it." Mr. Jaramillo answers, "Look, we are talking about you, not about Hillary." However, he lets the matter lie there and says no more if Clarisse doesn't participate. On this particular day, Deonne has come into the classroom looking very angry. He slams his pack down on his desk and sits without opening his textbook for reading. Although Mr. Jaramillo picks Deonne's card from the deck, he recognizes Deonne's mood and decides not to call on him. Will is in an opposite mood. Throughout the oral reading portion of the class, he continually giggles at every mispronounced word and at every reply students give to Mr. Jaramillo's questions. Will sits in the front row and turns around to laugh, seeing if he can get anyone else to laugh with him. Although most students either ignore him or give him disgusted looks, he keeps laughing. Mr. Jaramillo finally asks him what is so funny. Will replies, "Nothing," and looks back at the class and laughs. At the end of the period, there is time for sharing three posters. Will makes comments and giggles about each of them. Clarisse, who has not participated, says, "Will, how about shutting up!" As the students leave the room, Mr. Jaramillo takes Deonne aside. "What's the matter with you, Deonne?" he asks. "Nothing," Deonne replies. His jaws are clenched as he strides past Mr. Jaramillo.

Scenario 9: High School American Literature

The Class

Mr. Wong teaches an 11th-grade one-semester course in American literature. The course is required for graduation. Among Mr. Wong's 33 students are eight seniors who failed the course previously and are retaking it. The students at Mr. Wong's school are from middle-class affluent families, and many of them are highly motivated academically. At the same time, there is also a significant number who have little interest in school aside from the opportunity to be with their friends. Mr. Wong's teaching routine proceeds as follows: First, he begins the period with a three-question quiz over assigned reading. The quiz items focus on facts such as names, places, and description of plot. Second, when the quiz papers are collected, Mr. Wong conducts a question-and-discussion session about the assigned reading. He calls on individual students, many of whom answer, "I don't know." Third, Mr. Wong has the class begin reading a new chapter in the work under study. They take turns reading orally until the end of the period. The remainder of the assignment not read orally is to be completed as homework.

A Typical Occurrence

The students enter Mr. Wong's classroom lethargically and begin taking the quiz from questions written on the board. Mr. Wong notices that many of the answers are obvious guesses. He notices Brian in particular, who has already failed the class and must pass it now in order to graduate. Mr. Wong says, "Didn't any of you read your assignment?" When oral reading begins, Mr. Wong notices that Brian does not have his copy of *Huckleberry Finn*, the work being studied. This is nothing new. Mr. Wong lends Brian a copy. Brian follows along in the reading for a while, then begins doodling on a sheet of paper. Mr. Wong calls on Brian to read. Brian cannot find the place. Mr. Wong says, "Brian, this is simply unacceptable. You have failed the class once; fail it again now and you know you don't graduate."

Brian does not look up but says, "Want to make a bet on that?"

"What?"

"I guarantee you I'll graduate."

"Not without summer school, you won't!"

"That's okay by me. That will be better. This class is too boring, and the assignments are too long. I've got other things to do besides read this stupid story. Who cares about this anyway? Why can't we read something that has to do with real life?"

Mr. Wong, offended, replies, "You couldn't be more wrong! Other students enjoy this work, and it is one of the greatest books in American literature! There is nothing wrong with the book! What's wrong, Brian, is your attitude!"

Brian's eyes are hot, but he says nothing further. His book remains closed. Mr. Wong struggles through the final 10 minutes of class. Brian is first out of the room when the bell rings.

Scenario 10: Sixth Grade, Student Teacher

The Class

Denise Thorpe is a student teacher in an inner-city magnet school that emphasizes academics. Half of her students are African American, and the other half, of various ethnic groups, have been bused in to take advantage of the instructional program and rich resources. All are academically talented, and none has what would be called a bad attitude toward school. Mrs. Warde, the regular teacher of the class, does not seem to rely on any particular scheme of discipline, at least none obvious to Miss Thorpe. Mrs. Warde simply tells the students what to do and they comply. For the first few lessons that Miss Thorpe teaches, Mrs. Warde remains in the room, acting the role of aide to Miss Thorpe. The students work well, and Miss Thorpe feels happy and successful.

When Mrs. Warde Leaves the Room

Mrs. Warde tells Miss Thorpe that she will leave the room during the math lesson so that Miss Thorpe can begin getting the feel of directing the class on her own. Mrs. Warde warns her that the class might test her with a bit of naughtiness, though nothing serious is likely to occur. Just be in charge, Mrs. Warde counsels. The math lesson begins well, without incident. The lesson has to do with beginning algebra concepts, which Miss Thorpe approaches through a discovery mode. She tells the class, "I want you to work independently on this. Think your way through the following equations and decide if they are true for all numbers."

$$a + 0 = a$$
$$a + b = b + a$$
$$a(b + c) = ab + c$$
$$a + 1 = 1$$
$$a \times 0 = a$$

The students begin work, but within two minutes hands are shooting up. Miss Thorpe goes to help Alicia, who is stuck on the third equation. "What's the matter?" Miss Thorpe whispers.

"I don't understand what this means."

"It was like what I showed you on the board. The same."

"Those were numbers. I don't understand it with these letters."

"They are the same as the numbers. They take the place of the numbers. I showed you how they were interchangeable, remember? Go ahead, let me see. Tell me what you are doing, step-by-step."

Miss Thorpe does not realize it, but she spends almost five minutes with Alicia. Meanwhile, a few of the students have finished and are waiting, but most are holding tired arms limply in the air. Miss Thorpe rushes to the next student and repeats her questioning tutorial. Meanwhile, Matt and Alonzo have dropped their hands and are looking at each other's papers. They begin to talk, then laugh. Others follow, and soon all work has stopped and the classroom has become quite noisy. Miss Thorpe repeatedly says, "Shhh, shhh!" but with little effect. At last she goes to the front of the room, demands attention, and tells the class how disappointed she is in their rude behavior.

Synopses of Models of Discipline Analyzed in This Book

The following are brief sketches of discipline models presented in this book, arranged alphabetically by name of model.

Assertive Discipline (The Canters)

Assertive Discipline was set forth by Lee Canter and Marlene Canter in 1976 and has been continually modified since. For many years it has been the most popular of modern approaches to discipline, emphasizing students' right to learn and teachers' right to teach without disruption from misbehavior. It puts the teacher clearly in charge in the classroom but involves building rapport with students and involving them in making many class decisions, including rules of behavior and consequences to be applied when rules are broken.

Behavior as Student Choice (William Glasser)

Behavior as Student Choice was presented in 1969 by psychiatrist William Glasser in his book *Schools without Failure*. For a few years following its introduction it was the most influential of all modern discipline approaches. Believing that all students could behave properly if they wanted to, Glasser maintained that the best way to ensure proper behavior was to help students make good behavior choices. He advised teachers on how to work with students who chose to misbehave. Glasser also created and explained "classroom meetings" for discussing topics of concern to the class. Classroom meetings are now advocated by many authorities and are used in classrooms everywhere.

Beyond Discipline to Community (Alfie Kohn)

Beyond Discipline to Community was put forth in 1996 by Alfie Kohn, one of today's most astute educational critics. Kohn argues that virtually all discipline approaches, including those purported to be the most humane, produce effects the opposite of what is intended. He says educators want students to become responsible and self-directing, but their discipline systems are so coercive they take away student responsibility, do nothing to help students learn how to solve their own problems, and encourage students to see what they can get away with. Kohn suggests replacing discipline with "sense of community," in which all students are concerned about the interests of the group. This, says Kohn, will help students become more able to resolve problems, accept responsibility, show self-control, and work cooperatively with others.

Congruent Communication (Haim Ginott)

Haim Ginott clarified the role communication plays in discipline in his 1972 book *Teacher and Child*. He depicted true discipline not as a strategy that could be used to eliminate misbehavior in one fell swoop, but rather as a series of little victories through which the teacher slowly wins over student cooperation and support. These little victories are made possible, Ginott explained, by the manner in which teachers communicate with students while showing unwavering willingness to help. Ginott urged teachers to use congruent communication, which is harmonious with the situation and does not attack students, and I-messages, which indicate how the teacher feels in response to a situation in the classroom rather than you-messages, which attack the student.

Cooperative Discipline (Linda Albert)

Linda Albert brought Cooperative Discipline to international attention in her 1989 book *Cooperative Discipline*. Albert contends that student misbehavior occurs when students are unable to meet certain needs satisfactorily, primarily the need for belonging. Albert's model provides strategies for meeting that need, with emphasis on encouragement and activities that help students see themselves as capable, connected with others, and contributing members of the class. Albert also explains how to intervene effectively when misbehavior does occur.

Dealing with the Group (Fritz Redl and William Wattenberg)

This was the first organized alternative to traditional discipline. It was presented in 1951 by Fritz Redl and William Wattenberg in their book *Mental Hygiene in Teaching*. The approach focused on how groups function and how people in groups behave differently than they do individually. It emphasized identifying causes of misbehavior as the first step in deciding on corrective tactics. Redl and Wattenberg stressed supporting students' self-control through humor and personal attention, providing situational assistance such as hurdle help and familiar routines, appraising reality through frank discussions with students, and providing rewards and punishments judiciously.

Democratic Discipline (Rudolf Dreikurs)

Through a series of books published in the late 1960s through the 1970s, psychiatrist Rudolf Dreikurs championed the cause of democracy in the classroom, emphasizing democratic classrooms, democratic teachers, and democratic discipline. In all cases he urged teachers to focus on the concept of social interest, where students could see that their personal well-being contributed to, and was depended upon for, the well-being of the total class. He urged teachers to bring students into the picture as partners and contributors. He felt that this partnership would provide a democratic atmosphere and enable students to find their "genuine goal" of belonging.

Discipline as Self-Control (Thomas Gordon)

In 1989, Thomas Gordon published *Discipline That Works,* in which he described discipline as a quality of self-control that should be developed in students. He suggested that discipline imposed from without does nothing to help students make decisions, resolve problems, or assume responsibility for their actions. Gordon says if teachers are to be truly effective with students they must give up attempts to control them. He condemns the effects of praise and reward as detrimental to self-control. In their place, Gordon would have teachers use participative management in which students play strong roles in solving problems, determining how the class will function, and deciding how they will behave in order to make their time profitable.

Discipline with Dignity (Richard Curwin and Allen Mendler)

In 1988, Richard Curwin and Allen Mendler published *Discipline with Dignity,* an approach that highlighted student dignity as a prime factor in classroom discipline. Much misbehavior, they claimed, resulted from students' attempts to protect and enhance their sense of personal dignity. In 1992, Richard Curwin published *Rediscovering Hope: Our Greatest Teaching Strategy,* in which he pinpoints hope, and loss thereof, as prime motivators of student behavior in the classroom. In 1997, Curwin and Mendler published *As Tough as Necessary: Countering Violence, Aggression, and Hostility in our Schools,* in which they tell how to work productively with hostile or violent students who do not respond to ordinary discipline techniques.

Inner Discipline (Barbara Coloroso)

Inner Discipline, created and disseminated by Barbara Coloroso, is explained in her 1994 book *Kids Are Worth It!: Giving Your Child the Gift of Inner Discipline.* Coloroso has also produced a number of videos, audiotapes, and workbooks to help teachers develop discipline systems based on trust, respect, and success. Inner Discipline emphasizes treating students with respect, giving them power and responsibility, and providing guidance and support as they learn to manage their own behavior. Coloroso says teachers must make unconditional commitments to help students develop self-control, which students do through facing problems, developing plans for resolving those problems, and working through to a resolution.

Managing Lessons and the Class (Jacob Kounin)

Jacob Kounin's views on discipline, developed from studying hundreds of hours of videotapes made in classrooms at all levels, were first reported in his book *Discipline and Group Management in Classrooms* (1971). Kounin identified a number of teacher acts that strongly influence student behavior, including: (1) "withitness" in which the teacher is aware of everything that is going on in the room all the time; (2) momentum and smoothness in lesson delivery, to maintain student attention; (3) group alerting and accountability, to ensure student involvement in lessons; (4) "overlapping," in which the teacher attends to various classroom matters simultaneously; and (5) using tactics that prevent "satiation" or boredom.

Noncoercive Discipline (William Glasser)

William Glasser has the distinction of contributing both a historical model and an application model of discipline. The historical model, *Behavior as Student Choice*, was presented earlier in this section. It reflected Glasser's conclusions about discipline prior to 1985. *Noncoercive Discipline* is Glasser's present application model. Glasser observed that student behavior was progressively changing and that schools were finding it increasingly difficult to serve most students adequately. He therefore turned attention to what schools can do to counteract the problem of misbehavior. His conclusions are presented in books entitled *Control Theory in the Classroom* (1984) and *The Quality School: Managing Students without Coercion* (1992), in which he urges educators to organize the curriculum to meet students' needs for survival, belonging, power, fun, and freedom. He says teachers should try to befriend students, provide encouragement and stimulation, and show an unending willingness to help. He believes that doing these things will prevent most discipline problems. Problems that remain should be resolved by talking helpfully with the offending student.

Positive Classroom Discipline (Fredric Jones)

Fredric Jones has made four unique contributions to discipline, which are now presented in his 2001 book *Fred Jones's Tools for Teachers*. The first has to do with teaching in a manner that keeps students actively involved, thus limiting misbehavior. He calls this approach *Say See Do Teaching*. The second has to do with nonverbal communication. He contends that effective teachers say very little or nothing at all when inappropriate behavior occurs, instead using eye contact, body posture, and physical proximity. The third contribution concerns the use of incentive systems, in which all members of the class are given a stake in seeing that class disruptions do not occur. The fourth contribution concerns providing effective help to students in the shortest time possible.

Positive Discipline in the Classroom (Jane Nelsen, Lynn Lott, and H. Stephen Glenn)

Nelsen, Lott, and Glenn's approach to discipline is described in their book *Positive Discipline in the Classroom* (2000). They put faith in students' ability to control themselves, cooperate, assume responsibility, and behave in a dignified manner. These traits are furthered when concerns of students and teacher are discussed regularly in classroom meetings. As concerns arise they are written into a notebook and become agenda items for class meetings. Class members are taught intrapersonal, interpersonal, strategic, and judgmental skills which they bring to bear in resolving group problems. Through this process students come to see themselves as capable, significant, and able to control their own lives.

Shaping Desired Behavior (B. F. Skinner and his followers)

Skinner's paradigm of shaping behavior through reinforcement is still seen as a component of many application models. Followers of Skinner, sometimes called "Neo-Skinnerians," adapted Skinner's findings into a systematic approach called behavior modification, in which they use reinforcement to transform student behavior. This approach has been, and still is, widely used, despite being criticized for removing responsibility and teaching students to behave well only to gain the reward.

Synergetic Discipline (C. M. Charles)

In his book *The Synergetic Classroom: Joyful Teaching and Gentle Discipline* (2000), C. M. Charles points out that, from time to time, most teachers experience synergy in their classrooms, an energized state in which students happily and eagerly engage in a given class activity, with virtually no misbehavior. Charles explains how to produce these energized states by putting in place elements that contribute to synergy. Teachers are urged to work with students from a basis of trust, dignity, and helpfulness, and then call forth synergy by adding elements of teacher charisma, communication, interest, and coopetition (competing through cooperation). Synergy removes some of the major causes of misbehavior, such as boredom, lack of attention, feelings of powerlessness, and threats students perceive to their dignity. Should misbehavior occur, teachers correct it by identifying and removing its cause, in a gentle, helpful manner.

Win-Win Discipline (Patricia Kyle, Spencer Kagan, and Sally Scott)

Kyle, Kagan, and Scott, in their 2001 book *Win-Win Discipline: Structures for All Discipline Problems,* emphasize that teachers and students should recognize that they are on the same side when it comes to discipline—both are trying to find ways for students to meet their needs in nondisruptive ways. They treat discipline as a joint responsibility of teachers and students. When disruptive behavior occurs, teachers intervene to help students recognize the position they occupy, and from that basis find responsible ways of fulfilling their needs without producing disruptions. Win-Win Discipline also employs follow-up and long-term solutions to prevent recurrence of the problem.

Authorities in Discipline Included in This Book

The following is a list of the discipline authorities whose work is explored in this book.

Albert, Linda

Author, lecturer, television personality, and creator and disseminator of *Cooperative Discipline* (1996), which emphasizes character building and control of discipline problems by making students feel they are competent, connected with others, and contributing members of the class. Contributed the concept of the Three C's. Website: www.cooperativediscipline.com

Canter, Lee, and Marlene Canter

Former teachers and the creators and disseminators of *Assertive Discipline*, a program that resolves discipline concerns by relating positively with students while making sure that teachers' and students' needs are met in the classroom. Canter and Associates produces a large variety of materials for behavior management and making instruction more effective. Website: www.canter.net

Charles, C. M.

Professor, writer, international educator. Author of numerous books including *The Synergetic Classroom: Joyful Teaching and Gentle Discipline* (2000), which describes the desirable effects of the energized classroom and describes how teachers can assist students by limiting or removing known causes of misbehavior. Contributed the concepts of classroom synergy and coopetition. Email: cmcsdsu2@aol.com. Website: www.AWL.com

Coloroso, Barbara

Teacher, former Franciscan nun, author, and creator-disseminator of *Inner Discipline* in which she contends that the climate for a responsibility-oriented school is based upon trust cultivated by teachers and administrators. Website: www.kidsareworthit.com

Curwin, Richard, and Allen Mendler

Professors, private consultants, authors, and creator-disseminators of *Discipline with Dignity,* which presents strategies for improving classroom behavior through maximizing student dignity and hope. Contributed the concepts of student dignity and student hope. Website: www.disciplineassociates.com

Dreikurs, Rudolf (1897–1972)

Viennese-born psychiatrist, professor, director of the Alfred Adler Institute in Chicago, and author of various works on discipline. Dreikurs strongly urged education to become more democratic in nature. He contributed and popularized the concepts of basic goal, mistaken goals, social interest, and democratic classrooms, teaching, and discipline.

Ginott, Haim (1922–1973)

Teacher, professor, consultant, resident psychologist on the "Today" show, and syndicated columnist. Authored *Teacher and Child* (1972), in which he described how teachers could communicate most effectively with children and teenagers, as a means of promoting desirable behavior. Contributed the concepts of congruent communication and sane messages.

Glasser, William

Psychiatrist, lecturer, and author of acclaimed books on teaching and discipline. He first emphasized the role of student choice in discipline and later turned attention to quality in teaching and learning as the best means of involving students and avoiding discipline problems. Glasser contributed the concepts of class meetings, behavior as choice, and the role of student needs in teaching and discipline. Website: www.wglasserinst.com

Gordon, Thomas

Psychologist, lecturer, consultant, and author of award-winning approaches to communicating with the young. An honoree of the American Psychological Association, Gordon believed that self-discipline should be developed in all students. He contributed the concepts of communication roadblocks, communication door openers, win-win problem resolution, and problem ownership. Website: www.gordontraining.com

Jones, Fredric

Psychologist, professor, independent consultant, and developer-disseminator of *Positive Classroom Management*. Jones views discipline and instruction as inseparable. He has contributed the concepts of Say See Do Teaching, incentive systems, efficient help, and body language in discipline. Website: www.fredjones.com

Kohn, Alfie

Former teacher, now an author, lecturer, TV personality, and education critic. He is critical of most present-day models of discipline, saying they produce results the opposite of what is intended. He contends that discipline that controls students should be abandoned in favor of establishing a sense of community in the classroom. Website: www.alfiekohn.org

Kounin, Jacob

Professor and researcher in classroom management and lesson management. He presented evidence suggesting that management was the most important of all discipline techniques. He contributed the concepts of withitness, alerting, and overlapping.

Kyle, Patricia, Spencer Kagan, and Sally Scott

Two professors (Kagan and Kyle) and the principal of a nationally recognized school (Scott) who contend that effective discipline is a cooperative venture between teacher and student. They suggest strategies teachers can use to help students satisfy their legitimate needs through responsible, nondisruptive behavior. Website: www.KaganOnline.com

Nelsen, Jane, Lynn Lott, and H. Stephen Glenn

Educators, authors, consultants, and creator-disseminators of *Positive Discipline in the Classroom*. They urge teachers to foster student responsibility, mutual respect, and cooperation, as a means of doing away with most discipline problems. Website: www.empoweringpeople.com

Neo-Skinnerians

A term referring to popularizers of B. F. Skinner's findings about how human behavior is shaped through reinforcement. Their approach to discipline, which involves providing rewards for desired behavior, is commonly known as behavior modification.

Redl, Fritz, and William Wattenberg

Psychiatrist and educational psychologist, respectively, Redl and Wattenberg contributed the first systematic alternative to old-fashioned discipline. They focused on group dynamics and the causes of misbehavior, explaining how groups function differently from individuals. They contributed the concept of group dynamics and roles assigned by the group to teachers and students.

Major Themes in Discipline

The following are major themes in discipline, arranged alphabetically, that cross boundaries among models. Discipline authorities whose work notably contributed to these themes are identified.

Active Involvement: Students who are kept actively involved in learning they consider worthwhile seldom misbehave. Most authorities emphasize this.

Behavior as Choice: The belief that students are not forced by conditions to behave as they do, but willingly choose their behavior. This theme was central to William Glasser's earlier work and is still featured in the others' works, such as Linda Albert's Cooperative Discipline.

Behavior Modification: Refer to *Shaping Desired Behavior through Reinforcement*.

Body Language: Nonverbal communication in discipline, delivered through eye contact, facial expressions, gestures, posture, and physical proximity. A major feature of Fredric Jones's Positive Classroom Discipline.

Causes of Misbehavior: Factors such as boredom and threat to personal dignity that are believed to lead to student misbehavior. Preventive discipline limits the effect of those factors, while corrective discipline removes or ameliorates them. This theme is stressed in C. M. Charles's Synergetic Discipline, Linda Albert's Cooperative Discipline, and William Glasser's Noncoercive Discipline.

Communication: Deals with what teachers say to students, how they say it, how they draw students out, and how they reply to students. This theme is emphasized in most discipline systems, especially in Haim Ginott's Congruent Communication, Thomas Gordon's Discipline as Self-Control, and C. M. Charles's Synergetic Discipline.

Community, Sense of: Thinking in terms of "we" instead of "I" in the classroom. Individual well-being is seen to depend on the well-being of the class as a whole. This theme is basic to Alfie Kohn's Beyond Discipline and is stressed as well in Rudolf Dreikurs's Democratic Discipline, Linda Albert's Cooperative Discipline, and Jane Nelsen, Lynn Lott, and H. Stephen Glenn's Positive Discipline in the Classroom.

Concern for Others: Showing responsibility for others, interest in helping them, and building the class as a caring community. A strong current in various systems of discipline, such as Alfie Kohn's Beyond Discipline, Barbara Coloroso's Inner Discipline, and Rudolf Dreikurs's Democratic Discipline.

Dignity: See Student Dignity.

Energizing Teaching and Learning: A key aspect of C. M. Charles's Synergetic Discipline. Deals with factors and methods of producing synergism (energized conditions) in the classroom.

Enticement versus Coercion: The general view, expressed in most of today's application models, that it is much more effective to draw students into cooperating and abiding by class agreements rather than demanding they do so.

Group Dynamics: Has to do with how groups develop and function. The starting point in Fritz Redl and William Wattenberg's Understanding the Group.

Hope: The emotion that keeps today's students from giving up in education. Featured by Richard Curwin and Allen Mendler in their Discipline with Dignity.

Incentives: Tactics that entice students to cooperate, featured in Frederic Jones's Positive Classroom Discipline.

Management: Has to do with how lessons, environment, and behavior are organized, put into effect, and kept under control. Jacob Kounin put it at the center of his views on discipline.

Meeting Basic Needs: Various authorities in recent years have claimed that student needs are the best starting point for dealing with misbehavior. When needs are met, students have little reason to misbehave. This line of reasoning is featured in William Glasser's Noncoercive Discipline, C. M. Charles's Synergetic Discipline, Linda Albert's Cooperative Discipline, and Rudolf Dreikurs's Democratic Discipline.

Parental Involvement: Involving parents in helping approve and support, and sometimes even plan systems of discipline brings about better behavior in students overall. This is stressed in several application models, such as Linda Albert's Cooperative Discipline and Nelsen, Lott, and Glenn's Positive Discipline in the Classroom.

Participative Management: A concept introduced by Fritz Redl and William Wattenberg in which students are brought into close collaboration in making decisions about matters that affect the group. The concept was carried forth by Rudolf Dreikurs and Thomas Gordon and is now recommended by virtually all discipline authorities.

Responsibility: Increasingly, emphasis is being put on helping students to learn to behave responsibly on their own, recognizing that doing so contributes to their personal well-being. Responsibility is stressed in a number of models, such as Dreikurs's Democratic Discipline, Gordon's Discipline as Self-Control, Coloroso's Inner Discipline, and Kohn's Beyond Discipline.

Right to Learn: A fundamental tenet in Canters' Assertive Discipline: Students have the right to learn without interference from misbehaving classmates.

Right to Teach: A fundamental tenet in Canters' Assertive Discipline: Teachers have the right to teach as they think best without disruption from misbehaving students. An extremely popular concept with teachers.

Say, See, Do Teaching: Teaching in a series of short cycles of teacher input followed by student output, done to maintain student attention and active involvement. Featured in Jones's Positive Classroom Discipline.

Schoolwide Systems: Increasingly, schools are organizing and adopting systems of discipline that apply to all the classes in the entire school. This contributes to consistency. Most of the model authors would like to see their approach adopted by entire schools rather than just invidual teachers, in order to provide consistency and better overall results.

Self-Control and Self-Discipline: Many authorities today contend that the only valuable classroom discipline is that which leads to self-control or self-discipline. This theme is stressed strongly by Thomas Gordon, Alfie Kohn, and Barbara Coloroso, among others.

Shaping Desired Behavior through Reinforcement: This is the end purpose of Neo-Skinnerian behavior modification and is retained in discipline systems that use positive and negative consequences to influence student behavior. The approach is effective in the short term, but in the minds of many critics is counterproductive in the long run.

Shared Responsibility: The view that discipline is a responsibility students and teachers share equally, and that discipline plans should provide for joint responsibility. This view is emphasized in the works of Rudolf Dreikurs and is the cornerstone of Win-Win Discipline popularized by Patricia Kyle, Spencer Kagan, and Sally Scott.

Student Dignity: Student sense of self-respect. A great proportion of student misbehavior seems to occur as students attempt to defend and enhance their sense of self. Respecting student dignity was popularized by Ginott and is the central focus of Curwin and Mendler's Discipline with Dignity.

Teachers in Charge: Teachers' showing themselves to be positively but considerately in charge in the classroom. Stressed in Canters' Assertive Discipline.

Win-Win Conflict Resolution: A procedure of conflict resolution in which parties in dispute seek a common-ground answer to their dispute, one that gives both of them most of what they want. In this manner, neither side is seen to "lose," which helps prevent lasting animosity and the desire to get even. It is featured in many systems of discipline, including Thomas Gordon's Discipline as Self-Control, Jane Nelsen, Lynn Lott, and II. Stephen Glenn's Positive Discipline in the Classroom, and Kyle, Kagan, and Scott's Win-Win Discipline.

Glossary of Terms Related to Discipline

The following are terms featured in the models of discipline examined in this book, with indications of authors who originated and/or helped popularize them.

AAA-BCDE of student positions (Kyle, Kagan, and Scott): Attention-seeking, angry, avoiding failure, bored, control-seeking, don't know, energetic.

ABCD of disruptive behavior (Kyle, Kagan, and Scott): Aggression, breaking rules, confrontations, disengagement.

Acceptable choice (Nelsen, Lott, and Glenn): A behavior option the teacher considers worthwhile, made available to students.

Accomplishment albums and portfolios (Albert): Albums and portfolios in which students place samples of their best work, to document progress.

Accountability (Kounin): Holding each student responsible for active involvement in what is being taught.

Accountability mentality (Nelsen, Lott, and Glenn): Students' predisposition to accept responsibility for their shortcomings. Contrasts with victim mentality in which they place blame elsewhere.

Acknowledgment responses (Gordon): Teacher responses that show interest and attention when students are speaking.

Action dimension (Curwin and Mendler): Concerns what teachers should do when discipline problems occur.

Active listening (Gordon): Mirroring back what another person is saying, or otherwise confirming that one is attentive, interested, and nonjudgmental.

Activity movement (Kounin): The psychological and temporal progression of lessons.

Activity reinforcers (Skinner's followers): Activities that students prefer in school. They can be used as reinforcing stimuli.

Appraising reality (Redl and Wattenberg): Helping students examine their behavior, noting what is occurring, and anticipating probable consequences.

Appreciative praise (Ginott): Praise that expresses gratitude or admiration for effort.

Appropriate choices (Nelsen, Lott, and Glenn): Options that teachers make available to students, which further the educational program.

Assertive response style (the Canters): Responding to student behavior in a helpful manner while insisting that class rules be followed.

Assertive teachers (the Canters): Teachers who clearly, confidently, and consistently reiterate class expectations and attempt to build trust with students.

Attention-seeking behavior (Albert): Tactics such as pencil tapping, showing off, calling out, and asking irrelevant questions that students use to get attention from teacher and peers.

Autocratic teachers (Dreikurs): Teachers who boss students, command, demand cooperation, dominate, and criticize.

Authority (Gordon): A condition that allows one to control or exert influence over others.

Aversive discipline (Dreikurs): Controlling behavior through use of unreasonable constraints and harsh consequences.

Avoidance-of-failure behavior (Albert): Nonconstructive efforts students make to avoid being seen as stupid or incapable.

Backbone teachers and schools (Coloroso): Teachers and schools that have in place clear expectations and standards of conduct.

Backup system (Jones): The planned action teachers take when students misbehave seriously and refuse to comply with positive teacher requests—typically means being sent to the principal's office.

Barriers (Nelsen, Lott, and Glenn): Teacher behaviors that are disrespectful and discouraging to students.

Basic needs (Glasser): Psychological requirements for healthy functioning that students attempt to satisfy in school. In Glasser's view those needs are for survival, belonging, power, fun, and freedom.

Behavior: The totality of what people do, good or bad, right or wrong, helpful or useless, productive or wasteful.

Behavior contracts (Skinner's followers): Written agreements between teacher and students indicating what students are to do and what they will receive when they comply.

Behavior journal (the Canters): A log book in which students write accounts of their own misbehavior, why they broke a rule, and what a better behavior choice would have been.

Behavior modification (Skinner's followers): The use of Skinnerian principles of reinforcement to control or shape behavior.

Behavior shaping (Skinner): The process of gradually modifying behavior through reinforcement.

Behavior window (Gordon): A graphic device used to help determine whether a problem exists and if so who owns it.

Behaviorally at-risk (Curwin and Mendler): Students whose behavior prevents their learning and puts them in serious danger of failing in school.

Bell work (Jones): Work students do to begin a class period, such as reading, journal writing, and completion of warm-up activities, which do not require instruction from the teacher.

Belonging (Dreikurs): A basic student need that is met when students are made to feel they are valued and have an important role in the class. (Glasser, Dreikurs, Albert): A basic human need for legitimate membership in groups significant to the individual, with attendant security and comfort.

Big Three of discipline (Kyle, Kagan, and Scott): curriculum, instruction, and management.

Body carriage (Jones): Posture and movement that indicate to students whether the teacher is well, ill, in charge, tired, disinterested, or intimidated.

Body language (Jones): Nonverbal communication transmitted through posture, eye contact, gestures, and facial expressions.

Boss teachers (Glasser): Teachers who set the tasks, direct the learning activities, ask for little student input, and grade student work.

Brickwalls (Coloroso): Schools and teachers that rigidly use power and coercion to control students.

Builders (Nelsen, Lott, and Glenn): Teacher behaviors that show respect and encouragement to students.

Cause-effect relationship: A relationship between factors in which one that occurs earlier in time is seen logically to have produced the other. Example: Boredom (cause) produces misbehavior (effect).

Causes of misbehavior (Charles): Factors known to foster misbehavior, such as boredom and threat to personal dignity.

Challenge (Kounin): Teachers' giving puzzles, problems, or dares as a means of delaying satiation (boredom).

Charisma (Charles): Personal allure that invites attention and cooperation.

Choose their behavior (Glasser): The belief that students choose to behave as they do, rather than being forced to do so by background or other conditions.

Circle of friends (Albert): Organized group relationships that help all students feel they belong and are interconnected with others.

Class agreements: Codes composed jointly by teacher and students that indicate how behavior, instruction, and other matters are to occur.

Classroom meetings (Glasser): Meetings held in the classroom for addressing and solving problems.

Classroom structure (Jones): Classroom organization, including room arrangement, class rules, class routines, chores, and the like.

Class rules: Written code of conduct for classroom behavior.

Clients (Curwin and Mendler): The students in school, there to be helped by professionals, the teachers.

Climate: The feeling or tone that prevails in the classroom.

Code of conduct (Albert): Specification of how everyone is supposed to behave and interact, including the teacher. Preferable to lists of rules.

Collaborative rule-setting (Gordon): A procedure in which teachers and students work together to establish rules for making the classroom safe, efficient, and harmonious.

Communication (Ginott): Exchange of ideas, feelings, and opinions. One of the key elements for promoting good will in the classroom.

Community (Kohn): Classrooms and schools where students feel cared about and care about each other, are valued and respected, are involved in decision making, and have a sense of "we" rather than "I."

Conferring dignity (Ginott): Respecting students by putting aside their past history and being concerned only with the present situation.

Confrontive I-message (Gordon): An I-message used to ask students for input about a problem perceived by the teacher. "I need your help on this matter."

Confrontive skills (Gordon): A cluster of skills teachers can employ when they own a problem, used in a way that doesn't make students want to fight back or withdraw.

Congruent communication (Ginott): A style of communication in which teachers acknowledge and accept students' feelings about situations and themselves.

Connect (Albert): One of Albert's "Three C's"—forming bonds with other members of the class.

Consequences (Curwin and Mendler): Categories of interventions for misbehavior, such as reminders, warnings, and isolation from the group.
(the Canters): Penalties invoked by teachers when students interfere with others' right to learn.
(Glasser): Students' agreement that when they break rules, they will try, with the teacher's help, to correct the underlying problem.
(most authorities): Steps to be taken when rules are violated or complied with.
Also see *Instructional consequences*.

Constructivist theory: A theory of school learning which holds that students cannot receive knowledge directly from teachers but must construct it from experience.

Contribute (Albert): One of Albert's "Three C's"—student work or behavior that benefits the class and helps students see themselves in a more positive light.

Conventional consequences (Curwin and Mendler): Consequences commonly seen in practice, such as time out, removal from the room, and suspension from school.

Coopetition (Charles): Cooperation by members of a group in order that they might compete against other groups.

Coping mechanisms (Gordon): Strategies students use when confronted with coercive power—usually fighting, taking flight, or submitting.

Correcting by directing (Ginott): Teachers correcting student misbehavior simply by telling students respectfully what they should be doing, instead of what they are doing wrong.

Corrective discipline (Charles): The facet of discipline in which teachers stop student misbehavior and redirect it positively.

Democratic teachers (Dreikurs): Teachers who show friendly guidance and encourage students to take on responsibility, cooperate, and participate in making decisions.

Diagnostic thinking (Redl and Wattenberg): A process of analyzing misbehavior, by forming a first hunch, gathering facts, exploring hidden factors, taking action, and remaining flexible.

Dignity (Ginott; Curwin and Mendler): Respect for oneself and others.

Directions (the Canters): Statements that apply only to a given activity, in contrast to *rules*, which are always in effect.

Disciplinary problem: A situation provoked by transgression of class rules or agreements.

Discipline: What teachers do to prevent, suppress, and redirect student misbehavior.
(Coloroso): Helps students see what they have done wrong and gives them ownership of the problem.

Discipline approach: What teachers do to help students behave acceptably in school.
(Jones): Teacher efforts to engage students in learning in the most positive, unobtrusive fashion possible.
(Coloroso): What teachers do to help students become aware of their behavior and accept its consequences.
(Charles): Identifying and dealing with the causes of misbehavior.

Discipline hierarchy (the Canters): A list of consequences and the order in which they will be imposed within the period or day.

Discipline structures, types of (Kyle, Kagan, and Scott): language of choice, table the matter, student conference, spot the signs

Displaying inadequacy (Dreikurs): Student withdrawal and failure to try.

Door openers (Gordon): Invitations to students to discuss their problems, as when the teacher, sensing that a student is troubled, asks quietly, "Would you like to talk about what's bothering you?"

Educational value (Jones): A quality of class work that promotes academic learning rather than merely keeping students occupied.

Effective discipline, principles of (Curwin and Mendler): Five fundamental notions concerning the duty to deal with misbehavior, the ineffectiveness of short-term solutions, the need to treat students with dignity, the maintenance of student motivation, and the importance of responsibility rather than obedience.

Efficient help (Jones): Help given quickly to students that returns them to productive work.

Elements of synergetic teaching (Charles): Factors such as trust, communication, charisma, interest, and coopetition, that when used in conjunction can produce class synergy.

Encouragement (Dreikurs): Showing belief in students and stimulating them to try, as distinct from praising students for their accomplishments.

Evaluative praise (Ginott): Praise that expresses judgment about students' character or quality of work—considered to be detrimental by Ginott and various other authorities.

Extinction (Skinner): The gradual removal of a given behavior, accomplished by withholding reinforcement.

Eye contact (Jones): Teachers fixing their eyes on students' faces to show they are aware of students' behavior.

Facial expressions (Jones): Appearance of teachers' faces that communicates emotions such as appreciation, resignation, and annoyance.

Five A's (Albert): What teachers should supply to students in abundance: acceptance, attention, appreciation, affirmation, and affection.

Four essential skills (Nelsen, Lott, and Glenn): Intrapersonal, interpersonal, strategic, and judgmental skills that students need for success in life.

Four R's of consequences (Albert): Albert's reminder that any consequences teachers invoke for student misbehavior must be related to the offense, reasonable, respectful, and reliably enforced.

Four-step problem-solving process (Nelsen, Lott, and Glenn): A problem-solving strategy for students to use in resolving their disputes: (1) ignore the situation, (2) talk it over respectfully with the other student, (3) agree with the other student on a solution, (4) if no solution is found, put the matter on the class meeting agenda.

Freedom (Glasser): A basic student need that is met when students are allowed to make responsible choices concerning what they will study, how they will do so, and how they will demonstrate their accomplishments.

Fun (Glasser): A basic student need that is met when students are permitted to pursue activities they find intriguing and that allow them to interact with others.

General rules (Jones): Classroom rules that define the teacher's broad guidelines, standards, and expectations for work and behavior, as distinct from specific behaviors expected of students.

Generic consequences (Curwin and Mendler): Common reminders, warnings, choosing, and planning that teachers invoke when they see students misbehave.

Genuine discipline (Ginott): Proper behavior that comes from self-control, or self-discipline.

Genuine goal of belonging (Dreikurs): A fundamental desire to acquire a sense of place and value in a group.

Genuine incentives (Jones): Incentives that motivate all members of the class rather than just a few.

Genuine success: Student success based on true accomplishment.

Getting attention (Dreikurs): Student behavior, such as disruption and showing off, intended to gain attention of the teacher and other students.

Graceful exits (Albert): Steps teachers can take to distance themselves from confrontations with students who are very upset.

Grandma's rule (Jones): "First eat your vegetables, then you can have your dessert," or, "Finish your work first, then you can do something you especially enjoy."

Group alerting (Kounin): Getting students' attention and quickly letting them know what they are supposed to do.

Group concern (Jones): A condition in which every student has a stake in the behavior that permits the group to earn a promised incentive.

Group dynamics (Redl and Wattenberg): Psychological forces that occur within groups and subsequently influence the behavior of group members.

Helping skills (Gordon). A cluster of skills teachers can employ when the student owns a problem to be dealt with.

Helpless handraising (Jones): A condition in which a student sits, hand raised and not working unless the teacher is hovering nearby.

Hidden asset (Ginott): The following teacher question, when sincerely addressed to students: "How can I help you?"

Hope, sense of (Curwin and Mendler): Anticipation of success and well-being, which inspires us, enables us to live meaningfully, and provides courage and incentive to overcome barriers.

Hostile response style (the Canters): Bossing, putting-down, and ordering students about.

Hostile teachers (the Canters): Teachers who are openly disrespectful to students.

Hurdle help (Redl and Wattenberg): Assistance given to misbehaving students that helps them know what to do.

I-can cans (Albert): Decorated containers in which students place strips of paper to document accomplishments and progress.

I-can level (Albert): The degree of confidence students have when they believe they are capable of doing the work given them in school.

I-messages (Ginott; Gordon): Teachers' expressing their personal feelings and reactions to situations, such as "I have trouble teaching when there is so much noise in the room."

I-statements: Statements that begin with "I" and tell how the speaker feels. The same as I-messages.

Incentive (Jones): Something outside of the individual that entices the individual to act.

Inner discipline (Coloroso): The ability to control one's own behavior and make responsible decisions.

Instructional consequences (Curwin and Mendler): Consequences that teach students how to behave properly rather than punish.

Insubordination rule (Curwin and Mendler): If a student does not accept the consequence after breaking a class rule, then he or she will not be allowed to participate with the class until the consequence is accepted.

Interior loop (Jones): A classroom seating arrangement with wide aisles that allows teachers to move easily among students at work.

Interpersonal skills (Nelsen, Lott, and Glenn): Dialogue, sharing, listening, empathizing, cooperating, negotiating, and resolving conflicts—skills needed for working cooperatively with others.

Intrapersonal skill (Nelsen, Lott, and Glenn): Self-discipline and self-control, brought about by making distinctions between feelings, which are always acceptable, and resultant actions, which are not always acceptable.

Invite cooperation (Ginott): Encouraging and enticing students into activities and giving them choices, rather than demanding their participation.

Jellyfish teachers and schools (Coloroso): Teachers and schools that are wishy-washy, with unclear expectations or standards of conduct.

Judgmental skills (Nelsen, Lott, and Glenn): The ability to evaluate situations and make good choices.

Labeling is disabling (Ginott): Ginott's warning about the bad effects that occur when teachers label students verbally.

Laconic language (Ginott): Brevity of teacher's comments about misbehavior, such as "This is work time."

Lead teachers (Glasser): Teachers who explore with students what the students wish to learn and how they prefer to learn, provide necessary help, and encourage students to do quality work.

Logical consequences (Dreikurs): Conditions invoked by the teacher that are logically related to behavior students choose, such as making amends for what was done wrong.

(Coloroso): Positive behavior of students in response to breaking rules: The behavior is to be responsible and related to the rule broken.

Means-end relationship: A relationship in which focus is placed on a desired condition, then a factor is sought that might produce the desired end. Example: We want Sam to work productively (end). How do we get him to do so? (means).

Misbehavior: Behavior that is considered inappropriate for the setting or situation in which it occurs.

(Gordon): An adult concept in which a student's behavior causes a consequence that is unpleasant to the teacher.

(Charles): A violation of class rules or agreements.

(Kyle, Kagan, and Scott): Students meeting legitimate needs in a disruptive manner.

Misbehavior, types of (Coloroso): Mayhem, mischief, mistakes.

Mischief (Coloroso): Intentional misbehavior—presents an opportunity for teaching students that all actions have consequences, sometimes pleasant and sometimes not.

Mistaken goals (Dreikurs): Goals such as attention and power that students try to achieve in the mistaken belief they will bring positive recognition.

Mistakes (Coloroso): Errors in behavior, made without intent to break rules.

Modifying the environment (Gordon): A way of dealing with student misbehavior that involves changing the room or eliminating distractors.

Momentum (Kounin): Refers to teachers' getting activities started promptly, keeping them moving ahead, and bringing them to efficient closure or transition.

Need for extra attention (the Canters): A need evident in students who disrupt and call unnecessarily for the teacher's attention.

Need for extra motivation (the Canters): A need evident in students who do not engage in activities or complete work.

Need for firmer limits (the Canters): A need evident in students who disregard class rules.

Negative consequences. Something unpleasant that occurs, or is made to occur, to students when they misbehave.

Negative reinforcement (Skinner): Removing aversive stimuli, thereby strengthening desired behavior.

No-lose method of conflict resolution (Gordon): An approach that finds a mutually acceptable solution to a disagreement, so that neither party is made to feel a loser.

Nonassertive response style (the Canters): Teacher responses that let students get by with misbehavior in the classroom.

Nonassertive teachers (the Canters): Teachers who take a passive, hands-off approach in dealing with students.

Noncongruent communication (Ginott): Teacher communication that is not harmonious with students' feelings about situations and themselves.

Nondisciplinary problem (Charles): A difficulty affecting the class, such as noise from outside, that does not involve violations of class rules or agreements.

Obedience (Curwin and Mendler): Unquestioning compliance. Not the goal of discipline: Responsibility is the true goal.

Omission training (Jones): An incentive plan for an individual student who, by cutting down on undesired behavior, can earn preferred activity time for the entire class.

Operant behavior (Skinner): Any behavior that an organism produces voluntarily.

Operant conditioning (Skinner): The process of shaping behavior through reinforcement.

Overlapping (Kounin): Refers to teachers' attending to two or more issues in the classroom at the same time.

Participative classroom management (Gordon): An operating procedure in which teachers share power and decision making with their students.

Passive listening (Gordon): A helping technique teachers use with students; includes attention, eye contact, and alertness as the student speaks.

Permissive teachers (Dreikurs): Teachers who put few if any limits on student behavior and do not invoke consequences for disruptive behavior.

Perspective taking (Kohn): Doing one's best to see and understand a situation from another person's point of view.

Philosophy of discipline: The beliefs one has about the nature, purpose, and value of discipline.

Physical proximity (Redl and Wattenberg): The teacher's moving close to a student who is misbehaving.

Positive consequence. Something pleasant that occurs, or is made to occur, to students who behave in accordance with class rules.

Positive recognition (the Canters): Giving sincere personal attention to students who behave in keeping with class expectations.

Positive reinforcement (Skinner): Supplying reinforcing stimuli in order to strengthen a particular behavior.

Positive repetition (the Canters): Correcting a misbehaving student by commenting on what another student is doing properly—used in primary grades.

Power (Glasser): A basic student need for control, satisfied when students are given significant duties in the class and are allowed to participate in decisions about class matters.

Power-seeking behavior (Albert): Behaviors such as temper tantrums, back talk, disrespect, and defiance that students use to try to show they have power over the teacher.

Practice of discipline (Charles): How discipline is put into effect and conducted in the classroom—follows from one's philosophy and theory of discipline.

Praise: Laudatory comments, which teachers often use to encourage responsible behavior.
(Dreikurs; Ginott): Approval given to students for accomplishment: It is ineffective; encouragement should be used instead.

Preferred activity time (PAT) (Jones): Time allocated for students to engage in activities of their preference; used as an incentive to encourage responsible behavior.

Preventing escalation of conflicts (Curwin and Mendler): Employing tactics such as allowing a cool-off period or rescheduling the work for a more appropriate time.

Preventive discipline (Charles): The aspect of discipline that removes factors likely to lead to misbehavior.

Preventive I-messages (Gordon): I-messages teachers use to help prevent misbehavior.

Preventive skills (Gordon): A cluster of communication skills teachers can employ to prevent behavior problems.

Preventive you-messages (Gordon): Messages directed at student misbehavior and intended to prevent its recurrence, such as, "You behaved very badly on our last field trip. I certainly hope you do better this time." (Should not be used.)

Proactive teacher behavior (the Canters): Preplanned reactions to student misbehavior which, when practiced, can help teachers remain calm and effective in tense situations.

Problem (Gordon): A situation that causes discomfort for someone.

Problem ownership (Gordon): A term used to indicate who is troubled by a situation: The troubled person is said to "own the problem."

Problem resolution process (Coloroso): A process that resolves problems through three phases—*resolution* of the immediate problem, *restitution* to the person who has been damaged, and *reconciliation* between offender and the one offended.

Professionals (Curwin and Mendler): Refers to teachers, emphasizing that their primary purpose is to do what they can to help students.

Proper breathing (Jones): Breathing technique, slow and deep, that helps teachers remain calm when facing student misbehavior.

Proximity praise (the Canters): Giving praise to a properly behaving student who is seated near a misbehaving student.

Punishment (Dreikurs): Action taken by the teacher to get back at misbehaving students and show them who is boss.
(Gordon): Aversive treatment of students; has overall negative effects.
(Redl and Wattenberg): Planned, unpleasant consequences, not physical, the purpose of which is to change behavior in positive directions.
(Skinner): Supplying aversive stimuli, a process that may or may not result in behavior change.
(Coloroso): Psychologically harmful consequences applied by teachers to students; likely to provoke resentment and retaliation.

Quality curriculum (Glasser): A program of study that emphasizes excellence in learnings that students consider useful.

Quality education (Glasser): Education in which students acquire knowledge and skills that the students themselves see as valuable.

Quality learning (Glasser): Learning in which students attain high competency in knowledge and skills they judge to be important in their lives.

Quality schoolwork (Glasser): Learning activities centered around knowledge and skills that students find important and engaging.

Quality teaching (Glasser): Instruction in which teachers help students become proficient in knowledge and skills the students consider important.

Reactive teacher behavior (the Canters): Reactions to student behavior that are not thought through in advance. Frequently inappropriate and counterproductive.

Reasonable consequences (Coloroso): Consequences arranged by teacher and students that make sense and are appropriate to the violation of a given rule.

Reinforcement (Skinner): Supplying (or in some cases, removing) stimuli in such a manner that the organism becomes more likely to repeat a given act.

Reinforcing stimuli (Skinner): Stimuli received by an organism immediately following a behavior that increase the likelihood that the behavior will be repeated.

Resolution dimension (Curwin and Mendler): Focuses on helping chronically misbehaving students learn to make and abide by decisions that serve their needs.

Revenge (Dreikurs): A mistaken goal toward which students sometimes turn when thwarted in their desire to find acceptance in the group.

Revenge-seeking behavior (Dreikurs; Albert): Student behavior intended to harm the teacher, in retaliation for something the teacher has done.

Rewards (Gordon): Pay-offs used to control student behavior; considered ineffective in the long run.

Ripple effect (Kounin): The spread of effects to other students when a particular student is reprimanded.

Roadblocks to communication (Gordon): Things teachers say that inadvertently shut off student willingness to talk, such as preaching, advising, and analyzing.

RSVP of consequences (Coloroso): Consequences should be reasonable, simple, valuable, and practical.

Rules: Statements that indicate clearly how students are to behave.

Sane messages (Ginott): Teacher messages that address situations rather than students' character.

Satiation (Kounin): Getting all one can tolerate of a given activity, resulting in frustration, boredom, or listlessness.

Say, See, Do Teaching (Jones): A teaching method that uses repeated short cycles of teacher input followed by student output.

Scapegoating (Redl and Wattenberg): A phenomenon in which the group seeks to displace its hostility onto an unpopular individual or subgroup.

Seeking power (Dreikurs; Albert): Student behavior that attempts to gain control over teachers through arguing, lying, throwing temper tantrums, and refusing to follow directions.

Seeking revenge (Dreikurs; Albert): Student behavior intended to hurt the teacher or other students.

Self-discipline (Dreikurs; Albert): Self-control, which grows out of freedom to make decisions and having to live by the consequences.

Self-evaluation (Glasser): Students appraising the quality of their own work; a key step leading to improvement and quality work.

Sense of community (Kohn): Classes where students feel safe and are continually brought into making judgments, expressing their opinions, and working cooperatively toward solutions that affect themselves and the class.

Sense of hope (Curwin and Mendler): The belief that things will get better in the future, or that present tasks will be worthwhile. Many students have lost a sense of hope concerning the value of education.

Series of little victories (Ginott): Ginott's depiction of how teachers gradually develop good discipline in the classroom, through encouraging self-direction and responsibility while showing concern and helpfulness.

Setting limits: Clarifying with the class exactly what is expected of them.

Severe clause (the Canters): Invoking the most severe penalty in the discipline hierarchy when extreme behaviors such as fighting occur: usually means being sent to the principal.

Shaping behavior (Skinner): The process of using reinforcement to produce desired behavior in students.

Shifting gears (Gordon): A change teachers make—from an assertive posture to a listening posture in order to further communication.

Short-term solutions (Curwin and Mendler): Steps to stop misbehavior, such as scolding, lecturing, or detention: They are not likely to have lasting positive effect.

Significant seven (Nelsen, Lott, and Glenn): Three self-perceptions (personal capability, significance in primary relationships, and personal power) and four essential skills that contribute significantly to success in life (intrapersonal skill—understand and control self; interpersonal skill—communicate, cooperate, and work with others; strategic skill—flexible, adaptable, and responsible; and judgmental skill—ability to evaluate situations).

SIR (Glasser): An acronym standing for the process of self-evaluation, improvement, and repetition, used until quality is achieved.

Six-D conflict resolution plan (Albert): A six-step tool for helping resolve matters under dispute.

Smoothness (Kounin): Teachers' avoidance of abrupt changes that interfere with students' activities or thought processes.

Social contract (Curwin and Mendler): The agreement concerning rules and consequences that teacher and students have decided should govern behavior in the classroom.

Social contract test (Curwin and Mendler): A test to prevent students' using the excuse that they didn't understand the rules. This test deals with class rules and consequences.

Social interest (Dreikurs): The concept that one's personal well-being is dependent on the well-being of the group, thus one acts in ways that benefit the group.

Social reinforcers (Skinner's followers): Words and behaviors such as comments, gestures, and facial expressions that serve as reinforcing stimuli.

Specific rules (Jones): Classroom rules that detail specifically what students are to do and how they are to do it.

Strategic skills (Nelsen, Lott, and Glenn): Responding to the limits and consequences of everyday life with responsibility, adaptability, flexibility, and integrity.

Student accountability (Kounin): Students showing evidence they are attentive and actively involved in lessons.

Student needs (Glasser): A group of five basic needs—for survival, belonging, power, fun, and freedom—upon which curriculum and teaching should be based.

Student responsibility (Glasser): An earlier Glasser contention that students have the obligation to consider their behavior choices and live with the consequences.

Student roles (Redl and Wattenberg): Roles which students adopt, or are assigned, in the process of group dynamics.

Students' rights (the Canters): The opportunity to learn under the guidance of a caring teacher concerned about the best interests of students.

Successive approximations (Skinner): Behavior that, through reinforcement, moves progressively closer to the desired goal.

Supportive discipline (Charles): The facet of discipline in which teachers use reminders and encouragement to keep students behaving properly.

Survival (Glasser): A basic human need for providing for and protecting oneself.

Synergetic discipline (Charles): Discipline based on synergetic teaching, which removes most causes of misbehavior. Also the method of correcting misbehavior by dealing with whatever is causing the misbehavior.

Synergetic teaching (Charles): Teaching in a manner that energizes the class. Done by putting in place combinations of elements known to produce heightened classroom energy.

Synergy (Charles): A heightened state of energy that can occur when two or more entities feed energy to each other.

Talks about yesterday, today, and tomorrow (Albert): Chats with students about the progress they are making and what they will learn in the future.

Teacher enthusiasm (Kounin): Display of teacher interest and excitement which has a positive effect on student motivation and learning.

Teachers at their best (Ginott): Teachers when using congruent communication that addresses situations rather than students' character, invites student cooperation, and accepts students as they are.

Teachers at their worst (Ginott): Teachers when they name-call, label students, ask rhetorical "why" questions, give long moralistic lectures, and make caustic remarks to their students.

Teacher's own self-discipline (Ginott): One of the most important factors in class discipline, wherein teachers only rarely lose their composure and always treat students with respect.

Teachers' hidden asset (Ginott): Teachers' willingness to ask how they can be of most help to a given student at a given moment.

Teachers' rights (the Canters): The opportunity to teach in a classroom that is free from student disruption, with support from parents and administrators.

Theory of discipline: An overall explanation of the elements that comprise discipline and how they work together, influence each other, and produce certain outcomes.

Three C's (Albert): Albert's prescription for ensuring student sense of belonging in the class: feel capable, connect with others, and contribute to the class.

Three C committee (Albert): A school committee whose purpose is to think of ways to help all students feel more capable, connected, and contributing.

Three cons, student response to consequences (Coloroso): imploring, complaining, sulking.

Three F's (Coloroso): The three ways students typically respond to the threat of punishment—fear, fighting back, or fleeing.

Three perceptions (Nelsen, Lott, and Glenn): Perceptions of personal capability, significance in primary relationships, and personal power to influence one's own life.

Three Pillars of Win-Win Discipline (Kyle, Kagan, and Scott): Teacher and students are on the same side, share responsibility, and focus on behavior that meets students needs in a nondisruptive manner.

Three R's of Reconciliatory Justice (Coloroso): Restitution, Resolution, and Reconciliation.

Three R's of solutions (Nelsen, Lott, and Glenn): Solutions for correcting misbehavior that are related to what was done wrong, respectful of the persons involved, and reasonable.

True discipline: Defined by most authorities as inner discipline; self-discipline; self-control.

Trust (Charles): Students' confidence that the teacher is working in their best interest and will not harm them. Desirable in teaching and necessary for synergy.

Types of classroom misbehavior: In descending order of seriousness, as judged by social scientists, they are aggression, immorality, defiance of authority, class disruption, and goofing-off.
(Coloroso): Three types of student misbehavior are mistakes (unintentional), mischief (intentional light misbehavior), and mayhem (more serious misbehavior).
(Kyle, Kagan, and Scott): Four types of student misbehavior are aggression, breaking rules, confrontation, and disengagement.

(Dreikurs; Albert): Four types of student misbehavior are attention-seeking, power-seeking, revenge-seeking, and feigned helplessness.

Unequal treatment (Curwin and Mendler): The best discipline does not treat all students equally. It treats them differently in accordance with their individual needs.

Useful work (Glasser): Schoolwork that deals with skills and information that students deem valuable in their lives.

Value judgments (Glasser): In Glasser's earlier work, the contention that when students misbehave, they should be required to make judgments about their actions. Now refers to Glasser's insistence that students appraise the quality of their own work.

Victim mentality (Nelsen, Lott, and Glenn): A predisposition to blame others for one's own shortcomings. Contrasts with accountability mentality.

Violence (Curwin and Mendler): Verbal abuse, physical threat or action against a person, or damage done maliciously to the property of another person.

Why questions (Ginott): Counterproductive questions that teachers put to students, asking them to explain or justify their behavior. E.g., "Why did you...?"

Win–lose conflict resolution (Gordon): Conflict resolution in which one person emerges as "winner" and the other as "loser." This method is to be avoided in favor of "no-lose" or "win-win" conflict resolution.

Win–win discipline (Kyle, Kagan, and Scott): Discipline in which students learn to meet their needs in nondisruptive ways, thus allowing both teacher and students to be "winners."

Win-win solutions (Nelsen, Lott, and Glenn): Problem solutions that people in disputes with each other find acceptable.

Withitness (Kounin): The teacher's knowing what is going on in all parts of the classroom at all times.

You-messages (Ginott; Gordon): Teacher messages that attack students' character, such as "You are acting like barbarians." These messages carry heavy blame and put-downs.

Bibliography

A handbook of alternatives to corporal punishment. Fourth edition. 1994. Oklahoma City, OK: Oklahoma State Department of Education.

A place for problem students: Separate school proposed for disruptive teenagers. 1994. *Washington Post,* VAW, 1:5. January 13.

Agne, J., G. Greenwood, and L. Miller. 1994. Relationships between teacher belief systems and teacher effectiveness. *Journal of Research and Development in Education, 27*(3), 141–152.

Albert, L. 1992. *An administrator's guide to cooperative discipline.* Circle Pines, MN: American Guidance Service.

———. 1993. *Coping with kids.* Tampa, FL: Alkorn House.

———. 1994. *Bringing home cooperative discipline.* Circle Pines, MN: American Guidance Service.

———. 1994. *Responsible kids at school and at home: The cooperative discipline way.* (Videotape series). Circle Pines, MN: American Guidance Service.

———. 1996. *A teacher's guide to cooperative discipline.* Rev. ed. Circle Pines, MN: American Guidance Service.

———. 1996. *Cooperative discipline.* Circle Pines, MN: American Guidance Service.

———. 1996. *Cooperative discipline implementation guide.* Circle Pines, MN: American Guidance Service.

———. 1996. *Cooperative discipline staff development.* (Videotape series). Circle Pines, MN: American Guidance Service.

Black, S. 1994. Throw away the hickory stick. *Executive Educator, 16*(4), 44–47.

Blank, M., and C. Kershaw. 1993. Perceptions of educators about classroom management demands when using interactive strategies. Paper presented at the annual meeting of the American Educational Research Association (Atlanta, GA, April 12–16).

Blendinger, J. 1996. *QLM: Quality leading & managing. A practical guide for improving schools.* Dubuque, IA: Kendall Hunt.

Blumenfeld-Jones, D. 1996. Conventional systems of classroom discipline (the patriarchy speaks). *Journal of Educational Thought/Revue de la Pensee Educative, 30*(1), 5–21.

Boothe, J., L. Bradley, and T. Flick. 1993. The violence at your door. *Executive Educator 15*(1), 16–22.

Bozzone, M. 1994. Spend less time refereeing and more time teaching. *Instructor, 104*(1), 88–93.

Broder, J. 1998. Clinton blames Hollywood, access to firearms, and lax supervision for school violence. *The New York Times.* June 14.

Brownell, M., S. Smith, and J. McNellis. (1997). Reflections on "Attrition in Special Education: Why Teachers Leave the Classroom and Where They Go." *Exceptionality, 7*(3), 87–91.

Burton, M. 1998. Teachers action—students lives: The silent voice of discipline. Position Paper available from ERIC. ERIC Identifier: ED423215.

Byrne, J. 1998. Teacher as hunger artist: Burnout: Its causes, effects, and remedies. *Contemporary Education, 69*(2), 86–91.

Canter, L. 1976. *Assertive Discipline: A take-charge approach for today's educator.* Seal Beach, CA: Canter & Associates.

———. 1978. Be an assertive teacher. *Instructor, 88*(1), 60.

———. 1988. Let the educator beware: A response to Curwin and Mendler. *Educational Leadership, 46*(2), 71–73.

———. 1996. First, the rapport—then, the rules. *Learning, 24*(5), 12, 14.

Canter, L., and M. Canter. 1986. *Assertive Discipline Phase 2 in-service media package* [Videotapes and manuals]. Santa Monica, CA: Canter & Associates.

———. 1989. *Assertive Discipline for secondary school educators. In-service video package and leader's manual.* Santa Monica, CA: Canter & Associates.

———. 1992. *Assertive Discipline: Positive behavior management for today's classroom.* Second ed. Santa Monica, CA: Canter & Associates. Third edition, 1996.

———. 1993. *Succeeding with difficult students: New strategies for reaching your most challenging students.* Santa Monica, CA: Canter & Associates.

Carnegie, D. 1981. *How to win friends and influence people.* Revised edition. New York: Pocket Books.

Castle, K., and K. Rogers. 1993. Rule-creating in a constructivist classroom community. *Childhood Education,* 70(2), 77–80.

Charles, C. 1974. *Teachers' Petit Piaget.* Belmont, CA: Fearon.

Charles, C. 2000. *The synergetic classroom: Joyful teaching and gentle discipline.* New York: Longman.

Charles, C., and G. Senter. 1995. *Elementary classroom management.* Second ed. White Plains, NY: Longman.

Charles, M. 1996. A note on school reform. *Canadian Social Studies,* 30(3), 19–20.

Classroom discipline and lessons in social values. 1990. *The New York Times,* B, 7.3, January 31.

Clawson, P. 1995. Hispanic parents demonstrate to protest students' expulsions. *Chicago Tribune,* 2NW, 2:4, October 24.

Collins, R. 1995. Dover takes action. *Boston Globe,* NH, 1:1, November 12.

Collis, J. 1998. *When your customer wins, you can't lose.* Sydney, Australia: HarperBusiness.

Coloroso, B. 1989. *Winning at parenting...without beating your kids.* Booklet; video; audio. Littleton, CO: Kids are worth it!

———. 1990. *Discipline: Creating a positive school climate.* Booklet; video; audio. Littleton, CO: Kids are worth it!

———. 1990. *Winning at teaching...without beating your kids.* Booklet; video; audio. Littleton, CO: Kids are worth it!

———. 1994. *Kids are worth it!: Giving your child the gift of inner discipline.* New York: Avon Books.

———. 1999. *Parenting with wit and wisdom in times of chaos and confusion.* Littleton, CO: Kids are worth it!

Crossner, S. 1997. Helping young children to develop character. *Early Childhood News,* 9(2), 20–24.

Curwin, R. 1992. *Rediscovering hope: Our greatest teaching strategy.* Bloomington, IN: National Educational Service.

———. 1995. A humane approach to reducing violence in schools. *Educational Leadership,* 52(5), 72–75.

Curwin, R., and A. Mendler. 1988a. *Discipline with dignity.* Alexandria, VA: Association for Supervision and Curriculum Development.

———. 1988b. Packaged discipline programs: Let the buyer beware. *Educational Leadership,* 46(2), 68–71.

———. 1992. *Discipline with dignity* [Workshop participants handout]. Rochester, NY: Discipline Associates.

———. 1997. *As tough as necessary: Countering violence, aggression, and hostility in our schools.* Alexandria, VA: Association for Supervision and Curriculum Development.

Dao, J. 1995. Suspension now required for taking gun to school. *The New York Times,* B, 4:5, August 1.

Dowd, J. 1997. Refusing to play the blame game. *Educational Leadership,* 54(8), 67–69.

Dowdy, Z. 1995. School officers to merge with Boston police force. *Boston Globe,* 33:4, March 16.

Downing, J. 1996. Establishing a discipline plan in elementary physical education. *Journal of Physical Education, Recreation, and Dance,* 67(6), 25–30.

Dreikurs, R., and P. Cassel. 1972. *Discipline without tears.* New York: Hawthorn. Reissued 1995, New York: Penguin-NAL.

Dreikurs, R., B. Grunwald, and E. Pepper. 1982. *Maintaining sanity in the classroom.* New York: Harper & Row.

Egan, T. 1999. Violence by youths: Looking for answers. *The New York Times,* April 22.

Ehrgott, et al. 1992. A study of the marginal teacher in California. Paper presented at the annual meeting of the California Educational Research Association (San Francisco, November, 1992).

Elam, S. 1989. The second Gallup/Phi Delta Kappa poll of teachers' attitudes toward the public schools. *Phi Delta Kappan,* 70(10), 785–798.

Elam, S., L. Rose, and A. Gallup. 1995. The 27th annual Phi Delta Kappa/Gallup Poll of the public's attitudes toward the public schools. *Phi Delta Kappan, 76*(1), 41–56.

———. 1996. The 28th annual Phi Delta Kappa/ Gallup poll of the public's attitudes toward the public schools. *Phi Delta Kappan, 78*(1), 41–59.

Ellis, D., and P. Karr-Kidwell. 1995. A study of assertive discipline and recommendations for effective classroom management methods. Paper, 26 p. Washington, DC: U.S. Department of Education. ERIC Clearinghouse #35596.

Evertson, C., and A. Harris. 1992. What we know about managing classrooms. *Educational Leadership, 49*(7), 74–78.

Farner, C. 1996. Discipline alternatives. Mending the broken circle. *Learning, 25*(1), 27–29.

Feldman, D. 1994. The effect of assertive discipline procedures on preschool children in segregated and integrated settings: A longitudinal study. *Education and Training in Mental Retardation and Developmental Disabilities, 24*(9), 291–306.

Fighting violence with values. 1993. *Atlanta Journal,* A, 12:1, December 23.

Foltz-Gray, D. 1996. The bully trap: Young tormentors and their victims find ways out of anger and isolation. *Teaching Tolerance, 5*(2), 18–23.

Freiberg, H. 1996. From tourists to citizens in the classroom. *Educational Leadership 54*(1), 32–36.

Fuhr, D. 1993. Effective classroom discipline: Advice for educators. *NASSP Bulletin, 76*(549), 82–86.

Gardner, H. 1983. *Frames of mind: The theory of multiple intelligences.* New York: Harper and Row.

Gardner, P. 1996. The giant at the front: Young teachers and corporal punishment in inter-war elementary schools. *History of Education 25*(2), 141–163.

Gibbons, L., and L. Jones. 1994. Novice teachers' reflectivity upon their classroom management. Paper, 13 p. Washington, DC: U.S. Department of Education. ERIC Clearinghouse #SP036198.

Ginott, H. 1965. *Between parent and child.* New York: Avon.

———. 1969. *Between parent and teenager.* New York: Macmillan.

———. 1971. *Teacher and child.* New York: Macmillan.

———. 1972. I am angry! I am appalled! I am furious! *Today's Education, 61,* 23–24.

———. 1973. Driving children sane. *Today's Education, 62,* 20–25.

Glasser, W. 1965. *Reality therapy: A new approach to psychiatry.* New York: Harper & Row.

———. 1969. *Schools without failure.* New York: Harper & Row.

———. 1977. 10 steps to good discipline. *Today's Education, 66,* 60–63.

———. 1978. Disorders in our schools: Causes and remedies. *Phi Delta Kappan, 59,* 331–333.

———. 1986. *Control theory in the classroom.* New York: Harper & Row.

———. 1990. *The quality school: Managing students without coercion.* New York: Harper & Row. (Reissued with additional material in 1992)

———. 1992. The quality school curriculum. *Phi Delta Kappan, 73*(9), 690–694.

———. 1993. *The quality school teacher.* New York: Harper Perennial.

———. 1996. Then and now. The theory of choice. *Learning, 25*(3), 20–22.

Glasser, W., and K. Dotson. 1998. *Choice theory in the classroom.* New York: HarperCollins.

Glenn, H. 1989. *Developing capable people.* (Audio Cassette Tape Series). Fair Oaks, CA: Sunshine Press.

———. 1989. *Empowering others: Ten keys to affirming and validating people.* (Videotape). Fair Oaks, CA: Sunshine Press.

———. 1989. *Six steps to developing responsibility.* (Videotape). Fair Oaks, CA: Sunshine Press.

———. 1989. *Teachers who make a difference.* (Videotape). Fair Oaks, CA: Sunshine Press.

Glenn, H., and J. Nelsen. 1987. *Raising children for success.* Fair Oaks, CA: Sunshine Press.

———. 1988. *Raising self-reliant children in a self-indulgent world.* Rocklin, CA: Prima.

Glenn, H., J. Nelsen, R. Duffy, L. Escobar, K. Ortolano, and D. Owen-Sohocki. 1996. *Positive Discipline: A teacher's A–Z guide.* Rocklin, CA: Prima.

Good, P. 1996. Discipline alternatives: It's not your job. *Learning, 25*(3), 36–37.

Gootman, M. 1997. *The caring teacher's guide to discipline: Helping young students learn self-control, responsibility, and respect.* Thousand Oaks, CA: Corwin Press, Inc.

Gordon, T. 1970. *Parent Effectiveness Training: A tested new way to raise responsible children.* New York: New American Library.

———. 1976. *P. E. T. in action*. New York: Bantam Books.

———. 1987. *T. E. T.: Teacher Effectiveness Training*. New York: David McKay.

———. 1989. *Discipline that works: Promoting self-discipline in children*. New York: Random House.

Gottfredson, D., G. Gottfredson, and L. Hybl. 1993. Managing adolescent behavior: A multiyear, multi-school study. *American Educational Research Journal, 30*(1), 179–215.

Gratch, A. 1998. Growing teaching professionals: Lessons taught by first-year teachers. Paper presented at the Annual Conference on Qualitative Research in Education (Athens, GA, January 8–10.)

Greenlee, A., and E. Ogletree. 1993. Teachers' attitudes toward student discipline problems and classroom management strategies. Washington, DC: U.S. Department of Education. ERIC Clearinghouse #PS021851.

Halford, J. 1998. Easing the way for teachers. *Educational Leadership: 55*(5), 33–36.

Heaviside, S., C. Rowand, C. Williams, and E. Farris. 1998. *Violence and discipline problems in the U.S. public schools: 1996–97*. Evaluative Report. Washington, DC: U.S. Government Printing Office.

Henley, M. 1997. Six surefire strategies to improve classroom discipline. *Learning, 26*(1), 43–45.

Hill, D. 1990. Order in the classroom. *Teacher Magazine, 1*(7), 70–77.

Hindle, D. 1994. Coping proactively with middle years students. *Middle School Journal, 25*(3), 31–34.

Horne, A. 1994. Teaching children with behavior problems takes understanding, tools, and courage. *Contemporary Education, 65*(3), 122–127.

Hughes, H. 1994. *From fistfights to gunfights: Preparing teachers and administrators to cope with violence in school*. Paper presented at the annual meeting of the American Association of Colleges for Teacher Education (Chicago, February).

Johnson, D., K. Acikogz, and R. Johnson. 1994. Effects of conflict resolution training on elementary school students. *Journal of Social Psychology, 134*(6), 803–817.

Johnson, D., and R. Johnson. 1996. Peacemakers: Teaching students to resolve their own and school-mates' conflicts. *Focus on Exceptional Children, 28*(6), 1–11.

Johnson, V. 1994. Student teachers' conceptions of classroom control. *Journal of Educational Research, 88*(2), 109–117.

Jones, F. 1979. The gentle art of classroom discipline. *National Elementary Principal, 58*, 26–32.

———. 1987. *Positive classroom discipline*. New York: McGraw-Hill.

———. 1987. *Positive classroom instruction*. New York: McGraw-Hill.

———. 1996. Did not! Did, too! *Learning, 24*(6), 24–26.

———. 1996. *Positive Classroom Discipline—a video course of study*. Santa Cruz, CA: Fredric H. Jones & Associates.

———. 1996. *Positive classroom instruction—a video course of study*. Santa Cruz, CA: Fredric H. Jones & Associates.

———. 2001. *Fred Jones's tools for teaching*. Santa Cruz, CA. Fredric H. Jones & Associates.

Jones, J. 1993. *Instructor's guide: Positive classroom discipline—a video course of study*. Santa Cruz, CA: Fredric H. Jones & Associates.

———. 1996. *Instructor's guide: Positive classroom discipline—a video course of study*. Santa Cruz, CA: Fredric H. Jones & Associates.

———. 1996. *Instructor's guide: Positive classroom instruction—a video course of study*. Santa Cruz, CA: Fredric H. Jones & Associates.

Kagan, L., M. Kagan, and S. Kagan. 1998. *Teambuilding*. San Clemente, CA: Kagan Publishing.

Kagan, M., L. Robertson, and S. Kagan. 1998. *Classbuilding*. San Clemente, CA: Kagan Publishing.

Kohn, A. 1990. *The brighter side of human nature: Altruism and empathy in everyday life*. New York: Basic.

———. 1990. *You know what they say...: The truth about popular beliefs*. New York: HarperCollins.

———. 1992. *No contest: The case against competition*. Boston: Houghton Mifflin.

———. 1993. *Punished by rewards: The trouble with gold stars, incentive plans, A's, praise, and other bribes*. Boston: Houghton Mifflin.

———. 1994. Bribes for behaving: Why behaviorism doesn't help children become good people. *NAMTA Journal, 19*(2), 71–94.

———. 1995. Discipline is the problem—not the solution. *Learning 1995, 24*(2): 34.

———. 1996. *Beyond discipline: From compliance to community*. Alexandria, VA: Association for Supervision and Curriculum Development.

———. 1998. Beyond bribes and threats: How not to get control of the classroom. *NAMTA Journal,* 23(1), 6–61.

———. 1999. *The schools our children deserve: moving beyond traditional classrooms and "tougher standards."* Boston: Houghton Mifflin.

Kounin, J. 1977. *Discipline and group management in classrooms.* Revised edition. New York. Holt, Rinehart & Winston. (Original work published 1971)

Kyle, P., S. Kagan, and S. Scott. 2000. *Win-win discipline: Structures for all discipline problems.* San Clemente, CA: Kagan Publishing.

Kyle, P., S. Scott, S. and S. Kagan. 2000. *Win-win discipline course workbook.* San Clemente, California: Kagan Publishing.

La disciplina positive. 1994. ERIC Digest. Urbana, IL: ERIC Clearinghouse on Elementary and Early Childhood Education.

Landen, W. 1992. Violence and our schools: What can we do? *Updating School Board Policies, 23,* 1–5.

Lickona, T. 1966. Teaching respect and responsibility. *Reclaiming Children and Youth: Journal of Emotional and Behavioral Problems,* 5(3), 143–151.

Loucks, H. 1993. Teacher education: A success story. *Principal,* 73(1), 27–29.

Lowman, J. 1996. Characteristics of exemplary teachers. *New Directions for Teaching and Learning,* 65, 33–40.

Lumsden, L. 1996. Motivating today's students. The same old stuff just doesn't work. *Portraits of Success, 1*(2), November.

Mackenzie, R. 1997. Setting limits in the classroom. *American Educator,* 21(3), 32–43.

Martens, B., and S. Kelly. 1993. A behavioral analysis of effective teaching. *School Psychology Quarterly,* 8(1), 10–26.

Massey, M. 1998. *Early childhood violence prevention. ERIC digest.* ERIC identifier: ED424032.

Mazin, L., and J. Hestand. This gun is loaded. *Learning,* 25(2), 44, 46.

McCormack, S. 1989. Response to Render, Padilla, and Krank: But practitioners say it works! *Educational Leadership,* 46(6), 77–79.

Micklo, S. 1993. Perceived problems of public school prekindergarten teachers. *Journal of Research in Childhood Education,* 8(1), 57–68.

Milhollan, F., and B. Forisha. 1972. *From Skinner to Rogers: Contrasting approaches to education.* Lincoln, NE: Professional Educators Publications.

Miller, F. 1997. A class meetings approach to classroom cohesiveness. Perspectives. *Social studies and the younger learner,* 9(3), 18–20.

Morris, R. 1996. Contrasting disciplinary models in education. *Thresholds in Education,* 22(4), 7–13.

Nealon, P. 1995. *Boston Globe,* 17:2, March 14.

Nelsen, J. 1987. *Positive discipline.* New York: Ballantine. Revised edition, 1993.

———. 1988. *Positive discipline video* (Videotape). Fair Oaks, CA: Sunshine Press.

———. 1997. No more logical consequencs—At least hardly ever! Focus on solutions. *Empowering People Catalog,* Winter/Spring, 8.

———. 1999. *Positive time-out: And over 50 ways to avoid power struggles in the home and the classroom.* Rocklin, CA: Prima.

Nelsen, J., L. Lott, and H. Glenn. 1993. *Positive discipline in the classroom.* Rocklin, CA: Prima. Revised editions 1997, 2000.

N. H. schools begin program to teach ethics, values. 1989. *Boston Globe,* 67: 1, August 31.

Newman, M. 1995. 16 city schools are taken over by chancellor. *The New York Times, A,* 1:2, October 20.

Nolin, M. 1996. Student victimization at school. *Journal of School Health,* 66(6), 216–221.

O Harrow, R. 1995. Reading, writing, right and wrong. *Washington Post, D,* 1:1, September 8.

Ozvold, L. 1996. Does teacher demeanor affect the behavior of students? *Teaching and Change,* 3(2), 159–172.

Paradise, R. 1994. Spontaneous cultural compatibility: Mazahua students and their teachers constructing trusting relationships. *Peabody Journal of Education,* 69(2), 60–70.

Parents as partners. 1997. *Our Children,* 22(3), 36–37.

Peng, S. 1993. Fostering student discipline and effort: Approaches used in Chinese schools. Paper presented at the Annual Meeting of the American Educational Research Association (Atlanta, April 12–16).

Peterson, T. 1996. Discipline for discipleship. *Thresholds in Education,* 22(4), 28–32.

Petrie, G., P. Lindauer, B. Bennett, and S. Gibson. 1998. Nonverbal cues: The key to classroom management. *Principal,* 77(3), 34–36.

Phillips-Hershey, E., and B. Kanagy. 1996. Teaching students to manage personal anger constructively. *Elementary School Guidance & Counseling,* 30(3), 229–234.

Powell, T., and S. Taylor. 1994. Taking care of risky business. *South Carolina Middle School Journal,* Spring 1994, 5–6.

Rancifer, J. 1993. Effective classroom management: A teaching strategy for a maturing profession. Paper presented at the annual conference of the Southeastern Regional Association of Teacher Educators (Nashville, October 27–30).

———. 1995. Revolving classroom door: Management strategies to eliminate the quick spin. Paper presented at the annual meeting of the Southern Regional Association of Teacher Educators (Lake Charles, La., November 2–4).

Rardin, R. 1978. Classroom management made easy. *Virginia Journal of Education,* September, 14–17.

Redl, F., and W. Wattenberg. 1959. *Mental hygiene in teaching.* Revised edition. New York: Harcourt, Brace & World. (Original work published 1951)

Render, G., J. Padilla, and H. Krank. 1989. What research really shows about Assertive Discipline. *Educational Leadership, 46*(6), 72–75.

Rich, J. 1992. Predicting and controlling school violence. *Contemporary Education, 64*(1), 35–39.

Richardson, G. 1993. Student teacher journals: Reflective and nonreflective. Paper presented at the annual Mid-South Educational Research Association (New Orleans, November 10–12).

Richardson, R., D. Wilcox, and J. Dunne. 1994. Corporal punishment in schools: Initial progress in the bible belt. *Journal of Humanistic Education and Development, 32*(4), 173–182.

Rose, L., A. Gallup, and S. Elam. (1997). The 29th Annual Phi Delta Kappa/Gallup Poll of the Public's Attitudes toward the Public Schools. *Phi Delta Kappan,* 79: 41–56.

Ryan, F. 1994. From rod to reason: Historical perspectives on corporal punishment in the public schools. *Educational Horizons, 72*(2), 70–77.

Schaps, E. June, 1990. Cooperative learning: The challenge in the '90s. *Cooperative Learning Magazine,* June, 5–8.

Schimmel, D. 1997. Traditional rule-making and the subversion of citizenship education. *Social Education, 61*(2), 70–74.

Schmidt, S. 1996. Character in the classroom. *The San Diego Union,* May 19, 1:22.

Schneider, A. 1998. Insubordination and intimidation signal the end of decorum in many classrooms. *Chronicle of Higher Education, 44*(29), A12-A14.

Schneider, E. 1996. Giving students a voice in the classroom. *Educational Leadership, 54*(1), 22–26.

Schwartz, F. 1981. Supporting or subverting learning: Peer group patterns in four tracked schools. *Anthropology and Education Quarterly, 12*(2), 99–120.

Scott, B. 1997. *Positive discipline in the Classroom.* Video. Orem, Utah: Empowering People Productions.

Sesno, A. 1998. *97 savvy secrets for protecting self and school: A practical guide for today's teachers and administrators.* Thousand Oaks, CA: Corwin Press, Inc.

Shen, F. 1995. Educators get tough on violence. *Washington Post,* MDP, 1:1, August 24.

Sheviakov, G., and F. Redl. 1956. *Discipline for today's children.* Washington, DC: Association for Supervision and Curriculum Development.

Shreeve, W. 1993. Evaluating teacher evaluation: Who is responsible for teacher probation? *NASSP Bulletin, 77*(551), 8–19.

Skinner, B. F. 1948. *Walden two.* New York: Macmillan.

———. 1953. *Science and human behavior.* New York: Macmillan.

———. 1954. The science of learning and the art of teaching. *Harvard Educational Review, 24,* 86–97.

———. 1958. Teaching machines. *Science, 128,* 969–977.

———. 1968. *The technology of teaching.* New York: Appleton-Century-Crofts.

———. 1971. *Beyond freedom and dignity.* New York: Knopf.

———. 1973. The free and happy student. *Phi Delta Kappan, 55,* 13–16.

Slavin, R. 1991. Synthesis of research on cooperative learning. *Educational Leadership, 48,* 71–82.

Spence, G. 1995. *How to argue and win every time.* New York: St. Martin's Press.

Stein, N. 1996. From the margins to the mainstream: Sexual harassment in K-12 schools. *Initiatives, 57*(3), 19–26.

Stone, S. 1993. Issues in education: Taking time to teach social skills. *Childhood Education, 69*(4), 194–195.

Study backs induction schools to help new teachers stay teachers. 1987. *ASCD Update, 29*(4), 1.

Sudzina, M. 1997. From tourists to citizens in the classroom: An interview with H. Jerome Freiberg. *Mid-Western Educational Researcher, 10*(2), 35–38.

Susi, F. 1996. Becoming a behavior-minded art teacher. *Art Education, 49*(5), 62–68.

Taking action against violence. *Instructor, 103*(6), 41–43.

Teachers fear violence in schools. (1994). *Atlanta Journal Constitution,* E, 12:1, March 20.

Teaching children with attention deficit/hyperactivity disorder: Update 1998. *ERIC Digest* E569. ERIC Identifier: ED423633.

Teasley, A. 1996. Dealing effectively with student behavior (new teachers). *English Journal, 85*(4), 80–81.

Terry, Paul M. (1997). Teacher Burnout: Is It Real? Can We Prevent It? Paper presented at the Annual Meeting of the North Central Association of Colleges and Schools (Chicago, IL, April 8, 1997).

Wade, R. 1997. Lifting a school's spirit. *Educational Leadership, 54*(8), 34–36.

Wattenberg, W. 1955. *The adolescent years.* New York: Harcourt Brace.

———. 1967. *All men are created equal.* Detroit: Wayne State University Press.

Weinstein, C. 1992. Designing the instructional environment: Focus on seating. In *Proceedings of selected research and development presentations at the Convention of the Association for Educational Communications and Technology,* p. 7. Resources in Education, Phoenix, AZ: Oryx Press. (ERIC Document Reproduction Service No. IR 015 706).

Weirs, M. 1995. Clayton County adds boot camp to school program. *Atlanta Constitution,* XJI, 1:5, October 19.

Wesley, D., and D. Vocke. 1992. Classroom discipline and teacher education. Paper presented at the Annual Meeting of the Association of Teacher Educators (Orlando, FL, February 15–19).

Winik, L. 1996. Students want more discipline, disruptive classmates out. *American Educator, 20*(3) 12–14.

Woo, E. 1995. New math: Dividing school day differently. *Los Angeles Times,* A, 1:1, September 29.

Zeiger, A. 1996. 10 steps to a happier classroom. General music. *Teaching Music 4*(1), 38–39.

Zeitlin, E., and L. Parrilla. 1999. Malibu High has 'a coming of age.' *Los Angeles Times.* October 10.

Zeller, N., and M. Gutierrez. 1995. Speaking of discipline...: An international perspective. *Thresholds in Education, 21*(2), 60–66.

Index

AAA–BCDE: student positions directing behavior (Kyle, Kagan, and Scott), 172, 173, 175

ABCD's of disruptive behavior (Kyle, Kagan, and Scott), 172, 173, 175

Accountability (vs. victim) mentality (Nelsen, Lott, and Glenn), 107

Active listening (Gordon), 88, 95

AGM's (attention-getting mechanisms) Albert, 71

Albert, Linda
biographical sketch, 67–68, 271
contributions to discipline, 68
Cooperative Discipline, 67–84
principal teachings, 69

Apathy, student (Glasser), 124, 125

Assertive Discipline (Lee Canter and Marlene Canter), 33–49, 265
application exercises, 48
building trust and respect, 37, 43
defusing confrontations, 45
initiating Assertive Discipline in the classroom, 47
key terms, 47
needs and rights in the classroom, 34, 36, 43–44
positive recognition, 40
positive repetitions, 38
problem solving, 46
providing structure and limits, 38–39
questions and activities, 48–49
redirecting off-task behavior, 41, 45
strengths, 46–47
synopsis of model, 265
teaching expected behavior, 37
teaching the plan, 40

Authorities in discipline included in this book, alphabetical listing, 271–274

Barriers to relationships (Nelsen, Lott, and Glenn), 108

Behavior
definition, 2

Behavior modification, 20

Behavior window (Gordon), 90–91

Behaviorally at risk, students who are (Curwin and Mendler), 141–142

Belonging. See student needs.

Beyond Discipline (Alfie Kohn), 189–204, 265–266
application exercises, 203
caring supportive classrooms, 190
central focus, 190
changes that are needed, 196–197
class meetings, 191, 198–199
coercive discipline, 189
collaborative teacher-student partnerships, 189, 190
compliance, the trouble with, 195–196
conflict, the value of, 197
constructivist teaching, 189, 190–191
discipline, purpose of , 192, 194–195
good teaching, 193–194
implementing Beyond Discipline in the classroom, 201–203
making decisions, 199–200
participative classroom management, 189, 190
preview, 190
primary references, 204
principal teachings, 191

questions and activities, 204
review of selected terminology, 203
reward and punishment, 190
school as community, 200
selected terminology, 203
self-control and responsibility, 189
sense of community, 189, 191–192
strength of Beyond Discipline, 201
structure, criteria for judging, 198
teacher-made rules, 191
traditional instruction, shortcomings of, 192–193

Bibliography of references cited, 289–295

Boss teachers vs. lead teachers (Glasser), 125, 128–130

Builders of relationships (Nelsen, Lott, and Glenn), 108

Canter, Lee, and Marlene Canter
Assertive Discipline, 33–49, 265
biographical sketches, 34, 271
central focus, 34
contributions to discipline, 34
principal teachings, 35

Caring, importance of (Nelsen, Lott, and Glenn), 108

Charisma, teacher, 209

Charles, C. M.
biographical sketch, 206, 271
contributions to discipline, 206
principal teachings, 207–208
Synergetic Discipline, 205–219, 269

Circle of friends (Albert), 75

Class agreements, 207, 210

Class meetings
    building blocks to (Nelsen, Lott, and Glynn), 109–112
    format for (Nelsen, Lott, and Glynn), 114
    nature and purpose of (Glasser), 23, 122, 124
    value and use of (Kohn), 191, 198–199
Classroom scenarios for analysis and practice, 253–263
Classrooms
    types: autocratic, democratic, permissive, 29
Code of conduct, class, 76,
Collaboration, 97, 173, 189, 190
Coloroso, Barbara
    biographical sketch, 155–156, 272
    contributions to discipline, 156
    Inner Discipline, 155–170
    principal teachings, 156–158
Communication
    helpful, 209
    congruent, 26
    roadblocks to, 88, 95
Conflict
    dealing with conflict (Curwin and Mendler), 144–145, 149
    no-lose method for resolving (Gordon), 88, 94
    resolving (Charles), 211
    Six-D plan for resolving (Albert), 81
    value of (Kohn), 197
Confrontations
    avoiding and defusing (Albert), 79–81
    de-escalating (Curwin and Mendler), 139
Confrontive skills (Gordon), 86, 92
Consequences
    conventional, 143
    generic, 144
    hierarchy (Canters), 39–40
    instructional, 144
    invoking (Canters), 41, (Albert) 81, (Curwin and Mendler) 144
    logical, 29, 112, 143, 157, 182
    natural, 157, 165
    negative, 39–40, 238, 240
    positive, 39–40, 238, 240
    preplanned, 174
    reasonable, 157, 166

Cooperative Discipline (Linda Albert), 67–84, 266
    application exercises, 83
    attention seeking behavior, 70–71
    avoidance of failure behavior, 71–72
    avoiding and defusing confrontations, 79–81
    central focus, 68
    class code of conduct, 76
    goal of classroom discipline, 70
    helping students contribute, 75
    implementing consequences, 81
    initiating Cooperative Discipline, 82
    power seeking behavior, 71
    preview, 67
    primary references, 83–84
    principal teachings, 69
    questions and activities, 83
    revenge seeking behavior, 71
    selected terminology, 82
    Six-D conflict resolution, 81
    strengths of Cooperative Discipline, 82
    students and parents as partners in discipline, 78–79
    synopsis of model, 266
    teaching, enforcing, and reinforcing the class code of conduct, 76
    the Five A's of making connections, 74–75
    three c's of Cooperative Discipline, 72–75
    why students misbehave, 70
Coopetition, 210–211
Coping mechanisms (Gordon), 88, 93–94
Corrective discipline, 237, 241
Curwin, Richard, and Allen Mendler
    biographical sketches, 138, 272
    central focus, 138–139
    contributions to discipline, 138
    Discipline With Dignity, 137–153
    principal teachings, 139

Decision making, teaching, 163
Difficult students
    behaviorally at risk, 140–141
    Canters' suggestions, 42–46
    Curwin and Mendler's suggestions, 139, 142–143, 145, 146,

Dignity (Curwin and Mendler), 140
Discipline as Self Control (Thomas Gordon), 85–101, 267
    active listening, 88, 95
    application exercises, 100
    authority, 89
    behavior window, 90
    central focus, 86–87
    collaborative rule-setting, 97
    communication roadblocks, 88, 95
    confrontive I-messages, 88, 93
    confrontive skills, 86, 92
    coping mechanisms, 88, 93–94
    door openers, 88, 95
    helping skills, 86, 92, 94
    I-messages, 87, 93
    initiating Discipline As Self Control, 99
    listening skills, 95
    misbehavior, 90
    no-lose conflict resolution, 88, 94
    non-controlling methods, 89
    participative classroom management, 86, 88, 97–98
    preventive I-messages, 88, 97
    preventive skills, 86, 92, 97
    primary references, 101
    principal teachings, 87–89
    problem ownership, 87, 90
    questions and activities, 100
    reward and punishment, 89–90
    selected terminology, 100
    shifting gears, 88, 93
    strengths of Discipline As Self Control, 98
    you-messages, 87, 93, 97
Discipline, glossary of terms related to, 279–288
Discipline, major themes in, 275–277
Discipline, nature and aspects of
    corrective, 237, 241
    decline in effectiveness, 4
    definitions, 3, 159,
    formal systems of, 10
    helpful vs. coercive, 189, 207
    in the synergetic classroom, 212
    integral part of teaching, 207
    personal, 235, 237–250
    preventive, 228–229, 236, 240–241
    schools' and educators' efforts to cope, 6–10

seriousness of , 4
structures for, 178
supportive, 236–237
teaching decision making, 163
true discipline, 27, 30, 160, 162
Discipline plans, examples
  Dry Creek Elementary School
    (school-wide example),
    245–247
  examples of personal plans,
    237–250
  implementing your personal plan,
    250–251
  organizing your personal plan,
    235 ff
  The Emerald Way (school-wide
    example), 247–250
Discipline, purposes and goals of
  Albert's views, 70
  Charles's views, 207
  Coloroso's views, 159, 162
  Curwin and Mendler's views, 139
  Glasser's views, 123–124,
    131–132
  Gordon's views, 85
  in your philosophy, 221–224
  in your theory, 224–228
  Jones's views, 53
  Kohn's views, 190, 191, 192,
    194–195
  Kyle, Kagan, and Scott's views,
    174
Discipline, synopses of models
  analyzed in this book,
  265–270
Discipline With Dignity (Richard
  Curwin and Allen Mendler),
  137–153, 267
  application exercises, 151–152
  central focus, 138–139
  consequences, 139
  consequences: logical,
    conventional, generic,
    instructional, 143–144
  dealing with aggression, hostility,
    and violence, 146
  dealing with conflict, 149
  dealing with violence in the
    classroom, 148
  de-escalating potential
    confrontation, 139
  dignity, 140
  discipline based on core values of
    the school, 146–148

  disciplining difficult-to-control
    students, 142–143
  goal of discipline, 139
  helping teachers retrain
    themselves, 149
  hope, helping students regain, 142
  initiating Discipline With Dignity,
    149–150
  managing difficult students, 139
  motivating difficult-to-manage
    students, 145
  preventing escalation of conflicts,
    144–145
  preview, 137
  primary references, 152–153
  principal teachings, 139
  questions and activities, 152
  review of selected terminology,
    151
  strengths of Discipline With
    Dignity, 149
  students behaviorally at risk,
    140–141
  synopsis of model, 267
  underlying principles of effective
    discipline, 139
  value-guided behavior: four-phase
    plan for, 146–148
  why students misbehave, 139–140
Door openers (Gordon), 88, 95
Dreikurs, Rudolf
  biographical sketch, 28, 272
  major contributions, 30
  principal teachings, 29
  synopsis of model, 267

Empowering perceptions, the three
  (Nelsen, Lott, and Glenn), 106
Encouragement, 30, 75
Ethics, 207, 209

Five A's of making connections
  (Albert), 74–75
Four essential skills (Nelsen, Lott,
  and Glenn), 106
Four R's of consequences (Albert),
  81

Ginott, Haim
  biographical sketch, 25–26, 272
  major contributions, 27–28
  principal teachings, 26–27
  synopsis of model, 266
Glasser, William (earlier work)

  biographical sketch, 22, 272
  major contributions, 23
  principal teachings, 22–23
  synopsis of early model, 265
Glasser, William (later work)
  biographical sketch, 121, 272
  contributions to discipline, 121
  central focus, 121
  Noncoercive Discipline, 121–135,
    268
  principal teachings, 121–122
Glossary of terms related to
  discipline, 279–288
Gordon, Thomas
  biographical sketch, 85, 273
  central focus, 86–87
  Discipline As Self Control,
    85–101, 267
  contributions to discipline, 86
  principal teachings, 87–89
Graceful exits (Albert), 80

Helpful discipline procedure
  (Charles), 207, 212–213
Helping skills (Gordon), 86, 94
Hope, sense of, 142
Human relations skills, 211

I-can level (Albert), 72
I-messages 26, 88, 93, 97
Inner Discipline (Barbara Coloroso),
  155–170, 267–268
  application exercises, 168–169
  categories of misbehavior:
    mistakes, mischief, mayhem,
    156, 157, 159–60
  central focus, 156
  consequences, 157
  initiating Inner Discipline,
    166–167
  meaning of discipline, 159, 162
  natural consequences, 165
  preview, 155
  primary references, 170
  principal teachings, 156–158
  problem solving, 164–165
  questions and activities, 169
  reasonable consequences, 166
  RSVP test of consequences:
    reasonable, simple, valuable,
    practical, 158, 159
  selected terminology, 168
  strengths of Inner Discipline, 166
  synopsis of model, 267–268

Inner Discipline (Barbara Coloroso), *(continued)*
   teaching decision making, 162–163
   three con's that students use, 163–164
   three F's: fear, fighting back, fleeing, 159
   three R's of reconciliatory justice: restitution, resolution, reconciliation, 157, 160, 161–162
   three types of schools and teachers: brickwalls, jellyfish, backbones, 158
Interests of students, 209–210
Interpersonal skills (Nelsen, Lott, and Glenn), 107
Intrapersonal skills (Nelsen, Lott, and Glenn), 107

Jones, Fredric
   biographical sketch, 51–52, 273
   contributions to discipline, 52
   Positive Classroom Discipline, 51–66, 269
   principal teachings, 52
Jones, JoLynne Talbot, 60
Judgmental skills (Nelsen, Lott, and Glenn), 107

Kohn, Alfie
   Beyond Discipline, 189–204, 265–266
   biographical sketch, 190, 273
   contributions to discipline, 190–191
   principal teachings, 191–192
Kounin, Jacob
   biographical sketch, 23, 273
   major contributions, 24–25
   principal teachings, 24
Kyle, Patricia, Spencer Kagan, and Sally Scott
   biographical sketches, 172, 273
   contributions to discipline, 172–173
   principal teachings, 173–174
   Win-Win Discipline, 171–187, 270

Learning teams (Glasser), 126
Listening skills (Gordon), 95
Logical consequences, 29, 112,

Misbehavior
   as opportunity for learning, 172
   causes of and reasons for, 70, 111, 139–140, 172, 173, 175, 207, 212
   definitions of, 2, 90, 223
   intervening in, 230–232
   types of, 3, 155, 173,
Models of discipline analyzed in this book, synopses of, 265–270

Needs of students and teachers
   Charles's views, 207, 210
   Glasser's views, 123–124, 126
   needs and mistaken goals (Dreikurs), 29
   students' needs, 29, 123–124, 126, 207, 208, 210, 238
   teachers' needs, 239, 242
   universal need (Albert), 70
Nelsen, Jane, Lynn Lott, and H. Stephen Glenn
   biographical sketches, 104, 274
   central focus, 104–105
   contributions to discipline, 104
   Positive Discipline in the Classroom, 103–118, 269
   principal teachings, 105
No-lose conflict resolution (Gordon), 88, 94
Noncoercive Discipline (William Glasser), 121–135, 268
   application exercises, 134
   boss teachers vs. lead teachers, 125, 128
   central focus, 121
   classroom meetings, 122, 124
   initiating Noncoercive Discipline, 133
   intervening when students break rules, 131–132
   learning teams, 126
   preview, 121
   primary references, 135
   principal teachings, 121–122, 123–124
   quality curriculum, 127
   quality education, need for, 124, 125
   quality learning, 127, 128
   quality student work, 127
   quality teaching, 127
   questions and activities, 123–135

relation of quality teaching to discipline, 130–131
selected terminology, 133
SIR (self-evaluation, improvement, repetition), 128
strengths of Noncoercive Discipline, 132
student apathy, 124, 125
students' five basic needs, 123–124, 126
synopsis of model, 268
useful classwork, 127
what school offers students, 125
Non-punitive solutions (Nelsen, Lott, and Glenn), 112

Participative classroom management (Gordon), 86, 97–98
Personal capability (Nelsen, Lott, and Glenn), 106
Personal system of discipline, finalizing your, 235
   what you and other teachers want, 235
   preventive discipline, planning for, 236
   supportive discipline, planning for, 236–237
   corrective discipline, planning for, 237
   sample discipline plans, 237–250
Philosophy of discipline, clarifying your, 221, 221–224
Positive Classroom Discipline (Fredric Jones), 51–66, 268–269
   application exercises, 65
   backup systems, 61
   body language, 52–53, 56
   central focus, 52
   classroom structures, 54
   Grandma's rule, 58
   group concern, 60
   incentive systems, 57–58
   incentives, 53, 59
   initiating positive classroom discipline, 64
   lost teaching time, recouping, 53–54
   omission training, 61
   PAT (preferred activity time), 59
   preview, 51
   primary references, 66
   principal teachings, 52–53
   providing efficient help, 62–63

questions and activities, 65–66
Say, See, Do Teaching, 52, 57
selected terminology, 64
skill clusters, 54 ff
strengths 63,
student responsibility, 58
synopsis of model, 268–269
working the crowd, 53
Positive Discipline in the Classroom
    (Jane Nelsen, Lynn Lott, and H.
    Stephen Glenn), 103–118, 269
application exercises, 117–118
barriers to relationships, 108
beyond consequences, 112
builders of relationships, 108
building blocks to effective class
    meetings, 109–112
caring, importance of, 108–109
central focus, 104–105
class meetings, 105–106, 109–112
class meetings, standard format
    for, 114
developing the significant seven,
    106–107
four essential skills, 106
initiating Positive Discipline in the
    Classroom, 116–117
interpersonal skills, 107
intrapersonal skills, 107
judgmental skills, 107
nonpunitive solutions, 112
personal capability, 106
power and influence over one's
    own life, 107
preview, 103
primary references, 118
principal teachings, 105
questions and activities, 118
respectful classroom management,
    114
review of selected terminology, 117
significance in primary
    relationships, 107
significant seven, 106
strategic skills, 107
strengths of Positive Discipline in
    the Classroom, 116
synopsis of model, 269
three empowering perceptions, 106
Power and influence over one's own
    life (Nelsen, Lott, and Glenn),
    107
Practice of discipline, deciding on,
    228–233

Praise
    appreciative vs. evaluative, 26
    effective, 40
    encouragement vs. praise, 30
    undesirable effects of, 26, 30
Preventive discipline, 228–229, 236,
    240–241
Preventive I-messages (Gordon), 88,
    97
Preventive skills (Gordon), 86, 97
Problem solving, 164–165
Punishment, undesirable effects of,
    19, 21, 27, 90, 112, 159, 160,
    190, 191

Quality education (Glasser), 124,
    125, 127–128, 130–131

Redl, Fritz, and William Wattenberg
    biographical sketches, 18, 274
    major contributions, 19–20
    principal teachings, 18–19
    synopsis of model, 266
Respectful classroom management
    (Nelsen, Lott, and Glenn),
    114–116
Responsibility
    student, 58, 124, 126, 173
    teacher, 173
Responsible behavior, 232–233
Rewards, effects of, 90,
RSVP test of consequences:
    reasonable, simple, valuable,
    practical (Coloroso), 158, 159
Rules, class, 239–240, 242–243

Sarcasm, 27
Schools as communities (Kohn),
    191–192
Sense of community, 191–192, 233
Separate realities (Nelsen, Lott, and
    Glenn), 111
Shifting gears (Gordon), 88, 93
Significance in primary relationships
    (Nelsen, Lott, and Glenn), 107
Significant seven (Nelsen, Lott, and
    Glenn), 106–107
SIR (Glasser's self-evaluation,
    improvement, repetition), 128
Six-D conflict resolution (Albert), 81
Skinner, B. F.
    biographical sketch, 20
    major contributions, 21
    neo-Skinnerians, 274

principal teachings, 20–21
synopsis of the neo-Skinnerian
    model, 269
Strategic skills (Nelsen, Lott, and
    Glenn), 107
Student responsibility
    responsibility training (Jones),
    57–58
Supportive discipline, 236–237
Synergetic Discipline (C. M.
    Charles), 205–219, 269
adapting instruction to students'
    needs and traits, 208
application exercises, 218
causes of misbehavior, 207, 212
central focus, 206
charisma, 209
class agreements, 207, 210
communication, 209
conflict, addressing, 211
coopetition, 210–211
discipline as an integral part of
    teaching, 207
discipline in the synergetic
    classroom, 212
ethics and ethical qualities, 209
helpful nonconfrontive discipline,
    207, 212–213
human relations skills, 211
initiating Synergetic Discipline in
    the classroom, 214–217
interests, 209–211
preview, 205
primary reference, 219
principal teachings, 207–208
problems, addressing, 211
procedure in Synergetic Discipline,
    212–213
questions and activities, 219
selected terminology, 217–218
strengths of Synergetic Discipline,
    214
student needs that motivate
    behavior, 207, 210
students' natural resistance, 207
synergy, elements needed for, 207,
    208–211
synergy, nature of, 207, 208
synopsis of model, 269
trust, importance of, 207
Synergetic teaching, 206, 209,
    214–217
Synergy (Charles), 207, 208–211,
    233

Teachers, types and effectiveness
  at their best and at their worst
    (Ginott), 26
  boss teachers vs. lead teachers
    (Glasser), 125, 128–130
  charismatic, 209
  good teachers (Kohn), 190–191,
    193–194
  needs of,
  teachers' hidden asset, 26
  types of and their effects, 29,
    36–37, 158, 190–191,
    193–194, 209
Terms important in discipline
  Albert's Cooperative Discipline,
    82
  Charles's Synergetic Discipline,
    217–218
  Coloroso's Inner Discipline, 168
  Curwin and Mendler's Discipline
    With Dignity, 151
  Glasser's Noncoercive Discipline,
    133
  glossary of, 279–288
  Gordon's Discipline as Self
    Control, 100
  In the philosophy, theory, and
    practice of discipline, 234
  Jones's Positive Classroom
    Discipline, 64
  Kohn's Beyond Discipline, 203
  Kyle, Kagan, and Scott's Win-Win
    Discipline, 185
  Nelsen, Lott, and Glenn's Positive
    Discipline in the Classroom, 117
  pioneers of modern discipline, 31
  The Canters' Assertive Discipline,
    47
Themes in discipline, major, 275–277
Theory of discipline, clarifying your,
  221, 224–228

Three con's that students use
  (Coloroso), 163–164
Three F's associated with
  punishment: fear, fighting back,
  and fleeing (Coloroso), 159
Three pillars of Win-Win Discipline
  (Kyle, Kagan, and Scott), 172,
  174–175
Three R's of reconciliatory justice:
  restitution, resolution,
  reconciliation (Coloroso), 157,
  161–162
Trust, 207, 209

Underlying principles of effective
  discipline (Curwin and
  Mendler), 139
Useful classwork (Glasser), 127

Value-guided behavior: four-phase
  plan for (Curwin and Mendler),
  146–148

Win-Win Discipline (Patricia Kyle,
  Spencer Kagan, and Sally Scott),
  171–187, 270
  AAA-BCDE student positions in
    misbehavior, 172, 173, 175
  ABCD causes of misbehavior, 172,
    173, 175
  application exercises, 186
  applying the Win-Win process,
    175 ff
  big three of curriculum,
    instruction, and
    management, 183
  central focus, 173
  choosing language, 178–179
  conferencing, 179–180
  consequences, 174
  discipline structures, 178

follow-up structures, 174
identifying disruptive behavior,
  176–177
identifying the student's position,
  177–178
initiating Win-Win Discipline in
  the classroom, 185–186
logical consequences, 182
long-term solutions, 174
matching discipline structures to
  student positions, 180–182
parent and community alliances,
  174
parent and community alliances,
  184–185
preview, 171–172
primary reference, 187
principal teachings, 173–174
questions and activities, 187
school-wide programs, 184–185
selected terminology, 185
spotting the signs of misbehavior,
  178
strengths of Win-Win Discipline,
  185
synopsis of model, 270
tabling the matter, 179
teacher-student cooperation, 173
three pillars (same side, shared
  responsibility, learned
  responsibility), 173, 174–175
ultimate goal of Win-Win
  Discipline, 174
whole class patterns, dealing with,
  182–183
Win-Win Discipline process, 175 ff
Working the crowd (Jones), 53

You-messages, 26, 87–88, 93, 97